CRITICAL SURVEY OF POETRY

Feminist Poets

Editor

Rosemary M. Canfield Reisman
Charleston Southern University

SALEM PRESS
A Division of EBSCO Publishing, Ipswich, Massachusetts

Cover photo:
Margaret Atwood (© KC Armstrong/Corbis)

Copyright © 2012, by Salem Press, A Division of EBSCO Publishing, Inc.
All rights in this book are reserved. No part of this work may be used or reproduced in any manner whatsoever or transmitted in any form or by any means, electronic or mechanical, including photocopy, recording, or any information storage and retrieval system, without written permission from the copyright owner except in the case of brief quotations embodied in critical articles and reviews or in the copying of images deemed to be freely licensed or in the public domain. For information address the publisher, Salem Press, at csr@salempress.com.

ISBN: 978-1-42983-649-4

CONTENTS

Contributors iv

Feminist Criticism 1

Paula Gunn Allen 11
Margaret Atwood 17
Aphra Behn 31
Elizabeth Bishop 42
Eavan Boland 54
Lorna Dee Cervantes 71
Carolyn Forché 79
Alice Fulton 89
H. D. 97
Jane Hirshfield 107
Susan Howe 115
Denise Levertov 127
Charlotte Mew 141
Edna St. Vincent Millay 146
Marianne Moore 155
Thylias Moss 167
Alicia Suskin Ostriker 172
Sylvia Plath 177
Adrienne Rich 189
Muriel Rukeyser 203
Anne Sexton 214
Gertrude Stein 224
Alice Walker 237
Mitsuye Yamada 246
Yosano Akiko 253

Checklist for Explicating a Poem 261
Bibliography 264
Guide to Online Resources 268
Geographical Index 273
Category Index 274
Subject Index 276

CONTRIBUTORS

Karley K. Adney
University of Wisconsin, Marathon County

David Bromige
Sonoma State University

Peter Carravetta
Queens College, City University of New York

Caroline Collins
Quincy University

Heidi K. Czerwiec
University of North Dakota

Desiree Dreeuws
Sunland, California

Doris Earnshaw
University of California, Davis

Bernard F. Engel
Michigan State University

David L. Erben
University of South Florida

Howard Faulkner
Washburn University

Sarah Fedirka
Arizona State University

Lydia E. Ferguson
Clemson University

Kenneth E. Gadomski
University of Delaware

Ann D. Garbett
Averett University

Donna Gerstenberger
University of Washington

Keiko Matsui Gibson
Kanda University of International Studies

Morgan Gibson
Urbana, Illinois

Richard F. Giles
Wilfrid Laurier University

Sarah Hilbert
Pasadena, California

Earl G. Ingersoll
SUNY College at Brockport

Helen Jaskoski
California State University, Fullerton

Philip K. Jason
United States Naval Academy

Sheila Golburgh Johnson
Santa Barbara, California

Leslie Ellen Jones
Pasadena, California

Rebecca Kuzins
Pasadena, California

Roxanne McDonald
Wilmot, New Hampshire

Kevin McNeilly
University of British Columbia

Arthur E. McGuinness
University of California, Davis

Holly L. Norton
University of Northwestern Ohio

David Peck
Laguna Beach, California

Chapel Louise Petty
Stillwater, Oklahoma

Allene Phy-Olsen
Austin Peay State University

Carol Lawson Pippen
Goucher College

Samuel J. Rogal
Illinois State University

Jill Rollins
Trafalgar School

Karen F. Stein
University of Rhode Island

John Clendenin Townsend
Kalamazoo, Michigan

Paul Varner
Oklahoma Christian University

Barbara Wiedemann
Auburn University at Montgomery

FEMINIST CRITICISM

Any survey of feminist criticism will most likely be fraught with difficulties, the most serious of which is the attempt to avoid reductionism. This introduction to feminist criticism attempts to identify key figures, central concerns, and general movements. Such an attempt is a strategic move to organize a vital and growing body of work into some sort of scheme that can be collated and presented. Despite the existence of American, French, and British feminisms, for example, no such clear-cut schools or movements exist in a fixed way. The various writers included in this essay, and the various trends and movements discussed, share many positions and disagree on many important points. Such agreements and disagreements have less to do with nationality than with the rapid changes occurring in feminist criticism.

Three general perspectives on feminism are summarized here, as reflected in the work of American, French, and British writers. The work of two pivotal feminist writers, Simone de Beauvoir and Virginia Woolf, is discussed at some length, and there is also an attempt to isolate a few general trends and issues within the feminist movement.

Feminism has diverse goals, many of which overlap in the work of individual writers. This work is filled with pitfalls and temptations: Because women are participants in their cultures, the thinking (and writing) of women cannot be separated from the methods of the cultures in which they live, nor can women be separated from their races or sexual orientations. Furthermore, feminist criticism may be combined with other methods of criticism, such as deconstruction, psychoanalytic criticism, and Marxist criticism. Generally, however, feminist writers are concerned with the political, social, and cultural equality of women and with researching the effects of gender upon writing—determining how the writing of women differs from the writing of men.

Gender systems

Feminist critics have produced a variety of models to account for the production, reproduction, and maintenance of gender systems. They discuss the female writer's problems in defining herself in the conventional structures of male-dominated society, structures that restrict the possibilities of women and impose standards of behavior upon women personally, professionally, and creatively. Again, to generalize, once women experience themselves as subjects, they can attempt to undermine the social, cultural, and masculine subject positions offered them.

Feminist critics may, for example, reexamine the writing of male authors (an approach associated with American feminists) and, in particular, reexamine the great works of male authors from a woman's perspective in an attempt to discover how these great works reflect and shape the ideologies that subjugate women. Through this reexamination, feminist critics carefully analyze the depictions of female characters to expose the ideology implicit in such characterizations. They may also seek to expose the patriarchal ideology that permeates great works and to show how it also permeates the literary tradition. This particularly American approach is seen in the works of Kate Millett, Judith Fetterley, and Carolyn Gold Heilbrun.

GYNOCRITICISM

A second approach used by American feminists is termed "gynocriticism." This method of inquiry takes as its subject the writings of women who have produced what Elaine C. Showalter, who coined the term "gynocriticism," calls "a literature of their own." A female literary tradition is examined to discover how women writers have historically perceived themselves and their cultures. Other goals of gynocriticism are to preserve and chronicle the history of women's writing and to rediscover lost or neglected women writers. Showalter describes feminine writing as a form of the general experience of minority cultures, cultures that are also "Others" and whose members are struggling to find a place usually reserved for white males. This leads to the problem of multiple marginalization, since some men and women may be Others in terms of ethnicity and sexual orientation as well. In particular, the place within feminism of women of color is a controversial issue, as black writers such as Phillis Wheatley, Toni Morrison, Gwendolyn Brooks, and Nikki Giovanni challenge and enter the canon. Other practitioners of gynocriticism include Patricia Meyer Spacks and Susan Gubar.

LANGUAGE

Feminist writers may also focus on language, defining it as a male realm and exploring the many ways in which meaning is created. This language-based feminism is typically associated with French feminism. Such feminists may conceive of language as phallocentric, arguing that language privileges the masculine by promoting the values appreciated and perpetuated by male culture. Such a language-based approach typically attempts to reveal a relationship between language and culture, or, more specifically, the way the politics of language affects and even determines women's roles in a culture. Radical French feminists may associate feminine writing with the female body, so that the repression of female sexual pleasure is related to the repression of feminine creativity in general. French feminists insist that once women learn to understand and express their sexuality, they will be able to progress toward a future defined by the feminine economy of generosity as opposed to the masculine economy of hoarding. Such a position has drawn criticism from other feminists, because it seems to reduce women to biological entities and fosters (though it reverses) a set of binary oppositions—female/male. French feminists include Julia Kristeva, Annie Leclerc, Xaviere Gauthier, and Marguerite Duras.

Interestingly, differences between the French and English languages involve complicated feminist issues. The English language distinguishes between sex and gender, so that human beings are either female or male by sex and feminine or masculine by gender. The feminine/masculine opposition permits some fluidity, so that androgyny can become a central, mediating position between the two extremes. The distinction between male and female, however, is absolute. The way the English language categorizes people has itself created a debate within feminism, about naming. In the French language, by comparison, the concepts of femininity and femaleness are included in the same word.

Political and social agendas

Finally, British feminists have tended to be more historically oriented than have French and American feminists. British critics tend to be materialistic and ideological; they look carefully at the material conditions of historical periods and consider such conditions as central to understanding literature. Literature, in this model, is culturally produced. Some British feminists consider that an American opposition to male stereotypes has produced a feminine reaction that has led to an ignorance of real differences among women's races, social classes, and cultures. British feminists also emphasize that women's development of individual strategies to obtain real power within their political, social, or creative arenas is actually a negative move. They argue that such examples mystify male oppression and perpetuate the myth that, somehow, male oppression creates for women a world of special opportunities.

Generally, the British position encourages historical and political engagement to promote social change. This model of activism contrasts with the American and French models, which focus primarily on sexual difference. A typical strategy of the British approach is to examine a text by first placing the text in its historical context and then exposing the patriarchal ideologies that structure the text and govern the depiction of women characters. Because of historical oppression, the women characters tend either to be silent or to be mouthpieces for men's myths. British feminists include Judith Newton and Deborah Rosenfelt.

History

Feminist criticism owes much to the work of French philosopher and critic Beauvoir and to English writer and critic Woolf, two founders of contemporary feminist thought. Beauvoir, whose best-known and perhaps most important work is *Le Deuxième Sexe* (1949; *The Second Sex*, 1953), explored the many ways in which women are defined and limited in relation to men. Such limiting, Beauvoir contends, cannot be avoided in a male-dominated culture; even women perceived as independent are still negatively affected by the ideas and the relations of male society. Western society in general, for Beauvoir, is patriarchal and denies freedom of expression to women. In this patriarchal society, women become Others, viewed not as they are but as projections of male needs and subordinate to male expectations. Her approach tends toward a Marxist model in identifying an economic and political limiting of women with sexism in literature. Beauvoir finds in literature reflections of a more general socioeconomic oppression of women. Her approach emphasizes art's mimetic quality: Through its powers of reflection, art yields valuable insights into the sexism that is culturally prevalent.

The otherness examined by Beauvoir and other feminist writers is a condition of women, so that the characteristic of identity for women is separation. Constituted through a male gaze, the feminine exists as something that is inexpressible. Women function as objects of the male gaze. Therefore, women's bodies are vehicles for ambivalent feelings toward the mother. These problems extend into the Western philosophical tradition, so that Western (usually male) thinkers express their philosophical positions as essential and universal while embracing a center that is unexamined and male.

In her essay *A Room of One's Own* (1929), Woolf introduced many topics that have become vital to feminist critics. She contends that art is a collective product, incorrectly romanticized in theory as individual and personal. Woolf's conceptualization of a metaphorical "room," a female place, merges the introspection often associated with female discourse and the social sanctuary within which a woman may achieve her potential. Woolf helped to establish the broad range of feminist criticism, from cultural critique to discourse. The most important portion of *A Room of One's Own* ironically and satirically traces the lost career of William Shakespeare's "sister," whose creativity had no outlet in the sixteenth century. Woolf problematizes the structures of the male ego, its rituals, titles, and institutions, which are created at the expense of Others. This ironic introduction sets the stage in the text for a historical discussion of women writers and the problems they had in pursuing their careers. Furthermore, in her discussion of women novelists of the nineteenth century, especially George Eliot, Charlotte Brontë, and Jane Austen, Woolf foreshadows contemporary research on language.

Woolf further argues that a woman writer should write as a woman and as a woman who is not self-conscious of her gender. Ever-aware of the alienating and repressive effects of the myths created around women, Woolf also attempted to avoid creating alternative myths. She sets forth in her work the attempt to discover a collective concept of subjectivity that would foreground identity constructs, and she argues that such a concept of subjectivity is a characteristic of women's writing. Other women writers, however, seem more interested in the alienation created by structures that permit women restricted and repressive roles only, roles as Others, in society.

In her writing, Woolf is striving, like later feminists, to uncover the effects of a phallocentric culture that idolizes the autonomous and rational ego. She also attempts to offer an alternative to this idolatry, an alternative that emphasizes subjectivity and connectedness, if in a historically fluid context. Through her struggle to redefine women, she tries to avoid simply reversing the binary oppositions that polarize men and women into specific categories. She does not argue for a reversal of these categories.

Gender rules and relations

Since the time of Beauvoir and Woolf, the naming and interrogating of phallocentrism has become more assured. Feminist critics are challenging stereotypical masculine virtues, no longer accepting them as measures of virtue and excellence. One strategy many feminist critics adopt is to locate both men and women within a larger context; men and women are both captives of gender, in interrelated, but in vastly different, ways. Though men may appear to be the masters under the rules of gender, they are not therefore free, for like women, their gender expression is tightly controlled by sociocultural "rules."

If both men and women are influenced by gender, then the conceptualizations of women and the conceptualizations of men must be examined in terms of gender relations. Feminist critical models are complex and often contradictory. Claims about the centrality of gender relations in the formation of self, knowledge, and power relations, and the relationships of these areas to one another, continue to be debated. Feminist critics have developed many theories of how gender systems are created and perpetuated, how they dominate, and how they maintain themselves. Each of the theories, however, identifies a single process or set of processes as vital to gender relations. Influential feminist theorists have suggested the centrality of the sexual division of labor, childbearing and child-rearing practices, and various processes of representation (including aesthetic and language processes, for example). Such positions address the meanings and nature of sexuality and the relationship of sexuality to writing, the importance and implications of differences among women writers, and the effects of kinship and family organizations. Each of these many theories and debates has crucial implications for an understanding of knowledge, gender, power, and writing.

Juliet Mitchell has argued for the importance of Freudian theories to feminist theories of gender relations. Her work entails a defense of Lacanian psychoanalysis. She argues that Freud's work on the psychology of women should be read as a description of the inevitable effects on feminine psychic development of patriarchal social power. Dorothy Dinnerstein and Nancy Chodorow contribute to this psychoanalytical approach a larger account of the unconscious and its role in gender relations. They also examine the traditional sexual division of labor in the West, how this tradition has been passed on, and how it influences male-female relations.

Male versus female discourse

Hélène Cixous and Luce Irigaray find fundamental psychological differences between men and women. They have concluded that women are more influenced by pre-Oedipal experience and believe that the girl retains an initial identification with her mother, so that the relationship between mother and daughter is less repressed than that of the mother and son. This retention affects women's selves, so that they remain fluid and interrelational. As a result of this difference between men and women, masculine writing has an ambivalent response to women. Women tend to remain outside or on the fringes of male discourse, and feminine pleasure poses the greatest challenge to masculine discourse. Masculine discourse is also logocentric and binary; its meaning is produced through hierarchal, male-dominated, binary oppositions. Masculine discourse creates a situation in which feminine discourse is characterized by omissions and gaps. Latent in these gaps and omissions are conflicting feelings regarding sexuality, motherhood, and autonomy.

An important question raised by feminist criticism is whether there is a gender-based women's language that is significantly and inevitably different from the language of men. In *Language and Woman's Place* (1975), Robin Lakoff argues that there is more to "speaking like a woman" than simply vocabulary. Examining syntactical patterns of a typical female and evaluating the frequency with which women use tag questions, she concludes that the traditional powerlessness of women in Western society is reflected in many aspects of women's language. Other theorists who are interested in differences between male and female languages explore sociolinguistic issues, such as the practice of women assuming their fathers' names at birth and their husbands' names when married, the frequency with which women are addressed by familiar names, the frequency of interruption in speech between men and women, and the large number of pejorative terms applicable to women. Writers interested in these latter linguistic areas are Cheris Kramarae and Julia Penelope Stanley.

In this conflict between male and female discourse, writing may be an anticipatory, therapeutic experience of liberation. Writing may return to a woman her repressed pleasure. It may also create a collective space in which women writers may speak of and to women. Gayatri Chakravorty Spivak explores discourse and literature in general as discursive practices. In her *In Other Worlds: Essays in Cultural Politics* (1987) she shows the tendency in Western cultures to universalize particular examples into human examples. Spivak examines feminism in relation to British imperialism in India and then situates feminist criticism within middle-class academia. This approach argues that what has been assumed to be universal truth is in fact the Western colonial or male conception of truth, a perspective that distorts or ignores the experiences of Others. The goal of such a critical perspective is to authenticate the expression of Others based on individual experience and shared understanding and to call into question the accepted definitions of truth and meaningful discourse.

Differences among women

Another concern that has become important in feminist criticism is the differences among women themselves. A model that presumes a universal feminine experience requires that women, unlike men, be free from cultural and racial determination. Under such a model, the barriers to shared experience created by race, class, gender, and sexuality are somehow cleared away when one is a woman. Women of color, such as critic Barbara Smith, argue that one cannot assume that there is one universal feminine experience or writing. For example, the sexuality of black women tends to be represented as natural, primitive, and free from traditional cultural inhibitions; this assumption has been invoked both to justify and to deny the sexual abuse of black women and the lack of respect given to them. In general, Smith criticizes other feminists for excluding or ignoring women of color. She also observes that both black and white male scholars working with black authors neglect women.

Furthermore, it is not possible to discuss a universal experience of motherhood. Racism affects women of color differently from the way it affects white women, especially in the effort to rear children who can be self-sufficient and self-respecting. These troubles are inherent in a culture that holds as natural the binary opposition white/black, wherein white is the privileged term. This opposition is deeply rooted in the colonial history of Western civilization. Women of color cannot be exempt from the insidious consequences of this binary opposition, and white women cannot participate in productive dialogue with women of color whenever this traditional opposition is ignored.

Lesbian feminist criticism

Another friction within the feminist movement involves lesbian feminist criticism. Just as women of color have considered themselves excluded, lesbian feminists consider themselves excluded, not only by the dominant white male culture but also by heterosexual females. Authors concerned with this problem include Bonnie Zimmerman and Adrienne Rich. In fact, Rich provides a definition of "lesbianism" so broad that it encompasses most of feminine creativity.

Feminist psychoanalytic criticism

In the 1970's a general movement toward psychoanalysis and toward women reading men and one another occurred within feminism. This movement is exemplified in the writings of such feminists as Mary Jacobs, Jane Gallop, and Juliet Richardson. For feminist theorists, the limitations of traditional theories accounting for the origins of oppression had been uncovered. Writers in the 1970's became very interested in, for example, the positioning of women within repressive sexual and political discourses. Many feminist writers have become interested in the establishment of an identity that involves both separation and connection, so that a binary relationship is not created and one is not perceived as a threat. In such a new relationship, women would no longer need, for example, to attempt to create an Oedipal triangle through their children. Each gender might develop less threatening relations to the other.

Reading differences

In regard to women reading men and one another, Annette Kolodny investigated methodological problems from an empiricist stance. She concludes that women do read differently from men. Her essay "A Map for Rereading: Or, Gender and the Interpretation of Literary Texts" (1980) examines how the two contrasting methods of interpretation appear in two stories and how the differences between masculine and feminine perspectives are mirrored in the reaction of readers to the two stories (Charlotte Perkins Gilman's "The Yellow Wallpaper," 1892, and Susan Glaspell's "A Jury of Her Peers," 1927). Judith Fetterley's work also presents a model for gender differences in reading. In *The Resisting Reader: A Feminist Approach to American Fiction* (1978), she argues against the position that the primary works of American fiction are intended, and written, for a universal audience and that women have permitted themselves to be masculinized in order to read these texts. One of the first steps, Fetterley contends, is for women to become resisting, rather than assenting, readers.

Varieties of feminism

Feminism has engaged in and with other branches of criticism, including Marxist criticism and deconstruction. Nancy K. Miller and Peggy Kamuf, for example, have incorporated deconstructive approaches in their work. Judith Lowder Newton and Lillian Robinson have incorporated Marxism.

The movement toward alternative ways of writing, however, involves drastic changes in the relationship between public and private and the traditional opposition between emotional and rational. Such an attempt in literature was heralded by Woolf's writing (for example, *The Waves* in 1931 and *To the Lighthouse* in 1927) and may be read in the work of Muriel Spark (*The Hothouse by the East River*, 1973), Angela Carter (*The Passion of New Eve*, 1977), Toni Morrison (*The Bluest Eye*, 1970), Alice Walker (*Meridian*, 1976), Marge Piercy (*Woman on the Edge of Time*, 1976), Margaret Atwood (*The Edible Woman*, 1969), Joanna Russ (*The Female Man*, 1975), and Fay Weldon (*The Life and Loves of a She-Devil*, 1983), among others.

Perhaps the most agreed-upon accomplishment of feminist criticism (though even in this agreement there is caution) has been finding and identifying a variety of feminine traditions in literature. Numerous women writers have been "rediscovered," introduced into the literary canon, and examined as important to the literary tradition. This interest in expanding the study of literature by women has had a significant impact in colleges and universities. Indeed, feminist criticism, by the beginning of the twenty-first century, had joined with other traditions—Native American, African American, Asian American, lesbian and gay—in an ongoing effort to celebrate and express diversity in investigations of identity.

Bibliography

Beauvoir, Simone de. *The Second Sex*. 1949. Reprint. Introduction by Deirdre Blair. New York: Random House, 1990. In this famous work, the author considers thoughtfully just what it means to be a woman, thus setting the stage for the modern feminist movement. Includes an index.

Christian, Barbara. *New Black Feminist Criticism, 1985-2000*. Edited by Gloria Bowles, M. Guilia Fabi, and Arlene R. Keizer. Urbana: University of Illinois Press, 2007. A collection of essays and reviews by one of the founders of black feminist literary criticism, ranging in subject matter from pedagogical issues and questions of definition to analyses of specific writers. Includes bibliographical references and an index.

Eagleton, Mary, ed. *Feminist Literary Theory: A Reader*. Reprint. Cambridge, Mass.: Blackwell, 2000. A revised and expanded edition of a classic text, featuring additions to every section and an added chapter on postmodernist theories of subjectivity. Fully indexed.

Federico, Annette, ed. *Gilbert and Gubar's "The Madwoman in the Attic" After Thirty Years*. Columbia: University of Missouri Press, 2009. A thirty-year retrospective on a classic work of feminist literature and literary criticism (see below). Includes a foreword by Sandra M. Gilbert.

Frost, Elisabeth A. *The Feminist Avant-Garde in American Poetry*. Iowa City: University of Iowa Press, 2003. Discusses the works of Gertrude Stein, Mina Loy, Sonia Sanchez, Susan Howe, and Harryette Mullen. Includes a bibliography and an index.

Frost, Elisabeth A., and Cynthia Hogue, eds. *Innovative Women Poets: An Anthology of Contemporary Poetry and Interviews*. Iowa City: University of Iowa Press, 2006. Interviews in which fourteen diverse poets comment on their poetry and their poetic theories. Includes selections from their poetry. Each interview is preceded by a brief introduction.

Gilbert, Sandra M., and Susan Gubar. *The Madwoman in the Attic: The Woman Writer and the Nineteenth-Century Literary Imagination*. 2d ed. New Haven, Conn.: Yale University Press, 2000. A landmark work, reissued with a revealing new introduction by the original authors.

_____, eds. *Feminist Literary Theory and Criticism: A Norton Reader*. New York: W. W. Norton, 2007. Represents more than one hundred writers and scholars, dating from the Middle Ages to the twenty-first century. An indispensable collection.

Greer, Germaine. *Slip-Shod Sibyls: Recognition, Rejection, and the Woman Poet*. London: Penguin, 1996. A poignant account of the plight of women poets before the twentieth century, who were often treated as freaks of nature but because of their lack of education produced works that were neither original nor of high enough quality to be admitted to the canon.

Kinnahan, Linda A. *Lyric Interventions: Feminism, Experimental Poetry, and Contemporary Discourse*. Iowa City: University of Iowa Press, 2004. Examines how such social and cultural factors as nation, gender, and race influence the lyric subject. The author discusses linguistically experimental poetry by American and British writers, including Barbara Guest, Kathleen Fraser, Erica Hunt, Alison Saar, M. Nourbese Philip, and Carol Ann Duffy. Includes a bibliography and an index.

Langdell, Cheri Colby. *Adrienne Rich: The Moment of Change*. Westport, Conn.:

Praeger, 2004. A biographical and critical study of one of America's most important poets, showing how her poetry reflects each radical transformation in her ideology, including her adoption of radical feminism and her later conversion to postmodern Marxism. Includes biographical references and an index.

Lepson, Ruth, ed. *Poetry from "Sojourner": A Feminist Anthology.* Urbana: University of Illinois Press, 2004. A collection of nearly 150 poems published in the prominent feminist journal *Sojourner*, some by such well-known poets as Nikki Giovannni and Adrienne Rich, others by women whose only recognition has come from their work's appearance in *Sojourner*. Includes an index.

Mills, Sara. *Feminist Stylistics.* New York: Routledge, 2005. A study of feminist stylistics, utilizing both literary and nonliterary texts. In the first part of the volume, the author considers several theoretical issues; in the second section, she discusses analysis at the level of the word, the phrase or sentence, and the complete discourse. Includes a glossary, notes, a bibliography, and an index.

Rooney, Ellen, ed. *The Cambridge Companion to Feminist Literary Theory.* New York: Cambridge University Press, 2006. Provides extracts representing a wide range of historical periods and drawn from various disciplines to demonstrate how language reflects assumptions about gender. The book is divided into six thematic sections, each with an introduction. Includes a bibliography of extracts and an index. A well-organized, accessible guide to the subject.

Showalter, Elaine. *Inventing Herself: Claiming a Feminist Intellectual Heritage.* New York: Scribner, 2001. Examines the lives of famous women, from Mary Wollstonecraft to Princess Diana, many of them feminist writers and critics, but all, feminist or not, determined to be independent.

Smith, Barbara, ed. *Home Girls: A Black Feminist Anthology.* 1983. Reprint. New Brunswick, N.J.: Rutgers University Press, 2000. A collection of works by thirty-two black and lesbian activists from the United States and the Caribbean. Includes a new preface, updated biographies, and a bibliography.

David L. Erben

PAULA GUNN ALLEN

Born: Cubero, New Mexico; October 24, 1939
Died: Ft. Bragg, California; May 29, 2008

PRINCIPAL POETRY
The Blind Lion, 1974
Coyote's Daylight Trip, 1978
A Cannon Between My Knees, 1981
Star Child, 1981
Shadow Country, 1982
Wyrds, 1987
Skins and Bones: Poems, 1979-1987, 1988
Life Is a Fatal Disease: Collected Poems, 1962-1995, 1997

OTHER LITERARY FORMS

Paula Gunn Allen's writing helped establish the literature of her American Indian cultural heritage as a legitimate and recognized genre. In addition to her extensive and innovative catalog of poetry, Allen published fiction, nonfiction, biographies, collections of myth and oral tradition, critical essays, pedagogical articles concerning the education of native peoples, and gender and sexuality studies. Allen collected, wrote, and edited personal histories as well as myths and legends of various tribes in her books *The Sacred Hoop: Recovering the Feminine in American Indian Traditions* (1986), *Spider Woman's Granddaughters: Traditional Tales and Contemporary Writing by Native American Women* (1989), and *Grandmothers of the Light: A Medicine Woman's Sourcebook* (1991). Allen's motivation to raise awareness concerning American Indian literature, combined with her innovative academic endeavors, earned her acclaim from critics and readers alike, placing the author at the forefront of the American Indian, feminist, and gay and lesbian literary scenes.

ACHIEVEMENTS

Paula Gunn Allen's literary achievements began in 1978, when the National Endowment for the Arts awarded her a distinguished writing fellowship. She received two postdoctoral fellowships, the first from the University of California in 1981 and the second from the Ford Foundation-National Research Council in 1984. Allen received two awards for her groundbreaking work in 1990: the American Book Award from the Before Columbus Foundation for *Spider Woman's Granddaughters* and the Native American Prize for Literature.

Accolades for Allen's work increased throughout her career, in which she amassed honors such as the Susan Koppelman Award from the Popular Cultural Association and American Culture Association (1991), the Vesta Award for Essay Writing (1991), the Southern California Women for Understanding Award for Literature (1991), an honorary doctorate in humanities from Mills College (1995), the Hubbell Prize for Lifetime Achievement in American Literary Studies (1999), and the Lifetime Achievement Award from the Native Writers' Circle of the Americas (2001). In 2004, Allen's *Pocahontas: Medicine Woman, Spy, Entrepreneur, Diplomat* (2003) was nominated for a Pulitzer Prize, and in 2007, she received the Lannan Literary Fellowship, designed to honor writers whose impact on English-language literature promotes increased interest and readership in both prose and poetry.

Biography

Paula Gunn Allen was born Paula Marie Francis in 1939 in Cubero, New Mexico, and was raised by her mother and grandmother on the Cubero Land Grant, situated between the Laguna and Acoma Pueblo Reservations. The daughter of a Laguna-Sioux-Scottish mother and a Lebanese American father, Allen cultivated her love and appreciation of the myths and lore of her American Indian ancestors and would perpetuate her desire to be a lifelong student of native culture.

Allen began her higher education at Colorado Women's College, where the work of poet Robert Creeley would have a profound influence on her. She took time off from school to marry and have two children, but the marriage ended in divorce a few years later. She transferred to the University of Oregon, earning a B.A. in English in 1966 and an M.F.A. in creative writing in 1968. At the University of New Mexico, Allen wanted to pursue a doctorate in Native American literature, but the dean informed her that this was not possible as Native American literature was not a canonical genre. Instead, in 1975, Allen received a doctorate in American studies with a concentration on Native American literature.

Following the completion of her doctorate, two divorces, and the birth of three children, Allen began writing from a twentieth century lesbian-feminist perspective. She quickly established herself as a prolific writer and has since been acknowledged as the founder of American Indian literary studies. Seeking to rectify the canonical discrepancies regarding ethnic literature, Allen (after publishing five collections of poetry) turned her focus to the retelling of native myths and to lesbian-feminist literary criticism. In subsequent years, Allen kept working, writing many texts that would become staples in the classroom—providing future generations of students with the types of sources that were unavailable to her during her own education.

Analysis

Paula Gunn Allen's first book of poetry, *The Blind Lion*, contains some of the author's most personal work. The poems in its three sections—"The Blind Lion," "The

Amorclast," and "The Separation"— chronicle the dissolution of romantic love, while only subtly referencing her cultural background. The first section records a metamorphosis from the warm comfort of familiarity in "Definition" to colliding and opposing elements in "The Orange on Your Head Is on Fire," in which the man is the "fire/ bird" and the woman is the "cold wind." The lion of the title poem, an animal normally associated with dominance, pride, and courage, is made impotent by its blindness and is transformed into a weeping and pitiable creature. The lion thus becomes a metaphor for the relationship now reduced and defined by isolation. "Cool Life" further elucidates the couple's relationship complications, of which the narrator states: "between us/ we are ice . . ." and "outside of us/ dandelions bloom."

The second section of *The Blind Lion* denotes the irreparable breakage of traditional love and the institution of marriage. The language of the poems becomes increasingly dark and volatile, as the narrator in "The Amorclast" describes, "your fist expresses the rain-/ drops flying around us," culminating with the stark language and imagery of the lover "twisting the handle/ revealing the bone/ of your contempt." Other poems within this section similarly portray the escalating turbulence within the relationship—often represented by aspects of nature such as fog, frost, wind, and shadows. Here, Allen experiments with and reinvents the poetic form in order to fully portray the sporadic and often irrational ways in which people cope with failed relationships.

The third section, "The Separation," portrays the narrator's reclaiming and reinvention of herself, reflected in the increasingly prevalent spiritual and feminist tones of the poems. In "Shadows," the narrator struggles with her sense of identity as "The room comes to me a stranger,/ its familiar things turned/ unfamiliar, as though/ I, a visitor, had just walked in. . . ." Her former life having been forever altered, the narrator cannot recognize where she belongs in her newly realized solitude. "Liebestraume" (German for "dreams of love") is perhaps the darkest piece in the collection, wherein "pestilence," "plague," and "rotting velvet" lie under the covers that "half-hid the empty revolver you cocked and used/ to blow open the bone at the back of my skull. . . ." The romantic title belies the poet's emotions as her dreams of love are displaced by dreams of death. However, the narrator ends the poem expressing expectations of hope and rebirth, from which she will arise transformed.

A Cannon Between My Knees

A Cannon Between My Knees, Allen's third collection, builds on the feelings left unresolved at the end of *The Blind Lion*. The fourteen new poems are more noticeably concerned with spirituality, myth, creation, and the roles of women therein. Allen does include two poems dedicated to her father, "Durango Suite" and "Lament of My Father, Lakota," while further exploring the persistence of memory along with the harsh reality of reservation life in "Wool Season: 1973."

Allen's poetry shows a new maturity in this collection. Her feminist voice becomes increasingly impressive, as in "The Beautiful Woman Who Sings," which depicts a hardworking woman of nature who embodies true beauty. In "Poem for Pat," one of Allen's first pieces representing homosexual love and desire, the narrator reminisces, "we found each other again, she said,/ and we were shivering at what we contemplated/ locked together on the sandstone mesas. . . ." In "Suicid/ing(ed) Indian Woman," the poet retells four stories of jilted, misunderstood, and misused women from various native tribes. From their sadness, she creates strength, and as the collection progresses, so too do the references to woman as creator, mother, grandmother, provider, and nurturer.

Accompanying these representations of female empowerment are references to male weaknesses such as addictions to alcohol and gambling, brought on by the emasculation of native men, just two of the results of white colonization of native lands. These references make the phrase "a cannon between my knees" in the final poem of the collection, "Thusness Before the War," especially poignant, as the symbol of military domination and destruction becomes a phallic symbol of feminine virility and authority.

SHADOW COUNTRY

The meaning behind the title of Allen's fifth poetry collection, *Shadow Country*, welcomes reader interpretation, as its pages contain a world that is somehow universal, yet uniquely hers. Neither dark nor light, the title could represent Allen's feelings about her mixed heritage; it could imply the marginalization of native populations or the diminishing of the country's glory; or it could even signify, as in "Que Cante Quetzal," that the country is engulfed in shadow due to its ongoing participation in brutal military conquests worldwide. Allen does not limit herself by any boundaries in her poetic endeavors, as she explores the themes of creation, consumerism, revolution, apocalypse, resurrection, and celebration.

"Los Angeles, 1980" indicts American vanity and the consumerism that results from people's attempts to achieve the public "ideal." This "death culture" dominates the natural world and pollutes the air, then seeks to use the landscape's true beauty to create organic beauty products, natural-fiber clothes, and herbal nutritional supplements. Despite these urges to improve "naturally," signs reading "Weight and Smoking Control Center" and other such consumer fodder litter the sidewalks. A passerby notices her "average" reflection in the Center's smoky glass, and notes, ". . . death comes in pretty packages too,/ and all around me/ the dying air agreed."

The poems within *Shadow Country*, although certainly concerned with native spirituality, explore the issues of traditional and modern cultures, which are then juxtaposed with political issues. These comparative critiques produce powerful commentary in regard to the conflicting values of white and native societies. Relics and ruins of native cultures, military conquests, and forced removals are present in several poignant poems such as "Another Long Walk," "The Warrior," "Riding the Thunder," and "Off Reservation Blues," in which the dreaming narrator grieves over her imprisonment, which symbolizes the ongoing claustrophobia that resulted from the forced removal of native peoples to reservations, but which gives her poetry meaning: "Open words, openly said/ are not heard."

OTHER MAJOR WORKS
LONG FICTION: *The Woman Who Owned the Shadows*, 1983.

NONFICTION: *Studies in American Indian Literature: Critical Essays and Course Designs*, 1983; *The Sacred Hoop: Recovering the Feminine in American Indian Traditions*, 1986; *Grandmothers of the Light: A Medicine Woman's Sourcebook*, 1991; *As Long as the Rivers Flow: The Stories of Nine Native Americans*, 1996 (with Clark Smith); *Off the Reservation: Reflections on Boundary-Busting, Border-Crossing Loose Canons*, 1998; *Pocahontas: Medicine Woman, Spy, Entrepreneur, Diplomat*, 2003.

EDITED TEXTS: *From the Center—A Folio: Native American Art and Poetry*, 1981; *Spider Woman's Granddaughters: Traditional Tales and Contemporary Writing by Native American Women*, 1989; *Voice of the Turtle: American Indian Literature, 1900-1970*, 1994; *Song of the Turtle: American Indian Literature, 1974-1994*, 1996; *Hozho: Walking in Beauty*, 2001 (with Carolyn Dunn Anderson); *Outfoxing Coyote*, 2002 (with Anderson).

MISCELLANEOUS: *Columbus and Beyond: Views from Native Americans*, 1992 (with others); *Gossips, Gorgons, and Crones: The Fates of the Earth*, 1993 (foreword by Allen; text by Jane Caputi).

BIBLIOGRAPHY

Allen, Paula Gunn. "A Funny Thing Happened on My Way to Press." *Frontiers: A Journal of Women Studies* 23 (2002): 3-6. This short, autobiographical account of Allen's reactions to the stereotypes of American Indians is a quick yet insightful glimpse into the author's personality, both as an American Indian woman and as a poet.

Forbes, Jack. "Colonialism and Native American Literature: Analysis." *Wicazo Sa Review* 3 (1987): 17-23. Forbes's primary objective in this article is to address questions relating to the term "Native American literature." He examines what constitutes native or ethnic literature, who is "allowed" to write it, and what the literature infers or implies within the social construct of a colonial interpretation.

Jahner, Elaine A. "The Style of the Times in Paula Gunn Allen's Poetry." In *Speak to Me Words: Essays on Contemporary American Indian Poetry*, edited by Dean Rader and Janice Gould. Tucson: University of Arizona Press, 2003. In this article, Jahner writes on Allen's use of formal structures in her poems.

Koehler, Lyle. "Native Women of the Americas: A Bibliography." *Frontiers: A Journal of Women Studies* 6 (1981): 73-101. A comprehensive bibliography of authors and works related to various themes in Native American literature and an invaluable go-to guide for those interested in the genre. The author provides subsections on specific topics such as religion, sexuality, and craftswomen.

Rowley, Kelley E. "Re-inscribing Mythopoetic Vision in Native American Studies." *American Indian Quarterly* 26 (2002): 491-500. Mythopoetic vision refers to the process of making myths and how audiences come to perceive them. Rowley uses Allen's four characteristics of a sacred visionary narrative, "the supernatural characters, the nonordinary events, the transcendent powers, and the pour quoi elements," to further expound on the mythopoetics of Native American texts.

Ruppert, Jim. "Paula Gunn Allen and Joy Harjo: Closing the Distance Between Personal and Mythic Space." *American Indian Quarterly* 7, no. 1 (1983): 27-40. Ruppert discusses the poetry of Allen and Joy Harjo and the ways in which their works address the fusion of mundane and mystic/personal and universal spaces, in order to create harmony between earth, mind, and spirit.

Lydia E. Ferguson

MARGARET ATWOOD

Born: Ottawa, Ontario, Canada; November 18, 1939

PRINCIPAL POETRY
Double Persephone, 1961
The Circle Game, 1964 (single poem), 1966 (collection)
Kaleidoscopes Baroque: A Poem, 1965
Talismans for Children, 1965
Expeditions, 1966
Speeches for Dr. Frankenstein, 1966
The Animals in That Country, 1968
What Was in the Garden, 1969
The Journals of Susanna Moodie, 1970
Procedures for Underground, 1970
Power Politics, 1971
You Are Happy, 1974
Selected Poems, 1976
Two-Headed Poems, 1978
True Stories, 1981
Snake Poems, 1983
Interlunar, 1984
Selected Poems II: Poems Selected and New, 1976-1986, 1987
Selected Poems, 1966-1984, 1990
Poems, 1965-1975, 1991
Poems, 1976-1989, 1992
Morning in the Burned House, 1995
Eating Fire: Selected Poems, 1965-1995, 1998
The Door, 2007

OTHER LITERARY FORMS

Margaret Atwood's publishing history is a testimonial to her remarkable productivity and versatility as a writer. As well as a poet, she is a novelist, a short-fiction writer, a children's author, an editor, and an essayist. *The Edible Woman* (1969), Atwood's first novel, defined the focus of her fiction: mainly satirical explorations of sexual politics, where self-deprecating female protagonists defend themselves against men, chiefly with the weapon of language. Other novels include *Surfacing* (1972), *Lady Oracle* (1976), *Life Before Man* (1979), *Bodily Harm* (1981), *Cat's Eye* (1988), *The Robber Bride* (1993), *Alias Grace* (1996), *The Blind Assassin* (2000), *Oryx and Crake* (2003),

The Penelopiad: The Myth of Penelope and Odysseus (2005), and *The Year of the Flood* (2009). *The Handmaid's Tale* (1985), a dystopian novel set in a postnuclear, monotheocratic Boston, where life is restricted by censorship and state control of reproduction, is the best known of Atwood's novels and was made into a commercial film of the same title, directed by Volker Schlöndorff.

Dancing Girls, and Other Stories (1977) and *Bluebeard's Egg* (1983) are books of short fiction, as are *Wilderness Tips* (1991), *Good Bones* (1992), and *Moral Disorder* (2006). Atwood has written children's books: *Up in the Tree* (1978), which she also illustrated, *Anna's Pet* (1980, with Joyce Barkhouse), *For the Birds* (1990), *Princess Prunella and the Purple Peanut* (1995), *Rude Ramsay and the Roaring Radishes* (2003), and *Bashful Bob and Doleful Dorinda* (2004). A nonfiction book for young readers is *Days of the Rebels: 1815-1840* (1977).

Atwood's contributions to literary theory and criticism have also been significant. Her idiosyncratic, controversial, but well-researched *Survival: A Thematic Guide to Canadian Literature* (1972) is essential for the student interested in Atwood's version of the themes that have shaped Canadian creative writing over a century. Her *Second Words: Selected Critical Prose* (1982) is one of the first works of the feminist criticism that has flourished in Canada. She also produced *Strange Things: The Malevolent North in Canadian Literature* (1995). A related title is *Negotiating with the Dead: A Writer on Writing* (2002).

Achievements

Critical success and national and international acclaim have greeted Margaret Atwood's work since her first major publication, the poetry collection *The Circle Game*. Poems from that collection were awarded the 1965 President's Medal for Poetry by the University of Western Ontario in 1966, and after commercial publication, the collection won for Atwood the prestigious Governor-General's Award for poetry in 1967. In that same year, Atwood's *The Animals in That Country* was awarded first prize in Canada's Centennial Commission Poetry Competition. The Chicago periodical *Poetry* awarded Atwood the Union League Civic and Arts Poetry Prize in 1969 and the Bess Hokin Prize in 1974. Since that time, Atwood's numerous awards and distinctions have been more for her work in fiction, nonfiction, and humanitarian affairs. She has received several honorary doctorates and many prestigious prizes, among them the Toronto Arts Award (1986), *Ms.* magazine's Woman of the Year for 1986, the Ida Nudel Humanitarian Award from the Canadian Jewish Congress, and the American Humanist of the Year Award for 1987. In fact, at one time or another, Atwood has won just about every literary award for Canadian writers. In 2000, Atwood won the Booker Prize for the best novel by a citizen of the United Kingdom or British Commonwealth.

Biography

Margaret Eleanor Atwood was born into a family that encouraged inquiry and discovery. An important stimulus to her intellectual curiosity was certainly the family's yearly sojourns in the remote bush of northern Ontario and Quebec, where Atwood's father, an entomologist, carried out much of his study and research. It is likely that this environment shaped Atwood's ironic vision and her imagery. Atwood's writing, especially her poetry and her second novel, *Surfacing*, are permeated with her intimate knowledge of natural history and with her perception of the casual brutality with which the weak are sacrificed for the survival of the strong.

Studying between 1957 and 1961 for her undergraduate degree in English at Victoria College, University of Toronto, Atwood came under the influence of Canadian poet Jay MacPherson and especially of Northrop Frye, one of the twentieth century's preeminent critical theorists. They encouraged Atwood's early poetry and directed her toward biblical and mythological symbol and archetype, still strong forces in her writing.

Between 1961 and 1963, Atwood pursued graduate studies in English at Harvard University, receiving her M.A. in 1962. In 1963, she met fellow graduate student James Polk, whom she married in 1967, when after a period of writing and teaching, Atwood returned to Harvard to pursue a Ph.D. (beginning thesis work on the English metaphysical romance). In Canada, however, her burgeoning success as a writer and her involvement as a university teacher of creative writing soon superseded her formal studies.

In the early 1970's, Atwood traveled in Europe and then returned to Canada to continue writing and teaching. She became an editor at House of Anansi Press, one of the many Canadian publishing houses that sprang up in the fertile late 1960's to encourage young and sometimes experimental writers. She also met novelist Graeme Gibson, who may have influenced her own foray into experimental fiction, *Surfacing*. After her divorce from Polk in 1973, Atwood moved with Gibson to rural Alliston, Ontario, where their daughter Jess was born in 1976.

Throughout the 1980's and 1990's, Atwood's overall output was steady, though she did not continue to produce very much new poetry. In the latter 1980's, Atwood made successful forays into the field of screenwriting for film and the musical theater. Her increased involvement with world social and political issues is evident in her vice-chairmanship of the Writers' Union of Canada and her presidency of PEN International, where she has waged a vigorous battle against literary censorship. Her association with Amnesty International has prompted an increasingly strong expression of her moral vision. She has continued to publish regularly in Canadian, American, and European media and has received worldwide recognition as a major contemporary writer.

Analysis

Margaret Atwood's poetry deals essentially with paradox and struggle in both art and life. Her first (and now generally inaccessible) chapbook of poetry, *Double*

Persephone, contains the components of her vision, which she elucidates in her next nine poetry collections with more depth, conviction, and stylistic maturity, but whose elements she changes little. An overview of Atwood's poetry reveals patterns expressed through mythological and biblical allusion and recurring imagery relating to mutability, metamorphosis, near annihilation, and, ultimately, adaptation and definition. References to eyes, water, mirrors, glass, photographs, maps, and charts abound. The archetypal journey/quest motif is a vital component of Atwood's vision. It is worked out metaphorically in the historical context of European exploration and settlement of the Canadian wilderness, the pioneer's battle with alienation, loneliness, and the struggle to articulate a new self in a new world. If the pioneer masters the new "language," he or she will survive; his or her divided self will become whole. This life-and-death struggle is also carried out in the psychological arena of sexual politics. Much of Atwood's poetry (especially *Procedures for Underground* and *Power Politics*) explores—at first with anger, later with resignation, always with irony—the damage that men and women inflict on one another despite their interdependence. In Atwood's poetry, chaos is perceived as the center of things; it is the individual's quest, as both artist and natural being, to define order, meaning, and purpose—to survive.

THE CIRCLE GAME

The Circle Game, Atwood's first major poetry collection, represents the outset of an artistic and personal journey. The artist-poet (whose voice is personal, ironic, and female) struggles to shape chaos into order through language, whose enigmatic symbols she must master and control. Language is a set of tools, the key component of the poet's bag of tricks, packed for the (metaphoric) journey undertaken, for example, in *The Circle Game*'s "Evening Trainstation Before Departure":

> Here I am in
> a pause in space
> hunched on the edge
> of a tense suitcase.

Language, however, is duplicitous; it is a weapon that can rebound against the poet herself. She is engaged in a constant struggle to interpret and communicate without being subsumed, as suggested in "The Sybil": "she calls to me with the many/ voices of the children/ not I want to die/ but You must die."

In life, chaos comprises process, flux, and the temporal; the struggle for the individual is both to understand his or her own nature and to reconcile himself or herself to the processes of nature, history, and culture. The external, natural world mirrors the self; it speaks the siren language of the primitive and lies in wait to ambush with casual cruelty human beings' fragile civility. Through recognition, struggle, and reconciliation, the individual can transcend his or her destructive self, mirrored in the natural world.

Throughout *The Circle Game*, the self, both artistic and psychological, struggles to be born. The creative impulse is strong, the instinct for survival great, but *The Circle Game*'s "Journey to the Interior" says that the individual does not yet understand the ambiguous messages of either art or life and is in danger: "and words here are as pointless/ as calling in a vacant/ wilderness."

The opening poem, "This Is a Photograph of Me," presents a paradox. In the photograph, the speaker's image is barely discernible, suspended as if in a watery grave, yet awaiting redefinition, new birth: "I am in the lake, in the center/ of the picture, just under the surface." In "Camera," the artist is reviled for the impulse to capture life in a static form when the impulse to the kinesis, the process of life, is so compelling: "Camera man/ how can I love your glass eye? . . . that small black speck/ travelling towards the horizon/ at almost the speed of life/ is me." Who is "me"? It is the androgynous, divided self, defined metaphorically in the powerful poem "After the Flood, We." "We" are Deucalion and Phyrra, in Greek mythology the sole male and female survivors of the mythic flood, suspended over the misty shapelessness of the drowned old world, designated by Zeus as the only humans deserving of survival. The female speaker differentiates between "I" and "you," "you" being an intimate who is here (as elsewhere throughout Atwood's poetry) the male. These two are charged with creating a new world. The self-absorbed male is a casual progenitor, "tossing small pebbles/ at random over your shoulder," but the female persona perceives horror, a Frankenstein's monster rising up to overwhelm "the beauty of the morning." The threat to process and growth, both artistic and personal, is the strongest of perceived evils. A sense that the artist-speaker is not yet equal to the task, has not yet found the appropriate language, is particularly strong in "The Messenger," where "a random face/ revolving outside the window" fades into oblivion because, the poem's ironic tone implies, the message is brought to the inappropriate recipient; the messenger shouts "desperate messages with his/ obliterated mouth/ in a silent language."

In *The Circle Game*, a game motif is evident in the titles and metaphoric significance of several poems ("Playing Cards," "An Attempted Solution for Chess Problems," and the collection's title poem). Intelligence, even cunning, is required. Knowing the divided self is the key to becoming the artist fit to pass on the message vital for survival. The collection's final poem, "The Settlers," suggests that perhaps success will come in laying the foundation for future understanding. The poet-narrator optimistically envisions a transformation through natural evolution into messages for the future, though understanding is still in doubt: "children run, with green/ smiles (not knowing/ where)." As yet the tools, the language, are lacking. The simple innocence of a children's circle game becomes weighted with foreboding; critic Rosemary Sullivan observes, "The narcissism of the circle game claims the narrator, and confines Atwood herself in its prisoning rhythms. We have yet to see the circle effectively broken."

The Animals in That Country

The journey of discovery continues in *The Animals in That Country* and is undertaken in several metaphorical arenas: the natural, the historical, the cultural, and, above all, the arena of the self. Again, the artist-self is found wanting. Several poems such as "Provisions" and "The Surveyors" suggest that the pioneer brings the wrong equipment to the new world because he or she has a faulty concept of the terrain and its natural inhabitants. Later generations distance themselves as soon as possible from the natural interrelationship of human and animals, the hunt being transformed into a ritualized game and then an irrelevance, as the collection's title poem points out.

Self-definition in a modern cultural setting also eludes the speaker in this collection's poems. At its writing, Atwood was on the second of her two sojourns at Harvard. Her own dislocation in American society and her distaste (expressed in letters to friends and colleagues in Canada) for American materialism and the accelerating Vietnam War are expressed in poems such as "The Landlady" and "It Is Dangerous to Read Newspapers." Her sense of alienation, from both place and people, is sadly noted in "Roominghouse, Winter": "Tomorrow, when you come to dinner/ They will tell you I never lived here." An ironic view emerges in an encounter with a relief map of Canada in the poem "At the Tourist Centre in Boston." An increasingly irate narrator asks first herself and then the receptionist, "Do you see nothing/ watching you from under the water?// Was the sky ever that blue?// Who really lives there?" That series of ominous questions signals a return journey to the interior of both Canada and the still unmapped and undefined self.

The definitive exploration of people's relationship to the natural world, to history, and to their own warring selves takes place in two of the collection's most powerful poems, "A Night in the Royal Ontario Museum" and "Progressive Insanities of a Pioneer." In the former, the speaker is inadvertently locked in the museum, "this crazed man-made/ stone brain," and is compelled to undergo a metaphoric journey to the beginnings of natural and human history. The worst horror to contemplate is preexistence, nondefinition: "I am dragged to the mind's/ deadend, . . . lost/ among the mastodons." In "Progressive Insanities of a Pioneer," this struggle to redefine the self out of chaos is explored in a metaphorical battle between a pioneer and the wilderness. In seven sections, or chapters, the story of the pioneer's failure unfolds relentlessly, the poem's flat and terse diction underscoring the horror of his descent into insanity and death. Seeking to impose order on the perceived chaos of his surroundings, the pioneer fails to acknowledge the necessity of adapting to the wilderness rather than subjugating it. He does not learn the language; instead, he makes a futile effort to structure, to classify. He is doomed to failure and annihilation, drowning in a metaphorical flux of Leviathan proportions.

The Journals of Susanna Moodie

Success in these parallel journeys both into the physical wilderness and into the self is achieved, however, by the persona who informs and narrates Atwood's next collection of poems, *The Journals of Susanna Moodie*. J. W. Dunbar Moodie and his wife, Susanna, were impoverished English gentry who emigrated to Canada in 1832 and took up a land grant in the bush near what is now Peterborough, Ontario. Their seven-year sojourn in the bush before they settled in the town of Belleville was a searing experience for Susanna. Steeped in nineteenth century Romanticism and possessing to no small degree the arrogance of her class, Susanna arrived in Canada with the rosy expectations of vulnerable people unscrupulously lured from home by the promise of bountiful land, a temperate climate, congenial neighbors, and best of all, freedom from taxation. The harsh reality of life in the wilderness destroyed many; Susanna, though, was able to draw on a previously untapped toughness of spirit that eventually turned her from a homesick gentlewoman into a self-sufficient, grudgingly loyal Canadian who contributed much to a fledgling Canadian culture. She recorded her experiences in a pair of accounts entitled *Roughing It in the Bush: Or, Forest Life in Canada* (1852) and *Life in the Clearings Versus the Bush* (1853). In them, readers detect a duality of her attitude and personality that Atwood exploits to advantage in *The Journals of Susanna Moodie*. In her contemplation of the physical and spiritual wildernesses that confront her, Susanna's fear and despair is evident but so, increasingly, is a testy strength and a reluctant love for her new country.

The collection is divided into three sections that treat respectively Susanna's immigration, her sojourn in the bush, and her later years in Belleville and Toronto. Metaphorically, the "journals" chronicle the passages of Susanna's life: the rebirth and redefinition of the self that beginning in a new land requires; the trial by fire (in Susanna's case, literal) of life in the hostile wilderness; finally, reconciliation and death, where physical burial marks a spiritual intermingling with the new land, ironically becoming alien again through twentieth century urbanization.

In "Journal 1," Susanna repeatedly expresses the realization of her need for a new identity; familiar psychological landmarks are now irrelevant. In "Further Arrivals" she observes, "We left behind . . . our civilized/ distinctions// and entered a large darkness." At first, she is threatened at every level, perceiving her husband as "the wereman," her "first neighbours" as "speaking a twisted dialect," and the wilderness as consciously malicious. Despite the familiar human instinct to order, catalog, and impose, Susanna recognizes the need for compromise: "Resolve: to be both tentative and hard to startle/ . . . in this area where my damaged knowing of the language means/ prediction is forever impossible." Susanna survives seven years of loneliness and physical hardship that transform her. She departs for Belleville with a sense that she does not yet fully understand her relationship with the wilderness. In "Departure from the Bush," she observes, "In time the animals/ arrived to inhabit me./ . . . There was something they almost taught me/ I came away not having learned." From the relatively civilized perspective of Belleville, Susanna contemplates the relationship between pioneer and wilderness with a mixture of bitterness and resignation. In the three "dream" poems of the "Journal 2" section, she recognizes in the natural cycle the inexorable interrelationship of life and death (often violent) of which humankind is an integral part. Her own ambivalence is expressed in "The Double Voice": "Two voices/ took turns using my eyes"; while one saw "the rituals of seasons and rivers," the other pointed out "a dead dog/ jubilant with maggots." In "Journal 3," Susanna's reconciliation with her new self and with her harsh new land is completed; after her death, her defiant voice can still be heard over the roar of the twentieth century Toronto built over her bones. As Atwood says in the afterword to this collection, "Susanna Moodie has finally turned herself inside out, and has become the spirit of the land she once hated."

PROCEDURES FOR UNDERGROUND

Having left Susanna Moodie speaking prophetically from her underground grave, Atwood made the underground the shaping metaphor of her next poetry collection, *Procedures for Underground*. She returns to a theme that dominated *The Circle Game*: the power of the artist to shape and articulate both internal and external experience. Critic Jerome Rosenberg reminds readers of Atwood's observation that artists who experience the creative process make "a descent to the underworld"; the artist's role is a mystical and powerful one (and perhaps subversive, the collection's title suggests). The artist persona is set apart from ordinary human relationships, as a seer is, by the ability to interpret experience outside the literal. In the title poem, the expectations of the artist blessed (or cursed) with second sight are grimly described: "Few will seek your help/ with love, none without fear."

The artist's compulsion to define, shape, interpret, and preserve permeates the collection's imagery. In "Three Desk Objects," the writer's tools are transformed by this purpose: "My cool machines/ . . . I am afraid to touch you/ I think you will cry out in pain// I think you will be warm, like skin." Many of the poems describe the capturing of images, meanings, and moments through a variety of artistic media. "Woman Skating" ends with "Over all I place/ a glass bell"; "Younger Sister, Going Swimming" has her dive recorded on the poet's paper; "Girl and Horse, 1928" and "Projected Slide of an Unknown Soldier" explore time and history through the "freeze-frame" of photography. However, the artist fails to capture or interpret the "underground" aspect of the person. Human nature remains impenetrable, a language unlearned, a primeval mystery unsolved, as the poem "A Soul, Geologically" says. "Where do the words go/ when we have said them?" is the plaintive question in "A Small Cabin."

The most ominous note in the collection is struck by a poem that returns to the game motif of *The Circle Game* and makes a sad commentary on the passage from innocence to experience. In "Game After Supper," a memory of a happy children's game of twilight hide-and-seek turns macabre when the reader understands that the small child plays with spectral cousins long dead of diphtheria and that the seeker is a threatening, anonymous male figure. "He will be an uncle,/ if we are lucky," comments the speaker wryly, but the sexual threat is clear, and the stage is set for the largely sexual struggle that provides the primary focus in Atwood's next collection. From here onward, her concern is more with external relationships; it is probably fair to say that this shift in focus marks the end of her most powerful work as a poet.

POWER POLITICS

Power Politics, written when Atwood's first marriage was breaking up, focuses primarily on human relationships, though Atwood's parallel concerns with humans in natural and social history and with interpreting the dual self are also strongly present. Specifically, *Power Politics* chronicles the destructive love-hate relationship that can exist between incompatible men and women. In this pessimistic collection, signals are missed, messages are misinterpreted, and the battle is mutually lost. The menacing, shadowy "tall man" of "Game After Supper" resolves into an aggrieved male partner; the anguished female speaker explores their inability to fulfill each other sexually, intellectually, or spiritually. The inevitable failure of the relationship is evident from the collection's terse, vicious (and gratuitous) opening epigram: "you fit into me/ like a hook into an eye// a fish hook/ an open eye." The poems' titles provide an inexorable chronology of descent from love through suspicion, mutual betrayal, and accusation to sad resignation and parting. Much of the imagery is of battle; in the central, seven-section poem "They Are Hostile Nations," battle lines are drawn despite a perceived mutual need: "Instead we are opposite, we/ touch as though attacking." Ultimately, the speaker blames herself for bringing to bear the weight of her expectations, emotional and artistic, on a partner unable to carry them. In "Hesitation Outside the Door," she addresses him sadly: "Get out while it is/ open, while you still can." However, in the final poem, "He Is Last Seen," the speaker mourns her partner's seeming escape "towards firm ground and safety" and away from the still-unresolved conflict underlying all Atwood's poetry thus far: that of the divided, unreconciled self.

YOU ARE HAPPY

In *You Are Happy*, progress is made toward the resolution of this conflict. The ironic, pessimistic tone of *Power Politics* continues in the opening section. Human relationships fail once again for both emotional and artistic reasons; they cannot withstand the double assault of misunderstanding and misinterpretation. Imagery of water, ice, mirrors, eyes, and particularly cameras still prevails, as "Newsreel: Man and Firing Squad" shows: "No more of these closeups, this agony/ taken just for the record anyway." In the collection's middle sections, "Songs of the Transformed" and "Circe/Mud Poems," the poet confronts the limitations of art in controlling and interpreting human nature and behavior. Through the voice of the sorceress Circe, a compelling character in Homer's *Odyssey* (c. 725 B.C.E.; English translation, 1614) who transformed men into swine, Atwood acknowledges the limitations of mythmaking and the attraction of accepting life as it is, with its ambivalence and vitality: "I search instead for the others,/ the ones left over,/ the ones who have escaped from these/ mythologies with barely their lives." This positive realization is reiterated in the collection's last section. In "Late August," a new mood of voluptuous acceptance and fruitfulness is evident: "The air is still/ warm, flesh moves over/ flesh, there is no// hurry."

In this collection, Atwood's poetic skills show new direction. She intersperses her familiar spare, short poetic forms with more fluid prose poems. Indeed, the early 1970's marked the beginning of Atwood's shift away from poetry toward prose writing; the themes and imagery in many poems are explored more fully in novels from the same periods. There was a hiatus of four years until *Two-Headed Poems* appeared.

Two-Headed Poems

Interestingly, much of *Two-Headed Poems* relates closely in tone, theme, and imagery to *The Journals of Susanna Moodie*, but where the voice in the latter was objectified and dramatized as Moodie's, the voice in *Two-Headed Poems* is subjective and intimate. This relationship can perhaps be partly explained by the fact that Atwood gave birth to her daughter Jess in 1976, and her experience of motherhood is strongly reflected in this first collection of poems since her daughter's birth. There is a subtle softening of the irony of tone and vision and of terse diction, a perceptible turn toward acceptance rather than rejection. The poems in this work suggest that Atwood has experienced not only artistically, but also personally, Moodie's sense of purpose and place in human history; Atwood too belongs to "the procession/ of old leathery mothers/ / passing the work from hand to hand,/ mother to daughter,// a long thread of red blood, not yet broken" ("A Red Shirt"). Poems such as "You Begin" reflect a renewed emotional and artistic purpose; "All Bread," with its motifs of sacrifice, sacrament, and Communion, expresses on one level acknowledgment of the rhythms of life and death inherent in nature, and on a parallel level the interdependence of the sexes, which marriage sanctifies. The poet has reconciled herself to the sometimes violent paradoxes that define life: natural, human, and artistic.

True Stories

That emerging attitude of acceptance is put to the test in *True Stories*. This collection is Atwood's poetic response to her increasing political commitment; its focus is even more external and marks a renewed emphasis on social themes less markedly evident in earlier collections such as *The Animals in That Country*. The generalized setting of many of the poems is the dusty, brutal, and brutalized countries of the Caribbean and Central America. The central group of poems in *True Stories* deals with political torture:

The description of actual tortures is graphic and horrifying, emphasized rather than undercut by the spare, brutal, direct diction and imagery of Atwood's poetic style. Whether the original accounts themselves are true is a question with which Atwood grapples. In the three groups of poems in the collection (including a group of prose poems, "A True Romance"), she examines the role of artist as witness-bearer, and the ironies inherent in the examination of truth and reality through art. As in *Two-Headed Poems*, there is a final expression of a tentative faith in and acceptance of life, for all its paradoxes. "Last Day" declares, "This egg/ in my hand is our last meal,/ you break it open and the sky/ turns orange again and the sun rises/ again and this is the last day again." The collection's final allusion, then, is to the egg, universal symbol of immortality and hope.

INTERLUNAR

Interlunar returns to the strongly mythological themes, characters, and imagery of Atwood's first collections of poems. From the first, the components of Atwood's complex vision have been clear; reading her poetry in chronological order is an odyssey through the maturing and honing of her artistic skills rather than through a definition and articulation of vision.

The mysticism suggested in *Interlunar*'s title is confirmed in the poems themselves. They are arranged in subtitled groups, a favorite device of Atwood; the most fascinating is "Snake Poems," which explores the symbolism of snakes throughout human cultural and religious history. This includes their association with darkness, evil, destructiveness, and the male principle, as well as with wisdom, knowledge, creativity, and the female principle. Above all, their association with resurrection (for their ability to shed their skins) is explored and viewed (especially in "Metempsychosis") with Atwood's customary ambivalence. Resurrection is also a central theme of the title group of poems, "Interlunar." Intimations of mortality are seen to be on the poet's mind in such poems as "Bedside," "Anchorage," and "Heart Test with an Echo Chamber"; the doubtful comfort of resurrection is ironically considered in a set of poems titled for and concerned with the mythological figures of Orpheus, Eurydice, and Persephone. In this way, Atwood's poems and vision come full circle to her earliest poetic works, *Double Persephone* and *The Circle Game*.

The tone of the collection's title poem, "Interlunar," is uncharacteristically comforting and serene, the statement of a mature artist who recognizes that her odyssey toward understanding in art and life must be without end but need not be frightening: "Trust me. This darkness/ is a place you can enter and be/ as safe in as you are anywhere."

MORNING IN THE BURNED HOUSE

Morning in the Burned House is Atwood's first collection of new poems in a decade. It shows no falling off of skill or intensity and a continuation of all her familiar themes.

The poems in this volume tend to a darker lyricism, a sharper awareness of mortality. Although it is difficult to separate the personal from the political in Atwood's vision, the strongest newer poems seem to be those that are most intensely personal, such as the series on the death of her father. In other poems, the satiric, sardonic, and sometimes outrageously feminist Atwood is very much in evidence.

THE DOOR

The Door is Atwood's first book of new poems in twelve years, although before and after the publication of *Morning in the Burned House*, she published collections of selected poems from her earlier career—before other genres, especially the novel, began to compete so strongly for her attention. Like Thomas Hardy, Atwood may be returning to poetry now that she is a comfortably independent writer. Additionally, novels require a huge investment of time and energy, and following her "big novel" *The Blind Assassin*, she may have turned to writing poems, which produces the satisfaction of completion more quickly than other forms.

Concerns of time and energy are central to *The Door*, since a number of these poems deal with aging—no surprise coming from a poet born in 1939. The dust jacket says it all: The photograph on the front is of Atwood as a young girl, standing at her front door, while the publicity photograph of the author on the back flap reveals a woman approaching seventy. Thus, the photographs are graphic emblems of *The Door* and serve as an entry to the title poem. Throughout the persona's lifetime, ironically represented in everyday language and images, the door swings open, offering glimpses of darkness within before it closes. In the end, the persona steps in, and the door closes behind her, suggesting her death.

The earlier poems in *The Door* often range between memories of childhood and concerns of the present. For example, the opening poem of the first section, "Gasoline," seems to grow out of a sensory experience, allowing entry to the poet's childhood. Among the poet's more recent concerns are the advanced age of her parents, whose deaths will also move her toward the precipice. "My mother dwindles . . ." strikes a chord in all who have dealt with a parent's failing body and mind.

Another section of poems focuses on being a poet, especially an older poet. The tone is often unsentimental to the point of cynicism. In one poem, "The poet has come back . . ." from years of virtue to be a poet again. In another, "Owl and Pussycat, some years later," Pussycat reminds Owl of how they have achieved major reputations—won the prizes and written flattering blurbs about each other's work—but wonders what this "moulting owl" and "arthritic pussycat" have actually accomplished.

These are tough poems, not in their obscurity, but in their strong impulse toward the kind of realism readers more often expect in fiction than in poetry. "Nobody cares who wins"—wars, that is—although winning is better than losing. "Saint Joan of Arc on a postcard" looks like "a boned rolled leg of lamb." The opening line of the poem "The hurt child" ends with "will bite you." The persona here is reminiscent of Iris, the narrator of *The Blind Assassin*, or Penelope, the narrator of *The Penelopiad*—old and experienced enough to have lost the pleasures of sentimentalism, avoided the traps of self-delusion, and decided it is too late to do anything but tell the truth.

OTHER MAJOR WORKS

LONG FICTION: *The Edible Woman*, 1969; *Surfacing*, 1972; *Lady Oracle*, 1976; *Life Before Man*, 1979; *Bodily Harm*, 1981; *The Handmaid's Tale*, 1985; *Cat's Eye*, 1988; *The Robber Bride*, 1993; *Alias Grace*, 1996; *The Blind Assassin*, 2000; *Oryx and Crake*, 2003; *The Penelopiad: The Myth of Penelope and Odysseus*, 2005; *The Year of the Flood*, 2009.

SHORT FICTION: *Dancing Girls, and Other Stories*, 1977; *Bluebeard's Egg*, 1983; *Murder in the Dark: Short Fictions and Prose Poems*, 1983; *Wilderness Tips*, 1991; *Good Bones*, 1992 (pb. in U.S. as *Good Bones and Simple Murders*, 1994); *Moral Disorder*, 2006.

NONFICTION: *Survival: A Thematic Guide to Canadian Literature*, 1972; *Days of the Rebels: 1815-1840*, 1977; *Second Words: Selected Critical Prose*, 1982; *Margaret Atwood: Conversations*, 1990 (Earl G. Ingersoll, editor); *Strange Things: The Malevolent North in Canadian Literature*, 1995; *Deux sollicitudes: Entretiens*, 1996 (with Victor-Lévy Beaulieu; *Two Solicitudes: Conversations*, 1998); *Negotiating with the Dead: A Writer on Writing*, 2002; *Moving Targets: Writing with Intent, 1982-2004*, 2004 (pb. in U.S. as *Writing with Intent: Essays, Reviews, Personal Prose, 1983-2005*, 2005); *Waltzing Again: New and Selected Conversations with Margaret Atwood*, 2006 (with others; Ingersoll, editor).

CHILDREN'S LITERATURE: *Up in the Tree*, 1978; *Anna's Pet*, 1980 (with Joyce Barkhouse); *For the Birds*, 1990; *Princess Prunella and the Purple Peanut*, 1995 (illustrated by Maryann Kowalski); *Bashful Bob and Doleful Dorinda*, 2004 (illustrated by Dušan Petričić); *Rude Ramsay and the Roaring Radishes*, 2004 (illustrated by Petričić).

EDITED TEXTS: *The New Oxford Book of Canadian Verse in English*, 1982; *The CanLit Foodbook: From Pen to Palate, a Collection of Tasty Literary Fare*, 1987 (compiled and illustrated by Atwood).

MISCELLANEOUS: *The Tent*, 2006.

BIBLIOGRAPHY

Appleton, Sarah A., ed. *Once Upon a Time: Myth, Fairy Tales and Legends in Margaret Atwood's Writings*. Newcastle, England: Cambridge Scholars, 2008. Examines Atwood's use of myth and fairy tales in her fiction and poetry.

Atwood, Margaret. *Margaret Atwood: Conversations*. Edited by Earl G. Ingersoll. Princeton, N.J.: Ontario Review Press, 1990. Atwood discusses many aspects of her writing and life with various interviewers.

_____. *Waltzing Again: New and Selected Conversations with Margaret Atwood.* Edited by Earl G. Ingersoll. Princeton, N.J.: Ontario Review Press, 2006. Atwood discusses writing in interviews conducted after 1987.

Bloom, Harold, ed. *Margaret Atwood.* New York: Bloom's Literary Criticism, 2009. This volume includes an introduction by Bloom and provides critical analysis of Atwood's fiction and poetry.

Hengen, Shannon, and Ashley Thomson. *Margaret Atwood: A Reference Guide, 1988-2005.* Lanham, Md.: Scarecrow, 2007. Atwood's writings from 1988 to 2005 are covered in this resource, which includes listings of citations, reviews, quotations, and interviews. Also contains a guide to Atwood resources on the Internet and a chronology of her publishing career.

Howells, Coral Ann. *Margaret Atwood.* 2d ed. New York: Palgrave Macmillan, 2006. In this lively critical and biographical study, Howells elucidates issues that have energized all of Atwood's work: feminist issues, literary genres, and her own identity as a Canadian, a woman, and a writer. Focuses on the fiction.

_____, ed. *The Cambridge Companion to Margaret Atwood.* New York: Cambridge University Press, 2006. Contains an essay on Atwood's poetry and poetics as well as on her major themes.

McCombs, Judith, ed. *Critical Essays on Margaret Atwood.* Boston: G. K. Hall, 1988. This indispensable volume contains thirty-two articles and essays, including assessments of patterns and themes in her poetry and prose. The entries are arranged in the chronological order of Atwood's primary works, beginning with *The Circle Game* and ending with *The Handmaid's Tale.* It includes a primary bibliography to 1986 and a thorough index.

Nischik, Reingard M., ed. *Margaret Atwood: Works and Impact.* Reprint. Rochester, N.Y.: Camden House, 2002. This sturdy gathering of original (not reprinted) criticism includes Lothar Hönnighausen's comprehensive "Margaret Atwood's Poetry 1966-1995" as well as Ronald B. Hatch's "Margaret Atwood, the Land, and Ecology," which draws heavily on Atwood's poetry to make its case.

Wilson, Sharon Rose, ed. *Margaret Atwood's Textual Assassinations: Recent Poetry and Fiction.* Columbus: Ohio State University Press, 2003. This collection of essays examines Atwood's poetry, including *Morning in the Burned House,* as well as her fiction.

Jill Rollins; Philip K. Jason
Updated by Earl G. Ingersoll

APHRA BEHN

Born: Kent, England; July (?), 1640
Died: London, England; April 16, 1689
Also known as: Aphara Amis; Aphra Bayn; Aphra Johnson; *Astrea*

PRINCIPAL POETRY
Poems upon Several Occasions, with "A Voyage to the Island of Love," 1684 (including adaptation of Abbé Paul Tallemant's *Le Voyage de l'isle d'amour*)
Miscellany: Being a Collection of Poems by Several Hands, 1685 (includes works by others)
Selected Poems, 1993
The Poems of Aphra Behn: A Selection, 1994

OTHER LITERARY FORMS

Although Aphra Behn (bayn) wrote more than a dozen separate pieces of fiction that critics of her day called novels, only a portion may legitimately be labeled as such. Principal among these is her most noted work of fiction, *Oroonoko: Or, The Royal Slave, a True History* (1688); others worthy of consideration are *Agnes de Castro* (1688), *The Fair Jilt: Or, The History of Prince Tarquin and Miranda* (1688), *The History of the Nun: Or, The Fair Vow-Breaker* (1689), and *The Nun: Or, The Perjured Beauty* (1697). During her lifetime, Behn established her literary reputation by writing for the London stage, creating more than fifteen plays.

ACHIEVEMENTS

Critics may defend Aphra Behn's talent for drama and prose fiction as worthy of recognition beside that of her male contemporaries. As a writer of verse, however, she cannot claim a place among the poets of the first rank. This does not mean that her poetry has no value for the critic, the literary historian, or the general reader; on the contrary, her occasional verse is no worse than the political pieces of her colleagues (with the exception of John Dryden), while the songs and poems from her plays reflect her ability to manipulate verse as reinforcement for dramatic theme and setting.

In the nineteenth century, such poet-essayists as Leigh Hunt, Edmund Gosse, and Algernon Charles Swinburne recoiled initially from what they saw in Behn's occasional verse as indelicate and indecent language. They recovered sufficiently to find some merit in her songs. Hunt bemoaned her association with the rakes of the age, yet praised the songs as "natural and cordial, written in a masculine style, yet womanly withal." Gosse dubbed her "the George Sand of the Restoration"—an obvious reference that had nothing whatsoever to do with her literary abilities—although "she possessed an indis-

Aphra Behn (Library of Congress)

putable touch of lyric genius." Swinburne looked hard at a single poem, "Love in fantastic triumph sate," and concluded that "the virtuous Aphra towers above her sex in the passionate grace and splendid elegance of that melodious and magnificent song. . . ." The most attractive quality of her lyrical pieces is their spontaneity, demonstrating to the reader (or the theatergoer) that the best poetry need not be anchored to learning but can succeed because the lines are memorable, singable, and direct.

In her public verse, Behn had to compete with a large number of poets who tended to be more skilled mechanics and versifiers than she, and all of whom sought the same limited patronage and political favors as she. She found herself at a disadvantage because of her gender, which meant, simply, that her occasional verse did not always reach the widest possible audience. For example, such pieces as "A Pindarick on the Death of Charles II" (1685) and "A Congratulatory Poem to Her Most Sacred Majesty" (1688) may appear stiff and lacking in sincerity, but certainly no more so than the verses on the same subjects written by her contemporaries.

Behn's elegy on the death of Edmund Waller and her other contributions to a volume in memory of the departed poet in 1688 do, however, reflect a deep feeling of sorrow because of the occasion; these poems serve as a transition to her private verse, representing perhaps the highest level of Behn's poetic achievement. In "The Disappointment," for example, she reveals herself as a woman whose real desires have been obscured by frivolity and professionalism and who realizes that her laborious life is drawing to a close. The importance of such poems is that they provide the deepest insight into Behn; they draw a picture of the poet far more honestly and realistically than do the rumors, allusions, and innuendos set forth in countless biographical sketches and critical commentaries.

Biography

Although the details surrounding the life of Aphra Behn have at least become stabilized, they have not always been clear. Her earliest biographer, the poet Charles Gildon (1665-1724), maintained that she was born at Canterbury, in Kent, the daughter of a man named Johnson. In 1884, however, Edmund Gosse discovered a marginal note in a manuscript belonging to the poet Anne Finch, countess of Winchelsea (1661-1720), revealing that Behn had been born at Wye, near Canterbury, the daughter of a barber—which John Johnson certainly was not. The countess's note receives support from an entry in the parish register of the Saints Gregory and Martin Church, Wye, to the effect that Ayfara Amis, daughter of John and Amy Amis, was baptized there on July 10, 1640. Apparently Johnson, related to Lord Francis Willoughby of Parham, adopted the girl, although no one seems certain of the exact year. Nevertheless, Ayfara Amis accompanied her stepparents on a journey to Surinam (later Dutch Guiana) in 1658, Lord Willoughby having appointed Johnson to serve as deputy governor of his extensive holdings there. Unfortunately, the new deputy died on the voyage; his widow and children proceeded to Surinam and took up residence at St. John's, one of Willoughby's plantations. The exact length of their stay has yet to be determined; later biographers, though, have settled upon the summer of 1663 as the most probable date of return. The family's tenure at St. John's forms the background of Behn's most celebrated production, her novel *Oroonoko*.

By 1665, the young woman was established in London, married to a wealthy Dutch merchant (or at least a merchant of Dutch ancestry) who may well have had connections in or around the court of Charles II. In 1665 came the Great Plague and the death of Behn's husband; his death proved disastrous for Behn. For unknown reasons, the Dutch merchant left her nothing of substance—with the possible exception of his connections at court. Charles II, in the midst of his first war against the Dutch, hired Behn as a secret agent to spy against Holland; for that purpose, she proceeded to Antwerp. There she contacted another agent, William Scott, from whom she received various pieces of military information for forwarding to London. Although her work earned her little acknowledgment and even less money, Behn did conceive of the pseudonym Astrea, the name under which she published most of her poetry. Essentially, the venture into foreign intrigue proved a dismal failure for her; she had to borrow money and pawn her few valuables to pay her debts and provide passage back to England.

Once home, early in 1667, Behn found no relief from her desperate financial situation. Her creditors threatened prison, and the government ministers who had employed her refused any payment for espionage service rendered. Prison followed, most probably at Caronne House, South Lambeth, although again the specifics of time and length of term are lacking. Behn's later biographers speculate that she may have been aided in her release by John Hoyle (died 1692)—a lawyer of Gray's Inn, a wit, an intellectual, and bisexual, the principal subject and reason for Behn's sonnets, and the man with whom the writer carried on a long romance. In fact, Hoyle, to whom she refers often in her poems, is the only one of Behn's supposed lovers who can be identified with any certainty. When she finally gained her release from prison, she determined to dedicate the rest of her life to pleasure and to letters and to trust her own devices rather than to rely upon others whom she could not trust.

Behn launched her career as a dramatist in late December, 1670, at the New Duke's Theatre in Little Lincoln's Inn Fields, London. Her tragicomedy, *The Forced Marriage: Or, The Jealous Bridegroom* (pr. 1670), ran for six nights and included in the cast nineteen-year-old Thomas Otway, the playwright-to-be only recently in London from Christ Church, Oxford. The neophyte bungled his lines, and with that, his acting career came to a quick halt. Because of the length of the run, however, Behn, as was the practice, received the entire profit from the third performance; she could now begin to function as an independent artist. She followed her first effort in the spring of 1671 with a comedy, *The Amorous Prince: Or, The Curious Husband*, again at the New Duke's; another comedy, *The Dutch Lover*, came to Drury Lane in February, 1673, and by the time of her anonymous comedy, *The Rover: Or, The Banished Cavaliers, Part I*, in 1677, she had secured her reputation. Now she mixed easily with the likes of Thomas Killigrew, Edward Ravenscroft, John Wilmot, earl of Rochester, Edmund Waller, and the poet laureate, John Dryden—who would publish her rough translations from Ovid in 1683. With the reputation came offers for witty prologues and epilogues for others' plays, as well as what she desired more than anything—money. A confrontation, however, with the earl of Shaftesbury and the newly formed Whigs during the religiopolitical controversies of 1678, when she offended the opponents of Charles II in a satirical prologue to an anonymous play, *Romulus and Hersilia*, brought her once again to the brink of economic hardship; for the next five years, she was forced to abandon writing for the stage.

Fortunately, Behn could find other outlets for her art in popular fiction and occasional verse, although neither proved as profitable as the stage. Her series of *Love Letters Between a Nobleman and His Sister* (1683-1687) and *Poems upon Several Occasions* were well received, but the meager financial returns could not keep pace with her social expenses. When she did return to the stage in 1686 with a comedy, *The Lucky Chance: Or, An Alderman's Bargain*, she met with only moderate success and much public abuse. *The Emperor of the Moon*, produced the following year, fared somewhat better, although the London audience had seemingly lost its stomach for a woman playwright with Tory sympathies.

Behn continued to write fiction and verse, but sickness and the death of her one true artistic friend, Edmund Waller, both occurring in October, 1688, did little to inspire confidence in her attitudes toward life or art. Five days following the coronation of William III and Mary, on April 16, 1689, Behn died, the result, according to Gildon, of incompetent surgery. Nevertheless, she had risen high enough to merit burial in Westminster Abbey; in fact, her memorial, interestingly enough, lies near that of the famous actor Anne Bracegirdle (died 1748), whose acting skills prolonged Behn's popularity well after the playwright's death. The fitting epitaph to Behn was provided by her lover, John Hoyle, who declared, "Here lies proof that wit can never be/ Defense against mortality."

Analysis

The history of English poetry during the Restoration of Charles II and the reign of James II seems to have no room for Aphra Behn. The reasons, all having little or nothing to do with her true poetic abilities, are fairly obvious. To form a composite of the Restoration poet, one must begin with an outline of a gentleman who wrote verse for other gentlemen and a few literate ladies, who directed his efforts to a select group of coffeehouse and drawing-room wits, who wrote about politics, religion, scientific achievement, or war. He wrote poetry to amuse and to entertain, and even, on occasion, to instruct. He also wrote verse to attack or to appease his audience, those very persons who served as his readers and his critics. Thus, the Restoration poet vied with his colleagues for recognition and patronage—even for political position, favor, and prestige. He hurled epithets and obscenities at his rivals, and they quickly retorted. Of course, that was all done in public view, upon the pages of broadsheets and miscellanies.

Reflect, for a moment, upon the career of Dryden, who dominated the London literary scene during the last quarter of the seventeenth century. He stood far above his contemporaries and fulfilled the practical function of the Restoration man of letters: the poet, dramatist, and essayist who focused upon whatever subject or form happened to be current at a particular moment. Dryden succeeded because he understood his art, the demands of the times upon that art, and the arena in which he (as artist and man) had to compete. Around 1662 to 1663, he married Lady Elizabeth Howard, daughter of the earl of Berkshire and sister of Sir Robert Howard. Sir Robert introduced the poet to the reestablished nobility, soon to become his readers and his patrons. In 1662, Dryden joined the Royal Society, mainly to study philosophy, mathematics, and reason, in order "to be a complete and excellent poet." One result, in 1663, was a poem in honor of Walter Charleton, physician to Charles II; the poet praised the new scientific spirit brought on by the new age and lauded the efforts of the Royal Society and its support of such geniuses as Robert Boyle and Sir

Isaac Newton. In February, 1663, *The Wild Gallant*, the first of Dryden's twenty-eight plays, appeared on the stage; although the comedy was essentially a failure, it marked the beginning of an extremely successful career, for Dryden quickly recognized the Restoration theater as the most immediate outlet for his art.

Certainly Dryden became involved in the major religious and political controversies of his day, both personally and poetically, and his fortunes fluctuated as a result. His reputation, however—as critic, dramatist, and poet laureate of England—had been secured, and he remained England's most outstanding, most complete writer. As a poet, he headed a diverse group of artists who, although not consistently his equals, could compete with him in limited areas: the classicists of the Restoration, carryovers from an earlier age—Edmund Waller and Abraham Cowley; the satirists—Samuel Butler, John Oldham, Sir Charles Sedley, the earls of Rochester and Dorset; the dramatists—William Wycherley, Sir George Etherege, Nathaniel Lee, Thomas Otway, William Congreve, George Farquhar, and Behn.

The point to be made is that unlike Dryden and his male counterparts, Behn had little time and even less opportunity to develop as a poet. Sexism prevented her from fitting the prototype of the Restoration poet; she lacked access to the spheres of social and political influence, mastery of classical languages and their related disciplines, and the luxury of writing when and what she pleased. The need for money loomed large as her primary motive, and as had Dryden, she looked to the London stage for revenue and reputation. She certainly viewed herself as a poet, but her best poetry seems to exist within the context of her plays.

One problem in discussing Behn's poetry is that one cannot always catalog with confidence those pieces attributed to her and written by others. Also, there is confusion regarding those pieces actually written by her but attributed to others. For example, as late as 1926, and again in 1933, two different editors of quite distinct editions of the earl of Rochester's poetry erroneously assigned three of Behn's poems to Rochester, and that error remained uncorrected until 1939. Textual matters aside, however, Behn's poetry still provides substantive issues for critical discussion. Commentators have traditionally favored the songs from her plays, maintaining that the grace and spontaneity of these pieces rise above the artificiality of the longer verses—the latter weighed down by convention and lack of inspiration. True, her major poem (at least in terms of its length) of two thousand lines, *A Voyage to the Island of Love*, while carrying the romantic allegory to extremes, does succeed in its purpose: a poetic paraphrase of the French original, and nothing more. Indeed, Behn, as a playwright, no doubt viewed poetry as a diversion and exercise; she considered both activities useful and important, and both provided added dimensions to her art. She was certainly not a great poet; but few during her time were. Her poetic success, then, must be measured in terms of her competence, for which she may, in all honesty, receive high marks and be entitled to a permanent place on the roster of poets.

Abdelazar

At the head of the list are two songs from the play *Abdelazar: Or, The Moor's Revenge* (pr. 1676), the first a sixteen-line lyric known by its opening, "Love in fantastic triumph sate." Despite the trite (even by Restoration standards) dramatic setting—the usurper who murders his trusting sovereign and puts to death all who block his path to the throne—the poem reflects pure, personal feeling, as the poet laments over the misery of unrequited love. Behn depicts Love as a "strange tyrannic power" that dominates the amorous world; there is nothing terribly complicated, in either the sound or the sense of the language, for she relies upon simple sighs, tears, pride, cruelty, and fear. In the end, the poem succeeds because it goes directly to the central issue of the poet's personal unhappiness. "But my poor heart alone is harmed,/ Whilst thine the victor is, and free." The other song from *Abdelazar* is a dialogue between a nymph and her swain. The young lady, cognizant of the brevity of "a lover's day," begs her lover to make haste; the swain, in company with shepherds, shepherdesses, and pipes, quickly responds. He bears a stray lamb of hers, which he has caught so that she may chastise the creature ("with one angry look from thy fair eyes") for having wandered from the flock. The analogy between man and beast is obvious and nothing more need be said; the swain begs her to hurry, for "how very short a lover's day!"

Songs and Elegies

There are other songs of equal or slightly less merit, and they all seem to contain variations on the same themes. In one, "'Tis not your saying that you love," the speaker urges her lover to cease his talk of love and, simply, love her; otherwise, she will no longer be able to live. Another, a song from Lycidus beginning "A thousand martyrs I have made," mocks "the fools that whine for love" and unmasks the fashion of those who, on the surface, appear deeply wounded by the torments of love when they actually seek nothing from love but its shallow pleasures. In a third song, "When Jemmy first began to love," Behn returns to the shepherd and his flock motif. On this occasion, the nymph, overpowered by Jemmy's songs, kisses, and general air of happiness, gives herself completely to him. Then the call to arms beckons; Jemmy exchanges his sheep hooks for a sword, his pipes for warlike sounds, and, perhaps, his bracelets for wounds. At the end, the poor nymph must mourn, but for whom it is not certain: for the departed Jemmy or for herself, who must endure without him? Finally, in one of the longest of her songs, a 140-line narrative titled "The Disappointment," Behn introduces some of the indelicacies and indiscretions of which Victorian critics and biographers accused her. By late seventeenth century standards, the piece is indeed graphic (although certainly not vulgar or even indecent); but it nevertheless succeeds in demonstrating how excessive pleasure can easily turn to pain.

Although Behn, whether by choice or situation, kept outside the arena of poetic competition of the sort engaged in by Dryden and his rivals, she managed to establish personal relationships with the major figures of her age. Dryden always treated her with civility and even kindness, and there are those who maintain that a piece often attributed to Behn—"On Mr. Dryden, Renegade," and beginning "Scorning religion all thy lifetime past,/ And now embracing popery at last"—was not of her making. In addition, she remained on friendly terms with Thomas Otway, Edward Ravenscroft, Edmund Waller, and the earl of Rochester.

"On the Death of the Late Earl of Rochester"

Behn wrote elegies for Waller and Rochester, and both poems are well suited to their occasion; yet they are two distinctly different poems. "On the Death of the Late Earl of Rochester" (1685) is an appeal to the world to mourn the loss of a great and multifaceted personality: The muses must mourn the passing of a wit, youths must mourn the end of a "dear instructing rage" against foolishness, maidens the loss of a heaven-sent lover, the little gods of love the loss of a divine lover, and the unhappy world the passage of a great man. Draped in its pastoral and classical mantles, the poem glorifies a subject not entirely worthy of glorification; yet, if the reader can momentarily forget about Rochester, the piece is not entirely without merit. After all, the poet did demonstrate that she knew how to write a competent elegy.

"On the Death of Edmund Waller"

More than seven years later, on October 21, 1687, the aged poet Edmund Waller died, and again Behn penned an elegiac response, "On the Death of Edmund Waller." Her circumstances, however, had changed considerably since the passing of Rochester in July, 1680. Her health was poor, her finances low, her literary reputation not very secure. Apparently she had to write the piece in some haste, specifically for a collection of poems dedicated to Waller and written by his friends. Finally, Behn was deeply affected by Waller's death and chose the opportunity to associate that event with her own situation—that of the struggling, ailing, and aging (although she was then only forty-seven) artist. Thus, she sets the melancholy tone at the outset by identifying herself as "I, who by toils of sickness, am become/ Almost as near as thou art to a tomb." Throughout, she inserts references to an untuned and ignorant world, the muses' dark land, the low ebb of sense, the scanty gratitude and fickle love of the unthinking crowd—all of which seem more appropriate to her private and professional life than to Waller's. Still, the poem is not an unusual example of the elegy; Behn was not the first poet to announce her own personal problems while calling upon the world to mourn the loss of a notable person.

Midway through the elegy to Waller, Behn provides a clue that may well reveal her purpose as a poet and, further, may help to establish her legitimacy within the genre. She writes of a pre-Wallerian world of meaningless learning, wherein dull and obscure declamations prevented the blossoming of sensitive poets and true poetry and produced nothing that was "great and gay." During those barren years, she laments, there existed only thoughtless labor, devoid of instruction, pleasure, and (most important) passion. In a word, "the poets knew not Love." Such expressions and sentiments may appear, on the surface, as attempts to elevate the memory of her subject; in reality, they serve well to underline her own concerns for poetry as a means of bringing harmony to disorder, comfort to discord, and love to insensitivity. As a woman, she looked upon a poetic field dominated by masculine activity and masculine expression, by masculine attitudes and masculine ideals. Where, she must certainly have asked herself, could one find the appropriate context in which to convey to an audience composed of both males and females those passions peculiar to her sex and to her person?

Whether she actually found the form in which to house that passion—or whether she even possessed the craft and the intellect to express it—is difficult to determine. One problem, of course, is that Behn did not write a sufficient quantity of poetry beyond her plays and novels to allow for a reasonable judgment. Nevertheless, she never ceased trying to pour forth the pain and the love that dominated her emotions. She wrote (as in "'Tis not your saying that you love") that actions, not words, must reinforce declarations of love, for only love itself can sustain life. Without love, there is no life. Throughout her poems, that conclusion reverberates from line to line: Love is a triumph, a lover's day is short, the death of one partner means the spiritual (and automatic) death of the one remaining; a lover's soul is made of love, while the completion of an empty (and thus meaningless) act of love leaves a lover "half dead and breathless."

EXOTIC SETTINGS

Perhaps the most interesting aspect of Behn's poetry is her taste for exotic settings. These backdrops appear to contradict her very way of life. Behn was a woman of the city, of the urban social and intellectual center of a nation that had only recently undergone political trauma and change. She belonged to the theater, the drawing room, the coffeehouse, the palace—even to the boudoir. Not many of those settings, however, found their way into her poetry. Instead, she selected for her poetic environments a composite that she called the "amorous world" ("Love in fantastic triumph sate"), complete with listening birds, feeding flocks, the aromatic boughs and fruit of a juniper tree, trembling limbs, yielding grass, crystal dew, a lone thicket made for love, and flowers bathed in the morning dew.

Even the obviously human subjects, both alive and dead, rarely walk the streets of the town or meditate in the quiet of their own earthly gardens. Thus, Dryden, in the midst of religious disorientation, wanders about upon the wings of his own shame, in search of "Moses' God"; Rochester flies, quick as departing light, upon the fragrance of softly falling roses; and Waller, a heaven-born genius, is described as having rescued the chosen tribe of poetry from the Egyptian night. Of course, in the last two instances, Behn wrote elegies, which naturally allowed her departed subjects greater room for celestial meanderings. Love, however, had to be relieved from its earthly, banal confines. Love was very much Behn's real subject as a poet, but she was never prepared to discuss it within the context of the harsh and often ugly realities of her own time and place.

OTHER MAJOR WORKS

LONG FICTION: *Love Letters Between a Nobleman and His Sister*, 1683-1687 (3 volumes); *Agnes de Castro*, 1688; *The Fair Jilt: Or, The History of Prince Tarquin and Miranda*, 1688; *Oroonoko: Or, The Royal Slave, a True History*, 1688; *The History of the Nun: Or, The Fair Vow-Breaker*, 1689; *The Lucky Mistake*, 1689; *The Nun: Or, The Perjured Beauty*, 1697; *The Adventure of the Black Lady*, 1698; *The Wandering Beauty*, 1698.

PLAYS: *The Forced Marriage: Or, The Jealous Bridegroom*, pr. 1670; *The Amorous Prince: Or, The Curious Husband*, pr., pb. 1671; *The Dutch Lover*, pr., pb. 1673; *Abdelazer: Or, The Moor's Revenge*, pr. 1676; *The Town Fop: Or, Sir Timothy Tawdry*, pr. 1676; *The Rover: Or, The Banished Cavaliers, Part I*, pr., pb. 1677 (*Part II*, pr., pb. 1681); *Sir Patient Fancy*, pr., pb. 1678; *The Feigned Courtesans: Or, A Night's Intrigue*, pr., pb. 1679; *The Young King: Or, The Mistake*, pr. 1679; *The Roundheads: Or, The Good Old Cause*, pr. 1681; *The City Heiress: Or, Sir Timothy Treat-All*, pr., pb. 1682; *The Lucky Chance: Or, An Alderman's Bargain*, pr. 1686; *The Emperor of the Moon*, pr., pb. 1687; *The Widow Ranter: Or, The History of Bacon of Virginia*, pr. 1689; *The Younger Brother: Or, The Amorous Jilt*, pr., pb. 1696.

TRANSLATIONS: *Aesop's Fables*, 1687 (with Francis Barlow); *Of Trees*, 1689 (of book 6 of Abraham Cowley's *Sex libri plantarum*).

MISCELLANEOUS: *The Case for the Watch*, 1686 (prose and poetry); *La Montre: Or, The Lover's Watch*, 1686 (prose and poetry); *Lycidus: Or, The Lover in Fashion*, 1688 (prose and poetry; includes works by others); *The Lady's Looking-Glass, to Dress Herself By: Or, The Art of Charming*, 1697 (prose and poetry); *The Works of Aphra Behn*, 1915, 1967 (6 volumes; Montague Summers, editor); *The Works of Aphra Behn*, 1992-1996 (7 volumes; Janet Todd, editor).

BIBLIOGRAPHY

Altaba-Artal, Dolors. *Aphra Behn's English Feminism: Wit and Satire*. Cranbury, N.J.: Associated University Presses, 1999. An examination of Behn's writings from the perspective of feminism. Bibliography and index.

Hughes, Derek, and Janet Todd, eds. *The Cambridge Companion to Aphra Behn*. New York: Cambridge University Press, 2004. Replete with tools for further research, this is an excellent aid to any study of Behn's life and work.

O'Donnell, Mary Ann. *Aphra Behn: An Annotated Bibliography of Primary and Secondary Sources*. 2d ed. Burlington, Vt.: Ashgate, 2003. Contains a detailed description of more than one thousand primary works and more than six hundred books, articles, essays, and dissertations written about Behn after 1666. These works are listed chronologically. Indexed.

Spencer, Jane. *Aphra Behn's Afterlife*. New York: Oxford University Press, 2000. An examination of Behn's works with emphasis on her influence. Bibliography and index.

Stapleton, M. L. *Admired and Understood: The Poetry of Aphra Behn*. Newark: University of Delaware Press, 2004. This study of Behn's poetry examines, among other works, *A Voyage to the Island of Love*.

Todd, Janet. *The Critical Fortunes of Aphra Behn*. Columbia, S.C.: Camden House, 1998. This work focuses on the critical reception of Behn after her death.

———. *The Secret Life of Aphra Behn*. New Brunswick, N.J.: Rutgers University Press, 1996. The introduction summarizes efforts to study Behn's work and life, her place in literature, her ability to write in all the genres (except the sermon), and the biographer's efforts to overcome the paucity of biographical facts. Includes a bibliography of works written before 1800 and a bibliography of work published after 1800.

———, ed. *Aphra Behn Studies*. New York: Cambridge University Press, 1996. Part 1 concentrates on Behn's plays, part 2 on her poetry, part 3 on her fiction, and part 4 on her biography. Includes an introduction outlining Behn's career and the essays in the volume and an index.

Wiseman, Susan. *Aphra Behn*. 2d ed. Tavistock, England: Northcote House/British Council, 2007. A biography of Behn that examines her life and work. Bibliography and index.

Samuel J. Rogal

ELIZABETH BISHOP

Born: Worcester, Massachusetts; February 8, 1911
Died: Boston, Massachusetts; October 6, 1979

PRINCIPAL POETRY
North and South, 1946
Poems: North and South—A Cold Spring, 1955
Questions of Travel, 1965
Selected Poems, 1967
The Ballad of the Burglar of Babylon, 1968
The Complete Poems, 1969
Geography III, 1976
The Complete Poems, 1927-1979, 1983

OTHER LITERARY FORMS

In addition to her poetry, Elizabeth Bishop wrote short stories and other prose pieces. She is also known for her translations of Portuguese and Latin American writers. *The Collected Prose*, edited and introduced by Robert Giroux, was published in 1984. It includes "In the Village," an autobiographical revelation of Bishop's youthful vision of, and later adult perspective on, her mother's brief return home from a mental hospital. Like her poetry, Bishop's prose is marked by precise observation and a somewhat withdrawn narrator, although the prose works reveal much more about Bishop's life than the poetry does. Editor Giroux has suggested that this was one reason many of the pieces were unpublished during her lifetime. *The Collected Prose* also includes Bishop's observations of other cultures and provides clues as to why she chose to live in Brazil for so many years.

ACHIEVEMENTS

Elizabeth Bishop was often honored for her poetry. She served as consultant in poetry (poet laureate) to the Library of Congress in 1949-1950. Among many awards and prizes, she received an Award in Literature from the American Academy of Arts and Letters (1951), the Shelley Memorial Award (1953), the Pulitzer Prize in poetry (1956), the Academy of American Poets Fellowship (1969), the National Book Award in Poetry (1970), and the National Book Critics Circle Award in poetry (1976) for *Geography III*. She became a member of the American Academy of Arts and Letters in 1954 and served as chancellor for the Academy of American Poets from 1966 to 1979. However, as John Ashbery said, in seconding her presentation as the winner of the *Books Abroad*/Neustadt International Prize for Literature in 1976, she is a "writer's writer." Despite her continuing presence for more than thirty years as a major American poet, Bishop never achieved great popular success. Perhaps the delicacy of much of her writing, her restrained style, and her ambiguous questioning and testing of experience made her more difficult and less approachable than poets with showier technique or more explicit philosophies.

Bishop's place in American poetry, in the company of such poets as Marianne Moore, Wallace Stevens, and Richard Wilbur, is among the celebrators and commemorators of the things of this world, in her steady conviction that by bringing the light of poetic intelligence, the mind's eye, on those things, she would enrich her readers' understanding of them and of themselves.

Biography

Elizabeth Bishop is a poet of geography, as the titles of her books testify, and her life itself was mapped out by travels and visits as surely as is her poetry. Eight months after Bishop's birth in Massachusetts, her father died. Four years later, her mother suffered a nervous breakdown and was hospitalized, first outside Boston, and later in her native Canada.

Elizabeth was taken to Nova Scotia, where she spent much of her youth with her grandmother; later, she lived for a time with an aunt in Massachusetts. Although her mother did not die until 1934, Bishop did not see her again after a brief visit home from the hospital in 1916—the subject of "In the Village."

For the rest of her life, Bishop traveled: in Canada, in Europe, and in North and South America. She formed friendships with many writers: Robert Lowell, Octavio Paz, and especially Marianne Moore, who read drafts of many of her poems and offered suggestions. In 1951, Bishop began a trip around South America, but during a stop in Brazil she suffered an allergic reaction to some food she had eaten and became ill. She remained in Brazil for almost twenty years. During the last decade of her life, she continued to travel and to spend time in Latin America, but she settled in the United States, teaching frequently at Harvard, until her death in 1979.

Analysis

In her early poem "The Map," Elizabeth Bishop writes that "More delicate than the historians' are the map-makers' colors." Her best poetry, although only indirectly autobiographical, is built from those mapmakers' colors. Nova Scotian and New England seascapes and Brazilian and Parisian landscapes become the geography of her poetry. At the same time, her own lack of permanent roots and her sense of herself as an observer suggest the lack of social relationships one feels in Bishop's poetry, for it is a poetry of observation, not of interaction, of people as outcasts, exiles, and onlookers, not as social beings. The relationships that count are with the land and sea, with primal elements, with the geography of Bishop's world.

For critics, and certainly for other poets—those as different as Moore and Lowell, or

Randall Jarrell and John Ashbery—Elizabeth Bishop is a voice of influence and authority. Writing with great assurance and sophistication from the beginning of her career, she achieved in her earliest poetry a quiet, though often playful, tone, a probing examination of reality, an exactness of language, and a lucidity of vision that mark all her best poetry. Her later poetry is slightly more relaxed than her earlier, the formal patterns often less rigorous; but her concern and her careful eye never waver. Because of the severity of her self-criticism, her collected poems, although relatively few in number, are of a remarkably even quality.

History, writes Bishop in "Objects and Apparitions," is the opposite of art, for history creates ruins, while the artist, out of ruins, out of "minimal, incoherent fragments," simply creates. Bishop's poetry is a collection of objects and apparitions, of scenes viewed and imagined, made for the moment into a coherent whole. The imaginary iceberg in the poem of that name is a part of a scene "a sailor'd give his eyes for," and Bishop asks that surrender of her readers. Her poetry, like the iceberg, behooves the soul to see. Inner and outer realities are in her poetry made visible, made one.

"Sandpiper"

In Bishop's poem "Sandpiper," the bird of the title runs along the shore, ignoring the sea that roars on his left and the beach that "hisses" on his right, disregarding the interrupting sheets of water that wash across his toes, sucking the sand back to sea. His attention is focused. He is watching the sand between his toes; "a student of [William] Blake," he attempts to see the world in each of those grains. The poet is ironic about the bird's obsessions: He is "finical"; in looking at these details he ignores the great sweeps of sea and land on either side of him. For every point in time when the world is clear, there is another when it is a mist. The poet seems to chide the bird in his darting search for "something, something, something," but then in the last two lines of the poem the irony subsides; as Bishop carefully enumerates the varied and beautiful colors of the grains of sand, she joins the bird in his attentiveness. The reward, the something one can hope to find, lies simply in the rich and multivalent beauty of what one sees. It is not the reward of certainty or conviction, but of discovery that comes through focused attention.

The irony in the poem is self-mocking, for the bird is a metaphor for Bishop, its vision like her own, its situation that of many of her poetic personas. "Sandpiper" may call to mind such Robert Frost poems as "Neither out Far nor in Deep" or "For Once, Then, Something," with their perplexity about inward and outward vision and people's attempt to fix their sight on something, to create surety out of their surroundings. It may also suggest such other Bishop poems as "Cape Breton," where the birds turn their backs to the mainland, sometimes falling off the cliffs onto rocks below. Bishop does share with Frost his absorption by nature and its ambiguities, the ironic tone, and the tight poetic form that masks the "controlled panic" that the sandpiper-poet feels. Frost, however, is in a darker line of American writers: His emphasis is on the transitoriness of the vision, the shallowness of the sea into which one gazes, the ease with which even the most fleeting vision is erased. For Frost's poet-bird, "The Oven Bird," the nature he observes in midsummer is already 90 percent diminished. Bishop, rather, prefers the triumph of one's seeing at all. In her well-known poem "The Fish," when the persona finally looks into the eyes of the fish she has caught—eyes, the poet notes, larger but "shallower" than her own—the fish's eyes return the stare. The persona, herself now caught, rapt, stares and stares until "victory fill[s] up" the boat, and all the world becomes "rainbow, rainbow, rainbow." Like the rainbow of colors that the sandpiper discovers, the poet here discovers beauty; the victory is the triumph of vision.

Like the sandpiper, then, Bishop is an obsessive observer. As a poet, her greatest strength is her pictorial accuracy. Whether her subject is as familiar as a fish, a rooster, or a filling station, or as strange as a Brazilian interior or a moose in the headlights of a bus, she enables the reader to see. The world for the sandpiper is sometimes "minute and vast and clear," and because Bishop observes the details so lucidly, her vision becomes truly vast. She is, like Frost, a lover of synecdoche; for her, the particulars entail the whole. Nature is the matter of Bishop's art; to make her readers see, to enable them to read the world around them, is her purpose. In "Seascape," what the poet finds in nature, its potential richness, is already like "a cartoon by Raphael for a tapestry for a Pope." All that Bishop must accomplish, then, as she writes in "The Fish," is simply "the tipping/ of an object toward the light."

"Objects and Apparitions"

Although the world for the sandpiper is sometimes clear, it is also sometimes a mist, and Bishop describes a more clouded vision as well. She translated a poem by Paz, "Objects and Apparitions," that might indicate the fuller matter of her own work; the objects are those details, the grains of sand that reveal the world once they are tipped toward the light. The apparitions occur when one sees the world through the mist and when one turns vision inward, as in the world of dreams. Here, too, the goal is bringing clarity to the vision—and the vision to clarity. As Bishop writes in "The Weed," about drops of dew that fall from a weed onto a dreamer's face, "each drop contained a light,/ a small, illuminated scene."

Objects and apparitions, mist and vision, land and sea, history and geography, travel and home, ascent and fall, dawn and night—these oppositions supply the tension in Bishop's poetry. The tensions are never resolved by giving way; in Bishop's world, one is a reflection of the other, and "reflection" becomes a frequent pun: that of a mirror and that of thought. Similarly, inspection, introspection, and insight suggest her doubled vision. In "Paris, 7 A.M.," looking down into the courtyard of a Paris house, the poet writes, "It is like introspection/ to stare inside," and there is again the double meaning of looking inside the court and inside oneself.

"The Man-Moth"

No verbs are more prevalent or important in Bishop's poetry than those of sight: Look, watch, see, stare, she admonishes the reader. From "The Imaginary Iceberg," near the beginning of her first book, which compares an iceberg to the soul, both "self-made from elements least visible," and which insists that icebergs "behoove" the soul "to see them so," to "Objects and Apparitions" near the end of her last book, in which the poet suggests that in Joseph Cornell's art "my words became visible," one must first of all see; and the end of all art, plastic and verbal, is to make that which is invisible—too familiar to be noticed, too small to be important, too strange to be comprehended—visible.

In "The Man-Moth," the normal human being of the first stanza cannot even see the moon, but after the man-moth comes above ground and climbs a skyscraper, trying to climb out through the moon, which he thinks is a hole in the sky, he falls back and returns to life belowground, riding the subway backward through his memories and dreams. The poet addresses the readers, cautioning them to examine the man-moth's eye, from which a tear falls. If the "you" is not paying attention, the man-moth will swallow his tear and his most valuable possession will be lost, but "if you watch," he will give it up, cool and pure, and the fruit of his vision will be shared.

Questions of Travel

To see the world afresh, even as briefly as does the man-moth, to gain that bitter tear of knowledge, one must, according to Bishop, change perspectives. In *Questions of Travel*, people hurry to the Southern Hemisphere "to see the sun the other way around." In "Love Lies Sleeping," the head of one sleeper has fallen over the edge of the bed, so that to his eyes the world is "inverted and distorted." Then the poet reconsiders: "distorted and revealed," for the hope is that now the sleeper sees, although a last line suggests that such sight is no certainty. When one lies down, Bishop writes in "Sleeping Standing Up," the world turns ninety degrees and the new perspective brings "recumbent" thoughts to mind and vision. The equally ambiguous title, however, implies either that thoughts are already available when one is upright or, less positively, that one may remain inattentive while erect.

The world is also inverted in "Insomnia," where the moon stares at itself in a mirror. In Bishop's lovely, playful poem "The Gentleman of Shalott," the title character thinks himself only half, his other symmetrical half a reflection, an imagined mirror down his center. His state is precarious, for if the mirror should slip, the symmetry would be destroyed, and yet he finds the uncertainty "exhilarating" and thrives on the sense of "readjustment."

"Over 2000 Illustrations and a Complete Concordance"

The changing of perspectives that permits sight is the theme of Bishop's "Over 2000 Illustrations and a Complete Concordance." The poet is looking at the illustrations in a gazetteer, comparing the engraved and serious pictures in the book with her remembered travels. In the first section of the poem, the poet lists the illustrations, the familiar, even tired Seven Wonders of the World, moving away from the objects pictured to details of the renderings, until finally the "eye drops" away from the real illustrations, which spread out and dissolve into a series of reflections on past travels. These too begin with the familiar: with Canada and the sound of goats, through Rome, to Mexico, to Marrakech. Then, finally, she goes to a holy grave, which, rather than reassuring the viewer, frightens her, as an amused Arab looks on. Abruptly, the poet is back in the world of books, but this time her vision is on the Bible, where everything is "connected by 'and' and 'and.'" She opens the book, feeling the gilt of the edges flake off on her fingertips, and then asks, "Why couldn't we have seen/ this old Nativity while we were at it?" The colloquial last words comprise a casual pun, implying physical presence or accidental benefit. The next four lines describe the nativity scene, but while the details are familiar enough, Bishop's language defamiliarizes them.

The poet ends with the statement that had she been there she would have "looked and looked our infant sight away"—another pun rich with possibilities. Is it that she would have looked repeatedly, so that the scene would have yielded meaning and she could have left satisfied? Do the lines mean to look away, as if the fire that breaks in the vision is too strong for human sight? The gazetteer into which the poet first looked, that record of human travels, has given way to scripture; physical pictures have given way to reflected visions and reflections, which, like the imaginary iceberg, behoove the soul to see.

"THE RIVERMAN"

Bishop participates in the traditional New England notion that nature is a gazetteer, a geography, a book to be read. In her poem "The Riverman," the speaker gets up in the night—night and dawn, two times of uncertain light, are favorite times in Bishop's poetic world—called by a river spirit, though at first the dolphin-spirit is only "glimpsed." The speaker follows and wades into the river, where a door opens. Smoke rises like mist, and another spirit speaks in a language the narrator does not know but understands "like a dog/ although I can't speak it yet." Every night he goes back to the river, to study its language. He needs a "virgin mirror," a fresh way of seeing, but all he finds are spoiled. "Look," he says significantly, "it stands to reason" that everything one needs can be obtained from the river, which draws from the land "the remedy." The image of rivers and seas drawing, sucking the land persists in Bishop's poetry. The unknown that her poems scrutinize draws the known into it. The river sucks the earth "like a child," and the riverman, like the poet, must study the earth and the river to read them and find the remedy of sight.

Pictorial poetry

Not only do the spirits of nature speak, but so too for Bishop does art itself. Her poetry is pictorial not only in the sense of giving vivid descriptions of natural phenomena but also in its use of artificial objects to reflect on the self-referential aspect of art. Nature is like art, the seascape a "cartoon," but the arts are like one another as well. Bishop is firmly in the *ut pictura poesis* tradition—as is a painting, so a poem—and in the narrower tradition of ekphrasis: Art, like nature, speaks.

In "Large Bad Picture," the picture is an uncle's painting, and after five stanzas describing the artist's attempt to be important by drawing everything oversized—miles of cliffs hundreds of feet high, hundreds of birds—the painting, at least in the narrator's mind, becomes audible, and she can hear the birds crying.

In the much later "Poem," Bishop looks at another, much smaller, painting by the same uncle (a sketch for a larger one? she asks), and this time the painting speaks to her memory. Examining the brushstrokes in a detached and slightly contemptuous manner, she suddenly exclaims, "Heavens, I recognize the place, I know it!" The voice of her mother enters, and then she concludes, "Our visions coincided"; life and memory have merged in this painting as in this poem: "how touching in detail/ —the little that we get for free."

"The Monument"

Most explicitly in "The Monument," Bishop addresses someone, asking her auditor to "see the monument." The listener is confused: the assemblage of boxes, turned cattycorner one on the other, the thin poles hanging out at the top, the wooden background of sea made from board and sky made from other boards: "Why do they make no sound?... What is that?" The narrator responds with "It is the monument," but the other is not convinced that it is truly art. The voice of the poet again answers, insisting that the monument be seen as "artifact of wood" which "holds together better than sea or cloud or sand could." Acknowledging the limitations, the crudeness of it, the questions it cannot answer, she continues that it shelters "what is within"—presenting the familiar ambiguity: within the monument or within the viewer? Sculpture or poem, monument or painting, says the poet, all are of wood; that is, all are artifacts made from nature, artifacts that hold together. She concludes, "Watch it closely."

Thus, for Bishop, shifting perspectives to watch the natural landscape (what she quotes Sir Kenneth Clark as calling "tapestried landscape") and the internal landscape of dream and recollection are both the matter and the manner of art, of all arts, which hold the world together while one's attention is focused. The struggle is to see; the victory is in so seeing.

Poems of questioning

Bishop's poetry is not unequivocally optimistic or affirmative, however. There are finally more ambiguities than certainties, and—like her double-edged puns—questions, rhetorical and conversational, are at the heart of these poems. Bishop's ambiguity is not that of unresolved layers of meaning in the poetry, but in the unresolvable nature of the world she tests. "Which is which?" she asks about memory and life in "Poem." "What has he done?" the poet asks of a chastised dog in the last poem of *Geography III*. "Can countries pick their colors?" she asks in "The Map." *Questions of Travel* begins with a poem questioning whether this new country, Brazil, will yield "complete comprehension"; it is followed by another poem that asks whether the poet should not have stayed at home: "Must we dream our dreams/ and have them, too?" Bishop poses more questions than she answers. Indeed, at the end of "Faustina," Faustina is poised above the dying woman she has cared for, facing the final questions of the meaning that death gives to life: Freedom or nightmare?, it begins, but the question becomes "proliferative," and the poet says that"There is no way of telling./ The eyes say only either."

Knowledge, like the sea, like tears, is salty and bitter, and even answering the questions, achieving a measure of knowledge, is no guarantee of permanence. Language, like music, drifts out of hearing. In "View of the Capitol from the Library of Congress," even the music of a brass band "doesn't quite come through." The morning breaks in "Anaphora" with so much music that it seems meant for an "ineffable creature." When he appears, however, he is merely human, a tired victim of his humanity, even at dawn. However, even though knowledge for Bishop is bitter, is fleeting, though the world is often inscrutable or inexplicable, hers is finally a poetry of hope. Even "Anaphora" moves from morning to night, though from fatigue to a punning "endless assent."

Poetic form

Bishop's poetry is often controlled by elaborate formal patterns of sight and sound. She makes masterful use of such forms as the sestina and villanelle, avoiding the appearance of mere exercise by the naturalness and wit of the repetitions and the depth of the scene. In "The Burglar of Babylon," she adopts the ballad form to tell the story of a victim of poverty who is destroyed by his society and of those "observers" who watch through binoculars without ever seeing the drama that is unfolding. Her favorite sound devices are alliteration and consonance. In "The Map," for example, the first four lines include "shadowed," "shadows," "shallows," "showing"; "edges" rhymes with "ledges," "water" alliterates with "weeds." The repetition of sounds suggests the patterning that the poet finds in the map, and the slipperiness of sounds in "shadows"/"shallows" indicates the ease with which one vision of reality gives place to another. The fifth line begins with another question: "Does the land lean down to lift the sea?," the repeated sound changing to a glide. "Along the fine tan sandy shelf/ is the land tugging at the sea from under?" repeats the patterning of questions and the *sh* and *l* alliteration, but the internal rhyme of "tan" and "sandy," so close that it momentarily disrupts the rhythm and the plosive alliteration of "tan" and "tugging," implies more strain.

Being at the same time a pictorialist, Bishop depends heavily on images. Again in

49

"The Map," Norway is a hare that "runs south in agitation." The peninsulas "take the water between thumb and finger/ like women feeling for the smoothness of yard-goods." The reader is brought up short by the aptness of these images, the familiar invigorated. On the map, Labrador is yellow, "where the moony Eskimo/ has oiled it." In the late poem "In the Waiting Room," a young Elizabeth sits in a dentist's waiting room, reading through a *National Geographic*, looking at pictures of the scenes from around the world. The experience causes the young girl to ask who she is, what is her identity and her similarity, not only with those strange people in the magazine but also with the strangers there in the room with her, and with her Aunt Consuela, whose scream she hears from the inner room. Bishop's poetry is like the pictures in that magazine; its images offer another geography, so that readers question again their own identity.

Use of conceit

This sense of seeing oneself in others, of doubled vision and reflected identities, leads to another of Bishop's favorite devices, the conceit. In "Wading at Wellfleet," the waves of the sea, glittering and knifelike, are like the wheels of Assyrian chariots with their sharp knives affixed, attacking warriors and waders alike. In "The Imaginary Iceberg," the iceberg is first an actor, then a jewel, and finally the soul, the shifting of elaborated conceits duplicating the ambiguous nature of the iceberg. The roads that lead to the city in "From the Country to the City" are stripes on a harlequin's tights, and the poem a conceit with the city the clown's head and heart, its neon lights beckoning the traveler. Dreams are armored tanks in "Sleeping Standing Up," letting one do "many a dangerous thing," protected. In the late prose piece "12 O'Clock News," each item on a desk becomes something else: the gooseneck lamp, a moon; the typewriter eraser, a unicyclist with bristly hair; the ashtray, a graveyard full of twisted bodies of soldiers.

Formal control, a gently ironic but appreciative tone, a keen eye—these are hallmarks of Bishop's poetry. They reveal as well her limitation as a poet: a deficiency of passion. The poetry is so carefully controlled, the patterns so tight, the reality tested so shifting, and the testing so detached, that intensity of feeling is minimized. Bishop, in "Objects and Apparitions," quotes the painter Edgar Degas: "'One has to commit a painting . . . the way one commits a crime.'" As Richard Wilbur, the writer whom she most resembles in her work, has pointed out, Degas loved grace and energy, strain coupled with beauty. Strain is absent in Bishop's work.

Character sketches

Although there are wonderful character sketches among her poems, the poetry seems curiously underpopulated. "Manuelzinho" is a beautiful portrait of a character whose account books have turned to dream books, an infuriating sort whose numbers, the decimals omitted, run slantwise across the page. "Crusoe in England" describes a man suddenly removed from the place that made him reexamine his existence. These are people, but observers and outsiders, themselves observed. The Unbeliever sleeps alone at the top of a mast, his only companions a cloud and a gull. The Burglar of Babylon flees a society that kills him. Cootchie is dead, as is Arthur in "First Death in Nova Scotia," and Faustina tends the dying. Crusoe is without his Friday, and in "Sestina," although a grandmother jokes with a child, it is silence that one hears, absence that is present. There is little love in Bishop's poetry. It is true that at the end of "Manuelzinho," the narrator confesses that she loves her maddening tenant "all I can,/ I think. Or do I?" It is true that at the end of "Filling Station," the grubby, but "comfy" design of the family-owned station suggests that "Somebody loves us all," but this love is detached and observed, not felt. Even in "Four Poems," the most acutely personal of Bishop's poems and the only ones about romantic love, the subject is lost love, the conversation internal. "Love should be put into action!" screams a hermit at the end of "Chemin de Fer," but his only answer is an echo.

OTHER MAJOR WORKS
> SHORT FICTION: "In the Village," in *Questions of Travel*, 1965.
> NONFICTION: *The Diary of "Helena Morley,"* 1957 (translation of Alice Brant's *Minha Vida de Menina*); *Brazil*, 1962 (with the editors of *Life*); *One Art: Letters*, 1994; *Words in Air: The Complete Correspondence Between Elizabeth Bishop and Robert Lowell*, 2008 (with Robert Lowell).
> EDITED TEXT: *An Anthology of Twentieth Century Brazilian Poetry*, 1972 (with Emanuel Brasil).
> MISCELLANEOUS: *The Collected Prose*, 1984 (fiction and nonfiction); *Edgar Allan Poe and the Juke-Box: Uncollected Poems, Drafts, and Fragments*, 2006 (Alice Quinn, editor); *Poems, Prose, and Letters*, 2008.

BIBLIOGRAPHY

Bishop, Elizabeth. Interviews. *Conversations with Elizabeth Bishop*. Edited by George Monteiro. Jackson: University Press of Mississippi, 1996. These interviews with Bishop reveal the unusual artistic spheres in which she moved. Monteiro's lucid introduction respects the complexities of both Bishop and her repressive historical moment.

Bloom, Harold. *Elizabeth Bishop: Modern Critical Views*. New York: Chelsea House, 1985. Bloom has gathered fifteen previously published articles on separate poems and on Bishop's poetry as a whole, as well as a new article, "At Home with Loss" by Joanne Feit Diehl, on Bishop's relationship to the American Transcendentalists. "The Armadillo," "Roosters," and "In the Waiting Room" are some of the poems treated separately. A chronology and a bibliography complete this useful collection of criticism from the 1970's and early 1980's.

Costello, Bonnie. *Elizabeth Bishop: Questions of Mastery*. Cambridge, Mass.: Harvard University Press, 1991. Provides a comprehensive view of Bishop's visual strategies and poetics, grouping poems along thematic lines in each chapter. She examines the poet's relationship to spirituality, memory, and the natural world by exploring her metrical and rhetorical devices.

Goldensohn, Lorrie. *Elizabeth Bishop: The Biography of a Poetry*. New York: Columbia University Press, 1992. Analyzing Bishop's life through the lens of her verse, Goldensohn probes the lesbianism and alcoholism that Bishop wished to conceal in her life and examines the role that Brazil played in shaping Bishop's works.

Harrison, Victoria. *Elizabeth Bishop's Poetics of Intimacy*. New York: Cambridge University Press, 1993. Harrison's application of critical theory to Bishop's work reveals new facets of Bishop's art. She examines Bishop's language, poetics, and prosody via postmodern theory, feminist theory, and cultural anthropology. Takes advantage of the ample manuscript materials available.

Miller, Brett C. *Elizabeth Bishop: Life and the Memory of It*. Berkeley: University of California Press, 1993. The first critical biography of Bishop, this resource combines the subject's life and writings. Numerous notebook entries and letters are uncovered as sources for later poems, and Bishop's alcoholism is discussed.

_____. *Flawed Light: American Women Poets and Alcohol*. Urbana: University of Illinois Press, 2009. Miller studies how drinking and alcoholism affected certain prominent American women poets, and how their struggles were reflected in their poetry.

Parker, Robert Dale. *The Unbeliever: The Poetry of Elizabeth Bishop*. Urbana: University of Illinois Press, 1988. Parker has the advantage of a longer view of Bishop's writings and criticism. His wide grasp of her life and work leads him to shape her development into three stages: poems of wish and expectation, resignation into poems of place, and finally, as is natural with maturity, poems of retrospection. He focuses on the major poems in each area, with a last chapter on the later poems, some of which, such as "The Moose," had been in her mind for twenty years. Includes particularly fine notes and an index.

Schwartz, Lloyd, and Sybil P. Estess. *Elizabeth Bishop and Her Art*. Ann Arbor: University of Michigan Press, 1983. This indispensable source gathers critical articles from many admirers, as well as interviews, introductions at poetry readings, explications of specific poems, and a bibliography (1933-1981). Some of Bishop's journal passages demonstrate why she is a preeminent American poet—her realism, common sense, lack of self-pity over losses—as James Merrill calls her, "our greatest national treasure."

Travisano, Thomas. *Elizabeth Bishop: Her Artistic Development*. Charlottesville: University Press of Virginia, 1988. This comprehensive study of Bishop's career traces the evolution of her prose and poetry through three phases. The first, "Prison," uses enclosure as its metaphor; the second, "Travel," breaks through into engagement with people and places; and the third, "History," reconciles her life of loss and displacement to a calm, mature mood of courage and humor. Complemented by a chronology, a bibliography, and an index.

Howard Faulkner

EAVAN BOLAND

Born: Dublin, Ireland; September 24, 1944

PRINCIPAL POETRY
Twenty-three Poems, 1962
New Territory, 1967
The War Horse, 1975
In Her Own Image, 1980
Introducing Eavan Boland, 1981 (reprint of *The War Horse* and *In Her Own Image*)
Night Feed, 1982
The Journey, and Other Poems, 1983
Selected Poems, 1989
Outside History: Selected Poems, 1980-1990, 1990
In a Time of Violence, 1994
Collected Poems, 1995 (pb. in U.S. as *An Origin Like Water: Collected Poems, 1967-1987*, 1996)
The Lost Land, 1998
Against Love Poetry, 2001
Code, 2001
Three Irish Poets, 2003 (with Paula Meehan and Mary O'Malley; Boland, editor)
New Collected Poems, 2005
Domestic Violence, 2007
New Collected Poems, 2008

OTHER LITERARY FORMS

Eavan Boland (BOW-lahnd) collaborated with Micheál Mac Liammóir on the critical study *W. B. Yeats and His World* (1971). Boland has contributed essays in journals such as the *American Poetry Review*; she also has reviewed for the *Irish Times* and has published a volume of prose called *Object Lessons: The Life of the Woman and the Poet in Our Time* (1995). With Mark Strand, she prepared the anthology *The Making of a Poem: A Norton Anthology of Poetic Forms* (2000).

ACHIEVEMENTS

Ireland has produced a generation of distinguished poets since 1960, and the most celebrated of them have been men. Of this group of poets, Seamus Heaney is the best known to American audiences, but the reputations of Thomas Kinsella, Derek Mahon, Michael Longley, Paul Muldoon, and Tom Paulin continue to grow. Poetry by contemporary Irishwomen is also a significant part of the Irish literary scene. Eavan Boland is one of a group of notable women poets including Medbh McGuckian, Eithne Strong, and Eiléan Ní Chuilleanáin. In an essay published in 1987, "The Woman Poet: Her Dilemma," Boland indicates her particular concern with the special problems of being a woman and a poet. Male stereotypes about the role of women in society continue to be very strong in Ireland and make Irishwomen less confident about their creative abilities. Women also must contend with another potentially depersonalizing pressure, that of feminist ideology, which urges women toward another sort of conformity. Boland and the other female Irish poets previously mentioned have managed to overcome both obstacles and develop personal voices.

Boland has served as a member of the board of the Irish Arts Council and a member of the Irish Academy of Letters. Her honors and awards include the American Ireland Fund Literary Award (1994), the Lannan Literary Award for Poetry (1994), the Bucknell Medal of Distinction from Bucknell University (2000), the Smartt Family Foundation Prize for *Against Love Poetry*, the John Frederick Nims Memorial Prize from *Poetry* magazine (2002), the John William Corrington Award for Literary Excellence from Centenary College of Louisiana (2002-2003), and the James Boatwright III Prize for Poetry from *Shenandoah* (2006) for "Violence Against Women."

BIOGRAPHY

Eavan Boland was born on September 24, 1944, in Dublin, Ireland. Her parents were Frederick Boland and Frances Kelly Boland. Her father was a distinguished Irish diplomat who served as Irish ambassador to Great Britain (1950-1956) and to the United States (1956-1964). Her mother was a painter who had studied in Paris in the 1930's. Boland's interest in painting as a subject for poetry can be traced to her mother's encouragement. Because of her father's diplomatic career, Boland was educated in Dublin, London, and New York. From 1962 to 1966, she attended Trinity College, Dublin; beginning in 1967, she taught at Trinity College for a year. In 1968, she received the Macauley Fellowship for poetry.

In the 1980's, Boland reviewed regularly for the arts section of the *Irish Times*. In 1987, she held a visiting fellowship at Bowdoin College. She married Kevin Casey, a novelist, with whom she had two children: Sarah, born in 1975, and Eavan, born in 1978.

Boland began writing poetry in Dublin in the early 1960's. She recalls this early period: ". . . scribbling poems in boarding school, reading [William Butler] Yeats after lights out, revelling in the poetry on the course. . . . Dublin was a coherent space then, a small circumference in which to . . . become a poet. . . . The last European city. The last literary smallholding." After her marriage, Boland left the academic world and moved into the suburbs of Dublin to become "wife, mother, and housewife." *In Her Own Image* and *Night Feed* focus on Boland's domestic life in the suburbs and especially on her sense of womanhood. In the 1990's, Boland taught at several universities in the United States. In 1995, she became a professor at Stanford University, where she has served as Bella Mabury and Eloise Mabury Knapp Professor in the Humanities as well as the Melvin and Bill Lane Professor and chair of the creative writing program.

Analysis

Hearth and history provide a context for the poetry of Eavan Boland. She is inspired by both the domestic and the cultural. Her subjects are the alienating suburban places that encourage people to forget their cultural roots, her children with their typically Irish names, demystified horses in Dublin streets that can still evoke the old glories from time to time, and the old Irish stories themselves, which at times may be vivid and evocative and at others may be nostalgic in nature. Boland's distinctly female perspective is achieved in several poems about painting that note the dominance of male painters—such as Jan van Eyck, Edgar Degas, Jean Auguste Dominique Ingres, and Pierre-Auguste Renoir—in the history of art from the Renaissance to the Impressionists. Women were painted by these artists in traditional domestic or agrarian postures. Boland perceives women as far less sanitized and submissive. Her collection *In Her Own Image* introduces such taboo subjects as anorexia, mastectomy, masturbation, and menstruation.

Night Feed

Two of Boland's works, *In Her Own Image* and *Night Feed*, deal exclusively with the subject of women. *Night Feed* for the most part examines suburban women and positively chronicles the daily routine of a Dublin homemaker. The book has poems about diapers, washing machines, and feeding babies. The cover has an idyllic drawing of a mother feeding a child. However, *In Her Own Image*, published two years before *Night Feed*, seems written by a different person. Its candid and detailed treatment of taboo subjects contrasts sharply with the idyllic world of *Night Feed*. Boland's ability to present both worlds testifies to her poetic maturity.

The need for connection is a major theme in Boland's poetry. Aware of traditional connections in Irish and classical myths, she longs for an earlier period when such ties came instinctively. Her sense of loss with respect to these traditional connections extends beyond mythology to Irish history as well, even to Irish history in the twentieth century. Modern-day Dubliners have been cut off from the sustaining power of myth and history. Their lives, therefore, seem empty and superficial. Surrounded with the shards of a lost culture, they cannot piece these pieces together into a coherent system.

The alienation of modern urban Irish people from their cultural roots is the subject of Boland's "The New Pastoral" (from *Night Feed*). She considers alienation from a woman's perspective. Aware of the myths that have traditionally sustained males, Boland desires equivalent myths for females. She longs for a "new pastoral" that will celebrate women's ideals, but she finds none. She encounters many domestic "signs," but they do not "signify" for her. She has a vague sense of once having participated in a coherent ritual, of having "danced once/ on a frieze." Now, however, she has no access to the myth. Men seem to have easier access to their cultural roots than women do. The legends of the cavemen contain flint, fire, and wheel, which allowed man "to read his world." Later in history, men had pastoral poems to define and celebrate their place in the world. A woman has no similar defining and consoling rituals and possesses no equivalent cultural signs. She seems a "displaced person/ in a pastoral chaos," unable to create a "new pastoral." Surrounded by domestic signs, "lamb's knuckle," "the washer," "a stink/ of nappies," "the greasy/ bacon flitch," she still has no access to myth. Hints of connection do not provide a unified myth:

> I feel
> there was a past,
> there was a pastoral
> and these
> chance sights—
> what are they all
> but late amnesias
> of a rite
> I danced once
> on a frieze?

The final image of the dancer on the frieze echoes both John Keats's Grecian urn and William Butler Yeats's dancers and golden bird. The contemporary poet, however, has lost contact. Paradoxically, the poem constitutes the "new pastoral," which it claims is beyond its reach. The final allusion to the dancer on the frieze transforms the mundane objects of domestic life into something more significant, something sacred.

Boland seems in conflict over whether women should simply conform to male stereotypes for women or should resist these pressures to lead "lesser lives," to attend to "hearth not history." Many poems in *Night Feed* accept this "lesser" destiny, poems such as "Night Feed," "Hymn," and "In the Garden." The several poems in this volume that deal with paintings, "Domestic Interior," "Fruit on a Straight-Sided Tray," "Degas's Laundresses," "Woman Posing (After Ingres)," "On Renoir's *The Grape-Pickers*," all deal with paintings by male painters that portray women in traditional domestic or rural roles. The women in these paintings appear content with their "lesser lives." Poems such as "It's a Woman's World" seem less accepting, however, more in the spirit of *In Her Own Image*, which vigorously rejects basing one's identity on male stereotypes. "It's a Woman's World" complements "The New Pastoral" in its desire for a balance between hearth and history.

> as far as history goes
> we were never
> on the scene of the crime. . . .
> And still no page
> scores the low music
> of our outrage.

Women have had no important roles in history, Boland asserts. They produce "low music," rather than heroic music. Nevertheless, women can have an intuitive connection with their own "starry mystery," their own cosmic identity. The women in those paintings, apparently pursuing their "lesser lives," may have a sense of "greater lives." The male world (including male artists) must be kept in the dark about this, must keep believing that nothing mythic is being experienced.

> That woman there,
> craned to the starry mystery
> is merely getting a breath
> of evening air,
> while this one here—
> her mouth
> a burning plume—
> she's no fire-eater,
> just my frosty neighbour
> coming home.

In Her Own Image

The "woman's world" and the "starry mysteries" are presented far less romantically in *In Her Own Image*. The poems in this volume refuse to conform to male stereotypes of woman as happy domestic partner. They explore male-female conflicts in the deepest and most intimate psychic places. The title *In Her Own Image* indicates the volume's concern with the problem of identity. Boland wishes to be an individual, free to determine her own life, but other forces seek to control her, to make her conform to female stereotypes. A woman should be perfect, unchanging, youthful, pure—in short, she should be ideal. Male-dominated society does not wish women to explore their own deepest desires. Women transform these social messages into the voice of their own consciences, or, in Sigmund Freud's terms, their own superegos: "Thou shalt not get fat!" "Thou shalt not get old!" "Thou shalt not get curious."

These naysaying inner voices dominate the first three poems of *In Her Own Image*: "Tirade for the Mimic Muse," "In Her Own Image," and "In His Own Image." The "mimic muse" in the first poem urges the speaker to "make up," to conceal aging with cosmetics. The illustration for this poem shows a chubby and unkempt woman gazing into a mirror and seeing a perfect version of herself—thin, unwrinkled, and physically fit. The phrase "her own image" in the second poem refers to another idealization, the "image" of perfection that the speaker carries around inside herself. She finally frees herself from this psychic burden by planting the image outside in the garden. The illustration shows a naked woman bending over a small coffin.

The third poem, "In His Own Image," considers the pressures of a husband's expectations on a wife's sense of self. The speaker in this third poem does not try to reshape her features with makeup. She is battered into a new shape by a drunken husband. No illustration appears with this poem.

The speaker's "tirade" in "Tirade for the Mimic Muse" begins at once and establishes the intensely hostile tone of much of *In Her Own Image*: "I've caught you out. You slut. You fat trout." She despises the impulse in herself to conform to a stereotype, to disguise the physical signs of time passing: "the lizarding of eyelids," "the whiskering of nipples," and "the slow betrayals of our bedroom mirrors." In the final section of the poem, the authentic self has suppressed those conforming impulses: "I, who mazed my way to womanhood/ Through all your halls of mirrors, making faces." Now the mirror's glass is cracked. The speaker promises a true vision of the world, but the vision will not be idyllic: "I will show you true reflections, terrors." Terrors preoccupy Boland for much of this book.

"In Her Own Image" and "In His Own Image" deal with different aspects of the "perfect woman." The first poem has a much less hostile tone than does "Tirade for the Mimic Muse." The speaker seems less threatened by the self-image from which she wishes to distance herself. Images of gold and amethyst and jasmine run through the poem. Despite the less hostile tone, Boland regards this "image" as a burdensome idealization that must be purged for psychic health: "She is not myself/ anymore." The speaker plants this "image" in the garden outside: "I will bed her,/ She will bloom there," safely removed from consciousness. The poem "In His Own Image" is full of anxiety. The speaker cannot find her center, her identity. Potential signs of identity lie all around her, but she cannot interpret them:

> Celery feathers, . . .
> bacon flitch, . . .
> kettle's paunch, . . .
> these were all I had to go on, . . .
> meagre proofs of myself.

A drunken husband responds to his wife's identity crisis by pounding her into his own desired "shape."

> He splits my lip with his fist,
> shadows my eye with a blow,
> knuckles my neck to its proper angle.
> What a perfectionist!

> His are a sculptor's hands:
> they summon
> form from the void,
> they bring
> me to myself again.
> I am a new woman.

How different are these two methods of coping with psychic conflict. In "In Her Own Image," the speaker plants her old self lovingly in the garden. In "In His Own Image," the drunken husband reshapes his wife's features with violent hands. The wife in the second poem says that she is now a "new woman." If one reads this volume as a single poem, as Boland evidently intends that one should (all the illustrations have the same person as their subject), one understands that the desperate tone of other poems in the book derives from the suffering of this reshaped "new woman," a victim of male exploitation.

The next four poems of *In Her Own Image* deal with very private subjects familiar to women but not often treated in published poems: anorexia, mastectomy, masturbation, and menstruation. Both the poems and Constance Hart's drawings are startlingly frank. The poet wants readers to experience "woman" in a more complete way, to realize the dark side of being female. The poems further illustrate Boland's sense of alienation from cultural myths or myths of identity. She desires connections, but she knows that she is unlikely to have them. She is therefore left with images that signify chaos rather than coherence, absence rather than presence, emptiness rather than fullness.

Two of the four poems, "Anorexia" and "Mastectomy," read like field reports from the battle of the sexes. The other two poems, "Solitary" and "Menses," have a female perspective but are also full of conflict. In the illustrations for "Anorexia," a very determined and extremely thin naked woman, arms folded, looks disapprovingly at a fat woman lolling on a couch. An anorectic woman continues to believe that she is fat, despite being a virtual skeleton. Boland introduces a religious level in the first three lines: "Flesh is heretic./ My body is a witch./ I am burning it." The conviction that her body is a witch runs through the whole poem. Here, in an extreme form, is the traditional Roman Catholic view that soul and body are separate. The body must be punished because since the Fall, it has been the dwelling place of the devil. The soul must suppress the body in order for the soul to be saved. This tradition provides the anorectic with a religious reason for starving herself. In this poem, she revels in the opportunity to "torch" her body: "Now the bitch is burning." A presence even more disturbing than the witch is introduced in the second half of the poem, a ghostly male presence whom the anorectic speaker desires to please. To please this unnamed male presence, the speaker must become thin, so thin that she can somehow return to the womb imagined here paradoxically as male: "I will slip/ back into him again/ as if I had never been away." This return to the male womb will atone for the sin of being born a woman, with "hips and breasts/ and lips and heat/ and sweat and fat and greed."

In "Mastectomy," male-female conflict predominates. Male surgeons, envious of a woman's breasts (an effective transformation of the male-centered Freudian paradigm), cut off a breast and carry it away with them. The shocking drawing shows one gowned male surgeon passing the breast on a serving dish to another gowned male surgeon. The woman who has experienced this physical and psychological violation cries despairingly "I flatten to their looting." The sympathetic words of the surgeon before the operation belie the sinister act of removing the breast. It can now become part of male fantasy, as a symbol of primal nourishment and primal home:

> So they have taken off
> what slaked them first,
> what they have hated since:
> blue-veined
> white-domed
> home
> of wonder
> and the wetness
> of their dreams.

The next two poems, "Solitary" and "Menses," deal with equally private aspects of a woman's life, autoeroticism and menstruation. "Solitary" has a celebratory attitude toward self-arousal. The drawing shows a relaxed naked female figure lying on her stomach. Religious imagery is used in this poem as it is in "Anorexia," but here the body is worshiped rather than feared. The only negative aspect of "Solitary" is its solitude. The female speaker is unconnected with another person. Solitary pleasures are intense but less so than the pleasures of intercourse. The reader is taken on a journey from arousal to orgasm to postorgasmic tranquility. The religious language at first seems gratuitous but then perfectly appropriate. The speaker affirms the holiness of her body: "An oratory of dark,/ a chapel of unreason." She has a few moments of panic as the old words of warning flash into her mind: "You could die for this./ The gods could make you blind." These warnings do not deter her, however, from this sacred rite:

> how my cry
> blasphemes
> light and dark,
> screams
> land from sea,
> makes word flesh
> that now makes me
> animal.

During this period of arousal and climax, her "flesh summers," but then it returns again to winter: "I winter/ into sleep."

"Menses" deals with the private act of menstruation. A cosmic female voice addresses the speaker as menstruation begins, attempting to focus her attention solely on the natural powers working in her body. The speaker resists this effort. She feels simultaneously "sick of it" and drawn to this process. She struggles to retain her freedom. "Only my mind is free," she says. Her body is taken over by tidal forces. "I am bloated with her waters./ I am barren with her blood." At the end of the poem, the speaker seems more accepting of this natural cycle. She reflects on two other cycles that she has experienced, childbirth and intercourse. All three cycles, she begins to see, make her a new person: "I am bright and original."

The final three poems of *In Her Own Image*, "Witching," "Exhibitionist," and "Making-up," return to the theme that "Myths/ are made by men" (from "Making-up"). Much of a woman's life is spent reacting to male stereotypes. In "Witching," Boland further explores the idea of woman-as-witch, which was introduced in "Anorexia." Historically, women accused by men of being witches were doomed. The charges were usually either trumped-up or trivial. Boland's witch fantasizes about turning the table on her male persecutors and burning them first:

> I will
> reserve
> their arson,
> make
> a pyre
> of my haunch . . .
> the stench
> of my crotch

It is a grim but fitting fate for these male witch-burners.

Another male stereotype, woman-as-stripper, is treated in the poem "Exhibitionist." This poem has the last accompanying drawing, a young woman pulling her dress up over her head and naked to those watching her, perhaps as Boland feels naked toward those who have read through this volume. The male observers in "Exhibitionist" have in mind only gratifying their lusts. The speaker detests this exploitation and hopes to have a deeper impact on these leering males, hopes to touch them spiritually with her shining flesh:

> my dark plan:
> Into the gutter
> of their lusts
> I burn
> the shine
> of my flesh.

The final poem, "Making-up," returns to the theme of "Tirade for the Mimic Muse," that women must alter their appearances to please men, but that men have no such demands placed on them. The poem rehearses a litany of transformations of the speaker's "naked face." "Myths/ are made by men," this poem asserts. The goddesses men imagine can never be completely captured by that "naked face." A woman's natural appearance inevitably has flaws. Women are encouraged by men to disguise these flaws to make themselves look perfect. From these "rouge pots," a goddess comes forth, at least in men's eyes. Women should really know better.

> Mine are the rouge pots,
> the hot pinks, . . .
> out of which
> I dawn.

Boland is determined to make poetry out of her domestic life. *In Her Own Image* and *Night Feed* indicate that she has turned to the very ordinary subjects of hearth, rather than to the larger subjects of history, which she explored in her earlier volumes *New Territory* and *The War Horse*. In "The Woman Poet: Her Dilemma," Boland admits to uncertainty about this new orientation. She is encouraged especially, however, by the example of French and Dutch genre painters, whose work she calls "unglamorous, workaday, authentic," possessing both ordinariness and vision: "The hare in its muslin bag, the crusty loaf, the women fixed between menial tasks and human dreams." In her own equally ordinary domestic life, she believes that she has found a personal voice.

THE JOURNEY, AND OTHER POEMS

Boland's next major collection, *The Journey, and Other Poems*, explores more fully the poetic implications of this uncertainty. *In Her Own Image* and *Night Feed* offer opposed accounts of Boland's concerns as a woman and a writer, the former vehemently critical and openly outraged at sexual injustices, the latter more generously idyllic and positive about the domestic side of her femininity. In *The Journey, and Other Poems*, Boland incorporates this ambivalence into the fabric of her poems, channeling the tension between her contrary aspects into an antithetical lyric energy; each piece, that is, derives its form and force from a doubleness in the poet's mind, an impulse to be at once critical and affirmative. Instead of lamenting her inner confusions and contradictions, however, Boland builds a new sense of the lyric poem and engages with renewed vigor the vexed questions of gender, tradition, and myth that characterize her work.

The collection is divided into three sections, forming a triptych. In traditional religious painting, a triptych is composed of three canvases, side by side, the outer two either elaborating on or visually supporting the central portion, which usually contains the main subject of the work. In *The Journey, and Other Poems*, the first and third sections comment on, refocus, and expand the thematically dense matter of the central section, which contains "The Journey"—one of Boland's finest lyric achievements—and its "Envoi." Furthermore, Boland uses the structure of the triptych to underscore the ambivalence she feels. In the first section, the reader encounters memorial and idyll; in the third section, the reader finds the opposite, a vehement critique of inherited sexual mores and the patriarchal "tradition." Only in the central portion of the volume, "The Journey," does Boland take on both aspects at once and attempt, not to reconcile one to the other, but to reanimate and reenergize what she calls a dying, diminished poetic language.

The volume opens with "I Remember," a nostalgic tribute to the poet's mother. Boland recalls her mother's studio and her own almost irrepressible need, as a child exploring that room, "to touch, to handle, to dismantle it,/ the mystery." Boland longs for the mystery of innocence and the childlike wonder of a lost time—before the harsh realities of Irish economics and suburban alienation had taken root—when the world seemed balanced, "composed," and beautiful; but in the poem, that world is veiled and hidden from her, like the otherworldly elegance of her mother's "French Empire chairs" over which opaque cotton sheets have been draped. Similarly, in "The Oral Tradition," in which Boland overhears two women exchanging gossip—figures who, emblematically, "were standing in shadow"—she longs for "a musical sub-text," an "oral song" that seems only to express itself in "fragments and innuendoes," which nevertheless resonate with "a sense/ suddenly of truth." Boland wants to discover the archetypal "truth" buried under opaque surfaces, and, as she says in "Suburban Woman: A Detail," to find traces of the lost "goddess" within her instinctive, feminine memory. She expresses her need to be "healed into myth" through poetry and to recover the deeply ingrained, basic "patterns" of her womanhood.

The third section works negatively, upsetting traditional myths of the archetypal feminine. In "Listen. This Is the Noise of Myth," Boland starts to recount a "story" of a man and a woman setting the stage for a traditional version of domestic order, but she becomes self-conscious and critical, calling her own methods into question, making her characters—especially the woman—into "fugitives" from their traditional roles. Boland proposes to "set truth to rights," defiantly dismantling the old stories. She laments that even she must put "the same mirrors on the old magic" and return to the "old romances." Despite the sweet lure of storytelling, Boland wants to remake her own role as an author, and though she finds herself repeatedly thwarted by the "consolations of the craft," she struggles on.

Several poems in the third section echo Boland's other work. "Tirade for the Lyric Muse" recalls her "Tirade for the Mimic Muse," but here the subject is plastic surgery. The speaker addresses a sister "in the crime," an epithet that suggests a fellow poet, but one who, in Boland's view, has betrayed herself and her implicit commitment to "truth" by having the ordinary "surface" of her face altered to conform to a false notion of "skin deep" beauty. The true "music" of poetry, for Boland, cannot be captured by outward conformity to the "cruel" standards of a male world. Poems such as "Fond Memory" and "An Irish Childhood in England: 1951" respond to lyrics such as "I Remember" in the first section, rejecting nostalgia and finding in Boland's own indelible Irishness a sense of exile and insecurity. To be an English-speaking Irish native is to be a perpetual outcast. Irishness, for Boland, represents her own inability to settle on a given set of values or a certain appearance of "truth"; her nationality, paradoxically, undermines easy acceptance of the safe "myths" she craves.

If the first section works to rediscover the force of myth and the last section to dismantle the false safety net of traditional roles, the central portion—"The Journey"—springs directly from a double impulse. "The Journey" is a dream-vision, a description of a mental journey to the underworld undertaken in the poet's dreams. Many medieval poets, including Geoffrey Chaucer, wrote dream-visions. Like these poets, Boland depicts herself falling asleep over an open book of classical poetry. This connection to tradition, both medieval and ancient, is important to the poem, which describes a poetics, an account of how poems are or ought to be written. Boland searches for a new, vital form of writing. She begins by stating angrily that "there has never ... been a poem to an antibiotic...." She questions what is the proper subject for poetry, introducing antibiotics as something about which no one would bother to write. She espouses the ordinary and the domestic rather than the ethereal of the "unblemished" as a basis for poetry. To heal people and to repair their diminished relationship to "the language," poetry must look with renewed energy to the particulars of everyday life.

In her dream, Boland descends with Sappho—the greatest ancient female poet, whom she has been reading—to the land of the dead, where she meets the ghosts of mothers and housewives, women in whose experiences Boland has been trying to discover her mythical roots. Boland pleads with her mentor to let her "be their witnesses," but she is told that what she has seen is "beyond speech." She awakens, only to find "nothing was changed," despite her vision of "truth," and she weeps. This poetic "misery," taken up in the poem's "Envoi," comes from disappointment at being incapable of resuscitating the lost myths of womanhood, the anxiety of trying to bless "the ordinary" or to sanctify "the common" without the comfort of a traditionally sanctioned muse. Boland's work, to revive the feminine in poetry, results in a difficult mixture of discovery, desire, dissatisfaction, and rage. "The Journey" is a complex poem, and one of Boland's best works. It expresses both a naïve, dreamy faith in the power of myth and "truth" and a severe self-consciousness that calls the elements of her feminine identity into question. The ability to dwell poetically on such a problematic duplicity in a single poem truly indicates Boland's literary accomplishment.

IN A TIME OF VIOLENCE AND THE LOST LAND

Similar concerns, sometimes more deeply and darkly wrought, sometimes inscribed with a tonic humor, permeate Boland's poems of the 1990's. *In a Time of Violence* uses unusual and risky strategies to clarify the personal/political weave in Boland's vision. All those who lack autonomy are ultimately susceptible to victimhood and violence. This equation pertains to gender, nationhood, and any other form of identification. In *The Lost Land*, she continues to explore the issues and emotions of those who are victims of exile and colonialism. These are especially the burdens of "Colony," a major poem that makes up the first half of the book. Colonization, Boland says, is not just an act of governments, but an act of individuals—any exercise of power and dominance at the expense of the independence of others. It even applies to the relationships of parents and children, husbands and wives. These echoes weave their way more noticeably through the shorter poems in the collection. Along with the losses of place that Boland records—"place" having political, cultural, and psychic significance—she expresses here the loss of motherhood—another "place" of position that vanishes with time. Boland's constantly growing artistry, her ability to fasten on the telling concrete detail, and her hard-won personal and public authority make this collection outstanding.

AGAINST LOVE POETRY

Against Love Poetry deftly reconciles the sacrifice of freedom necessary for a lasting marriage with "the idea of women's freedom." If such a move seems unexpected or contradictory, it nonetheless arises from the same impulse as Boland's earlier work: the desire to delineate the true experience of women's lives. The book's first half, a section entitled "Marriage," clarifies the book's title. The sentimental ideal of romantic love, by now a well-known part of the poetic tradition, cannot begin to render adequately the truths of married life: "It is to mark the contradictions of a daily love that I have written this. Against love poetry." Throughout the volume, Boland draws on history, myths, folktales, and memory, continually subverting clichéd versions of romantic love in favor of a more complex, if often more stark, reality. For example, the poem "Quarantine," the fourth poem in the "Marriage" section, follows the route of a married couple walking during the Irish potato famine. Ultimately, after the man struggles unsuccessfully to keep his ill wife warm, both die "Of cold. Of hunger. Of the toxins of a whole history." Here the narrative shifts, echoing the book's title briefly to declare that "There is no place here for the inexact/ praise of the easy graces and sensuality of the body." What is important, the poem emphasizes, is the ordinary yet striking reality of what happens: "Their death together in the winter of 1847. Also what they suffered. How they lived./ And what there is between a man and a woman./ And in which darkness it can best be proved."

As in her earlier work, Boland continues to blend personal history, folktale, and classical myth to overturn past and present stereotypes of women's lives. "Called," an entry in the section half of the book, describes the author's unsuccessful search for the grave of her grandmother who died young. With Boland's resolve to "face this landscape/ and look at it as she was looked upon:// Unloved because unknown./ Unknown because unnamed," the familiar landmarks are stripped away, the earth returns to its essences, and the poet drives home as constellations appear, "some of them twisted into women." Even as Boland notes the vital role of women within the cosmos, those who "single-handedly holding high the dome/ and curve and horizon of today and tomorrow," she acknowledges the pain of being marginalized: "All the ships looking up to them./ All the compasses made true by them./ All the night skies named for their sorrow." Not surprisingly, in "Suburban Woman: Another Detail," she aptly describes her writing as the process of selecting words "from the earth,/ from the root, from the faraway/ oils and essence of elegy:/ Bitter. And close to the bone."

Interestingly, Boland extends her range of subjects to include poetry about the little-known accomplishments of historical women from the remote and recent past. The first poem in the "Marriage" section portrays Hester Bateman, a British silversmith who in the nineteenth century took on the trade of her husband, engraving marriage spoons for an Irish customer. In the book's second section, "Code," Boland directly addresses Grace Murray Hopper, who verified the computer language known as COBOL: "Let there be language—/ even if we use it differently:/ I never made it timeless as you have./ I never made it numerate as you did." In both poems, Boland identifies strongly with her protagonists, demonstrating the ability of the woman artist to create the future and to reconcile oppositions: "composing this/ to show you how the world begins again:/ One word at a time./ One woman to another" ("Code").

DOMESTIC VIOLENCE

In *Domestic Violence*, the late-night quarrels of a neighbor couple, the sectarian strife that erupted in Ireland in the 1960's, the poet's personal history, and the plight of Irish women become inextricably entwined. The title poem recalls how Boland and her husband, then newly married, watched the civil unrest known as the Troubles unfold in the grainy images of a small black-and-white television set, "which gave them back as gray and grayer tears/ and killings, killings, killings,/ then moonlight-colored funerals." In the same section, another poem, "How It Was Once in Our Country," evokes Ireland's turbulent history from previous centuries, relating the story of a mermaid who, according to some storytellers, "must have witnessed deaths" and remained below the water "to escape the screams." As always, there is the note of exile: "What we know is this/ (and this is all we know): we are now/ and we will always be from now on—/ for all I know we have always been—// exiles in our own country."

In the book's second section, Boland explores both past and present as she considers "last things," pondering what she will bequeath to her daughters. "Inheritance" expresses the poet's regret that she never learned the crafts of her predecessors: "the lace bobbin with its braided mesh,/ its oat-straw pillow and the wheat-colored shawl/ knitted in one season/ to imitate another." She also recalls a long night of tending to her first child: "When dawn came I held my hand over the absence of fever,/ over skin which had stopped burning, as if I knew the secrets of health and air, as if I understood them// and listened to the silence/ and thought, I must have learned that somewhere." In the entries that conclude this section, the poet's voice becomes more strident. "Windfall," an imagined rendering of the funeral for the grandmother whose grave she could not locate, describes "the coffin of a young woman/ who has left five children behind. There will be no obituary." The tragedy resides not only in her ancestor's unrecorded death, but also the insidious ways that language can be appropriated to justify ignoring lives that a culture or a country may consider insignificant:

> We say *Mother Nature* when all we intend is
> a woman was let die, out of sight, in a fever ward.
>
> Now say *Mother Ireland* when all that you mean is
> there is no need to record this death in history.

In "Letters to the Dead," the "signs and marks" used to inscribe ancient Egyptian pottery laid at the entrance of tombs become the poet's telling metaphor for a similar communication with her own ancestors. Ultimately, however, Boland's frank question reaches deep into Irish history:

> How many daughters stood alone at a grave,
> and thought this of their mothers' lives?
> That they were young in a country that hated
>   a woman's body.
> That they grew old in a country that hated
>   a woman's body
>
> They asked for the counsel of the dead.
> They asked for the power of the dead.
> These are my letters to the dead.

In a similar poem, "Violence Against Women," Boland mourns the female casualties of the Industrial Revolution, "women who died here who never lived:// mindless, sexless, birthless, only sunned/ by shadows, only dressed in muslin." For the poet, they resemble "shepherdesses of the English pastoral" trapped in traditional poetry, "waiting for the return of an English April/ that never came and never will again." Boland's closure questions and indicts the cultural and historical institutions that so often connive in the fate of women like Boland's grandmother.

Like her fellow poet and countryman Heaney, Boland's poetry has become a search for the images, symbols, and language that could adequately, realistically portray the struggles of women throughout history and her own pain at feeling like an exile in her own country. Throughout a career of patiently and carefully crafting poems, Boland has achieved an eloquence that is truly superlative.

OTHER MAJOR WORKS
NONFICTION: *W. B. Yeats and His World*, 1971 (with Micheál Mac Liammóir); *Object Lessons: The Life of the Woman and the Poet in Our Time*, 1995.
TRANSLATION: *After Every War: Twentieth-century Women Poets*, 2004.
EDITED TEXT: *The Making of a Poem: A Norton Anthology of Poetic Forms*, 2000 (with Mark Strand).

BIBLIOGRAPHY
Boland, Eavan. Interview by Patty O'Connell. *Poets and Writers* 22 (November/December, 1995). A lengthy conversation that ranges through Irish and American poetry, Dublin as an image in Boland's work, her mother, and poetry workshops.
Collins, Floyd. "Auspicious Beginnings and Sure Arrivals: Beth Ann Fennelly and Eavan Boland." *West Branch* 52 (Spring, 2003): 108-123. Contains an excellent discussion of *Against Love Poetry* and a comparison of Boland and Beth Ann Fennelly.
Constantakis, Sara, ed. *Poetry for Students*. Vol. 31. Detroit: Thomson/Gale Group, 2010. Contains an analysis of Boland's "Outside History."
Gonzalez, Alexander G., ed. *Contemporary Irish Women Poets: Some Male Perspectives*. Westport, Conn.: Greenwood Press, 1999. Enthusiastic responses by male critics to a wide range of Irish women poets include two strong essays on Boland: Thomas C. Foster's "In from the Margin: Eavan Boland's 'Outside History' Sequence" and Peter Kupillas's "Bringing It All Back Home: Unity and Meaning in Eavan Boland's 'Domestic Interior' Sequence."
Haberstroh, Patricia Boyle. *Women Creating Women: Contemporary Irish Women Poets*. Syracuse, N.Y.: Syracuse University Press, 1996. Compares Boland, Eithne Strong, Eiléan Ní Chuilleanáin, Medbh McGuckian, and Nuala Ní Dhomhnaill.
Keen, Paul. "The Doubled Edge: Identity and Alterity in the Poetry of Eavan Boland and Nuala Ní Dhomhnaill." *Mosaic* 33, no. 3 (2000): 14-34. Setting his investigation within the political and cultural upheavals in contemporary Ireland, Keen attends to Boland's theoretical writings to approach her poems. He sees her as rewriting Irish myths about the country and women rather than subverting them. Several key poems are examined with clarity and compassionate care. The comparative approach is fruitful.
McElroy, James. "The Contemporary Fe/Male Poet: A Preliminary Reading." In *New Irish Writing*, edited by James Brophy and Eamon Grennan. Boston: Twayne, 1989. McElroy defends Boland against critical charges of "stridency" and overstatement, arguing that her recurrent confrontations with the Irish domestic woman constitute a crucial part of her poetics of recovery and renewal, and that her willful reiterations of "female miseries" form a powerful catalog of matters that must be treated emphatically if Irish poetry is to recover its potency.
Randolph, Jody Allen, ed. *Eavan Boland: A Critical Companion*. New York: Norton,

2008. This volume, one of the first book-length studies of Boland, includes poetry and prose by Boland, interviews with her, and criticism of her work.

Villar-Argáiz, Pilar. *Eavan Boland's Evolution as an Irish Woman Poet: An Outsider Within an Outsider's Culture*. Lewiston, N.Y.: Edwin Mellen Press, 2007. Focuses on Boland as a female poet, presenting analysis of male-female relationships in her poetry. Includes an analysis of "Anorexic."

_____. *The Poetry of Eavan Boland: A Postcolonial Reading*. Dublin: Maunsel, 2008. This volume places Boland squarely within the context of postcolonial literature.

Kevin McNeilly; Arthur E. McGuinness;
Philip K. Jason
Updated by Caroline Collins

LORNA DEE CERVANTES

Born: San Francisco, California; August 6, 1954

PRINCIPAL POETRY
Emplumada, 1981
From the Cables of Genocide: Poems on Love and Hunger, 1991
Drive: The First Quartet, 2006

OTHER LITERARY FORMS

Nearly all the literary work of Lorna Dee Cervantes (sur-VAHN-tehz) is poetry. She was the founder and editor of Mango Publications, which published the literary review *Mango*, and she also founded and has edited the literary magazine *Red Dirt*.

ACHIEVEMENTS

Lorna Dee Cervantes's first collection of poems, *Emplumada*, won the American Book Award from the Before Columbus Foundation in 1982. Her second collection, *From the Cables of Genocide*, won the Paterson Poetry Prize and the Latino Literature Award and was nominated for a National Book Award in 1992. In 1995, she received the Lila Wallace-*Reader's Digest* Writers' Award. *Drive* was nominated for a Pulitzer Prize in poetry and won the Balcones Poetry Prize (2006). Cervantes has also been named Outstanding Chicana Scholar by the National Association of Chicano Scholars.

BIOGRAPHY

Lorna Dee Cervantes was born in 1954 in San Francisco and moved to San Jose (the setting for several of her best-known poems) after her parents' divorce in 1959. Her ethnic identification is not only Mexican American but also Native American, and she draws on this dual heritage in her poetry. She began writing poetry at an early age and first came to notice reading "Refugee Ship" at a drama festival in Mexico City in 1974. Her poems began to appear in Chicano journals such as *Revista Chicano-Riquena* and *Latin American Literary Review*, and in 1981, the University of Pittsburgh Press published her first volume of poetry, *Emplumada*, to widespread praise.

Cervantes gained her B.A. from San Jose State University in 1984, studied for four years as a graduate student in the history of consciousness program at the University of California, Santa Cruz, and has taught creative writing at the University of Colorado at Boulder. In addition to her academic position, Cervantes has done a good deal of editorial work, encouraging other Chicano writers, and has read her poetry at numerous national and international literary festivals.

Analysis

Lorna Dee Cervantes is one of the major Latina poetic voices writing in English, and at least half a dozen of her poems have been reprinted widely. Although she has written on a variety of topics, including a number of love poems, she is best known for those poems that define the situation for Mexican Americans at the end of the twentieth century, poems that are feminist and political. More than any other poet, Cervantes describes what it is like to live in two cultural worlds—or between them—and the tensions and difficulties such a limbo creates for a woman.

Emplumada

Many of Cervantes's best-known poems were printed in her first collection, published in 1981. *Emplumada* immediately established Cervantes as a major voice in contemporary American poetry, and its best poems raised the themes and issues with which many women were struggling. Although her language is simple and direct, Cervantes uses a number of Spanish words and phrases (and includes a two-page "glossary" at the end of the book that translates them into English). What is most striking in the collection is its colorful imagery; the poems are filled with visuals of birds and flowers. For example, the collection's title, *Emplumada*, comes from the combination of two Spanish words: *emplumado*, meaning "feathered or in plumage, as in after molting," and *plumada*, a "pen flourish." The title thus implies both change and growth and the flourish of a pen. The two emerge in this collection in a woman defining her new self through her poetry. As she writes at the end of "Visions of Mexico While at a Writing Symposium in Port Townsend, Washington,"

> as pain sends seabirds south from the cold
> I come north
> to gather my feathers
> for quills.

Poet Lynette Seator has written that *Emplumada* contains "poetry that affirms Mexican-American identity as well as the identity of the poet as woman coming-of-age." Although this collection also contains love poems ("Café Solo," "The Body Braille"), the best poems ("Lots: I," "Lots: II," "Poema para los Californios Muertos") have larger feminist, ethnic, and historical subjects.

"Refugee Ship"

"Refugee Ship" (from *Emplumada*) is the poem that first gained notice for Cervantes. It is a remarkable work for such a young poet, for its brief fourteen lines capture the feelings of many immigrants caught between two cultures. The first stanza establishes her Latina identity and her link to her *abuelita* (grandmother). In the five lines of the second stanza, she describes her estrangement from her native culture in language and in name:

> Mama raised me without language.
> I'm orphaned from my Spanish name.
> The words are foreign, stumbling
> on my tongue. . . .

Even her physical appearance, she concludes in this stanza, looks alien: "I see in the mirror/ my reflection: bronzed skin, black/ hair." The four lines of the third and final stanza give the image of the title that so perfectly describes her situation and dilemma:

> I feel I am a captive
> aboard the refugee ship.
> The ship that will never dock.
> *El barco que nunca atraca.*

The third and fourth lines, which repeat the same phrase first in English and then Spanish, emphasize her estrangement, her sense not only of dislocation but also of being caught between two places, two lives, and never able to land or reside in either. "Refugee Ship" captures that feeling of estrangement for generations of immigrants to the United States, who were torn between two cultures and completely at home in neither.

"OAXACA, 1974"

Closely linked to "Refugee Ship" is "Oaxaca, 1974," which was included in *Emplumada* under that title, but appeared originally and in some anthologies as "Heritage." In the poem, the narrator looks for her Mexican heritage "all day in the streets of Oaxaca," but the children laugh at her, calling to her "in words of another language." Although she has a "brown body," she searches "for the dye that will color my thoughts," or make "this bland pochaseed" ("an assimilated Mexican American," as Cervantes translates the phrase in the glossary) more Latino in her thinking. She did not ask to be brought up "tonta" (stupid), she concludes, but "Es la culpa de los antepasados" (It is her ancestors' fault):

> Blame it on the old ones.
> They give me a name
> that fights me.

If the name is Lorna, it is obviously English in derivation and says nothing of her Mexican American heritage. The poem was first titled "Heritage," and although Cervantes dropped the poem's original first word, "Heritage," when it became "Oaxaca, 1974," the idea embodied in that word still runs beneath the poem's lines and images. The poem, like "Refugee Ship," is an evocative description of the immigrant living uncomfortably between two cultures.

"Freeway 280"

Two other poems in this first collection, "Freeway 280" and "Beneath the Shadow of the Freeway," complement each other and have been reprinted in several anthologies. Deborah L. Madsen wrote, "Cervantes's poetry reveals an acute sense of the importance of geographical and cultural place," and that is nowhere more true than in these two related poems. "Freeway 280" has the theme of human versus nature: In spite of the "raised scar" of the freeway, the narrator tells readers, life thrives. Once, she wanted to leave on the same freeway, but now she has returned.

> Maybe it's here
> en los campos extraños de esta ciudad ["in the strange fields of this city"]
> where I'll find it, that part of me
> mown under
> like a corpse
> or a loose seed.

The opposition between humans and nature has become the means of the narrator's finding her own identity in a hometown destroyed by urban development, but where "wild mustard remembers, old gardens/ come back stronger than they were."

"Beneath the Shadow of the Freeway"

"Beneath the Shadow of the Freeway" is a longer and more complex poem (and probably Cervantes's best-known single poem) that starts in the same San Jose setting. In spite of its title and all its natural imagery, however, "Beneath the Shadow of the Freeway" is really a celebration of the power of women. In language that lifts her thoughts to a mythic level, Cervantes creates a powerful statement of Latina strength, and a reminder about those—particularly men—who so often take it away.

The poem is broken into six numbered parts; all except the first contain verse stanzas themselves. In the first section, the narrator describes the house she lives in with her mother and her grandmother, who "watered geraniums/ [as] the shadow of the freeway lengthened." "We were a woman family," the narrator declares in the next stanza, and introduces her main theme. Her mother warns her about men, but the narrator models herself more on her grandmother, who "believes in myths and birds" and "trusts only what she builds/ with her own hands." A drunken intruder (perhaps the mother's former husband) tries to break into the house in the fifth section but is scared away. In the final stanza, the mother warns the narrator, "Baby, don't count on nobody," but the narrator confesses to the reader that "Every night I sleep with a gentle man/ to the hymn of the mockingbirds," plants geraniums, ties her hair up like her grandmother, "and trust[s] only what I have built with my own hands." The poem is thus a celebration of three generations of women and contains the promise that women can be independent and still find love.

"POEM FOR THE YOUNG WHITE MAN..."

"Poem for the Young White Man Who Asked Me How I, an Intelligent, Well-Read Person Could Believe in the War Between Races" may be Cervantes's most blatantly political poem in *Emplumada*, but it mirrors ideas and images found throughout the collection. "I believe in revolution," she tells the Anglo man who has questioned her, "because everywhere the crosses are burning" and "there are snipers in the schools." They are not aimed at her interrogator, she says, but "I'm marked by the color of my skin."

> Racism is not intellectual.
> I can not reason these scars away.
>
> Outside my door
> there is a real enemy
> who hates me.

"I am a poet," the persona declares, "who yearns to dance on rooftops." Her "tower of words," however, cannot silence "the sounds of blasting and muffled outrage." This contradiction is continued in the poem's last lines:

> Every day I am deluged with reminders
> that this is not
> my land
> and this is my land.
>
> I do not believe in the war between races
>
> but in this country
> there is war.

As in "Refugee Ship" and "Oaxaca, 1974," the narrator is torn between two lands—but here within her own country.

FROM THE CABLES OF GENOCIDE

Cervantes's second collection of poems, *From the Cables of Genocide*, failed to match the quality and power of *Emplumada*. The poems in the book's four sections—"From the Cables of Genocide," "On Love and Hunger," "The Captive Verses," and "On the Fear of Going Down"—tend to be longer and written in a more complex style. Cervantes also makes less use of Spanish. At least four of the poems are written "after Neruda," several others "after García Lorca," and there are more classical allusions here than in *Emplumada*. Although the distinctively sharp Cervantes language and intense imagery grace the poems in this collection, fewer of them have been reprinted.

Many of the poems in *From the Cables of Genocide* record the pain and loss suffered at the ending of love, and "My Dinner with Your Memory" may be representative of this recurrent subject and situation. The imagery of a feast (bread, butter, cheese, plum brandy) works counter to the sense of pain here: "when the moon slivers my heart/ into poverty's portions." The concluding lines are ambiguous at best but certainly convey the poem's sense of loss:

> Who would hunger at the brink of this
> feast? Who would go, uninvited,
> but you and your ghost of a dog?

Other poems in the collection, such as "On Love and Hunger" and "Macho," continue this theme. There are fewer poems here that deal with ethnic or multicultural issues ("Flatirons" and "Pleiades from the Cables of Genocide" are two strong exceptions) and more that deal with the personal plight of a woman ("On Finding the Slide of John in the Garden"). Some of the best poems in the second collection—like "Shooting the Wren"—are reminiscent of poems in the first, such as "Uncle's First Rabbit."

DRIVE

Fifteen years elapsed between the publication of *From the Cables of Genocide* and Cervantes's third volume of poetry, *Drive: The First Quartet.* In spite of its subtitle, the volume actually contains five separate collections, each set off by a heavy black page and introduced by a painting or photograph. In the author's note that concludes the volume, Cervantes writes that she has always been influenced by painters and describes the paintings by her friend Dylan Morgan that introduce four of the sections. The fifth is introduced by a black-and-white photograph of Robert F. Kennedy.

The first collection, *How Far's the Water?*, contains the most political poems, dealing with topics such as genocide and injustice. The first poem in the collection is "For My Ancestors Adobed in the Walls of the Santa Barbara Mission"; others include "Coffee," "Bananas," and "Portrait of a Little Boy Feeding a Stray in Sarajevo." The second collection, *BIRD AVE*, shifts to more personal subjects: Cervantes growing up in the barrio in the 1960's and early 1970's ("On the Poet Coming of Age") and young people at a Summer Youth Leadership Institute in 1999 ("Collages"). The third collection, *PLAY*, contains three sections of spontaneous poetry workshop exercises on a wide variety of subjects that generate what Cervantes calls seven-minute poems ("Manzanita," "Thelonious Monk," "Ghosts"). The fourth collection, *Letter to David: An Elegiac Mass in the Form of a Train,* is dedicated to Robert F. Kennedy's son, David A. Kennedy, who drank himself to death on April 25, 1984. As Cervantes explains in her prefatory "Note to David" that follows photos of both the young man and his father, the poet remembers vividly the day his father was assassinated. Each of the fourteen poems in this collection is a numbered station, as in the Roman Catholic stations of the Cross, and most are preceded by a parenthetical date. For example, "Fourteenth Station" begins "*(June 5, 1968)*" and links the elder Kennedy with the poet's mother. The fifth collection, *Hard Drive*, consists of three parts: "Striking Ash," "On Line," and "Con una poca de gracia." This collection contains mostly love poems but it also includes two photographs of the poet, one accompanying the poem "Portrait of the Poet at Thirty-three." *Drive* reveals an amazing range of poetic subjects and voices, and many of the poems demonstrate Cervantes's belief in the key relationship between language and power.

"Coffee" and "Bananas"

"Coffee" centers on the massacre of forty-five men, women, and children by paramilitary units in Acteal in Chiapas, Mexico, in 1997. In six sections of the ten-page poem, Cervantes denounces the slaughter—section 3 is a simple recital of the names of the victims—and the imperialism represented by U.S. corporations in Central America. The theme of the poem is best captured in the repeated cry, "No more genocide in my name." "Bananas" uses the fruit to illuminate the international sociopolitical network of plenty and poverty running from Boulder, Colorado, to the Baltic country of Estonia. In both poems, the stark language and images are at the same time personal and political.

Bibliography

Candelaria, Cordelia. *Chicano Poetry: A Critical Introduction*. Westport, Conn.: Greenwood Press, 1986. In an early evaluation of Cervantes's poetry, Candelaria writes that *Emplumada* reveals a "fresh, forceful, and multifaceted" talent and places her work in the third and final phase of Chicano poetry, after protest poetry and the development of a "Chicano poetics."

Harris-Fonseca, Amanda Nolocea. "Lorna Dee Cervantes." In *Latino and Latina Writers*, edited by Alan West-Duran et al. Vol. 1. New York: Scribner's, 2004. Harris-Fonseca provides a detailed discussion of Cervantes's first two collections of poetry and the differences between them, with analyses of several key poems.

"Lorna Dee Cervantes." In *After Aztlán: Latino Poets of the Nineties*, edited by Ray González. Boston: David R. Godine, 1993. Contains a section providing a basic biography of the poet and analysis of her works, and also places her among other Latino poets.

"Lorna Dee Cervantes." In *The Bloomsbury Guide to Women's Literature*, edited by Claire Buck. New York: Prentice Hall, 1992. This entry provides basic information on Cervantes's life and works, while placing her in the feminist context.

McKenna, Teresa. "'An Utterance More Pure Than Word': Gender and the Corrido Tradition in Two Contemporary Chicano Poems." In *Feminist Measures: Soundings in Poetry and Theory*, edited by Lynn Keller and Cristanne Miller. Ann Arbor: University of Michigan Press, 1994. Detailed analyses of Juan Gomez-Quinoñes's "The Ballad of Billy Rivera" and Cervantes's "Visions of Mexico While at a Writing Symposium in Port Townsend, Washington." Also touches on several other key poems in *Emplumada*.

Madsen, Deborah L. *Understanding Contemporary Chicana Poetry*. Columbia: University of South Carolina Press, 2000. An overview of Cervantes's poetry in the final chapter of this study finds that she uses angry language, passionate expression of emotions, and complex, interwoven imagery to portray the Mexican American woman's life from a feminist perspective.

Rodriguez y Gibson, Eliza. "'Tat Your Black Holes into Paradise': Lorna Dee Cervantes and a Poetics of Loss." *MELUS* 33 (Spring, 2008): 139-155. This critical analysis of "To We Who Were Saved by the Stars" and "Pleiades from the Cables of Genocide," both in *From the Cables of Genocide*, shows how Cervantes provides a way to understand losses, both historical and cultural, and shows how women deal with these losses.

Savin, Ada. "Bilingualism and Dialogism: Another Reading of Lorna Dee Cervantes' Poetry." In *An Other Tongue: Nation and Ethnicity in the Linguistic Borderlands*, edited by Alfred Arteaga. Durham, N.C.: Duke University Press, 1994. Using the linguistic theory of Mikhail Bakhtin, Savin finds that Cervantes's "poetic discourse is fragmented, divided, lying somewhere in the interspace between two cultures," but that *Emplumada* eloquently expresses the Chicano quest for self-definition.

Seator, Lynette. "*Emplumada*: Chicana Rites-of-Passage." *MELUS* 11 (Summer, 1984): 23-38. Reads Cervantes's first collection as poems that not only affirm Mexican American identity but also present a woman in the process of coming of age. Contains detailed analyses of many of the best poems in the collection, including "Lots: I," "Lots: II," "Caribou Girl," "For Edward Long," and "For Virginia Chavez."

Wallace, Patricia. "Divided Loyalties: Literal and Literary in the Poetry of Lorna Dee Cervantes, Cathy Song, and Rita Dove." *MELUS* 18 (Fall, 1993): 3-19. Wallace argues that these three poets use language creatively to overcome barriers. He sees Cervantes's poems as "often acts of assertion against restrictive social and linguistic structures."

David Peck
Updated by Peck

CAROLYN FORCHÉ

Born: Detroit, Michigan; April 28, 1950

PRINCIPAL POETRY
Gathering the Tribes, 1976
The Country Between Us, 1981
The Angel of History, 1994
Blue Hour, 2003

OTHER LITERARY FORMS

Carolyn Forché (fohr-SHAY) has provided translations of the poems of Central American writers Claribel Alegría (*Flowers from the Volcano*, 1982; *Sorrow*, 1999) and, working with William Kulik, Robert Desnos (*The Selected Poems of Robert Desnos*, 1991). In addition, she wrote the text for a series of photographs of El Salvador, covering the period from 1979 to 1982, in *El Salvador: The Work of Thirty Photographers* (1983). Her essays, reviews, and poems have appeared in major publications, including *The New York Times Book Review*, *Atlantic*, *Ms.*, *American Poetry Review*, *The New Yorker*, *Antaeus*, and *Virginia Quarterly Review*. Forché edited the influential anthology *Against Forgetting: Twentieth-Century Poetry of Witness* (1993) and coedited *Writing Creative Nonfiction: Instruction and Insights from Teachers of the Associated Writing Programs* (2001) with Philip Gerard. She translated and edited the collection by Mahmoud Darwish, *Unfortunately, It Was Paradise: Selected Poems* (2003), with Munir Akash.

ACHIEVEMENTS

Carolyn Forché's poems focus on people—her ancestors, her childhood friends, Native Americans, and Salvadorans, to name a few—and emphasize place—often Detroit, the Southwest, or Central America. Her commitment to speaking for those who have been silenced, whether for economic, ethnic, racist, or political reasons, has won for her many readers and much critical acclaim. Her first book, *Gathering the Tribes*, concerning a girl's initiation into adulthood, was selected for the Yale Series of Younger Poets in 1975. Her second, *The Country Between Us*, concerning a young woman's development of a social conscience, was the Lamont Poetry Selection of the Academy of American Poets (1981) and won the Poetry Society of America's Alice Fay di Castagnola Award. The commitment to politics that surfaced clearly in the second volume is also evident in *El Salvador* and in many of her essays. She has received numerous awards for her poetry and various fellowships, including a National Endowment for the Arts Fellowship (1977) and a John Simon Guggenheim Memorial Fellowship (1978). She received the Lannan Literary Award for Poetry in 1990 and the Los Angeles Times Book Prize for poetry in 1994 for *The Angel of History*. Forché also won the Edita and Ira Morris Hiroshima Foundation for Peace and Culture Award for 1998, which was presented to her in recognition of her work on behalf of human rights and the preservation of memory and culture. Forché's *Blue Hour* was a finalist for the National Book Critics Circle Award in 2003 and a finalist for the Lenore Marshall Poetry Prize of 2004.

Forché has been a member of several literary organizations, including the International Association of Poets, Playwrights, Editors, Essayists, and Novelists (PEN) and the Academy of American Poets, and of political and government groups such as Amnesty International, the Institute for Global Education, and the Commission on United States-Central American Relations. The poet and professor has accepted invitations to judge literary contests, reading for such competitions as the Discovery/The Nation's Joan Leiman Jacobson Poetry Prize of 2002.

Biography

Born in 1950 to Michael Joseph Forché, a tool and die maker, and Louise Nada Sidlosky Forché, a homemaker, Carolyn Louise Forché, the oldest of seven children, spent her first five years in Detroit, Michigan, before moving to the suburbs with her family. With the encouragement of her mother, Forché began writing poems at the age of nine, often as an escape, much like daydreaming. At the age of eighteen, she published her first poem, "Artisan Well," in the October, 1968, issue of *Ingenue*.

At Justin Morrill College, an experimental college of Michigan State University, she attracted the attention of several professors, who became mentors and encouraged her writing. In 1970 and again in 1971, she won first prize in Michigan State University's poetry competition. At college, she majored in creative writing and minored in English literature and French but also took courses in international relations, philosophy, and history. In addition to French, she studied Russian, Spanish, Serbo-Croatian, and Tewa (Pueblo Indian)—perhaps following an interest generated by her Slavic-speaking relatives. After receiving her B.A. in 1972, she entered the M.F.A. program at Bowling Green State University in Ohio; she received her degree in 1975. Her thesis, "Secret Histories," suggests the direction that her poetry would take: the chronicling of the lives of those who have been forgotten.

As a student she worked on the poems that formed her first collection, *Gathering the Tribes*, and she completed it at age twenty-four. The collection was well received, entering its third printing only a year after its publication. She then turned her attention to the period involving the Vietnam War. In high school, she and her working-class friends had been supportive of the war, but in college, she joined the antiwar movement. She struggled to understand Vietnam partly because her first husband, whom she married when she was nineteen, was psychologically scarred by the war and partly because her political conscience had been stimulated by Terrence Des Pres's *Survivors: An Anat-*

omy of Life in the Death Camps (1976), which she had read while convalescing from viral meningitis in 1976. She made Des Pres's acquaintance, and the two writers entered into a correspondence that lasted until his death in 1987. His last work, *Praises and Dispatches* (1988), explores the relationship between poetry and politics, a subject that is of importance in understanding Forché's poems.

During the 1970's, Forché developed an interest in Central America. In 1977, when she was translating the poems of Claribel Alegría, she traveled to Spain to consult the exiled poet. There she met a number of Latin American writers and began to learn about the region's human rights problems. Returning to California, she taught English at San Diego State University but also worked for Amnesty International. When she received a Guggenheim Fellowship, Leonel Gomez, Alegría's nephew, suggested that she use it to travel in El Salvador; other friends, however, suggested Paris. Gomez argued, "Do you want to write poetry about yourself the rest of your life?" Answering in the negative, she chose El Salvador. From 1978 to 1980, as a journalist and human rights activist reporting to Amnesty International, she traveled in El Salvador, witnessing the poverty of the peasants, the ill health of the children, the rural hospitals where operations were often performed without anesthesia, and also the luxurious homes of members of the military. During this period, the notorious death squads were becoming active, and she learned about the missing people and the torture of political dissidents. Once back in the United States, she lectured and wrote articles concerning her experiences, following the Salvadorans' plea: "Document it. . . . go back and tell them what you've seen." Her poems on El Salvador are included in *The Country Between Us*, which gained for Forché a reputation as a political poet. Perhaps that designation is not, or should not be, unusual, for as Forché points out, "History and politics affect everyone's life, everywhere, always."

As she had after her first collection, she again took a hiatus from poetry, explaining that reflection and solitude were necessary for writing poetry and the political situation allowed her neither. Instead, she turned to writing a series of essays on places she had visited. The first, on El Salvador, appeared in *American Poetry Review* in 1981, and she planned additional essays on Lebanon and on Northern Ireland. While in Lebanon, she presented a series of news documentaries on Beirut (parts of which reminded her of Detroit) for National Public Radio's program *All Things Considered*.

Forché was married on December 27, 1984, to Henry E. Mattison, a photographic correspondent with *Time* magazine whose assignments included Nicaragua, El Salvador, Lebanon, and South Africa. They were together in South Africa but left in 1986 for the birth of their son, Sean Christophe, for they did not want their child to be born under the apartheid system.

In 1974, Forché began to teach English and writing, becoming a writer-in-residence at various universities, including Michigan State University, San Diego State University, the University of Virginia, New York University, Vassar College, and Columbia

University. In 1989, she settled at George Mason University, which became her academic home for the next nine years. In the fall of 2008, after being invited as visiting professor to Georgetown University's Lannan Center for Poetry and Social Practice, Forché accepted a permanent position in the school's English Department.

Analysis

In her first collection, *Gathering the Tribes*, Carolyn Forché recounts the experiences of her youth and maturation, focusing on places and people of importance to her development. She writes of her grandmother and Michigan but also of Teles Goodmorning (a Pueblo Indian) and the Southwest, claiming a spiritual kinship. Her second volume, *The Country Between Us*, is marked by a similar emphasis on places and people, but this time, the place is often El Salvador or Czechoslovakia and the people are victims of oppression.

Her first collection charts the growth of a child entering adulthood, and the second completes the process, chronicling the development of a social conscience with an emphasis on commitment and responsibility. Criticized for being an activist poet, Forché counters, "There is no such thing as a nonpolitical poetry." Her belief that "we are, as a species, now careening toward our complete destruction with ever-greater velocity" explains her political involvement and her commitment to speak out.

Gathering the Tribes

In *Gathering the Tribes*, Forché links the process of her maturation to the influence of specific people and places. These poems display a strong sense of place, whether it be the Michigan of her childhood, the Wakhan region of northern Afghanistan, or the Pueblo villages of New Mexico. However, there is also a strong sense of dislocation: Her Slavic ancestors left their homeland, and the narrator can never be part of the Southwest. Thus strong bonds between people are essential; the tribes must be gathered together. The people whom she cherishes might be her Slavic ancestors, her childhood friends, or those she considers spiritual ancestors—the American Indians of the Southwest. It is often women who provide guidance—her peasant grandmother; the Indians Rosita and Alfansa; the narrator's lover, Jacynthe. Reinforcing the prominent position of women in the collection are many domestic images, such as bread making and pea shelling, and images drawn from nature and the natural cycles. This emphasis on women has led to questions about Forché's position on the women's movement; she responds, "I think any intelligent woman would have to consider herself a feminist."

Gathering the Tribes is divided into three parts. The first, "Burning the Tomato Worms," focuses primarily on the narrator's Slavic ancestors and their history, including their probable forced migration from northern Afghanistan, across Turkey, to the region where Russia borders Czechoslovakia. The poems suggest a connection between the past of the ancestors and the present of the narrator's girlhood. In other words, her life is a continuation of their lives, especially that of the peasant grandmother, Anna. The poems are imbued with Anna's wisdom and knowledge of the Old World's folkways and folklore, knowledge that the narrator needs: "Grandma, come back, I forgot/ How much lard for these rolls" ("The Morning Baking"). Throughout the poems, there is a transference of the past to the present. Eventually the narrator becomes, in a sense, her grandmother: "But I'm glad I'll look when I'm old/ Like a gypsy dusha hauling milk."

The strong bond between the speaker and her grandmother is evident in the central poem "Burning the Tomato Worms." The poem is set in the Midwest, with its "ploughed land" and "horse-breath weather," reminding the narrator of her deceased grandmother Anna. The narrator is directly linked to her grandmother's ancestors:

> Before I was born, my body as snowfat
> Crept over Wakhan
> As grandfathers spat into fires and thawed
> Their tarpaulin
> Sending crackled paths of blood
> Down into my birth.

She inherits these memories and those of her grandmother's youth in Eastern Europe, when political oppression forced her family to leave home:

> When time come
> We go quick
> I think
> What to take.

Carrying nothing but the bare essentials, the grandmother eventually settled in Michigan.

It is Anna who, "shelling snow peas" with Uzbek hands that once were "known for weaving fine rugs," teaches the narrator and guides her, relying on Old World maxims such as "Eat bread and salt and speak the truth." Anna wants the speaker to confront "something/ That was sacred and eternal." The meaning of this "something" is left ambiguous until the final section of the poem, when the reader understands that the grandmother is leading the speaker to an acceptance of the natural cycles of life. Her grandmother shapes the speaker's life, yet the narrator is not frozen to the past but is part of the present and future. Her life is a counterbalance to her grandmother's death. Thus the poem tells of the younger woman's sexual awakening and ends with a transferring of life from the grandmother to the speaker.

Just as the first part of *Gathering the Tribes* examines the influence of Forché's biological ancestors, the second, "Song Coming Toward Us," shows the influence of her spiritual forebears, primarily the American Indians of the Southwest. The bonds are again clear: "What has been/ and what is becoming/ are all of the same age" ("Calling Down the Moose"). The American Indians, such as Alfansa (in "Alfansa") and Rosita ("Mientras Dure Vida, Sobra el Tiempo"), are her teachers, just as her grandmother was. This section ends with "Plain Song," which expresses her acceptance of her eventual death, since death, like sex, is part of the natural cycle:

> When it happens, let the birds come.
> Let my hands fall without being folded.
> . . . .
> Close my eyes with coins, cover
> my head with agave baskets
> that have carried water.

The final section, "The Place That Is Feared I Inhabit," draws predominantly on Forché's personal experiences rather than on her ancestors. The poems chronicle the development of the narrator's sexuality, from her infatuation with Joey, a childhood boyfriend, in "Taproot" and "This Is Their Fault," to a more adult understanding of sexuality as a young mother in "Year at Mudstraw," followed by a sense of disillusionment in "Taking Off My Clothes"; here the speaker voices the suspicion that her lover cannot appreciate her, just as he could not appreciate a Ming bowl. One of the final poems, "Kalaloch," presents a lesbian relationship against the backdrop of nature. The first few stanzas of the erotic poem focus on Jacynthe and the speaker's stay at the coast, where they gather mussels, pick berries, and watch the fog and the tide at day and the moon and the campfire at night. Their love is as natural as the setting in which it is expressed.

THE COUNTRY BETWEEN US

If *Gathering the Tribes* can be said to chronicle an initiation into adulthood, Forché's second volume, *The Country Between Us*, explores the responsibilities and commitments of that adulthood. The catalyst for this collection was Forché's stay in El Salvador. Eight of the poems in the volume have to do with that experience, and the first section of the volume is dedicated to Oscar Romero, the archbishop who, in 1980, was murdered as he said Mass in San Salvador. Vietnam and Czechoslovakia are also highlighted in this collection. As in the first collection, people are central. Included are a steelworker troubled by Vietnam; a woman with whom the speaker shared childhood dreams and who now lives in a trailer with her husband and children, wondering what happened to her life; Des Pres, Forché's confidant and mentor; and a dissident from Eastern Europe.

The prose poem "The Colonel," the most frequently quoted piece in *The Country Between Us*, is autobiographical, like much of Forché's work, and is based on an encounter with a Salvadoran military officer. At first, the evening described seems unexceptional, even ordinary. The speaker and her friend have dinner (lamb, wine, and fruit) with the colonel and his wife. Typical household items such as newspapers, a pet dog, and a television set make the setting comfortable and tranquil—yet the broken glass embedded in the wall surrounding the compound suggests otherwise. The family's activities—one child files her nails, the other goes out for the evening, the wife serves coffee—are also familiar. Nevertheless, the horror of the situation is soon apparent. The colonel dumps a sackful of human ears on the dining table, emphasizing his intolerance for human rights activists:

> He spilled many ears on the table. They were like dried peach halves. There is no other way to say this. He took one of them in his hands, shook it in our faces, dropped it into a water glass. It came alive there. I am tired of fooling around he said.

While the colonel might have power now, the poem suggests that the situation will not last: "Some of the ears on the floor caught this scrap of his voice. Some of the ears on the floor were pressed to the ground." The ears assume a life of their own and a memory, and they will be avenged.

While the volume's first part, "In Salvador, 1978-80," focuses on that country, the second, "Reunion," examines oppression found elsewhere: Turkey ("Expatriate"), Czechoslovakia ("Letter from Prague, 1968-78"), and the United States with its economic oppression. In "As Children Together," Victoria and the speaker grow up together and speak of their girlish dreams; Victoria envisions herself in Montreal, living a romantic life filled with flowers, "a satin bed, a table/ cluttered with bottles of scent." She wants desperately to escape her parents' house with "its round tins of surplus flour,/ chipped beef and white beans, relief checks," where her father whittles aimlessly on soap cakes. Victoria becomes promiscuous and eventually marries a serviceman, who returns from Vietnam "broken/ cursing holy blood at the table/ where nightly a pile of white shavings/ is paid from the edge of his knife." Her life, a legacy of Vietnam and poverty, is circumscribed by the trailer in which she lives. Still, the poem ends on a note of hope. One of the girls, the speaker, has broken the cycle: "If you read this poem, write to me./ I have been to Paris since we parted."

In "Joseph," the narrator's childhood companion and first boyfriend, Joseph, has also lost his dreams. His life now consists of working in the steel mill, meeting women in bars ("You take her panties to your face/ and it is all you have and all/ your father had and all your brothers"), and fishing. The narrator recognizes the emptiness of his working-class life: "It is not enough, the fish,/ the white heads of beer, your winnings." His youth held a promise that was not fulfilled because of the oppression of poverty. Now the gap between the two former friends prevents communication.

The final part of the collection, "Ourselves or Nothing," contains one long poem of the same title, dedicated to Des Pres. The poem suggests the importance of remembering, of not letting "Belsen, Dachau, Saigon, Phnom Penh/ and the one meaning Bridge of Ravens,/ Sao Paulo, Armagh, Calcutta, Salvador" be forgotten, and the importance of not remaining behind the "cyclone fence," of not hovering "in a calm protected world like/ netted fish, exactly like netted fish." It is crucial to become involved, for, as the poem concludes, "It is either the beginning or the end/ of the world, and the choice is ourselves/ or nothing."

THE ANGEL OF HISTORY

In *The Angel of History*, Forché's ambition and accomplishment reach new heights. Read either as a single, long poem or a sequence of related poems, this dazzling volume breaks away from the techniques of her earlier work. Forché's own comment, in her notes to the volume, says it best:

> The first-person, free-verse, lyric-narrative poem of my earlier years has given way to a work which has desired its own bodying forth: polyphonic, broken, haunted, and in ruins, with no possibility of restoration.

There may be some overstatement here; something that is fragmentary is not necessarily in ruins. However, the ruined moral landscape that Forché's persona annotates is projected with a "terrible beauty." Through the voice (or voices) of the recording angel, the poet absorbs and releases visions and echoes of the disasters that humans of the twentieth century have wrought on themselves. Readers are forced to witness and respond to the Holocaust, to Hiroshima, and to genocide in Latin America. At once angry and compassionate, devastated and distanced, the angel forces the reader to accept the harsh reality and guides him or her toward a thin but luminous possibility of redemption. Forché's poem is like the bell in "The Garden Shukkei-en," devastated by the atomic bomb though since restored: "It is the bell to awaken God that we've heard ringing."

BLUE HOUR

Forché's fourth collection, *Blue Hour*, is named for the French phrase *l'heure bleu*, that twilight moment between dark and dawn in which utter darkness and pure light meet, resulting in a Rayleigh scattering that turns the sky blue. To the poet, who woke with her infant son at this hour, it is the moment associated with "hovering." In the endnotes, she writes that this sort of interstice of time also is the blue that is the second *sefirah* in Kabbala, as well as that moment of luminosity or clear light "arising at the moment of death" in Tibetan Buddhism. The title thus sets the tone that runs through the eleven poems, a tone of dream-state meeting poetic-state, tinting the abstractions and atrocities with a conjured beauty that renders the concrete tolerable.

The speaker in the poems, almost always unobtrusively reporting events of history, offers thoughtful insights into destruction and death as well as the lack of language and the "language of lack." In "Nocturne," the speaker announces "These are the words no longer." The abandoned house becomes that which soon "give[s] itself back . . . , its walls becom[ing] as unreadable as symbols on silk." Nevertheless, the speaker, in "Sequestered Writing," calls to the world to engage, to "*Come here and know*," and, in "On Earth," to "open the book of what happened." However, unlike the speaker in *The Angel of History*, the poetic voice in *Blue Hour* also suggests that people let go of history, bidding "*Adieu*, Franco-Prussian War," and "*Adieu*, country." As if oversaturated by war, death, and the past, and filled with a vision of the future "wrapped in a shroud" (in "Hive"), the poetic voice calls for total absorption and ephemeral suspension at the same time. In "In the Exclusion Zones," a poem about areas of earth contaminated by the nuclear incident at Chernobyl, the speaker calls for something more than remembering, because the "bees of the invisible" (a line borrowed from Maria Rainer Rilke) do that and the "white towel hung in an open door" is enough to bring back memories. In *Blue Hour*, Forché treats memory not only as a binding element but also as something to be transcended. As the poetic voice suggests in abecedarian form in the collection's longest poem, "Of Earth," there is ultimately a "stepping back into an earlier life." The "clouds return . . . to the sky from the past," and "what you see" is a "beginning of life after death." In all the past atrocity remembered in the present, there is a blue hour moment—a French, Kabbala, Buddhist, or everyone-on-Earth instant when light reflecting against dark inspires a bardic state of near metaphysical transcendence—or in Forché's words, at least a hovering in the meantime.

Forché has been praised by some critics for her ability to blend the political with a personal poetic mode. Others disagree, claiming that Forché is too much a part of her poems and that her poetic diction is unsuited to her subject. However, others suggest that in *Blue Hour*, she is working against the subjective "I" in favor of the image until it reaches almost metaphysical status. Forché has stated that all subjects should be appropriate for poetry and that she has a responsibility to speak as a witness: "In my own life, the memory of certain of those who have died remains in very few hands. I can't let go of that work if I am of that number." Forché includes the political in her work, but most important, she never forgets that she is writing poetry, poetry that is lyrical, honest, sensual, tender, courageous, and intelligent.

OTHER MAJOR WORKS

NONFICTION: *El Salvador: The Work of Thirty Photographers*, 1983 (text for photographs).

TRANSLATIONS: *Flowers from the Volcano*, 1982 (of Claribel Alegría); *The Selected Poems of Robert Desnos*, 1991 (with William Kulik); *Sorrow*, 1999 (of Alegría); *Unfortunately, It Was Paradise: Selected Poems*, 2003 (of Mahmoud Darwash; with Munir Akash).

EDITED TEXTS: *Against Forgetting: Twentieth-Century Poetry of Witness*, 1993; *Writing Creative Nonfiction: Instruction and Insights from Teachers of the Associated Writing Programs*, 2001 (with Philip Gerard).

Bibliography

Bedient, Calvin. "Passion and War: Reading Sontag, Viola, Forché, and Others." *Salmagundi* 141/142 (Winter, 2004): 243-262. Bedient examines how war is treated by several writers and offers a close reading of *Blue Hour*.

_____. "Poetry and Silence at the End of the Century." *Salmagundi* 111 (Summer, 1996): 195-207. Bedient compares *The Angel of History* to Charles Wright's *Chickamauga* (1995) and T. S. Eliot's *The Waste Land* (1922).

Bogan, Don. "The Muses of History." *The Nation* 24 (October, 1994): 464-469. This brief but careful reading of *The Angel of History* attends to its structure and tone. Bogan sets Forché's work alongside James Fenton's collection *Out of Danger* (1994).

Doubiago, Sharon. "Towards an American Criticism: A Reading of Carolyn Forché's *The Country Between Us*." *American Poetry Review* 12 (January/February, 1983): 35-39. Doubiago faults other critics who have no tolerance for a political message in poetry and suggests that any aesthetic has a political basis.

Forché, Carolyn. Interview by David Montenegro. *American Poetry Review* 17 (November/December, 1988): 35-40. Forché discusses a number of issues, including her work in progress, the influence of her grandmother on her poetry, her childhood, and the Vietnam War.

Gleason, Judith. "The Lesson of Bread." *Parnassus: Poetry in Review* 10 (Spring/Summer, 1982): 9-21. Gleason finds Forché effective in transmitting the horror of El Salvador in *The Country Between Us*, but also effective in suggesting a hope for the future by the use of the image of bread making in this volume and in *Gathering the Tribes*.

Greer, Michael. "Politicizing the Modern: Carolyn Forché in El Salvador and America." *Centennial Review* 30 (Spring, 1986): 125-135. Greer presents a useful critical discussion of the eight Salvadoran poems in *The Country Between Us*, showing how Forché employs modernist poetics to examine political events.

Grieve-Carlson, Gary. "'Where Is Your God?' Theophany and *The Angel of History*." *Renascence: Essays on Values in Literature* 58, no. 4 (2006): 289-304. Grieve-Carlson poses the problem of misreadings of *The Angel of History*.

Logan, William. "Out on the Lawn." *New Criterion* 22, no. 4 (December, 2003): 85-93. Logan critiques what he views as the alarming fragmentation of half-thoughts that make up the ten poems of *Blue Hour*.

Ostriker, Alicia. "Beyond Confession: The Poetics of Postmodern Witness." *American Poetry Review* 30, no. 2 (March/April, 2001): 35-39. Offers a look at what may be termed the poetics of postmodern witness by examining Forché's *The Angel of History* and works by Adrienne Rich and Sharon Doubiago. Ostriker notes how "the fragmentary quality of Forché's writing registers the way consciousness cracks under the weight" of witnessed horrors.

Barbara Wiedemann; Philip K. Jason
Updated by Roxanne McDonald

ALICE FULTON

Born: Troy, New York; January 25, 1952

PRINCIPAL POETRY
Anchors of Light, 1979
Dance Script with Electric Ballerina, 1983
Palladium, 1986
Powers of Congress, 1990
Sensual Math, 1995
Felt, 2001
Cascade Experiment: Selected Poems, 2004

OTHER LITERARY FORMS

Alice Fulton has published her essays in journals, as well as a collection of essays, *Feeling as a Foreign Language: The Good Strangeness of Poetry* (1999). A collection of her short stories, *The Nightingales of Troy: Stories of a Family's Century*, was published in 2008. She has also contributed to audio recordings of her poetry accompanied by music, including *Poets in Person: American Poets and Their Art* (1991), *I Will Breathe a Mountain: A Cycle from American Women Poets* (1991), *Turbulence: A Romance* (1997), *Mail: From Daphne and Apollo Remade* (2000), *Turns and Turns into the Night* (2001), and *The Etiquette of Ice* (2005).

ACHIEVEMENTS

Alice Fulton's poetry has been published in many anthologies since 1982. She has also won numerous honors, including fellowships from the MacDowell Colony, the Millay Colony, the Michigan Society of Fellows, the Yaddo Colony, the Bread Loaf Writers' Conference, the Guggenheim Foundation, the National Endowment for the Arts, the Ingram Merrill Foundation, and the John D. and Catherine T. MacArthur Foundation. She received the Emily Dickinson Award (1980) and the Consuelo Ford Award for "Terrestrial Magnetism" from the Poetry Society of America (1984), an Academy of American Poets College Poetry Prize (1982), and the Rainer Maria Rilke Prize (1984). *Palladium* was selected for the National Book Series by Mark Strand in 1985 and won the Society of Midland Authors Award in 1987. Fulton won the Bess Hokin Prize from *Poetry* magazine (1989), the Robert Chasen Poetry Prize from Cornell University, the Henry Russel Award from the University of Michigan (1990), the Elizabeth Matchett Stover Award from *Southwest Review* (1994), the Editor's Prize in Fiction from the *Missouri Review* (1997), and the Bobbitt National Prize (2002) for *Felt*.

Biography

Born in 1952 in Troy, New York, Alice Fulton attended Catholic schools in her hometown. She began writing poetry during the 1970's. In 1978, she earned a bachelor of arts degree in creative writing from Empire State College in Albany, New York, and, in 1982, a master of fine arts degree from Cornell University, where she studied with A. R. Ammons. She married artist Hank De Leo in 1980.

In 1983, she became an assistant professor of English at the University of Michigan, where she remained until 2001. Fulton has also been a visiting professor of creative writing at Vermont College; the University of California, Los Angeles; Ohio State University; and the University of North Carolina, Wilmington. During the 1990's, Fulton served as a judge for many poetry prizes, including the National Book Award, the Lamont Poetry Selection, the Akron Poetry Prize, and the Walt Whitman Award. In 2002, she joined the faculty of Cornell University, becoming the Ann S. Bowers Professor of English in 2004.

Analysis

Like both Emily Dickinson and Annie Dillard, Alice Fulton is an explorer of the mind, individuality, societal roles, and ultimately the cosmos. Fulton is sometimes even called a postmodern Dickinson because of her dense vocabulary, her spasmodic pace, and her mingling of the personal and the abstract. Fulton also shares with Dickinson a view of poetry as the play of the mind. Words are tried on like dresses to offer new explanations for old situations. With only a vocabulary and a different grammar, Fulton holds up old verities to new light: Like Dickinson, she "tell[s] the truth but tell[s] it slant."

With this technique, Fulton casts societal suppositions and inherited myths into different frames as she goes about with a new vocabulary, making the familiar unfamiliar and strangely making the unfamiliar familiar. Questions become more important than answers in her vocabulary for a world ever more unstable, fragmented, and formless. Like Dickinson, she seeks to redefine life by emphasizing the periphery, thereby rearranging the focus of the reader's attention; the expected is never there.

Although Dillard operates primarily in a different genre (nonfiction), Fulton, like Dillard, wants to go beyond the seen and the normal to relocate herself in a larger milieu that reaches beyond time and currency. To place herself in a different sphere as she redefines her world, Fulton uses different references for her explorations. She uses terms from chaos theory, fractal forms, and physicist Werner Heisenberg's theory of indeterminacy to map out the concealed elements of life that shape people because poems, as she said in 1986, "are linguistic models of the world's working [and] our knowledge of form includes the new concept of manageable chaos, along with the ancient categories of order and chaos." Fulton the poet is like a fish noticing and defining water for the first time. To this end, in her essay "Inconvenient Knowledge" (1997, 1998), she calls for writers to "become cultural outsiders.... Imagination [poetry] is the transfiguring force ... pressing against cultural assumptions in order to reinvent them."

Another common element that Fulton shares with Dickinson and Dillard, besides their pushing against type, is an association with Catholicism. Although Dickinson is seen as a prototype of the New England Protestant, she actually spent much household time talking with the Irish workers employed with her family. Because of these conversations, she dropped her negative attitude toward Catholicism. In fact, the pallbearers for her coffin were the family's Irish Catholic workmen. Dillard, also born a Protestant of Calvinist origins, converted to Catholicism in her adult life, and Fulton was born Catholic with Irish ancestors.

Like other poets in the line of writers who do not produce the norm and follow tradition, Fulton has to be read and reread. Her poems present spaces that lyrical poetry has overlooked. In a course description of Fulton's English 535, "Postmodern Fractal Poetics: Writing in Three Dimensions," which appeared on the University of Michigan's Web site, Fulton provides her own, best guide to her poetics:

> Fractal poetics is composed of the disenfranchised aspects, the dark matter of Tradition: its blind spots, recondite spaces, and recursive fields.... [I]t exists on a third ground between "high" and "low" terrain, resistant to those classifications.... Fractal poetics has dispensed with fidelity to the "normal" and the "natural," to "simplicity" and "sincerity." Instead of reproducing speech, the poem makes a sound-unto-itself; its music is not so much voiced as built.... The disjunctive shifts of fractal poetry ... are akin to nonlinear interactions [an allusion to mathematics] in which the value of the whole cannot be predicted by summing the strength of its parts. A fractal poem might contain purposely insipid or flowery lines that would be throwaways if taken out of context. When juxtaposed with other inclusions, however, these debased lines establish a friction or frame greater than their discrete presence would predict.

"Fix"

In "Fix" (from *Felt*), Fulton reaffirms her ties to Dickinson. She comments on science and natural forces, as does Dickinson, but the clearest parallel is contained in her first line, "There is no caring less," which she repeats three times throughout the course of the poem. The line is metrically identical to the opening lines of Dickinson's poems; it is also stylistically identical, making a seemingly uncomplicated, blanket statement about the nature of things without obvious justification. It is a thoroughly ambiguous sentiment, devoid of any clear meaning, and it is this ambiguity that works to Fulton's advantage as she explores the various ramifications of there being "no caring less" throughout the poem. However, despite the different meanings she tries on—which lead the reader to view the idea through the screen of the universe's indifference to humanity, the apathy of the "you" she addresses in the beginning of the poem, and her own devotion to the same—what is left at the poem's conclusion is still a statement that can be played with semantically any number of ways, but it does not provide closure. There clearly exists "no caring less," but at the final moment both subject and object are absent.

"THE ORTHODOX WALTZ"

"The Orthodox Waltz" (from *Powers of Congress*) is a slow poem, full of suggestion and implication. In this, as in her other poems, Fulton feels no need to provide her reader with background information, preferring to begin in medias res and allowing the readers to sort out the situation for themselves. The poem is a metaphor for the typical pattern of courtship; it is a dance and a highly orthodox one at that, as the man leads and the woman must follow. However, although the man may lead, there is a necessary give-and-take in such a dance, and each party seeks response from the other in order to continue. This highly complex back-and-forth action is symbolized in part by Fulton's description of the man's actions:

> He kept his ear pressed
>
> like a safecracker's
> stethoscope against
> her head, kept his
>
> recombinant endearments
> tumbling toward a click.

It is this "click" that is the necessary culmination of courtship, the connection of two people that enables them to edge past the first hesitant phase and form a relationship. So often, Fulton points out, this is a step that must finally be taken alone, without the approbation or input of others, as the woman in her poem is distracted by her partner's "clasp and lust-/ spiel . . ." from all her mother's years of good advice.

"FUZZY FEELINGS"

Just as all people live multiple lives, Fulton shows herself similarly to be layered. In "Fuzzy Feelings" (from *Sensual Math*, also in *Cascade Experiment*), she is a dental patient, a consumer of the popular women's magazine *Glamour*, a sister, and an aunt, thinking of events occurring at the moment, a few moments ago, and last year, which blend together in some unplanned pattern and texture. The blending begins in the dentist's chair as Fulton stares at the ceiling, waiting for her dental work to begin. Her staring leads to thoughts of nature's colors mixed with the colors in the office, without a perceivable break. Interspersed are words from the dentist, "sinking one into another" while Fulton "fak[es] Lamaze and ancient mantras" to take her out of the chair and out of the room and away from dental pain. Her mind takes her to questions about sex that she read in the magazine while waiting for her appointment and to thoughts of the world's textures.

However, the thoughts of being somewhere else, home, lead her to the emotional pain from the death of her niece, her sister Sandy's child. This kind of pain cannot be stopped by Novocaine. It is too deep, too strong. It hinders her sister Sandy from being layered; she is just pain. To hide the pain that identifies her on only one layer, Sandy "blends some body/ veil into herself. Gets ready to flex/ the verbal abs and delts and hopes/ she won't be up till dawn." Like Fulton, who will have "a refined smile" and "a headache" when she leaves the dental office, Sandy will hide "The fissures = = [the] vacancies inside." Both Fulton and her sister strive for some kind of "grace" in living despite the pain: "Right now I'm trying to open wide." The multiple meanings of the images and the abstractions in the poem lead the reader to a visual picture, more poignant because of the poet's lack of straight narration and tone about the events.

CASCADE EXPERIMENT

Cascade Experiment, which consists of a wide sampling of poems culled from Fulton's previous five books of poetry, amply demonstrates not only her broad range of interests but also her continually evolving sense of how to use the most seemingly insignificant details to illuminate the nuances of difficult moral ideas. Gathered together, these poems provide an opportunity to see both the larger trends evident across her work and how her theory of fractal poetics has developed. Such seminal poems as "Palladium Process," "Cherry Bombs," "= = ," "Maidenhead," "Give: A Sequence Reimagining Daphne & Apollo," and "The Permeable Past Tense of Feel," trace over the course of her career such signatures of her style as the appearance of screens, veils, masks, or prosthetics; the use of "superclusters" of words; her use of fractal poetics (contradictions or images to create liminal spaces or to represent possibility, negation, or transition); and the continuing influence of Dickinson.

In her essay "Screens: An Alchemical Scrapbook" (from *Feeling as a Foreign Language*), Fulton explains that screens and veils are mediators that, although they are transparent, call attention to the space between, which allows for new possibilities. She also uses certain words—such as "veil," "bride," "lace," and "white"—repeatedly over the course of a poem, a book, or even several books. She calls these words "superclusters": words not interesting in themselves, but that accumulate multiple layers of meaning each time they appear. For example, the word "white" in various contexts in Fulton's poetry may be merely a color, it may represent the possibility of a blank page or canvas, or it may signify oppressive notions of purity or innocence imposed on women in the form of a confirmation or wedding dress.

In the title poem, "Cascade Experiment" (also in *Powers of Congress*), Fulton's growing unease with received religious information, where "childhood catechisms all had heaven," leads her to search for answers in science:

> Because faith creates its verification
> and reaching you will be no harder than believing
> in a planet's caul of plasma
> or interacting with a comet.

By line 28, however, she is calling herself "an infidel of amplitude" as she "discard[s] and enlarge[s]" both received religion and received science. She recognizes that science, like religion, permits only some information to be known. Other information, such as the "thirteen species/ of whiptail lizards composed entirely of females/ stay undiscovered due to bias/ against such things existing." If Fulton is to discover the truth of the world for herself, she will have to become an independent, passionate explorer, who will "meet the universe halfway . . . move toward what/ looks to us like nothing."

The central idea in "Cherry Bombs" (also in *Powers of Congress*) is the knowledge that young girls learn as they grow (or perhaps that which they are born knowing) about their growing up, whether they wish to acknowledge the information or not. That future is almost set like the "Lilt perms . . . [into] an unfixable forever" that the poet does not want. Fulton rejects the future war planned for her with its "training bras," "GI Joe advances," the combat of "Labor," and "monuments for women/ dead of children." Like Dillard in *An American Childhood* (1987), the poet wants to be herself as she defines herself. "No one could make me/ null and void," she vows at age five, as her childhood quickly passes.

"Maidenhead" (also in *Felt*) is one of Fulton's longer poems, and one of her more complex as well. Into it she weaves Dickinson, her own likewise reclusive aunt, the Catholic school she attended, and her white graduation dress, which she compares to Dickinson's. She identifies herself at the age of seventeen as markedly different from the rest of the girls in her school: She sits alone reading Dickinson on the bus and is teased on account of her aunt, while the other girls read wedding magazines and sunbathe. In this poem, as in others, Fulton freely uses imagery relating to science and nature:

> There's an optical effect,
> *interference,*
> I think it's called, that puts the best
> light on a gem's flaws
>
> . . . .
>
> wave trains of light collide
> from aberrations
>
> . . . . . .
>
> There is a lace
> of nerves, I've learned, a nest of lobe and limbic
> tissue around the hippocampus, which on magnetic resonance
> imaging resembles a negative of moth.

She ties such imagery predominantly to her thoughts on the inner workings of Dickinson's and her aunt's troubled minds; at times she directly addresses Dickinson, commenting on how she compares to her aunt. In addition to this, she also uses imagery relating to Catholicism, mentioning the nuns at her high school changing their habits, the uniform she is forced to wear every day, the different connotations of a veil, and the stitches in her newly made white dress that are "so uncatholic and so—/ made for me." It is a poem in which Fulton feels no remorse about simply moving on without any clear transition to another subject, returning only later and just as suddenly.

"Give: A Sequence Reimagining Daphne & Apollo" (also in *Sensual Math*) provides a clear example of Fulton's theory of fractal poetics: its jarring juxtapositions of content (the source myth of the title with Ninja Turtles, bobbin lace with an electron cloud), shifting pronouns, and use of white space and Fulton's idiosyncratic symbol "= =" all merge to create a portrait of the nymph Daphne, trapped between states, neither woman nor laurel tree. It is perhaps for using this hallmark symbol "= =," her own version of Dickinson's signature dashes, that Fulton is best known. She attempts to define the symbol in a poem actually titled "= =": "It's a seam made to show/ . . ./ The double equal that's nowhere to be found/ in math. The dash/ to the second power = = dash to the max.// It might make visible the acoustic signals/ of things about to flame. . . ." She concludes the poem with the following metaphor: ". . . = = the wick that is// the white between the ink" before the poem dissolves into white space with no concluding punctuation. In *Cascade Experiment*, as Fulton negotiates between the concrete and the abstract, literal and ambiguous meanings, form and metamorphosis, she evokes the subversive genius of Dickinson, who famously claimed "I dwell in Possibility—"

OTHER MAJOR WORKS

SHORT FICTION: *The Nightingales of Troy: Stories of a Family's Century*, 2008.

NONFICTION: *Feeling as a Foreign Language: The Good Strangeness of Poetry*, 1999.

BIBLIOGRAPHY

Frost, Elisabeth A., and Cynthia Hogue, eds. *Innovative Women Poets: An Anthology of Contemporary Poetry and Interviews.* Iowa City: University of Iowa Press, 2006. Contains an interview of Fulton by Cristanne Miller, one of the leading critics on Fulton's poetry, as well as a brief biography and some representative poems.

Fulton, Alice. "Alice Fulton." http://alicefulton.com. The official Web site for Fulton provides information on her life and works as well as links to interviews.

_____. "Fractal Amplifications: Writing in Three Dimensions." In *The Measured Word: On Poetry and Science*, edited by Kurt Brown. Athens: University of Georgia Press, 2001. The poet provides an explanation of her fractal poetics.

_____. "Fractal Poetics: Adaptation and Complexity." *Interdisciplinary Science Re-*

views 30, no. 4 (December, 2005): 323-330. Fulton provides further explanation of her theory as it applies to her own and others' poetry.

Keller, Lynn. "The 'Then Some Inbetween': Alice Fulton's Feminist Experimentalism." *American Literature* 71, no. 2 (1999): 311-340. Explores Fulton's nonalignment with any particular school of poetry and discusses the problems for poet and reader because of her of lack of a traditional identity.

Marcus, Ben. "The Safety Net." Review of *Cascade Experiment*. *Poetry* 184, no. 5 (September, 2004): 381-385. Marcus finds Fulton to be more of a technician than a messenger, producing beautiful poems that have everyday messages. Nevertheless, he feels that sometimes she is able to transcend the narrative with her poetic skills.

Miller, Cristanne. "'The Erogenous Cusp': Or, Intersections of Science and Gender in Alice Fulton's Poetry." In *Feminist Measures: Soundings in Poetry and Theory*. Ann Arbor: University of Michigan Press, 1994. Miller explores Fulton's use of quantum physics to reinvent poetic discourse.

_____. "Questioning Authority in the Late Twentieth Century." In *Marianne Moore: Questions of Authority*. Cambridge, Mass.: Harvard University Press, 1995. Fulton is placed in a tradition with Emily Dickinson and Marianne Moore.

_____. "Wonder Stings Me More than the Bee." *Emily Dickinson International Society Bulletin* 8, no. 2 (1996): 10-11. Fulton is discussed as a descendant of the nineteenth century poet Dickinson via the Fulton poem whose title comes from a Dickinson letter. The implicit idea is the lack of clear boundaries in life, despite societal attempts to maintain them.

Carol Lawson Pippen
Updated by Heidi K. Czerwiec

H. D.

Born: Bethlehem, Pennsylvania; September 10, 1886
Died: Zurich, Switzerland; September 27, 1961

PRINCIPAL POETRY
Sea Garden, 1916
Hymen, 1921
Heliodora, and Other Poems, 1924
Collected Poems of H. D., 1925
Red Roses for Bronze, 1931
The Walls Do Not Fall, 1944
Tribute to the Angels, 1945
The Flowering of the Rod, 1946
By Avon River, 1949
Selected Poems of H. D., 1957
Helen in Egypt, 1961
Hermetic Definition, 1972
Trilogy, 1973 (includes *The Walls Do Not Fall*, *Tribute to the Angels*, and *The Flowering of the Rod*)
Collected Poems, 1912-1944, 1983
Selected Poems, 1988

OTHER LITERARY FORMS

Although H. D. is known chiefly for her poetry, she did produce works in other genres, including novels, a verse drama, a screenplay, and a children's novel. The nonfiction trilogy *Tribute to Freud, Writing on the Wall, Advent* (1974) presents an account of her psychoanalysis with Sigmund Freud in the 1930's. In *End to Torment: A Memoir of Ezra Pound by H. D.* (1979), she profiles her mentor.

Other posthumous publications have included *HERmione* (1981), an autobiographical novel that was written in 1927, and *The Gift* (1982), a memoir about her childhood that was written in London during the Blitz of World War II. *HERmione* contains fictionalized depictions of young Pound and others, and it lyrically describes young H. D.'s acceptance of herself as a woman and an artist. *The Gift*, as it shifts between recollections of childhood and descriptions of the destruction and fear in London wrought by the bombing during World War II, presents revealing looks at H. D.'s view of life.

ACHIEVEMENTS

Hilda Doolittle, or H. D. as she signed her pseudonym, was at the center of the pre-World War I literary movement known as Imagism. It had a profound influence on twentieth century poetry, insisting on direct treatment through concrete imagery, freshness of language, economy of expression, and flexible versification. H. D. was a protégée of Pound, and the images in her poems best demonstrated Pound's definition of the image as "that which presents an intellectual and emotional complex in an instant of time." "Priapus" and "Hermes of the Ways," H. D.'s first Imagist poems, published in 1913, were hailed as innovative breakthroughs; with the publication of *Collected Poems of H. D.* in 1925, she came to be regarded as the finest of the Imagists. A number of these early poems, such as "Orchard," "Oread," "Heat," and "Sea Gods," have been repeatedly anthologized. (Unless otherwise noted, all poems cited are from *Collected Poems of H. D.*).

H. D.'s productive literary career spanned some fifty years. Her later poetry, somewhat neglected, included *Red Roses for Bronze*; the World War II trilogy, *The Walls Do Not Fall*, *Tribute to the Angels*, and *The Flowering of the Rod*; her long "epic" poem, *Helen in Egypt*; and *Hermetic Definition*.

H. D. has received less critical attention than others of her generation. Although her early Imagist poetry was highly acclaimed, critical response to her later work has been mixed. Some critics have argued that this later work is marred by patches of triteness and sentimentality and a too-narrow focus; others have praised its spiritual richness and the undeniable beauty of many of its passages, and later critics have called attention to its feminist aspects. Although she was awarded *Poetry*'s Levinson Prize in 1938, she was near the end of her life before there were signs of renewed interest in her work: She received the Harriet Monroe Memorial Prize in 1958, the Brandeis Award in 1959, and the prestigious Award of Merit Medal from the American Academy of Arts and Letters in 1960—a prize given only once every five years. Several books appraising H. D. appeared in the 1960's, and since the mid-1970's, numerous articles and the first full-length biography have been published. Her *Collected Poems, 1912-1944* was published in 1983.

BIOGRAPHY

Hilda Doolittle was born in Bethlehem, Pennsylvania, the first Moravian community in America, on September 10, 1886. Her mother, Helen Wolle Doolittle, was artistic and musical; her father, Charles Leander Doolittle, was professor of mathematics and astronomy at Lehigh, later director of the Flower Observatory at the University of Pennsylvania. Hilda had a rich childhood in a setting of mystical Moravianism that exerted a lasting influence on her poetry.

At the age of fifteen, she met Pound, the first of several extraordinary figures who profoundly influenced her life. Pound, then a precocious graduate student at the University of Pennsylvania, encouraged her to become broadly read, and together they studied Latin, Greek, the classics, yogic texts, and a great diversity of authors. Pound, according to their fellow student William Carlos Williams, "was wonderfully in love with her," but their relationship was somewhat stormy. In 1908, he proposed that they elope to Europe, but her family ties and her suspicions of his other romantic liaisons deterred her. This estrangement was equivocal, however, and in 1911, Hilda joined Pound and his literary circle in London, never again to live in the United States. Her first Imagist poems were published in *Poetry* (January, 1913), under the signature that Pound suggested, "H. D., Imagiste." Active in the Imagist movement, she published her first collection, *Sea Garden*, in 1916.

The intense experiences of the World War I years forever after dominated H. D.'s life and art. Although still attached to Pound, in 1913, she married fellow Imagist Richard Aldington. Their marriage, initially happy, was troubled by infidelity and the turmoil of war. In 1914, H. D. met D. H. Lawrence. Their strong mutual attraction persisted through the war years, and their relationship was ever afterward present in H. D.'s life and work. In 1915, her first child was stillborn; in 1916, Aldington enlisted and at the same time began an extramarital affair. In 1917, H. D.'s favorite brother was killed in France, and in 1919, her father died. In 1919, gravely ill with pneumonia, she gave birth to her daughter, Perdita; H. D. never revealed who the father was, and she and Aldington separated. Distressed by these events to the point of collapse, she was aided by a young woman from a wealthy English family, Winifred Ellerman, known by her pen name Bryher. For a time they lived together, and traveled to Greece, America, and Egypt. In 1922, H. D. settled near Zurich, with Bryher nearby, to rear her daughter and write. Her literary reputation established by the 1925 publication of *Collected Poems of H. D.*, she lived an active though secluded life, dedicated to her art.

In 1933, dissatisfied with her imperfect understanding of the events of her life and how they related to her art, she entered analysis under Freud. This experience, together with her experiences in London during World War II, permitted her to crystallize her own "legend," to expand on the multiple meanings in her writing. She wrote much during the last fifteen years of her life, including her most ambitious long poem, *Helen in Egypt*, and the autobiographical novel, *Bid Me to Live* (1960). Following a brief visit to America to accept an award for her poetry, she was disabled by a stroke and died on September 27, 1961, at a clinic near Zurich, at the age of seventy-five.

ANALYSIS

H. D. was a lyric poet with one overarching dramatic theme: a heroine's quest for love and spiritual peace. Her poetry about this one central drama, although written in concise and crystalline images, is an evocative and often enigmatic reworking of scenes, a retelling of tales, where new characters fuse with old, where meanings subtle shift with the perspective, and where understanding interchanges with mystery.

"OREAD"

The early poem, "Oread"—one of the most often anthologized of H. D.'s poems—has been celebrated as the epitome of the Imagist poem. First published in February,

1914, this deft six-line poem not only illustrates the essence and freshness of the Imagist approach but also foreshadows and reflects many of the themes to which H. D. would turn and return in her art. The six lines of the poem rest on a single image:

>Whirl up, sea—
>whirl your pointed pines,
>splash your great pines
>on our rocks,
>hurl your green over us,
>cover us with your pools of fir.

The image in this poem is a "presentation," not a representation; it is a tangible, immediate manifesting of a physical thing, not a description of a scene or an abstract feeling. On the immediate level, the poem is an image of a stormy sea whose wave crests are like forest pines as they crash against the shore and recede, leaving rocky pools in their wake. The image evokes a complex picture suggesting color, the beating of waves on a coast, sounds crashing and hushed, and even fragrance.

"Oread" has, as the Imagists insisted free verse should have, a rhythmic and linguistic development that is musical rather than metrical, corresponding to the sense of the poem. The first three lines describe an active, thrashing sea advancing on a rocky coast, and the last three suggest a lessening forcefulness, still powerful but withdrawing. The rising and falling movement is created in part by emphatic, initial-stress spondees and trochees in the beginning lines of the poem, which then give way to the more yielding dactyls, anapest, and iambic of the last two lines. These prosodic modifications are paralleled by the vowel and consonantal sounds: rough plosives and fricatives dominate the first half; the last half employs liquid continuants to suggest waning flow and submarine calm. This shift in tone is also underscored by the appearance of back vowel sounds in the last three lines only, giving the lines a more sonorous and less frenzied sound.

Various devices give unity to the poem. It is set as one sentence, in lowercase. The imperative mood of the verbs that begin all but the fourth line emphasizes the thrusting force of the waves. Internal rhymes subtly reinforce the central metaphor, fusing sea and forest: the aspirated *h* and the liquid *r* and *l* of "whirl" are repeated in "hurl"; and the last word, "fir," is a partial assonantal echo of the first word, "whirl," and "green" similarly echoes "sea." Consonants are repeated with like effect. For example, the *h*, *l*, *p*, and *s* of "whirl up, sea" are forcibly compressed in "splash," and quietly recapitulated in "pools of fir." Line 4 ("on our rocks"), which introduces character and location, is distinguished from the preceding lines by its lack of a verb, its use of back vowel sounds, and its triseme (or anapest); yet it is yoked to line 3 by enjambment, again subtly sustaining the fusion metaphor.

"Oread" has an elusiveness that is typical of H. D.'s poetry: The identity of the speaker is obscure, the location of the seacoast is unspecified. Who is "us"? Why are the rocks "our rocks"? The answers lie hidden in the title, which contains much that is enigmatic and unspoken. An oread is a nymph of Greek myth—in particular, a mountain nymph. Like naiads, nereids, dryads, sylphs—the nymphs of rivers, the sea, woods, air— oreads were usually personified as beautiful young girls, amorous, musical, gentle, and shy virgins, although occasionally identified with the wilder aspects of nature and akin to satyrs. The oread is one of the multiple forms that H. D. used to develop the central feminine consciousness in her writings. The oread inhabits the lonelier reaches of nature, rocky places of retreat; as H. D. put it in her children's novel, *The Hedgehog* (1936), "The Oreads are the real mountain girls that live furtherest up the hill."

Mountain nymphs were especially identified in myth as companions of the goddess Artemis, the virgin huntress associated with the moon; Artemis guarded the chastity of her nymphs as jealously as her own. It is one of the finer aspects of H. D.'s poetry that she can evoke the presence of things that are not mentioned yet shimmer ghostlike somewhere just out of poetic range: The goddess Artemis is an offstage presence in this poem, as in others. Her figure, white, distant, cold, virginal, yet passionate, is another of the complex manifestations of consciousness that appear in odd guises throughout H. D.'s poetry. In *Helen in Egypt*, for example, the moon goddess is symbolized by the white island in the sea where Helen encounters her lover Achilles. Artemis is embodied in the form of another island in "The Shrine" (subtitled "She Watches over the Sea," and dedicated to Artemis when initially published); it is an island whose difficult approaches can wreck mariners but can also reward those who reach "the splendor of your ragged coast": "Honey is not more sweet/ than the salt stretch of your beach." There is a sexuality, even a bisexuality, about this Artemis apparent in such lines as these, or as in the opening lines of "Huntress": "Come, blunt your spear with us,/ our pace is hot."

THE CLASSICAL WORLD

The title "Oread" is an allusion to both the moon goddess Artemis, the virgin huntress, and her nymph-companions, wild and free in the mountains. This allusion is but one of many in H. D.'s poems to the Greek world, which was, along with Egyptian, Roman, and other civilizations of antiquity, a frame of reference and an abiding source of inspiration for her. A reader with only a slight familiarity with H. D.'s writings will thus recognize in a title such as "Oread" resonances of the classical world. Virtually all her poems and prose writings allude to it, either directly or by implication. Many of her early poems are explicitly set in the ancient world; others, such as "Sea Iris" and "Sea Lily," are located there only by reference to "temple steps" or "murex-fishermen," or, like "Oread" and "Lethe," have their settings implied solely by their titles.

In the classical world, H. D. found a metaphor for her own loneliness; as she once wrote to Williams, "I am, as you perhaps realize, more in sympathy with the odd and the lonely—with those people that feel themselves apart from the whole. . . ." It was a far country of the imagination where she could find retreat both from the pain of love and from the strain of war and modern life. Ancient Greece or Egypt is envisioned as a stark and beautiful world, a world of cold purity in harmony with nature, where an austere peace could be found in the harsher aspects of the natural landscape. Cities are squalid (as in "The Tribute"), crowded, hideous, and menacing (as in "Cities"); H. D. finds the starker elements of sea, rocky coasts and mountains, trees and wildflowers, storms and wind, the moon and stars, rain, snow and frost, to be sympathetic as well as remote. "I go," she says in the epigraph to *The Flowering of the Rod*, "where I love and where I am loved: Into the snow." The wild seacoast of "Oread" is a manifestation of this nameless land. Linked to the classical world, it appears and reappears throughout H. D.'s work, a dense metaphor for the mental landscape of the particular feminine consciousness present in her writings.

LAYERS OF MEANING

This piling up of associations to be evoked by allusion, as in "Oread," is a stylistic device that H. D. used in both poetry and prose. Her object was to create a many-layered work, dense with meaning, rich with metaphor, and evocative of mystery and legend. She labeled this style *Palimpsest* (also the title of her 1926 novel), a palimpsest being a parchment on which earlier writing has been erased but is still faintly discernible under new writing. H. D. thought of her writing as a superimposition of recurring, almost archetypal feelings and behaviors, like photographic negatives placed on top of one another, yielding a new yet old picture or pattern.

"Oread" illustrates this style. Against the background of rich allusion that is implied in the title, "Oread" is seen to have many layers of superimposed meaning. One step beyond the level of the surface imagery, the poem becomes an incantation, a prayer almost, spoken by the remote-dwelling oread on behalf of herself and her cloistered sisters. They seek, through communion with the elemental natural forces that sustain them in their retreat from the world of men, to be cleansed and strengthened, purified and rededicated to the harmonies of the natural world they have chosen for their refuge. There is also, in the call to the sea to "cover us with your pools," an implied wish to be suspended oblivious in the healing waters, to be reunited with the seamatrix. This hint is echoed in many poems, such as the similar plea found in "Lethe" for release from the pain of loveless existence: "The roll of the full tide to cover you/ Without question,/ Without kiss." The subject of women hurt and deserted by men whom they loved recurs throughout H. D.'s poems about goddesses, demigoddesses, and other women of antiquity (of whom there are many in her verse—Demeter, Simaethea, Circe, Leda, Phaedra, Helen, Thetis, Cassandra, Calypso, Eurydice, and more). These poems present passionate women ill-treated by men.

SEXUAL METAPHOR

Many of H. D.'s poems are about the foundering of a passionate impulse through indecision or rejection and the compensating retreat to colder climes that are clean and pure and white, yet haunted by memories of what was and what might have been. These poems are not only about retreat from the pitch and toss of emotion, but also about immersion in the salt flood of passionate entanglement.

This is the case with "Oread": At the same time that the poem invokes purification by a sort of baptismal rite, it is on yet another level wryly and compellingly sexual. In the first two lines of "Oread," the sea, traditionally a feminine metaphor, takes on masculine attributes as the image fuses sea and tree: "Whirl up, sea—/ whirl your pointed pines." (A reader familiar with H. D.'s Attic wit will not be surprised to note that "pines" is an anagram of "penis," although there is no direct evidence that H. D. intended this play on words—or the equally suggestive pun on "fur" in "pools of fir." She often referred to her poems, as in *The Walls Do Not Fall*, as "anagrams, cryptograms,/ little boxes, conditioned/ to hatch butterflies.")

The sea-crests, hardened by their fanciful merging with thrusting pines, are urged to "whirl up," to "splash," to "hurl" themselves against a rocky coast, to "cover us," as male animals cover the female, perhaps to inseminate (insinuated by the oblique reference to fertility in the word "green"). The natural rhythm of the poem, abetted, as previously noted, by various prosodic and grammatical devices, suggests arousal, climax, and commingled torpor. On an elementary level, "Oread" is about events in the natural world; on another level, the landscape pictured evokes the austere classical world to which consciousness may retreat; and, on still another level, the natural landscape becomes a metaphor for the landscape of the body.

The superimposition of sexual metaphor occurs again and again throughout H. D.'s poetry. For example, the pubescence implied by "pools of fir" is an echo of the earlier poem, "Hermes of the Ways," where Hermes is invoked in his original form as a god of fertility: "Hermes, Hermes,/ the great sea foamed,/ gnashed its teeth about me;/ but you have waited,/ where seagrass tangles with shore-grass." "Priapus" (later retitled "Orchard"), a poem addressed to the Greek fertility god usually represented with an exaggerated phallus, celebrates the bounty of nature in lines transparent with reference to female genitalia: "grapes, red-purple,/ their berries/ dripping with wine,/ pomegranates already broken,/ and shrunken figs/ and quinces untouched,/ I bring you as offering."

Feminine anatomy is also likened to coastal recesses or rocky chambers, as in the aforementioned "The Shrine," or in "Circe," a poem about the legendary enchantress who would "give up/ rock-fringes of coral/ and the inmost chamber/ of my island palace" for a glance from Odysseus. In H. D.'s metaphors for the sexual landscape, love and lovers meet where sea meets shore, on salt beaches, as in the refrain that haunts *Helen in Egypt*, on "the ledge of a desolate salt beach." This unusual coupling of rocky clefts with female sexuality and genitalia—perhaps suggested by the analogous promontory of the mons veneris—is typical of H. D.'s use of contrarieties and oxymorons. Fire in ice, sweet in salt, soft and hard, male and female—these contrasts are used to create images of great vitality.

Feminine consciousness

As H. D.'s art evolved, she developed a central feminine consciousness through a variety of images and personas and events, each of which lent associational meaning to the others. This feminine spirit is both delicate and durable, beautiful but tough, capable of surviving great buffeting, much as the "weighted leaf" in the poem "Storm," broken off by the vaguely masculine storm, "is hurled out,/ whirls up and sinks,/ a green stone." This spirit or consciousness may appear as an oread, as Helen of Troy or other figures from classical myth, or as a green stone, a seashell, a worm on a leaf, a hardy sea flower, a chrysalis—or as a melding of several of these. An image from *The Walls Do Not Fall* presents the poet as an "industrious worm" that survives calamity to tell its story, to "spin my own shroud." In *Helen in Egypt*, Theseus (the character modeled on Freud) calls Helen "Psyche with/ half-dried wings." The portrayal of Psyche—in Greek myth, the personification of the soul, beloved by Eros—as a newly formed butterfly is a complex image into which are telescoped links to the figure of the oread and to other chrysalis-like manifestations of H. D.'s poetic consciousness.

This consciousness grew out of the events and situations and characters of H. D.'s life, and each of her poems is a symbolic re-creation of some part of her life, thus giving a further, hidden meaning to the poetry. For example, the knowledge that the nickname bestowed upon H. D. by the green-eyed Ezra Pound was "Dryad" adds another dimension to "Oread." A dryad is a wood nymph, and the nickname was perhaps a token of their early love among the apple trees of Pennsylvania, where H. D. was a virgin and Pound something of a satyr. Early poems such as "Oread" and "Priapus," with their bold sexual undercurrents, can thus also be read as amusing, half-mocking secret messages to the principal men in her life. Although not confessional poetry, H. D.'s work was intimately bound to her personal experiences, especially those of the period from 1911 to 1920, and though her poems may be grasped without knowing these circumstances, even a slight familiarity with them enhances the reader's pleasure and understanding. H. D. had no hesitation in acknowledging this autobiographical dimension: as she said of her thinly disguised autobiographical novel, *Bid Me to Live*, "It is a roman à clef, and the keys are all easy enough to find."

Creating her own legend

By poeticizing the story of her life, H. D. was consciously attempting, as she indicated in *Tribute to Freud* (1956), to create her own legend, to universalize her own experiences and emotional states, not for idiosyncratic self-glorification, but rather to capture a timeless expression of an age-old quest—a quest through the labyrinth of memory for enlightenment and love, for the truth of the soul, for mystical union, for her womanhood, for the purpose of her art. The goal was to "justify all the spiral-like meanderings of my mind and body," as she said of her analysis with Freud. She was concerned with preserving the intricate setting of her memories: "We wander in a labyrinth," she observed in *By Avon River*; "If we cut straight through, we destroy the shell-like curves and involutions." This quest motif furnishes a final, ontological, or even religious layer of meaning to "Oread" and other poems. The oread's venturing from her forested retreat to the sea ledges can be interpreted as seeking the love of lover, mother, and father—and perhaps the godhead, since the image of merged sea and trees is suggestive of the Moravian doctrine of mystical union with Christ's body that influenced H. D. as a child and later as a poet.

H. D.'s poetry was original and manifested a new development in Western literature. Reversing the usual form of allegory, she drew images from the natural world and characters and situations from classical sources to transmute the story of her own life into poems expressing universal human experience. Exemplified by "Oread," her poems are like ideographic pictures or signs with many meanings coiled in single images—images that, in their distilled essence, contain the world seen by a gifted poet.

OTHER MAJOR WORKS

LONG FICTION: *Palimpsest*, 1926; *Hedylus*, 1928; *Kora and Ka*, 1934 (includes *Mira-Mare*); *The Usual Star*, 1934 (includes *Two Americans*); *Nights*, 1935; *Bid Me to Live*, 1960; *HERmione*, 1981; *Pilate's Wife*, 2000 (wr. 1929); *Majic Ring*, 2009 (wr. 1944); *The Mystery*, 2009 (wr. 1951); *White Rose and the Red*, 2009 (wr. 1948).

NONFICTION: *Tribute to Freud*, 1956; *Tribute to Freud, Writing on the Wall, Advent*, 1974; *End to Torment: A Memoir of Ezra Pound by H. D.*, 1979; *The Gift*, 1982; *A Great Admiration: H.D./Robert Duncan Correspondence, 1950-1961*, 1992 (Robert J. Bertholf, editor); *Richard Aldington and H.D.: The Early Years in Letters*, 1992 (Caroline Zilboorg, editor); *Between History and Poetry: The Letters of H.D. and Norman Holmes Pearson*, 1997 (Donna Krolik Hollenberg, editor).

TRANSLATIONS: *Choruses from "Iphigenia in Aulis" and the "Hippolytus" of Euripides*, 1919; *Hippolytus Temporizes*, 1927 (adaptation of classical text); *Euripides' Ion*, 1937.

CHILDREN'S LITERATURE: *The Hedgehog*, 1936.

BIBLIOGRAPHY

Bloom, Harold, ed. *Hilda Doolittle (H. D.)*. Broomhall, Pa.: Chelsea House, 2002. A collection of essays examining the poet and her works.

Burnett, Gary Dean. *H. D. Between Image and Epic: The Mysteries of Her Poetics*. Ann Arbor, Mich.: UMI Research Press, 1990. This study deals with H. D.'s poetry between the wars (1916-1944). Burnett refers to this period as her middle period between the Imagist years and the later epics. Her concerns about her life, her response to the war, her research on ancient mystery cults, and her interest in the work of her contemporaries are traced and shown as a context for reading these poems. Includes bibliography and index.

Camboni, Marina, ed. *H. D.'s Poetry: "The Meanings That Words Hide: Essays."* Brooklyn, N.Y.: AMS, 2003. This collection examines topics such as the gender issues in H. D.'s trilogy, H. D.'s uses of language, and the poet's influence on other poets.

Collecott, Diana. *H. D. and Sapphic Modernism, 1910-1950.* New York: Cambridge University Press, 1999. This critical study argues for recognition of H. D. as a key figure in the shaping of Anglo-American modernism. The development of a homoerotic strand within H. D.'s distinctively modernist poetics comes together in Collecott's central concept of sapphic modernism.

Fritz, Angela DiPace. *Thought and Vision: A Critical Reading of H. D.'s Poetry.* Washington, D.C.: Catholic University of America Press, 1988. Fritz attempts to cover H. D.'s entire poetic canon and in doing so reaffirms her eminence as a modernist and feminist poet. Ths study suggests throughout that H. D.'s thought and vision are best defined in her poetry. Includes bibliography and index.

Guest, Barbara. *Herself Defined: The Poet H. D. and Her World.* Garden City, N.Y.: Doubleday, 1984. In this highly experimental biography, Guest ignores such conventions as footnotes and chronological tables. She includes no bibliography and few dates. Her tremendous scholarship, however, is evident, and her book is a successful evocation of the ambiance, the people, and the places that made up H. D.'s world. The book is thus a reliable account of H. D.'s life, even though critics have pointed out that in Guest's book, H. D. herself remains a more shadowy figure than many of the people who surrounded her.

Korg, Jacob. *Winter Love: Ezra Pound and H. D.* Madison: University of Wisconsin Press, 2003. An examination of the personal and professional relationship between two of the most significant poets of the twentieth century. This book is especially worthwhile for those beginning study on H. D.

Laity, Cassandra. *H. D. and the Victorian Fin de Siècle: Gender, Modernism, Decadence.* New York: Cambridge University Press, 1996. Argues that H. D. shaped an alternative poetic modernism of female desire from the "feminine" personas. An examination of female modernism to demonstrate extensively the impact of the Decadents on a modernist woman writer.

Taylor, Georgina. *H. D. and the Public Sphere of Modernist Women Writers, 1913-1946: Talking Women.* New York: Oxford University Press, 2001. This study places H. D. within the greater community of women writers in which she lived.

Vetter, Lara Elizabeth. *Modernist Writings and Religio-scientific Discourse: H. D., Loy, and Toomer.* New York: Palgrave Macmillan, 2010. Examines religion and science in the writings of H. D., Mina Loy, and Jean Toomer.

John Clendenin Townsend

JANE HIRSHFIELD

Born: New York, New York; February 24, 1953

PRINCIPAL POETRY
Alaya, 1982
Of Gravity and Angels, 1988
The October Palace, 1994
The Lives of the Heart, 1997
Given Sugar, Given Salt, 2001
After, 2006

OTHER LITERARY FORMS

Besides her work as a poet, Jane Hirshfield has written a major work on the craft and philosophy of poetry: *Nine Gates: Entering the Mind of Poetry* (1997). *Nine Gates* treats the gates through which readers and writers pass as they learn what poetry brings to life and how it works. Patricia Kirkpatrick considers this volume of essays as addressing "not only ways to read and write, but a way to live." *The Ink Dark Moon: Love Poems by Ono no Komachi and Izumi Shikibu, Women of the Ancient Court of Japan* (1988, expanded 1990) is a series of translations from the Japanese with cotranslator Mariko Aratani, and *Women in Praise of the Sacred: Forty-three Centuries of Spiritual Poetry by Women* (1994) is ananthology of inspirational poetry by women from 2300 B.C.E. to the twentieth century. Both of these collections attempt to make more widely known the works of historical women poets whose work has often been neglected and marginalized. They are attempts to contradict the lingering myth that women throughout history have not written significant poetry.

ACHIEVEMENTS

Jane Hirshfield's honors include fellowships from the Guggenheim and Rockefeller Foundations, Columbia University's Translation Center Award, two Silver Medals from the Commonwealth Club of California (1988, 1994), the San Francisco State University Poetry Center Book Award (1994), and two Northern California Book Awards in poetry (1994, 2001). She won Pushcart Prizes for *Of Gravity and Angels* and *Given Sugar, Given Salt*. For the latter volume, she was also a finalist for the National Book Critics Circle Award in 2001. The Academy of American Poets gave her an academy fellowship for distinguished achievement in poetry in 2004. *After* was named a best book of 2006 by *The Washington Post*, *The San Francisco Chronicle*, and the *Financial Times*.

Biography

Jane Hirshfield was born in New York City to Robert Hirshfield and Harriet Hirshfield. Her father was a clothing manufacturer, and her mother was a secretary. From her childhood, Hirshfield wanted to be a writer. After her first book was published, her mother showed Hirshfield a note written on large lined paper from the first grade in which the young Hirshfield had written, "I want to be a writer when I grow up." Her first poem was published in 1973, after she graduated magna cum laude from Princeton University with an independent major in creative writing and literature in translation. She was part of Princeton's first graduating class to include women. Despite early publication, she withdrew from the writing life to study at the San Francisco Zen Center for eight years. In 1979, she was lay-ordained in the lineage of Soto Zen and left the life of withdrawal. After that time, Hirshfield devoted her life to writing, translation, and editing, earning numerous awards and grants. From 1991 to 1998, she served as lecturer in creative writing at the University of San Francisco and served as visiting associate professor at the University of California, Berkeley, in 1995. In 1999, she joined the core M.F.A. faculty of Bennington College. In 2000, she was Elliston Visiting Poetry Professor at the University of Cincinnati.

Analysis

Jane Hirshfield became a distinct voice in poetry at the turn of the twenty-first century through her sensitive observation of the significance of ordinary details of daily life. Unlike most poets of the Western tradition, Hirshfield tends not to be human centered in her poetry. In other words, her poetry usually does not deal with human relationships, character, or direct interaction. Instead, her poetry objectifies the material of existence and relates matter to the individual or abstracted human nature. A typical poem of Hirshfield's mature work, for example, will note an utterly mundane object such as a grouping of broken seashells; the concept of rooms, crickets, cucumbers; or the nature of leather, and then proceed to relate it to the human soul. Her poetry, in short, resembles Impressionist still lifes.

Although her work as translator and editor of women's poetry indicates Hirshfield's strong feminist nature, little of her poetry is political in the usual sense of direct comment on specific issues. All her work is political, however, in the sense of integrating the stirrings of the heart, one of her favorite images, with the political realities that surround all people.

Undoubtedly, the source for these characteristics of her poetry and for her very concept of poetry as the "magnification of being" derives from her strong Zen Buddhist training. The themes of her poetry and its emphasis on "compassion, on the preexistent unity of subject and object, on nature, on the self-sufficient suchness of being, and on the daunting challenge of accepting transitoriness," Peter Harris notes, are derived from Buddhist concepts. Hirshfield does not, however, burden her poetry with heavy, overt

Zen attitudes. Only occasionally is there direct reference to Buddhism.

Hirshfield considers herself an eclectic poet not tied to any one tradition. Her earliest influences developed from English sonnets and Latin lyrical verse, but early on, she developed an interest in Japanese poetry, first through haiku, and later she was influenced by Aztec, Eskimo, and ancient Indian court poetry. She has mentioned her chief American influences as Walt Whitman, Emily Dickinson, Galway Kinnell, Elizabeth Bishop, Gary Snyder, and Robert Hass.

ALAYA

Jane Hirshfield's first book of poetry was part of the *Quarterly Review of Literature* poetry series of 1982. "Alaya" on one hand means "home" but also is, Hirshfield has said, "a Buddhist term meaning 'the consciousness which is the storehouse of experience,' of memory . . . the place where seed-grain is kept."

"The Gift" from *Alaya* points in the direction of Hirshfield's tendency in her later work to objectify all reality, even the personal: "From how many hands/ your body comes to me,/ and to how many will I pass it on." Here the body comes, not "you come to me," and the speaker will pass "it," the body, on, instead of passing on such things as his memory, his influence, or even his love. The poem is remarkable for its early mature handling of imagery and phrasing. The person addressed, for example, exaggerates "nothing" and leans "into the wind" and is "lost/ but like a flock of geese." However flocks of geese do not really get lost. The poem ends as many of Hirshfield's poems do, and as many poems written in writing workshops often do, with a significant metaphor to draw meaning from the experience of this poem: "Slowly now,/ lift the lid of the box:/ there is nothing inside./ I give this to you, love."

The movement of the poem, then, would ordinarily be seen as a movement from the physical, the body, to the immaterial, the soul, but a Hirshfield poem, perhaps because of the poet's Zen beliefs, will not distinguish between physical and immaterial. The soul and body are indistinguishable. Despite the objective displacement of the self in "The Gift," however, much of Hirshfield's early poetry maintains a personal point of view, both in *Alaya* and in her next book.

OF GRAVITY AND ANGELS

Jane Hirshfield's second book of poetry, *Of Gravity and Angels*, continues to demonstrate her mastery of language, yet nearly half of the poems in this volume include the pronoun "I." For most of the poems, the self remains integral to the text.

At her public readings and in her interviews, the poet talks frequently of her love for horses and her use of horses in her poems. "After Work" is a typical Hirshfield horse poem. The poem takes a straightforward description of a habitual moment in her life, the after-work feeding of the horses, and transforms the experience into meaning:

> I stop the car along the pasture edge,
> gather up bags of corncobs from the back,
> and get out.
> Two whistles, one for each,
> and familiar sounds draw close in darkness—

The horses come and eagerly devour corncobs brought by the speaker. However, despite the personal nature of this ordinary experience, Hirshfield objectifies it. The horses do not "just" come. They come "conjured out of sleep"; they come with "each small noise and scent/ heavy with earth, simple beyond communion."

One of the more memorable poems from *Of Gravity and Angels* is "Dialogue," which begins: "A friend says,/ 'I'm always practicing to be an old woman.'" Another friend considers herself differently: "'I see myself young, maybe fourteen.'" The speaker, however, identifies with neither friend.

Another often read poem is "The Song." In it, Hirshfield implies that all material nature has its own spirit. Here the spirit leaves the tree but never completely. In the same way that the tree will grieve its lost spirit, "the wood, if taken too quickly, will sing/ a little in the stove," still remembering her.

THE OCTOBER PALACE

In *The October Palace*, Hirshfield reveals herself to be a fully mature poet, no longer a developing talent. She moves beyond the formulas of writers' workshop poems and finds the unique voice and range of experiences that has brought her the prizes and grants necessary for a sustainable poetic career.

Perhaps the overall theme of *The October Palace* is that every moment of one's life possesses its own meaning. This theme can be seen, perhaps most obviously, in "Percolation." The speaker is in the midst of wasting a day confined inside because of the rain. As she meditates on her confinement and as she becomes aware of a frog croaking "a tuneless anthem," she develops serenity from the conviction that "surely all Being at bottom is happy:/ soaked to the bone, sopped at the root." She discovers that life-giving peace must be wrung out of all experience, "yielding as coffee grounds/ yield to their percolation, blushing, completely seduced,/ assenting as they give in to the down-rushing water."

In many of her poems, Hirshfield enjoys relating narratives from various folk and historical legends. For example, in "A Plenitude," she considers the nature of fullness, completeness—plenitude—by relating a common story from Renaissance art:

> But there is the story, too,
> of a young painter meeting the envoy of a Pope.
> Asked for a work by which his art
> could be weighed against others', he dipped his

stylus—
with great courtesy, according to Vasari—
in red ink, and drew a single, perfect O.

THE LIVES OF THE HEART

In *The Lives of the Heart*, Hirshfield develops fully a new imagery of the lion and of the heart. Lions appear with mythic power in such poems as "Knowing Nothing," "Spell to Be Said upon Waking," "Lion and Angel Dividing the Maple Between Them," and "Each Happiness Ringed by Lions." In an interview with Katherine Mills, Hirshfield explained her idea about the lions: "The lion is fierceness and beauty; undeniable presence; danger; power; passionate love; transformation. Perhaps, for me . . . lions are the earthly answer to Buddhism." Thus, in "Knowing Nothing," "The lion has stalked/ the village for a long time." However, it does not want a goat in a clearing; "The goat is not the reason." Instead,

> The reason is the lion,
> whose one desire is to enter—
> Not the goat, which is
> only the lure, only excuse
> but the one burning life
> it has hunted for a long time
> disguised as hunger. Disguised as love.
> Which is not the reason.

Here the paradox of the lion's ferocity and its longing to assert itself—of its love—keep the reader searching but not finding the reason of life experience: "Love is not the reason./ Love is the lure."

In a similar way, these poems celebrate the heart, the center of human nature that keeps all people at the core of their existence. Hirshfield explained to Katie Bolick of *The Atlantic* "that for some years a central task in my life has been to try to affirm the difficult parts of my experience; that attempt is what many of the heart poems address. . . . At some point I realized that you don't get a full human life if you try to cut off one end of it, that you need to agree to the entire experience, to the full spectrum of what happens." For example, in "Secretive Heart" at its center, the heart, is one of the most mundane material objects, an old Chinese cauldron "still good for boiling water" but evidently not for much else. "The few raised marks/ on its belly/ are useful to almost no one."

GIVEN SUGAR, GIVEN SALT

Hirshfield's fifth volume of poetry, *Given Sugar, Given Salt*, continues with the old themes but proves her most expansive volume: "As water given sugar sweetens, given salt grows salty,/ we become our choices." Thus, this collection explores choices for meaningful living. In "Bone," for example, the speaker's dog unearths an old bone, the toy of her previous dog—for whom she still grieves. The new dog knows nothing of the old dog:

> My memories,
> my counting and expectations,
> mean nothing to her;
> my sadness, though,
> does puzzle her a moment.

However, the new dog does not remain puzzled for long. She just keeps chewing and then readies herself for a game of catch.

Choices control all people's lives. In "Happiness Is Harder," Hirshfield considers even happiness a choice. Sadness can be cured perhaps: "A person has only to choose./ *What* doesn't matter; just *that*-." However, "Happiness is harder."

Hirshfield has, then, developed a unique voice among contemporary American poets. Her work has the quiet yet persistent vision characteristic of Zen. Life often is a question with no answer, but the question must be asked. Hirshfield continually asks.

After

After continues Hirshfield's examination of experience that lies beyond the power of words and rational answers, as the volume's initial poem, "After Long Silence," illustrates. The poem begins with details that suggest an empty kitchen at night. A pot rests in the dish rack; the soup has been put away. Even the moon has retreated from the window. The poem asks about the significance of such moments. "Distinctions matter," Hirshfield asserts. The very impossibility of applying language to such moments demands most of the writer: "The untranslatable thought must be most precise," the poet says, concluding that words are only the beginning point; thought is what comes after words.

The limitations of language explain this volume's emphasis on what Hirshfield calls "assays" in the titles of many of the poems. The word means "appraisal," "evaluation," and is etymologically related to "essay" or "trial." Hope, judgment, and translucence are some of the abstractions subtitled as assays. "To Judgment: An Assay" examines how judgment (the you of the poem) evaluates. Judgment may make a violent invader decide to burn a village or make a mild biologist express a fondness for beetles, but in either case, judgment's evaluation is foreign to Hirshfield's detached willingness to allow the world to be what it is. She may admire judgment, but she will not love it until it can lose its insistence on adjectives that categorize the world's beings as good or bad, beautiful or ugly.

These assays are particularly interesting when they examine bits of linguistic structure. The word "to," for example, is seen in assay as always leaning forward, "transience and transformation." In "'And': An Assay," Hirshfield says the conjunction embodies simultaneity: "*Before* disappears./ *After* transforms into others./ 'And'—that strong rock—stays standing."

Hirshfield's Buddhism is always a binding thread in these poems' acceptance of the world as it is. In "Burlap Sack," the poet offers the sack as a metaphor for a sorrowing person. The sack may be filled with rocks or sand, but the heavy weights are not the sack itself any more than the one who grieves is grief. Instead, the sorrowful person carries grief the way a mule carries a burden, and the poem concludes with the suggestion that one might let the mule alone so that it can graze, its ears waggling in joy.

The mule of "Burlap Sack" is just one of the many animals in this volume, reminding the reader of Hirshfield's connection to the natural world. The poems are full of dogs, wolves, panthers, birds, and horses, as well as other parts of nature—sand, stones, leaves, and lemons.

Many of the seventeen short poems of "Seventeen Pebbles" are haiku-like, using single images to evoke the mystery of things that are beyond articulation. "Lighthouse," for example, pictures the sweep of the beacon, comparing it to a monk's sweeping a garden. The monk has somehow left his question behind and focuses on his sweeping. The "pebble" concludes with an image of horses grazing at night as the beam first reveals them and then sweeps on to leave them in the dark as if they have disappeared. Much of the appeal of Hirshfield's work lies in such joining of clarity and mystery, the powerful "after" of the volume's title.

OTHER MAJOR WORKS

NONFICTION: *Nine Gates: Entering the Mind of Poetry*, 1997.

TRANSLATION: *The Ink Dark Moon: Poems by Ono no Komachi and Izumi Shikibu, Women of the Ancient Court of Japan*, 1988, expanded 1990 (with Mariko Aratani).

EDITED TEXT: *Women in Praise of the Sacred: Forty-three Centuries of Spiritual Poetry by Women*, 1994.

BIBLIOGRAPHY

Eaton, Mark A. "Jane Hirshfield." In *Twentieth-Century American Nature Poets*, edited by J. Scott Bryson and Roger Thompson. Vol. 342 in *Dictionary of Literary Biography*. Detroit: Gale, 2008. Examines Hirshfield's career-long involvement with the natural world and includes discussions of poems from each volume of her work.

Elkins, Andrew. "California as the World in the Poetry of Jane Hirshfield." In *Another Place: An Ecocritical Study of Selected Western American Poets*. Forth Worth: Texas Christian University Press, 2002. This work on place in literature examines how Hirshfield treats her adopted state in her poetry.

Galens, David M., ed. *Poetry for Students*. Vol. 16. Detroit: Gale, 2002. This volume includes three essays offering close readings of Hirshfield's "Three Times My Life Has Opened."

Harris, Peter. "About Jane Hirshfield: A Profile." *Ploughshares* 24, no. 1 (Spring, 1998): 199-205. Particularly valuable is Harris's study of the Zen influence in Hirshfield's work.

Hirschfield, Jane. "A Conversation with Jane Hirschfield." In *Rattle Conversations*, edited by Alan Fox. Los Angeles: Red Hen Press, 2008. In an interview first published in *Rattle* magazine in 2005. Hirshfield discusses why she writes and how she does it.

Hirschfield, Jane, and Meredith Monk. "Buddhism and Creativity:" A Conversation with Jane Hirschfield and Meredith Monk." Interview by Pat Enkyō O'Hara. In *Women Practicing Buddhism: American Experiences*, edited by Peter N. Gregory and Susanne Mrozik. Boston: Wisdom, 2008. Hirshfield and Meredith Monk discuss creativity and Buddhism. Hirshfield states that she feels art arises out of a question.

Hoey, Allen. *Contemporary Women Poets*. Detroit: St. James Press, 1997. Hoey considers Hirshfield's career from a variety of perspectives. Perhaps most valuable is his examination of the influence of the poet James Wright on Hirshfield's poetry.

Ratiner, Steven. "Transcendence: Verse That Conveys the Humble Profundity of Buddhism." Review of *After. The Washington Post*, August 6, 2006, p. T12. The reviewer praises Hirshfield's work, which he says reflects a modern trend toward simpler poems. Notes that "After Long Silence" exhibits "precise vision and rigorous thought."

Paul Varner
Updated by Ann D. Garbett

SUSAN HOWE

Born: Boston, Massachusetts; June 10, 1937

PRINCIPAL POETRY
Hinge Picture, 1974
The Western Borders, 1976
Secret History of the Dividing Line, 1978
Cabbage Gardens, 1979
The Liberties, 1980
Pythagorean Silence, 1982
Defenestration of Prague, 1983
Articulation of Sound Forms in Time, 1987
A Bibliography of the King's Book: Or, Eikon Basilike, 1989
The Europe of Trusts: Selected Poems, 1990
Singularities, 1990
The Nonconformist's Memorial, 1993
Frame Structures: Early Poems, 1974-1979, 1996
Pierce-Arrow, 1999
Bed Hangings, 2001
The Midnight, 2003
Souls of the Labadie Tract, 2007

OTHER LITERARY FORMS

Because the poetry of Susan Howe (how) poetry is engendered both by a close attention to the minims of language and by a constant examination of the ground from which the language stems, she has come into association with the group known as the Language Realists, or the school known as Language poetry, publishing in the magazines of that movement as well as in several anthologies predominantly or wholly of Language Realism: *The L= A= N= G= U= A= G= E Book* (1984, edited by Bruce Andrews and Charles Bernstein), *21 + 1 American Poets Today* (1986, edited by Emmanuel Hocquard and Claude Royet-Journoud), *In the American Tree* (1986, edited by Ronald Silliman), and *"Language" Poetries: An Anthology* (1987, edited by Douglas Messerli).

Howe has also published several reviews and *My Emily Dickinson* (1985). This last, a book-length consideration of Dickinson's work, elucidates the poetry not only of its subject but also of its author, and it is central to an understanding of her oeuvre. She explains her fascination with fragments from history in *Incloser* (1992): "By choosing to install certain narratives somewhere between history, mystic speech, and poetry, I have

115

enclosed them in an organization although I know there are places no classificatory procedure can reach where connections between words and things we thought existed break off. For me, paradoxes and ironies of fragmentation are particularly compelling." Howe's particular interest in nineteenth century Americans is shown in her collection of literary criticism, *The Birth-Mark: Unsettling the Wilderness in American Literary History* (1993), in which references to Anne Hutchinson, Mary Rowlandson, Cotton Mather, Nathaniel Hawthorne, Herman Melville, Ralph Waldo Emerson, and Dickinson show her dedication to recapturing the pioneer and transcendental spirits that built the American character.

Achievements

In the years since Susan Howe began to publish her poetry, she has established herself as a poet of profound engagement with the problematic of Being in the era she confronts. Her work also addresses the meaning of being American and being a woman, in order to strip away obsolete ideas and to discover the realities of these conditions.

Howe has twice received the American Book Award from the Before Columbus Foundation, in 1981 for *Pythagorean Silence* and again in 1986 for *My Emily Dickinson*. She received a Pushcart Prize in 1980 for "The Art of Literary Publishing," an interview she conducted with James Laughlin, and a second Pushcart Prize in 1989. In 1985, she participated in the Colloquium on New Writing held by the Kootenay School for Writers in Vancouver, Canada, and in that same year was writer-in-residence at New College in San Francisco. In 1986, she was awarded a writer's fellowship by the New York State Arts Council, and she spoke on the poet Dickinson at a conference on H. D. and Dickinson held at San Jose State University. In 1989, a complete issue of *The Difficulties* was devoted to discussion of her work. *The Birth-Mark* was named one of the International Books of the Year by the *Times Literary Supplement* in 1993. She was a John Simon Guggenheim Memorial fellow and won the Ray Harvey Pearce Award, both in 1996, and was a recipient of the New York State Council Writers in Residency grant for a poetry workshop at Lake George, New York. Howe was a distinguished fellow at the Stanford Institute of the Humanities in 1998, and her work appeared in 1999's *Anthology of American Poetry*, edited by Cary Nelson, the same year that Howe was elected to the American Academy of Arts and Sciences. She served as a chancellor of the Academy of American Poets (2000-2006).

Biography

Susan Howe was born in Boston, Massachusetts, on June 10, 1937. With the exception of a relatively brief period in Buffalo, New York, her childhood and adolescence were spent in Boston and Cambridge, where she attended the Beaver Country Day School, from which she was graduated in 1955. Also in 1955, she began a year's study at the Gate Theater, Dublin, Ireland, acting and designing sets. From 1957 to 1961, she attended the Museum School of Fine Arts in Boston. She next took up residence in New York City, working as a painter and exhibiting her paintings at a number of galleries, including the Kornblee. In 1961, she married Harvey Quaytman, and their daughter Rebecca was born that same year. When her marriage ended in 1966, Howe began living with the sculptor David von Schlegell, and in 1967, their son Mark was born. The couple was married from 1976 to 1992, when Schlegell died.

In 1971, Howe moved to Guilford, Connecticut. From 1975 to 1980, she produced the program *Poetry* for WBAI, New York City's Pacifica Radio station. In 1988-1989, she was Butler Fellow at the State University of New York, Buffalo. In 1990-1991, she was a visiting professor of writing at Temple University in Philadelphia. Howe was a professor of English at the State University of New York, Buffalo, from 1989 to 2007 and served as the Samuel P. Capen Chair of Poetry and the Humanities. She was the 2007 Sherry Memorial Visiting Poet at the University of Chicago. Her third husband, Peter Hewitt Hare, died in 2008. Howe served as the Anna-Maria Kellen Fellow for fall, 2009, at the American Academy in Berlin.

Analysis

Susan Howe's poetry challenges habitual assumptions on many levels, but the level the reader is most likely to notice first is the syntactic; what Howe says of Dickinson can with equal force be applied to herself: "In prose and poetry she explored the implications of breaking the law just short of breaking off communication with a reader." Generally, Howe's poems make much use of the page, where the white space is allowed to interrupt the sequence of print, so that a variety of statements may be derived from relatively few phrases, and the overall thrust of the syntax is continually thwarted. Denied easy access to an overarching meaning, the reader must work with smaller units (phrase, line, couplet) and can only gradually constitute the meaning of the whole. This process parallels the approach to Being advocated both explicitly and implicitly in Howe's work. The presumptions of categorical value that modern Western culture persists in advocating are resisted at every turn, for Howe sees (and reveals) just how damaging such presumptions and categories can be. Often, she labors to construct a fresh view of her subject, be it Esther Johnson (known to Jonathan Swift's readers as Stella), Dickinson, or American theologian Jonathan Edwards. To this end, Howe employs the various devices of deconstruction, notably the fracturing of sentence, phrase, or even word.

Such a project inevitably must challenge received notions of the poetic. It is for this reason that traditional forms are absent from Howe's poetry. Such forms by their very ease of recognition would defeat her purpose. To arouse the critical faculties in her reader, Howe must abjure whatever constructions might encourage a reader to glide effortlessly onward: The work must be difficult, not only to reflect accurately the difficulty of living but also to remind the reader at each turn of his or her preconceptions concerning the nature of reality, art, and the very act of reading. For Howe, as for other poets wedded to this task, the question then becomes, What portion of the inherited conceptions of beauty, truth, and the good ought to be retained (as inherent to the art of poetry), and what portion uprooted and discarded (as inimical to a faithful representation of the present)? Language, derived from Being, comes then to govern Being; the reader projects back onto the world expectations previously drawn therefrom: However, the world is always in process, always changing, always endangering one's assumptions and rendering them obsolete. It is therefore to language itself, argue poets who share Howe's address, that the poet ought to draw attention; the reader must be kept aware of the ways in which language governs not only one's concepts but also one's perceptions, and it is for this reason that Howe through "parataxis and rupture" never lets her readers forget the effect of words and phrases on content. Content, in fact, always includes the agony of choice, whether it be the deliberations as to formal procedure or their counterparts in other modes of action.

Inescapably, Howe is, by birth and gender, both American and a woman, subject to the assumptions of those categories, and at once in revolt against such predications and eager to discover their underlying realities. In *My Emily Dickinson*, she would rescue the Dickinson of her particular vision from the several inadequate characterizations that prevent, to Howe's view, a full experience of the poetry. To this end, Howe, in a work that is cousin to both William Carlos Williams's *In the American Grain* (1925) and Charles Olson's *Call Me Ishmael* (1947), rereads the contribution of figures vital to Dickinson's production: Elizabeth Barrett Browning and Robert Browning, James Fenimore Cooper, Emily Brontë, Charles Dickens, Jonathan Edwards, Ralph Waldo Emerson, Cotton Mather, Mary Rowlandson, William Shakespeare, Henry David Thoreau, and Thomas Wentworth Higginson. Howe finds that, approached from this rich assortment of angles, Dickinson's poetry yields a wealth of information about Being in general, but also about being American and being a woman, and about how a poetry grows consanguineously. Howe is severe with certain feminist critics who, while lauding Dickinson, laud a Dickinson who is essentially the creation of patriarchal vision, swallowing whole this distortion. Toward the end of *My Emily Dickinson*, Howe observes: "Victorian scientists, philosophers, historians, intellectuals, poets, like most contemporary feminist literary critics—eager to discuss the shattering of all hierarchies of Being—didn't want the form they discussed this in to be shattering." Howe's poetic practice is the negation of this widespread and persistent error.

"The lyric poet," Howe writes in *My Emily Dickinson*, "reads a past that is a huge imagination of one form," and while the labor of precursors in one sense is enormously beneficial, providing as it does countless elucidations of Being, in another sense it becomes a mighty burden, because of the irresistible nature of preexisting formulations, whether to the poet or to her audience, formulations which nevertheless demand to be resisted if one is to come to a personal definition of one's epoch. Howe, then, in her determination to "make it new," aligns herself with such high modernists as Ezra Pound, Gertrude Stein, and Williams, although she must also—for the reasons given above—keep her project distinct from theirs. The world in the 1970's and 1980's is far from the world of the 1910's and 1920's; Howe is among those who see the poet's calling as a demand to make forms consonant with her own day.

THE LIBERTIES

The analysis provided during the 1960's and 1970's of dominant patriarchal elements in Western society is one example of this altered ideology to which Howe would be responsible. Therefore, *The Liberties*, a book of poetry whose sufficient cause is the largely masculine-engendered version of Esther Johnson, known— and it is the commonality of this means of recognition Howe intends to attack—as Swift's Stella. Howe would liberate from this patriarchal version another picture of this historical personage. As she writes in another context (in her analysis of the received idea termed "Emily Dickinson"): "How do I, choosing messages from the code of others in order to participate in the universal theme of Language, pull SHE from all the myriad symbols and sightings of HE?" In *The Liberties*, Howe begins by providing a prose sketch, "Fragments of a Liquidation," whose import can best be summarized by repeating the last two sentences of its first paragraph: "Jonathan Swift, who gave allegorical nicknames to the women he was romantically involved with, called her 'Stella.' By that name she was known to their close friends, and by that name she is known to history." The poems that follow spring from Howe's desire to liberate Esther from Stella and, by extension, Howe's own self from equally pernicious assumptions. In practice, it is not always possible to distinguish from each other these twin liberations, and so a composite woman, struggling to be freed from the roles provided for her by men and a male-dominated history, becomes the shadow heroine of Howe's pages.

If the method is to question in this manner and to reconstitute a truer history, the technique that Howe develops and that is consonant with her method is to call meaning into question not only at the level of the sentence (these poems are so severely underpunctuated that the reader usually must decide the limits of the sentence) but also at the level of the phrase or even the word. One poem, for example, begins "and/ she/ had a man's dress mad/ e/ though her feet ble/ d/ skimming the surf/ ace," a series of ruptures that militates against any "skimming of the surface" on the reader's part.

In a subsequent section of *The Liberties*, Howe extends her attention to Shakespeare's Cordelia, surely attractive to Howe for her refusal to accede to the patriarchal demand to accord with the picture of herself that her father wished to perpetuate. This section, titled "White Foolscap," puns on "fool's cap" and thus reminds the reader that Cordelia is a dramatic character whose only "real" context is the play *King Lear* (pr. c. 1605-1606), complete with Fool. However, the title also refers to the blank page that the writer addresses: metaphorically, the nothingness into which she throws herself, composing. In the next section, "God's Spies," a playlet, Stella and Cordelia meet, together with the ghost of Swift; the women are dressed as boys in their early teens. The action is fragmented, the dialogue sparse, truncated, enigmatic. The longest speech is Stella's, a poem the historical Stella wrote, very much in the manner of Swift: When it is done, Stella shoots herself. To so sink herself in the style of another, Howe is saying, is tantamount to suicide.

The third and final section of *The Liberties*, "Formation of a Separatist, I," is prospective, as the previous sections were retrospective. Howe has composed these poems of isolated words—single words with white space between each, arranged in blocks—and celebrates their individual tones, rather than their syntactic possibilities. There are, however, other poems in this section that depend on phrases and sentences; in fact, the book ends with these lines: "Tear pages from a calendar/ scatter them into sunshine and snow." The nightmare of history disperses into a present that is subject to elements in their own nature.

Pythagorean Silence

Pythagorean Silence is divided into three sections: The first, "Pearl Harbor," opens with a poem titled "Buffalo, 12.7.41" and the announcement of the cataclysm that has unleashed such terrible forces upon the second half of the century, the cataclysm that has so thoroughly trammeled survivors and inheritors in an ethical dilemma that becomes, for the artist, an aesthetic dilemma as well. Theodor Adorno, the German theoretician of art and society, averred that it has become impossible, since the deaths at the Nazi concentration camp at Auschwitz, to write poetry; the tens of millions murdered since 1941 cry out whenever Being is addressed. A character in Howe's poem, who is called TALKATIVE, "says we are all in Hell": Howe suggests that a truer use of language, one less suspect (in Howe's world and work, all talking about things is seen as vitiated by its own remove), can be found in biblical Rachel's inconsolable cry: "her cry/ silences/ whole/ vocabularies/ of *names*/ for *things*." The problem with the declaration that "we are all in Hell" arises from the clichéd nature of the phrase, which works against an experience of its meaning. Howe's "negative poetry" would undo prior namings where these have become impenetrably familiar. This is why she nudges her poems along through puns: In the pun, other meanings break through the intended singularity of usage, the law of logical syntax is transgressed by the play of several possibilities. "Connections between unconnected things are the unreal reality of Poetry," she asserts in *My Emily Dickinson*.

In section 2, the title section of *Pythagorean Silence*, the initial poem opens with a pun arising from the fracturing of a single word: "He plodded away through drifts of i/ ce." "Drifts of i" suggests the accumulation of personal, even egocentric, experience, with "drifts" implying the contingent nature of such accumulations, accrued as "the wind listeth." The line's extension equates "i" with "ice"—a frozen lump of such subjectivity. Still, Pythagoras broke through the amassed subjectivity of his experience to accomplish, with his theorem, the objective; to the extent that he is the hero of this sequence and this book, Howe implicitly urges emulation of his persistence. The "silence" of her title—which Howe discovered in a footnote in E. R. Dodd's *The Greeks and the Irrational* (1951)—refers to the silence maintained by initiates of the Pythagorean rites prior to their more active worship, a form of meditation. Indeed, the impression of her poetry is of (to echo William Butler Yeats) "speech after long silence", a use of language directly opposed to unthinking, unfeeling chatter.

Notice should be taken, however, of Howe's statement in *My Emily Dickinson*:

> at the center of Indifference I feel my own freedom . . . the Liberty in wavering. Compression of possibilities tensing to spring. Might and might . . . mystic illumination of analogies . . . instinctive human supposition that any word may mean its opposite. Occult tendency of opposites to attract and merge.

Taking this as a rule of thumb and applying it to the claim that Pythagoras is the hero in her book, the reader will consider the possibility that he is also the villain, capable of leading the unsuspecting into frozen wastes of abstruse speculation. This afterthought will not annul the previous reading, but rather coexist with it. Howe's greatest clarity lies in her ability to imply and exemplify the insupportable partiality of any single answer.

Single answers, after all, like universal concepts, are acts of enclosure, a delimiting of the possible; historically, they have been imposed by men on women and children, by imperialists on territories hitherto regarded as "unknown," terra incognita, full of hidden terrors—even as women and children for the dominant man. Howe herself, in an article published in *Politics and Poetic Form* (1989, edited by Charles Bernstein), addresses these issues, remarking that that sum of single answers, knowledge, "no matter how I get it, involves exclusion and repression." She continues:

> National histories hold ruptures and hierarchies. On the scales of global power what gets crossed over? Foreign accents mark dialogues that delete them. . . . When we move through the positivism of literary canons and master narratives, we consign our lives to the legitimation of power, chains of inertia, an apparatus of capture.

It has become part of the burden of Howe's poetry to make plain enough these concerns, to confront, although at oblique angles, readers with modes of capture and unfreedom of which they may have been unaware. Her method is to locate the mortmain of the past in documents—demotic narratives of escape and capture, for example—of the past, and in instanced persistence of past patterns into the conduct of the present. In this second endeavor, she may take herself as instance, although the work never resembles autobiography in any of its conventional senses. When all is said and done, however, a poem itself is a form of enclosure, even as the choice of a place of one's own, an affirmation of belonging (as in Howe's case, being a New Englander). Clearly, then, such acceptance of limitation can be a source of strength, succor, and enabling. Even though Howe admits that all power is unstable, she does not deny its existence. There is a push-pull in her poetry, then, between the need for limits and a suspicion of them: Are they freely elected? Or are they imposed from without?

THE NONCONFORMIST'S MEMORIAL

The Nonconformist's Memorial challenges traditional beliefs and conceptions of history from both a nonconforming feminist and a deconstructionist point of view. The book has four long sequences that are divided into two sections, "Turning" and "Conversion." The book's structure, as well as Howe's thematic approach and her use of expressionism, echoes T. S. Eliot's *Four Quartets* (1943). She imitates his style, however, in an ironic way, acting as a counterpoint in many instances to his religious themes and suggestions for bringing the soul closer to God. For example, the two poems in "Turning" describe female speakers' struggle with their religious faith. In "The Nonconformist's Memorial," the speaker raises questions about the practice of "true submission and subjection," because "self-concealment" (Eliot's proposal) has failed to lead the speaker to the anticipated union with God; it has, instead, thrown her into bewilderment and physical darkness. The sense of estrangement is created by the harsh tone in lines such as "Stop clinging to me" and "Don't touch me" and by Howe's use of large gaps between stanzas, ruptures that visually display the poet's thematic concerns.

In another of the collection's notable poems, "Melville's Marginalia," Howe explores the contributions of an Irish poet—that history has deemed "minor"—to Herman Melville's research. In her teaching of Melville's *Billy Budd, Foretopman* (1924) in the early 1990's, Howe discovered a book titled *Melville's Marginalia*, a collection of marginal notations and annotations that Melville marked in books from his library. She learns that in fact, James Clarence Mangan was "a rebel politically, and a rebel intellectually and spiritually—a rebel with his whole heart and soul singing against the spirit of the age." Her poem of this subject follows the structural pattern that Howe has established in other poems in the book. They objectify the speaker's struggle to decipher the meaning of the words in Melville's comments on Magnan, as well as the meaning of Magnan's own writings. The chaotic movements of lines in the beginning of the poem again make certain parts hardly readable. The first half of the poem is also frequently disrupted by prose sections that include works from Magnan's writings and the speaker's meditation. Literally and figuratively then, Howe's deconstructionist exploration of Magnan brings his work and persona out of the margins and into a concrete place in history.

PIERCE-ARROW

Six years after *The Nonconformist's Memorial*, Howe produced a collection of new poems, *Pierce-Arrow*. The book brings historiography and poetry together, focusing on nineteenth century pragmatist philosopher Charles Sanders Peirce and Juliette, his wife. Howe addresses her first section, "Arisbe," to a biographical essay on Peirce and poems about his work. The middle section, "The Leisure of the Theory Class," is full of allusions to philosophers and literary figures whose relations are both blurred and solidified in Howe's poems. The final section, "Ruckenfigur," takes as its theme the legend of Tristan and Isolde, the tragic lovers. A mixture of prose and poetry, full of dense and at times pedantic references, *Pierce-Arrow* is a tour de force of history, biography, poetry, and scholarship.

THE MIDNIGHT

In *The Midnight*, Howe's fragmentation is in full force. The work begins with a facsimile of a tissue interleaf from Robert Louis Stevenson's *Master of Ballantrae* (1889). Howe explains how the paper creates a "mist-like transcience" and "quick rustling," the type of scene and sound that one might imagine as her characters from history appear and disappear in this volume. The poems have the appearance of found poetry accented with artifacts, such as the bed hangings that are the focus of the first section, representing the "revisionist work in/ historic interiors" and "other documentary evidence" that she collects as she explores the nooks and crannies of history, wishing to "glide" her "shadow through time." These bed hangings are not merely symbolic to Howe but objects that she desires, remnants of a time and place with different textures than today. When she refers to an nineteenth century curtain fabric called "moreen" and a swatch described as "harateen," owned by John Holker, 1850, one can feel Howe running her fingers over the fabric, admiring its subtle weave. As she describes "Some prepared cloth or other/ left simply in the hair 'glazed'/ or 'lustred' a kind of twilled/ lasting . . ." and Malachy Postlethwayt's defininition of Calamanco as ". . . 'a woolen/ stuff manufactured in Brabant/ in Flanders . . . ,'" the reader sees the scholar studying the fabric for clues to its origin. In this way, Howe combines the sensual and cerebral.

This is followed by a section of prose entitled "Scare Quotes," which begins with a confession: "I am an insomniac who goes to bed in a closet." Howe ruminates on the meaning of wakefulness or awakening in the religious sense, consistent with her interest in Calvinism. She segues into definitions of "bed" and then the curtains that would be placed around the bed of someone such as Queen Elizabeth I, whose favorite lace was called "Opus scissum," with elaborate cutwork of lilies "set with small seed pearl" on her ruffs, mimicking the scrapbook effect that Howe achieves with her inclusion of print artifacts interspersed with her poetry and prose, like the copy of a page from Nathan Bailey's *An Universal Etymological English Dictionary* (1721), showing English, Saxon, Greek and Hebrew alphabets. It evokes a longing for another time, as in "Bed Hangings II," a later section of poetry, in which Howe refers to "cobweb gossamer ephemera" in "The Age of Resplendent Lace."

Also included in this section is information about Howe's mother, particularly how she was described in an excerpt from a director's unpublished memoirs called "Some Talented Women," in which he referred to a young Dublin actress named Mary Manning "whose brain, nimble and observant as it was, could not yet keep pace with a tongue so caustic that even her native city . . . was a little in awe of her." Not only an actress but also a theater critic, magazine editor, and author of two plays and a novel before becoming what Howe describes as "a faculty wife and mother," Howe's mother passed her wit to her daughter as well as her love of books, bringing her up on Yeats, Howe says, "as if he were Mother Goose." Howe's great-aunt Louie Bennett, who became the first woman president of the Irish Trade Union Congress, eventually being memorialized on an Irish stamp and having a bench in Stephen's Green dedicated to her memory, also makes several appearances, most notably in Howe's inclusion of a flyleaf from one of Bennett's books in which she has inscribed, "This book has a value for Louie Bennett that it cannot have for any other human being. Therefore let no other human being keep it in his possession." Howe confides that she recently secured the spine of her great-aunt's beloved *Irish Song Book* with duct tape due to "damage control—its cover was broken." Howe taunts, "So your edict flashes daggers—so what." This is one of the ironies of Howe's work: her reverence for words and frustration with those who would keep her from them, like the "humiliation and angry despair" she feels when she is told that the Dickinson manuscripts that she has requested from the Houghton Library Reading Room are not there, despite the arrangements she had made to gain access to them.

Howe also shows an abiding interest in Frederick Law Olmsted, landscape architect and designer of Parkside in Buffalo, New York, among other famous urban oases such as Central Park in New York City. She includes some of the passages he wrote as a result of insomnia, including one about how much he enjoyed walks and rides with his father in the woods and fields, taking "tours of the picturesque," similar to the ones that Howe gives to visiting poets to show them Buffalo's golden age. This longing to recapture the past is also shown in the closing with a sequence of poems that refer several times to a "faded gown sleeve flung open," perhaps signifying the age and elegance of a garment that is available for inspection but still concealing a history to which the viewer might gain access through reading and writing words but can never truly know.

Souls of the Labadie Tract

Howe's experimentation with fragmentation continues in *Souls of the Labadie Tract*, inspired by a group of utopians called Labadists, Dutch followers of Jean de Labadie's teachings. They left the Netherlands in 1684 to spread his vision and settled in Cecil County, Maryland. The 3,750 acres where they lived came to be known as the Labadie Tract and, more informally, New Bohemia. Among the Labadist beliefs were, according to Howe, "the necessity of inner illumination, diligence and contemplative reflection." Like the Shakers, they also renounced marriage and held all property (including children) in common, supporting themselves with manual labor and commerce.

Howe's interest in this group seems to lie in their relatively unknown status as well as the quietude that was part of their culture. Her poems inspired by them evoke serenity and spirituality but also feelings of isolation. Howe describes how the "Green cloud conceals green/ valley nothing but green/ continually moving then// silk moth fly mulberry tree/ Come and come rapture." However, she notes, "We are strangers here/ on pain of forfeiture," even referring to a rupture: "She left the sect which split."

In the book's final section, "118 Westerly Terrace," Howe reflects on the home life of Wallace Stevens, speculating on how words and images could have come to a poet whose day job was as a surety claims lawyer and later vice president of the Hartford Accident and Indemnity Company. The ideas that Howe describes him jotting down the backs of old laundry bills and envelopes are similar to those she mentions Jonathan Edwards writing on pieces of paper that he pinned to his clothing as he traveled on horseback from parish to parish. Perhaps these are the "silk dresses" made out of worms that Stevens described poets making. Howe herself has woven these dresses with her collection of remnants, her words becoming the thread that holds them together.

OTHER MAJOR WORKS
NONFICTION: *Religious Literature of the West*, 1971 (with John Raymond Whitney); *My Emily Dickinson*, 1985; *Incloser*, 1992; *The Birth-Mark: Unsettling the Wilderness in American Literary History*, 1993; "Sorting Facts: Or, Nineteen Ways of Looking at Marker," 1996.

BIBLIOGRAPHY
Back, Rachel. *Led by Language: The Poetry and Politics of Susan Howe*. Tuscaloosa: University of Alabama Press, 2002. A set of essays that examines Howe's experimentation with language and interest in Puritanism, American colonial history, and her own Irish ancestry.
Collis, Stephen. *Through Words of Others: Susan Howe and Anarcho-scholasticism*. Victoria, B.C.: ELS Editions, 2006. A critical analysis of Howe's works, from the viewpoint of anarcho-scholasticism.
Crown, Kathleen. "'This Unstable I-Writing': Susan Howe's Lyric Iconoclasm and the Articulating Ghost." *Women's Studies* 27, no. 5 (1998): 483-505. In-depth analysis of Howe's poem "Articulation of Sound Forms."
Daly, Lew. *Swallowing the Scroll: Late in a Prophetic Tradition with Poetry of Susan Howe and John Taggart*. Buffalo, N.Y.: M Press, 1994. A critical study comparing the work of Howe and John Taggart.
Freitag, Kornelia. *Cultural Criticism in Women's Experimental Writing: The Poetry of Rosmarie Waldrop, Lyn Hejinian, and Susan Howe*. Heidelberg: Universitätsverlag Winter, 2006. The works of Rosmarie Waldrop, Lyn Hejinian, and Howe are compared and contrasted, with emphasis on their cultural perspectives.

Gelpi, Albert. "Emily Dickinson's Long Shadow: Susan Howe and Fanny Howe." *The Emily Dickinson Journal* 17, no. 2 (Fall, 2008): 100-112. A comparison of Susan Howe's and Fanny Howe's poetry in relation to the poetry of Dickinson, who influenced both of them. Gelpi contends that Susan Howe's poetry is fragmented and historically influenced, while Fanny Howe's poetry is lyrical and theologically oriented.

Green, Fiona. "'Plainly on the Other Side': Susan Howe's Recovery." *Contemporary Literature* 42, no. 1 (2001): 78-101. Analyzes the effect of Howe's father's death on her poetry.

Joyce, Elisabeth W. *"The Small Space of a Pause": Susan Howe's Poetry and the Spaces Between.* Cranbury, N.J.: Associated University Presses, 2010. Provides an analysis of Howe's poetry, with an emphasis on space and time.

Naylor, Paul. *Poetic Investigations: Singing the Holes in History.* Evanston, Ill.: Northwestern University Press, 1999. A critical survey of English Commonwealth and American experimental and avant-garde literature of the twentieth century. Covers the work of Howe, Kamau Brathwaite, Nathaniel Macky, and Lyn Hejinian. Includes bibliographical references and index.

Nicholls, Peter. "'The Pastness of Landscape': Susan Howe's *Pierce-Arrow*." Review of *Pierce-Arrow*. *Contemporary Literature* 43, no. 3 (2002): 441-460. A close reading of Howe's collection, exploring themes and associations that run throughout the work.

Wilkinson, Jessica. "Resurrecting Absence: Susan Howe's *A Bibliography of the King's Book: Or, Eikon Basilike* and the Historically Unspoken." *Cultural Studies Review* 14, no. 1 (March, 2008): 161-176. Describes Howe's probing of the gaps, blanks, and spaces in history to reconstruct a literary history and present it in a contemporary setting.

David Bromige; Sarah Hilbert
Updated by Holly L. Norton

DENISE LEVERTOV

Born: Ilford, Essex, England; October 24, 1923
Died: Seattle, Washington; December 20, 1997

PRINCIPAL POETRY
The Double Image, 1946
Here and Now, 1957
Five Poems, 1958
Overland to the Islands, 1958
With Eyes at the Back of Our Heads, 1959
The Jacob's Ladder, 1961
City Psalm, 1964
O Taste and See: New Poems, 1964
Psalm Concerning the Castle, 1966
The Sorrow Dance, 1966
A Marigold from North Vietnam, 1968
Three Poems, 1968
A Tree Telling of Orpheus, 1968
The Cold Spring, and Other Poems, 1969
Embroideries, 1969
Summer Poems, 1969, 1970
A New Year's Garland for My Students: MIT, 1969-1970, 1970
Relearning the Alphabet, 1970
To Stay Alive, 1971
Footprints, 1972
The Freeing of the Dust, 1975
Chekhov on the West Heath, 1977
Modulations for Solo Voice, 1977
Life in the Forest, 1978
Collected Earlier Poems, 1940-1960, 1979
Pig Dreams: Scenes from the Life of Sylvia, 1981
Wanderer's Daysong, 1981
Candles in Babylon, 1982
Poems, 1960-1967, 1983
The Menaced World, 1984
Oblique Prayers: New Poems with Fourteen Translations from Jean Joubert, 1984
Selected Poems, 1986
Breathing the Water, 1987

Poems, 1968-1972, 1987
A Door in the Hive, 1989
Evening Train, 1993
Sands of the Well, 1996
The Stream and the Sapphire: Selected Poems on Religious Themes, 1997
The Great Unknowing: Last Poems, 1999
Making Peace, 2006 (Peggy Rosenthal, editor)

OTHER LITERARY FORMS

The Poet in the World (1973) gathers prose articles, reviews, criticism, statements to the press, and tributes to fellow poets by Denise Levertov (LEHV-ur-tawf). *Light Up the Cave* (1981), her second volume of prose pieces, includes three short stories, articles on the nature of poetry and politics, speeches and political commentary, and memoirs and notes on other writers—Hilda Morley, Michele Murray, Bert Meyers, Rainer Maria Rilke, and Anton Chekhov. Of particular interest are the pages on dream, memory, and poetry and the details of her arrest and imprisonment experience as a war protester.

Levertov also wrote a novella, *In the Night: A Story* (1968), and the libretto for an oratorio, *El Salvador: Requiem and Invocation* (pr. 1983). With Kenneth Rexroth and William Carlos Williams, she edited *Penguin Modern Poets Nine* (1967). She produced translations of other poets' works, including *In Praise of Krishna: Songs from the Bengali* (1967, with Edward C. Dimock, Jr.), *Selected Poems*, by Eugene Guillevic (1969), and *Black Iris*, by Jean Joubert (1988). Her final prose work, *Tesserae* (1995), consists of autobiographical fragments that composed a "mosaic" of the poet's life.

ACHIEVEMENTS

Denise Levertov's first book of poems, *The Double Image*, was published in England in 1946. It brought her to the attention of British and American critics and poets such as Kenneth Rexroth and Robert Creeley. Eleven years later, her first American book was published, followed by many volumes of poems and several translations of other poets' work. She taught at many institutions, including Vassar College; Drew University; City College of New York; University of California, Berkeley; Massachusetts Institute of Technology; Brandeis University; Tufts University; and Stanford University. As the poetry editor of *The Nation* in the 1960's, she influenced the critical reception of new poets. She was elected to the American Academy of Arts and Letters. Her many awards include the Bess Hokin Prize from *Poetry* magazine in 1960, a Guggenheim Foundation Fellowship in 1962, a National Institute of Arts and Letters Award in 1965, the Lenore Marshall Poetry Prize in 1976 for *The Freeing of the Dust*, both the Elmer Holmes Bobst Award and the Shelley Memorial Award in 1983, the Frost Medal in 1990, the Lannan Literary Award for Poetry in 1993, an Academy of American Poets Fellowship in 1995, and a Washington State Book Award in 1996.

Biography

Born near London, England, in 1923, Denise Levertov was reared in a multicultural environment: Welsh and Russian, Jewish and Christian. On her mother's side, her lineage was Welsh. Beatrice Spooner-Jones, her mother, was a daughter of a physician and great-granddaughter of a tailor, teacher, and preacher, Angell Jones, made famous by Daniel Owen, "the Welsh Dickens," in the novel *Hunangofiant Rhys Lewis* (1885). Beatrice Spooner-Jones had a beautiful singing voice and a stock of stories to tell of Welsh life. She loved to travel, and in Constantinople, where she was a teacher in a Scottish mission, she met a young Russian Jew, Paul Peter Levertoff, who had converted to Christianity. They were married in London, where he was ordained to the Anglican priesthood. His great passion in life was reconciliation between Christians and Jews. A daughter, Olga, was born to the couple, and seven years later, a second daughter, Denise.

In some ways, Denise felt like an only child. She never attended a public or private school; her mother, her only teacher, read many classic works of fiction to her. She visited museums and libraries in London and studied ballet for many years; for a time, she considered a career in dance. When World War II came, she entered nurse's training and worked in a number of London public hospitals caring for children, the aged, and the poor. She had been writing poems since childhood and published her first volume of poems in England shortly after the war.

Levertov met and married an American writer, Mitchell Goodman, who was studying abroad. They lived in Europe until 1948, returning to Europe from New York for a period in 1950-1951. Her son Nikolai was born in 1949. In 1956, she became an American citizen. For the next thirty years, she published more than a dozen volumes of poetry with the same publisher, New Directions. During the Vietnam era, she wrote and spoke passionately against the war; in 1972, with Muriel Rukeyser and Jane Hart, she traveled to Hanoi. In the years of nuclear bomb testing in the air, she participated in the movement toward a test-ban treaty and the elimination of nuclear weapons. Later, she vigorously supported protests against American involvement in civil wars in El Salvador, Honduras, and Nicaragua. She lived in Mexico for a number of years: Indeed, her mother grew to love Mexico and remained with a family in Oaxaca for twenty years before her death in 1977. After spending much of the last decade of her life in the Pacific Northwest, Levertov died in Seattle, Washington, on December 20, 1997.

Analysis

Denise Levertov published about six hundred poems. Despite this large number of works, her poems revolve around a few preoccupations and questions that continuously engaged her attention: the meaning of life, the issues of justice that have arisen in the twentieth century, and more personal concerns that have to do with friendships, family relationships, and immediate thoughts and feelings. Since the lyric poem captures a moment of intense feeling and thought (it is the most compressed form of literature), chronological analysis of Levertov's work gives access to a record of the poet's unfolding life. Levertov seems to have been uniquely placed in her family and time to inherit two great streams of lyric power—the Welsh gift of song and speech and the profound religious thought of her priest father's Jewish-Christian search for truth.

With such a combination of parental influences, the themes that prevail in Levertov's poetry—the nature and form of poetry, and the moral obligations of the poet to society—are hardly surprising. She once said that the Hasidic or mystical beliefs in her father's Jewish heritage gave her an ease and familiarity with spiritual mysteries. For the purpose of analysis, one can study these three areas of her concern—poetry, morality, and mystery—but in her poems they often appear not separately but together, coloring the mosaic of her words. She combines the skills of a craftsperson and those of an artist, the vision of moral integrity and spiritual insight.

EARLY INFLUENCES

A young poet must establish her voice and style. Levertov learned from modernist poets such as Charles Olson and William Carlos Williams, who used concrete, everyday words and familiar settings and events to convey profound truths. She drew also from Welsh hymn-singing lines. Lines and line breaks are essential to the sound quality of her poetry. Some of her inspiration comes from dreams, images, and dream sounds. Naturally, the technical apparatus of poetry-making absorbs her interest as a poet and teacher of poetry writing: How should journals be used? How should a poet revise drafts? How does one evaluate poetry and distinguish what is good from what is bad? Who are the great poets of the twentieth century?

As to the second preoccupation in Levertov's poetry, the integrity of moral vision, the twentieth century has provided abundant evidence of the human capacity for sin as well as visionary leadership in the fight against evil. The age-old oppression of Jews by Christians flared into monstrous proportions as millions of innocent women, children, and men were gassed in death camps in Europe. The shock of this discovery in 1945 as World War II came to a close must have been intense for the young poet-nurse whose father was both Jew and Christian. In later decades, she felt an imperative to protest the horror and injustice of war. The effort to end the Vietnam War brought women together before the women's movement had gathered full force. The sight of children mutilated and burned by napalm aroused the conscience of many "unpolitical" people. Levertov's actions and her words expressed the outrage of many citizens. She explored the relevance of poetry to politics and questioned the moral responsibility of the poet in a time of peril. What use should be made of the gift of speech?

Early in her career, Levertov expressed her vision of unity in the physical and spiritual worlds. "Taste and See," the title poem of her seventh volume, has a biblical sound. Insisting that one cannot know a divinity apart from what is given to the senses, she probes the meaning of physical experience—a life affirmation—and considers its relationship to religious values. Decades before the general public awakened to the need to respect the physical world, Levertov spoke of the mystery in the objects people taste, touch, and see: the Moon, food, a glass of water. She found both happiness and wisdom in the realization of mystery. Increasingly, in her later poetry, the value of mystical and religious experience became her theme.

Religious significance

Levertov links the imagination with truth in poetry; thus, the poem has a religious significance. As "religion" literally means "binding anew," she finds connections to be the essence or truth of imagination. In the poem "A Straw Swan Under the Christmas Tree," she writes, "All trivial parts of/ world-about-us speak in their forms/ of themselves and their counterparts! . . . one speech conjuring the other." The human emotion of sympathy depends on understanding the connections in animate and also inanimate life. "May the taste of salt/ recall to us the great depths about us," she writes in "The Depths." The principle of interrelated form applies even in the extreme case of Nazi leader Karl Adolf Eichmann. In "During the Eichmann Trial," she says that if one looks accurately into another face, or into a mirror, one sees "the other," even Eichmann. This oneness is a mystery, and something Eichmann did not know: "We are members/ one of another."

One should not conclude, however, that the truth of imagination Levertov seeks is an intellectual truth. Unlike the poet Dante, who moves from love and care in the physical world to a spiritual and intellectual understanding of love, Levertov remains firmly based in the physical realm, however far along the mystical path she may travel. Perhaps in the modern age the presence of evil within and without is so strong that the poet dares not abandon her mooring in the physical "real" world that needs so much assistance. Humanity is "a criminal kind, the planet's nightmare" (as she quotes Robinson Jeffers in the poem "Kith and Kin"). The truth she continually explores remains the connection in the patterns of human and natural life. Courage is a necessity, and models of courage may be found in her lean, economical poetic voice.

Diction and imagery

A "speaking-voice" quality in Levertov's poems results from the open form of uneven line lengths. In keeping with the tone of a human voice in natural and varied cadences, her diction neither startles nor challenges the reader with rare and exotic words in the manner of Marianne Moore or Edith Sitwell. She "tunes up" or increases the vibrancy of her poems by making them "tight," with no excess words or phrases. She often omits subjects and verbs, punctuating a fragment as though it were a sentence, and alternates or intersperses fragments with complete sentences. Another skill is accuracy in word choice, using the best word to evoke the scene, the object, the person, or the feeling she is describing. She can change the feeling of a line by inserting words from another collocation—sets of words often found together. For example, in a late poem, "Those Who Want Out," from *A Door in the Hive*, she describes people who are designing permanent colonies in space—their optimism, their love of speed and machines that are "outside of nature." Then a closing line judges them with icy and stern tone in six one-syllable words with biblical power: "They do not love the earth." This use of sparse, plain Anglo-Saxon English for a "stopper" of great power is found frequently in William Shakespeare.

Along with devices of diction, poetic speech uses images to convey truth. Levertov's images are most frequently from the natural world—plants, animals, and landscapes—and of everyday household objects. "In the Unknown" takes the reader to the poet's home: "As if the white page/ were a clean tablecloth,/ as if the vacuumed floor were a primed canvas." In "To the Muse," she describes the body as the house one lives in and the place to find one's inner poetry. There are many rooms in this house, and when the Muse seems to have departed, she is hiding, like a lost gold ring. One has forgotten to make a place for her, and to bring her back, one needs to attend to the house, find some flowers to decorate it, and be alert to the Muse with all one's senses. Images of caves, mirrors, water, cloud, shadow, and moon fill her poems to make her feelings and ideas accessible to the common reader.

ROLES OF THE POET

In harmony with her use of diction and form, Levertov expressed a modest view of the poet: a person who can articulate feeling through the medium of language. She refused the exalted aura of a supersensitive person whose feelings are beyond the reach of ordinary human beings. Glorification by "temperament" was never attractive to her and was as suspect as misplaced romantic adulation—not a twentieth century ideal. It was the process of writing, not the result, that fascinated her. She saw poems as structures of meaning and sound that convey feelings accurately. The poet must revise and polish until the poem is complete. Technical skill with diction, form, rhythm, syntax, and sound—above all, sound—raises a poem from mediocrity to perfection. As a teacher, she had much experience to share. From her essays and articles on the subject of poetry one can gain information about many technical aspects of her craft. Her poems are more readily understood when one is familiar with these principles.

VERSIFICATION

Like many young poets, Levertov experimented in her early writings with various rhyme schemes, tones, and forms. A 1946 poem, "Folding a Shirt," uses Dante's interlacing terza rima rhyme pattern for six stanzas: *aba bcb cdc ded efe fgf.* "Midnight Quatrains" rhymes the second and fourth end words of each stanza. There are dramatic poems in dialogue form and ballads. Typically, however, Levertov's poems have no end rhyme or regular meter. (The lack of regular rhyme and stressed beats in most modern poetry has been attributed to the chaos and irregularity in the twentieth century—poetry reflects life.) Her rhythm is subtle, moving with the line break. Uneven lines are the rule, not the exception. The placement of words and indentations create rhythmic ebb and flow, abrupt interruptions, slow pauses, and dramatic suspense. The eye follows a varied typography that signals rhythm with blank space and black ink, like a design for reading aloud. The "melos" or song quality of such an open form comes from the rightness of the line length—the line's appropriate length in the poem's internal system of meanings.

As well as obtaining rhythm by a masterful use of line breaks, Levertov excels in the construction of sentences within the poem. Often a poem is built like an argument: a proposition followed by a rebuttal, in the way of a sonnet. The poem's syntax often matches the idea of the poem. In "The Prayer," the poet is praying to Apollo at Delphi for the flame of her poetry to be maintained. As if the poem were the flame, it keeps going until the poet breaks the sentence when she begins to wonder whether the god is mocking her. The sentence ends at the same time that her belief in the god falters. The second sentence, a reprise, says that the flame is flickering, and perhaps it is some other god at work. In a very sensual poem, "Eros at Temple Stream," she pictures lovers bathing near a river, soaping each other with long, slippery strokes—their hands as flames. The poem's syntax—one long sentence with no punctuation at its close—mirrors the meaning.

NARRATIVE AND DRAMATIC POEMS

In Levertov's narrative and dramatic poems, she set the stage quickly. A mini-play, "Scenario," opens bluntly: "The theater of war. Offstage/ a cast of thousands weeping." A poem about animal life at the dump begins, "At the dump bullfrogs/ converse as usual." Often these poems begin with brief noun phrases, as in "A Hunger": "Black beans, white sunlight." Levertov's impulse for story and drama resulted in a number of long poem sequences and poetic plays. "Staying Alive," with its prologue and four parts with entr'actes, vividly recalls events and feelings at the height of the Vietnam War protests and the People's Park struggle in Berkeley, California, in 1969. In 1983, an oratorio, *El Salvador: Requiem and Invocation*, was performed at Harvard University; the text by Levertov was set to music by the composer W. Newell Hendricks. Using the structures of the Johann Sebastian Bach passions and George Frideric Handel and Franz Josef Haydn oratorios, Levertov wrote voices for a narrator, Archbishop Oscar Romero, a questioner, nuns, and a chorus. She studied the speeches of the murdered archbishop and quoted his words as well as passages from Mayan prayers. The work was given to help fund-raising efforts of relief organizations active in Central America.

Political poems

That the poet should be also a political person came as an early and natural revelation to Levertov. Her first published poem, "Listening to Distant Guns" (1940), tells of hearing "a low pulsation in the East" that "betrays no whisper of the battle scream." She actually heard the guns of World War II from the south coast of England, to where she, along with many young people, had been evacuated from the city of London. She herself was safe, but the war was very near. She describes the dismal feelings of the English people in "Christmas 1944," when no celebration could hide the blackout curtains on the windows, the knowledge of "fear knocking on the door" of so many Europeans. She gives a welcome: "Come in, then poverty, and come in, death:/ This year too many lie cold, or die in cold." During her impressionable teens and early twenties, she was surrounded with war. Although two decades would pass before her active involvement in the American antiwar movement, she had already expressed her grief at the mass destruction war brings.

In "On the Edge of Darkness: What Is Political Poetry?" (originally a lecture delivered at Boston University in 1975), Levertov defends the idea that a lyric poem can be simultaneously intimate, passionate, and political. Indeed, there is a long history of poets speaking out their political ideas—generally, though not always, in defense of liberty and peace. Contemporary "political" poets usually participate actively in the struggles of which they write. Specific issues give rise to topical poetry on race, class, environment, and gender problems. These poems, like the songs associated with the struggles, change the feelings of the listeners and readers; they alter the awareness of a community. The standards of aesthetic value apply to this poetry as to all other; it should arouse the whole being of the listener: mind, senses, and spirit.

Antiwar poetry

By 1966, Levertov was writing poems about the war in Vietnam. The most influential and famous of these is probably "Life at War." Speaking for her contemporaries, she tells of war's pervasive influence in her century—"We have breathed the grits of it in, all our lives"—and then begins a long lament over the damage war has done to people's imaginations. The modern imagination, she argues, is "filmed over with the gray filth of it," because humankind (and here she lists wonderful and praiseworthy achievements and powers of human beings) "whose language imagines *mercy* and *lovingkindness*," can schedule the burning of children's bodies. "Burned human flesh/ is smelling in Vietnam as I write." As a former nurse, Levertov can bring her sensual awareness into her passionate denunciation of modern war. The poem closes with a statement that humankind needs the "deep intelligence" that living at peace can give. The violence to human imagination from war comes from its insult to intelligence.

Other antiwar poems were composed in the form of dialogues such as questions and answers about Vietnamese people or a narrator questioning a bomber pilot. Levertov's poems also protest the false language of war communiqués. She pays tribute to the young men and women antiwar activists—those who die, those who live, those who go to jail. One poem honors her friend and fellow poet Muriel Rukeyser, who went to Vietnam with her in 1972. Both women had sons who were teenagers at the time and faced the possibility of being drafted into the military.

MARRIAGE AND FAMILY LIFE

Family life, and in particular marriage, inspired many of Levertov's most memorable poems. In keeping with her insistence on the beauty of sensual experience, she celebrated the joy of marriage. The short poem "Bedtime" puts the contentment of fulfilled love in natural terms: "We are a meadow where the bees hum,/ mind and body are almost one." "Hymn to Eros" praises the "drowsy god" who quietly circles in "a snowfall hush." Two beautiful poems to her son, Nikolai, are spaced years apart—one before his birth, "Who He Was," and one, "The Son," as he becomes a man. The first tells of his conception, gestation, and birth, and the second of skills he has gained.

The death of love and the contemporary difficulties in male-female relationships also provide subjects for notable poems. The much-quoted "About Marriage" begins with a cry for freedom, "Don't lock me in wedlock, I want/ marriage, an/ encounter," and concludes, "I would be/ met/ and meet you/ so,/ in a green/ airy space, not/ locked in." As the women's movement and the antiwar movement seemed to merge, the desire for peace and independence became the message of many women writers and poets. "The Ache of Marriage" compares marriage to Jonah's life in the belly of a whale; the poet and her spouse are looking for joy, "some joy/ not to be known outside it." Marriage is not discarded as an ideal, but its confinement brings problems to women who feel an urge to work in a wider field. In "Hypocrite Women," Levertov tells women that they should not be ashamed of their "unwomanly" traits but should admit boldly the truth of their lives.

The nature of another woman-to-woman relationship is explored in the "Olga" poems. Levertov's sister, older by seven years, was estranged from her family for many years. Her death brought a recollection and definition of the two lives that were linked in dream and memory but separated by behavior, circumstances, and distance. The gaze of her sister's eyes haunts the poet: "eyes with some vision/ of festive goodness in back of their hard, or veiled, or shining,/ unknowable gaze." Poems to her mother and father join poems to other poets as Levertov continually seeks and writes about the connections in her life. Rilke, Rukeyser, Boris Pasternak, Robert Duncan, and Pablo Neruda are some of the poets she addressed in poems.

TRAVEL AND DREAMSCAPES

Reflecting the world consciousness typical of Americans in the second half of the twentieth century, Levertov traveled widely. Many of her poems describe the people

135

and places she visited in Europe, Mexico, the United States, and Asia. Distant places remain alive in memory with sensual evocations—dreamscapes. The perfume of linden trees in blossom in an ancient European town is recalled in "The Past." Feelings of comfortable married happiness mingle with the beauty of the setting. The poem "In Tonga" describes the life of sacred bats hanging in their caves, squeaking in night flight. The poet muses about them, "If they could think/ it would not be of us." "Poem from Manhattan" builds a prayer and invocation to New York City through its power, energy, and hope—"city, act of joy"—to its desolation—"city, gesture of greed." Moral and spiritual awareness accompanies the poet's sensory connections to the world.

MYSTICISM

The mystical and religious tones of Levertov's poetry can be traced from their beginnings to their full flowering in the poems of the 1980's collected in two volumes, *Breathing the Water* and *A Door in the Hive*. The daughter of a clergyman who was steeped in mystical Jewish Hasidism, Levertov showed her familiarity with religious texts in early poems. "Notes of a Scale" gives four moments of wonder; its reference note directs the reader to Martin Buber's *Tales of the Hasidim: The Early Masters* (1975). The poem "Sparks" includes passages from the Old Testament book of Ecclesiastes. In this work, Levertov moves easily from the ancient Hebrew text to the circumstances of a modern life. Not only Jewish mysticism but also Christian tradition inspired her poetry. Later poems take as their themes the annunciation to Mary, Jesus' parable of the mustard seed, and the path of Calvary.

Levertov's religious poetry is deeply imbued as well with thoughts on the lives and works of religious saints and writers. Saint Thomas Didymus, Julian of Norwich, William Blake, William Everson, and W. H. Auden are evoked in various poems. One should remember, also, that she translated religious poetry of the Bengali Vaishnava faith. Collaborating with the scholar Edward C. Dimock, Jr., she published this fascinating poetry under the title *In Praise of Krishna: Songs from the Bengali*. The warm emotional and erotic content of these poems has a kinship to Levertov's sensual approach to religious mysticism.

DREAM-BASED POEMS

Access to religious symbols often comes in dreams. The immensely influential biblical accounts of dream visions (those of Ezekiel, Daniel, and John of Patmos, among others) echo in texts from every century. Many of these dream visions were part of Levertov's own home educational fare. She wrote of two childhood dreams. One consisted of a violent transformation from a rustic scene of happiness to a scene of burning and devastation. The other recurring dream was of a large country house made of a warm pink stone; its name was Mazinger Hall. These two dreams, like the later ones she used in poems, carry emotional content of joy and sorrow, gain and loss, security and terror. Gradually, her dream material was transformed into poems that evoke similar feelings in her readers.

In Levertov's early dream-based poems, the process of transferring a dream to a poem involved describing the dream content. The poet explained that later, after analytical work on her dreams, she abandoned that objectivity and gave her images stronger and clearer emotional force to present the dream content more directly to the reader. A third stage in this process came with the realization that the dream needs a literary form that cannot be imposed but must be listened for. Several times she found that a dream worked only as a prose tale. The stories "Say the Word" and "A Dream" began as poems that she transformed to a rhythmic prose. The experience of using dream material for a work of art teaches the poet that the poem must be not only visually clear but also morally or emotionally significant for the reader. An expression that is too private does not make an effective poem.

Another kind of dream poem may result from an auditory message received in a dream state, or as a combined visual and auditory dream. Levertov experienced each type and made poems of them. In "The Flight," she retells a vision of the poet and mystic William Blake, who spoke the words, "The will is given us that we may know the delights of surrender." She waited several years before composing a poem about that experience, to avoid a too-literal transcription. Again, an auditory message was received in a dream about Pasternak. The visual scene disappeared from memory, but the words remained. In both instances, as Levertov explains, the quality of the resulting poem came from the poet's willingness to recognize and absorb a hidden quality that lay beyond the superficial appearances. Some dream images may indicate the questions or problems present at that moment in the poet's life. In that case, the truth of the life and the truth of the dream provide an interplay that makes a powerful poem.

HONEY OF THE HUMAN

The religious message that hums (a favorite Levertov verb) throughout her poetry is the oneness of all life: all human beings, animals, trees, and the great elements of earth, air, fire, and water. The vision of air and water blended comes in poems about bees, honey, and ocean currents that hold "my seafern arms." The cleansing properties of honey in the hive, she writes in "Second Didactic Poem," neutralize even the poison of disease organisms. That hive with its transforming power may be the same as human activity—"honey of the human." Transformation may also move in the opposite direction, from a joyful morning self-confidence to a rapid pace that diminishes the person ("Remembering"). These apparent divisions between good and evil in a person's emotional life can be harmonized from a point of view that is wide enough to encompass the other side, or opposite, in what is experienced.

Certain lines of Levertov's poetry shine as lighthouse beacons across the restless waters of human experience: for example, "We are one of another" ("A Vision"), the lovely love song "We are a meadow where the bees hum" ("Bedtime"), and "To speak of sorrow/ works upon it" ("To Speak"). Why do these lines hum in the mind years after they are first encountered? In them one finds three qualities that characterize Levertov's poetic work: music, morality, and mysticism. Her best poems are true lyrics—songs, in their flowing rhythms and enchanting sound patterns of vowel and consonant combinations. Moreover, she teaches the lessons modern Americans need to hear, about respect for natural life and for unprotected, helpless human beings, especially children and the elderly. Then there is the wonder she shares in the magic of common things—the "gleam of water in the bedside glass" ("Midnight Gladness") and the moonlight crossing her room ("The Well"). Levertov said, "There is no magic, only facts"; her magic is found in accurate and loving observation of everyday shapes, colors, and sounds.

Legacy

Beyond her mastery of the poem's form and even beyond the thought content, Levertov's poetry nevertheless can be appreciated for the qualities of the poet herself. During the 1960's, before the women's movement had strengthened the fragile position of women poets, when a cult of death followed the suicides of Anne Sexton and Sylvia Plath, Levertov lamented their loss, not only because they were fine poets but also because their deaths would confirm a popular conception of the poet as abnormally sensitive, often on the edge of madness. For her, alcoholism and nervous breakdowns were not signs of poetic talent. Creativity, she wrote, belongs to responsible, mature adults who take citizenship seriously. In the late 1960's and 1970's, she put this antiromantic view to the service of the peace and women's rights movements—marching, protesting, speaking against social injustices. She called attention to the political poets imprisoned in many countries. In the 1980's, she produced poetry of great beauty on the human and material sources of her spiritual inspiration.

Indeed, one of her last volumes of poetry, *Sands of the Well*, showed the beginning of a pronounced shift from her poems of social engagement to a more all-encompassing focus on a spirituality that transcended simple Christianity. Her lasting legacy was to show that a poet in the United States can support herself economically. Generously and with humor, she shared with students the fruits of her years of practicing her craft. In all these ways, she modeled a high standard for both poetry and the poet.

Other major works

LONG FICTION: *In the Night: A Story*, 1968.

PLAY: *El Salvador: Requiem and Invocation*, pr. 1983 (libretto; music by W. Newell Hendricks).

NONFICTION: *The Poet in the World*, 1973; *Light Up the Cave*, 1981; *New and Selected Essays*, 1992; *Tesserae*, 1995; *The Letters of Robert Duncan and Denise Levertov*, 2004 (Robert J. Bertholf and Albert Gelpi, editors).

TRANSLATIONS: *In Praise of Krishna: Songs from the Bengali*, 1967 (with Edward C. Dimock, Jr.); *Selected Poems*, 1969 (of Eugene Guillevic); *Black Iris*, 1988 (of Jean Joubert).

EDITED TEXTS: *Penguin Modern Poets Nine*, 1967 (with Kenneth Rexroth and William Carlos Williams); *The Collected Poems of Beatrice Hawley*, 1989.

BIBLIOGRAPHY

Felstiner, John. "Poetry and Political Experience: Denise Levertov." In *Coming to Light: American Women Poets in the Twentieth Century*, edited by Diane Wood Middlebrook and Marilyn Yalom. Ann Arbor: University of Michigan Press, 1985. Shows that Levertov awakens human sensitivity—male and female—by insisting on the sacramental quality of all physical presence. In poetry, she finds hope while facing the horrors of war in Central America, in Vietnam, and in American cities. Felstiner's words on the oratorio *El Salvador: Requiem and Invocation* are particularly worthwhile.

Gelpi, Albert, and Robert J. Bertholf, eds. *Robert Duncan and Denise Levertov: The Poetry of Politics, the Politics of Poetry*. Stanford, Calif.: Stanford University Press, 2006. This collection of essays discusses the friendship between Duncan and Levertov that was broken up during the Vietnam War by their differing viewpoints of the role of the poet in politics.

Lacey, Paul A. "Denise Levertov: A Poetry of Exploration." In *American Women Poets*, edited by Harold Bloom. New York: Chelsea House, 1986. Considers the influence of Hasidism in Levertov's poetry: She treats the miraculous in a matter-of-fact tone. Her weakness in the early poetry, Lacey says, stemmed from an inability to deal seriously with evil in the world. Later, however, she grew into the political consequences of what it means to be, as she says, "members one of another."

Levertov, Denise. Interviews. *Conversations with Denise Levertov*. Edited by Jewel Spears Brooker. Jackson: University Press of Mississippi, 1998. Collects interviews with Levertov conducted by various interviewers from 1963 to 1995. The most common themes addressed are faith, politics, feminism, and poetry.

Marten, Harry. *Understanding Denise Levertov*. Columbia: South Carolina University Press, 1988. One of the most important studies of Levertov in book form, Marten's analysis covers four decades of poetry. Individual chapters give an overview, a history of the earliest poetry, an analysis of the volumes that established her reputation, a consideration of her public voice, and a discussion of spiritual dimension in her later development. The annotated bibliography of critical articles is particularly helpful.

Rodgers, Audrey T. *Denise Levertov: The Poetry of Engagement*. Rutherford, N.J.: Fairleigh Dickinson University Press, 1993. Examines Levertov's political commitment to antiwar themes in particular, placing poems on this topic in relation to

Levertov's earlier work and her life. The author had access to Levertov herself and to previously unpublished letters in the preparation of this study.

Wagner-Martin, Linda. *Denise Levertov*. New York: Twayne, 1967. Although written when Levertov was in mid-career, this biography, survey of poems, and bibliography provide an excellent introduction to the poet's life and work. Seven chapters discuss Levertov's family and education in England, her poetic themes and forms, and influences from modernist poets. Includes a chronology and notes.

Doris Earnshaw
Updated by Leslie Ellen Jones

CHARLOTTE MEW

Born: London, England; November 15, 1869
Died: London, England; March 24, 1928

PRINCIPAL POETRY
The Farmer's Bride, 1916, 1921 (also known as *Saturday Market*, 1921)
The Rambling Sailor, 1929
Collected Poems of Charlotte Mew, 1953
Collected Poems and Prose, 1981
Selected Poems, 2008

OTHER LITERARY FORMS

Though primarily known for her poetry, Charlotte Mew (myew) also wrote short stories and essays. Her first story to appear in print was "Passed" (1894), published in John Lane and Elkin Mathews's *The Yellow Book*, which also published works by Henry James and Max Beerbohm and the drawings of Aubrey Beardsley. From 1899 to 1905, Mew was a regular contributor to *Temple Bar*, a magazine for middle-class Victorians, which published the stories "The China Bowl" (1899), "An Open Door" (1903), "A White Night" (1903), and "Mark Stafford's Wife" (1905), as well as the essays "Notes in a Brittany Convent" (1901) and "The Poems of Emily Brontë" (1904). "An Old Servant" (1913), Mew's tribute to her childhood nurse, Elizabeth Goodman, appeared in *The New Statesmen*. Mew rewrote "The China Bowl" as a one-act play, which was broadcast by the British Broadcasting Corporation posthumously in 1953. That same year, *Cornhill Magazine* published her story "A Fatal Fidelity."

ACHIEVEMENTS

Although Charlotte Mew's work never won any awards, her poetry did win accolades from major literary figures, including Virginia Woolf, Thomas Hardy, Siegfried Sassoon, Rebecca West, H. D., and novelist May Sinclair. In 1923, Hardy, John Masefield, and Walter de la Mare secured for her a Civil List pension of seventy-five pounds per year.

BIOGRAPHY

Charlotte Mew was born in 1869 in the Bloomsbury section of London, where she would live her whole life, much of it at 9 Gordon Street. She was the first girl born to Frederick Mew and Anna Maria Kendall. Originally from the Isle of Wight, Frederick Mew had been sent to London by his father to train as an architect. He became an assistant to architect H. E. Kendall, Jr. In 1863, he married Kendall's daughter, Anna Maria.

Anna Maria, an invalid much of her life, saw her marriage as beneath her. Frederick's death in 1898 put the family into financial crisis. Of the seven Mew children, only Charlotte, her older brother, Henry, and two younger siblings, Anne and Freda, survived to adulthood. Henry and Freda were both institutionalized for mental illness, a situation that strained the family's limited resources and haunted Mew's poetry.

Following her father's death, Mew lived with her sister Anne and her mother at Gordon Street. Eventually they lived in the basement, having rented out the upper rooms for additional income. Mew was particularly devoted to Anne, a painter who attended the Royal Female School of Art and later rented a studio, 6 Hogarth Studios. In 1909, the year Mew published "Requiescat," her sister Anne had a painting accepted by the Royal Academy. As girls, they attended the Gower Street School and later lectures at University College, London.

At Gower Street, Mew developed a crush on Miss Lucy Harrison, the school's headmistress. Mew's unrequited love for Harrison anticipates her most important adult female relationships. Of particular importance were her relationships with Ella D'Arcy, assistant literary editor of *The Yellow Book*, whom she met in 1894, a year before composing "The China Bowl," and novelist and suffragette May Sinclair, whom she met in 1913 through Mrs. Dawson "Sappho" Scott, an arts patron and founder of International PEN. Sinclair brought Mew's work to the attention of Ezra Pound, who published "The Fête" in *The Egoist*. Mew wrote "Madeleine in Church," which many consider her best poem, during the years of her friendship with Sinclair. While in love with both D'Arcy and Sinclair, Mew repressed her desire because of a strict sense of sexual propriety. Perhaps for the same reason and out of fear that any offspring would suffer mental illness, Mew and her sister Anne decided to never marry.

In 1915, Mew met Alida Monro (née Klemantaski), whose husband, Harold, owned the Poetry Bookshop (Bloomsbury), where Mew read her work. After reading Mew's poem "The Farmer's Bride" in *The Nation* (1912), Monro convinced her husband to publish a collection of Mew's poetry. In 1916, the Poetry Bookshop printed five hundred copies of *The Farmer's Bride*. Five years later, it brought out a revised edition with eleven additional poems. Despite unflagging support from the Monros and positive reviews from H. D. and West, the book did not sell well. In 1929, the Poetry Bookshop posthumously published Mew's poetry collection, *The Rambling Sailor*.

In 1923, the same year Mew was awarded the Civil List pension, her mother died of bronchial pneumonia. Unable to continue paying rent on their house, now in Delancey Street, Mew and her sister Anne lived temporarily at Anne's studio. Anne's health was seriously declining, and in June, 1927, she died of cancer. On February 15, 1928, devastated by the loss of her sister and perhaps fearing for her own mental health (she had become obsessed with germs and the possibility that her sister had been buried alive), Mew agreed to enter a nursing home near the Baker Street Station. Less than one month later, on March 24, 1928, she committed suicide by drinking half a bottle of Lysol.

Analysis

At times autobiographical, Charlotte Mew's poetry frequently takes the themes of longing, death, insanity, and loneliness. It often addresses passion, religious and sexual, as well as sin and the distance between a heavenly God and individual human suffering on Earth. Her work frequently contains tensions created through binaries of inside/outside, freedom/confinement, nature/society. Her deeply emotional verse contains jarring juxtapositions of images and is marked by irregular rhyme and meter. Writing in the last decade of the nineteenth century and the first decades of the twentieth, Mew's poetry straddles the fin de siècle and early modernist periods.

The Farmer's Bride

The poems in *The Farmer's Bride* reflect Mew's dominant themes. "Ken" and "On the Asylum Road" provide moving depictions of madness and the isolation that results from mental illness. "Ken" closes with the lines, "... when they took/ Ken to that place, I did not look./ After he called and turned on me/ His eyes. These I shall see—" The final dash suggests that the speaker remains haunted by Ken's gaze. In "The Narrow Door," death disrupts a game of "shop" as a coffin is carried out through the narrow door before which the "café children" play. Images of death appear in the partially autobiographical "The Changeling," in which "the little pale brother" has been "called away," and "The Quiet House," which opens with "the old Nurse" and concludes with the speaker's revision of the famous line from René Descartes, "some day I *shall* not think; I shall not *be*!" In "Fame," Mew's speaker mediates on whether she could renounce her fame, represented by "the over-heated house," "Where no one fits the singer to his song,/ Or sifts the unpainted from the painted faces," and return to her previous life, symbolized in "The folded glory of the gorse, the sweet-briar air." Choosing Fame, the speaker fantasizes taking her "To our tossed bed." A still birth, "A frail, dead, new-born lamb," "The moon's dropped child," results from their union, a consequence of ambition and sexual passion.

The title poem, "The Farmer's Bride," tells of a young bride, who, having developed a fear of men, runs away. Chased after and returned by the villagers, she is locked away where she "does the work about the house" "like a mouse." The bride's imprisonment, symbolic of women's confinement in marriage, is contrasted against her natural self, which the narrator associates with "wild violets" and the "beasts in stall." In the lines "Sweet as the first wild violets, she,/ To her wild self. But what to me?," the break between "self" and "me," illustrates this broken and unconsummated union. The farmer laments that there are no children: "What's Christmas-time without there be/ Some other in the house than we!" The poem ends with the farmer overcome by his grief and sexual desire: "Oh! my God! the down,/ The soft young down of her, the brown,/ The brown of her—her eyes, her hair, her hair!"

The Farmer's Bride also contains the two-hundred-line free-verse poem, "Madeleine in Church," a dramatic monologue spoken by a woman who prefers to kneel not before Jesus, but rather a "plaster saint" ". . . more like [her] own clay,/ Not too divine." Too high on the cross, Jesus appears distant from the realities of her life, her marriage and divorce, the death of her child, her fading youth. She challenges him, "What can You know, what can You really see/ Of this dark ditch, the soul of me!" Unlike the traditional "fallen woman," Mew's Madeleine is unrepentant, insisting twice, "We are what we are" and that she will not be among the "broken things" held in God's "everlasting wings." The poem offers two versions of love through which Mew repeats the human/divine binary represented by the saint and Jesus. Mew invites readers to compare the perfect yet unattainable passion of Mary Magdalene for Jesus, "a passion" "so far from earthly cares and earthly fears" that one can only look "at it through tears," to the marriage of the speaker's mother, who was "yoked to the man that Father was." Looking to bridge this chasm between the heavenly and the earthly, the speaker longs for a human Jesus, who would notice or even speak to her: "If He had ever seemed to notice me/ Or, if, for once, He would only speak."

The Rambling Sailor

This posthumous collection of thirty-two poems was edited by Alida Monro and contains six of Mew's "Early Poems," including "Requiescat." While the collection continues themes of loss, loneliness, and death, particularly the death of children, these poems express resignation and a fragile hope. They are poems of remembrance, of things, places, and people lost. The speaker in "The Trees Are Down" observes the cutting down of "the great plane-trees at the end of the gardens," and in "Fin de Fête," the speaker recalls how she and an anonymous "you" "should have slept" together like children in a fairy tale, but now there is only the speaker's "lonely head."

Stylistically these poems are more restrained; there are more sonnets, and fewer free-verse lines overspill the page. In a mirroring of form and content, the sexual and religious passion, the grief and despair is also contained, though tentatively. The speakers in these poems appear less consumed with earthly desires, meditating instead on the afterlife. The speaker in "In the Fields," reflecting the "lovely things which pass," asks, "Can I believe there is a heavenlier world than this?," and "Not for That City" claims, "We strain our eyes beyond this dusk to see/ What, from the threshold of eternity/ We shall step into. . . ." Facing their own death or the death of someone they love, the speakers in these poems look to nature, particularly spring, for solace. Having previously ". . . liked Spring last year/ Because you were here," the speaker of "I So Liked Spring," decides, "I'll like Spring because it is simply Spring/ As the thrushes do," and the war poem, "May, 1915," assures its readers, "Let us remember Spring will come again."

Bibliography

Dowson, Jane, and Alice Entwistle. "'I Will Put Myself, and Everything I See, upon the Page': Charlotte Mew, Sylvia Townsend Warner, Anna Wickham and the Dramatic

Monologue." In *A History of Twentieth-Century British Women's Poetry*. New York: Cambridge University Press, 2005. Contains considerable analysis of Mew's poetry, finding the poet's hallmark to be an ability to summon "felt absence."

Fitzgerald, Penelope. *Charlotte Mew and Her Friends*. 1992. Reprint. London: Flamingo, 2002. In this book-length biography, Fitzgerald examines Mew's life in the context of her friendships with Ella D'Arcy, Mrs. Dawson Scott, and May Sinclair. Contains selected poems and bibliography.

Goss, Theodora, ed. *Voices from Fairyland: The Fantastical Poems of Mary Coleridge, Charlotte Mew, and Sylvia Townsend Warner*. Seattle: Aqueduct Press, 2008. Presents the poetry of Mew, Coleridge, and Warner, with some critical analysis.

Hamilton, Ian. *Against Oblivion: Some Lives of the Twentieth-Century Poets*. New York: Viking, 2002. Contains a biography essay on Mew that looks at her poetry. Hamilton edited a selection of Mew's poetry.

Katz, Jon, and Kevin Prufer, eds. *Dark Horses: Poets on Overlooked Poems—An Anthology*. Urbana: University of Illinois Press, 2007. Contains Mew's poem "The Trees Are Down," with a commentary by Molly Peacock.

Kendall, Tim. *Modern English War Poetry*. Oxford: Oxford University Press, 2006. The chapter on Mew compares her war poetry to that of Edward Thomas, analyzing the trope of spring in each.

Leighton, Angela. *Victorian Women Poets: Writing Against the Heart*. New York: Harvester Wheatsheaf, 1992. The chapter on Mew in this introduction to eight nineteenth century women poets provides a biography and analysis of her work, identifying her as a Victorian and drawing comparisons to writer and artist Christina Rossetti.

Rice, Nelljean McConeghey. *A New Matrix for Modernism: A Study of the Lives and Poetry of Charlotte Mew and Anna Wickham*. New York: Routledge, 2003. Rice views both Mew and Wickham, who both published through the Poetry Bookshop, to be modern poets.

Sarah Fedirka

EDNA ST. VINCENT MILLAY

Born: Rockland, Maine; February 22, 1892
Died: Austerlitz, New York; October 19, 1950
Also known as: Nancy Boyd

PRINCIPAL POETRY
Renascence, and Other Poems, 1917
A Few Figs from Thistles, 1920
Second April, 1921
The Ballad of the Harp-Weaver, 1922
The Harp-Weaver, and Other Poems, 1923
The Buck in the Snow, and Other Poems, 1928
Edna St. Vincent Millay's Poems Selected for Young People, 1929
Fatal Interview, 1931
Wine from These Grapes, 1934
Conversation at Midnight, 1937
Huntsman, What Quarry?, 1939
Make Bright the Arrows, 1940
There Are No Islands Any More, 1940
Collected Sonnets, 1941
Invocation to the Muses, 1941
The Murder of Lidice, 1942
Collected Lyrics, 1943
Poem and Prayer for an Invading Army, 1944
Mine the Harvest, 1954
Collected Poems, 1956

OTHER LITERARY FORMS

Edna St. Vincent Millay was known during her early career for her verse plays, the most successful being *Aria da Capo*, first produced in 1919 and published in 1921, followed by *The Lamp and the Bell* (pr., pb. 1921) and *Two Slatterns and a King* (pr. 1917), and *The Princess Marries the Page* (pr. 1917). Her reputation as a writer of verse for the stage was such that she was invited to write the libretto for a Deems Taylor opera commissioned by the Metropolitan Opera Company of New York. The result of her collaboration with Taylor was a successful presentation of *The King's Henchman* (pr., pb. 1927), a variation of the Tristan story. Millay tried to rework the material of the opera libretto into a drama but finally condemned the result as hopelessly contaminated; she was never able to rid it of the influence of the libretto.

Edna St. Vincent Millay
(Library of Congress)

Conversation at Midnight and *The Murder of Lidice* are sometimes classified as plays, the former receiving performance after Millay's death and the latter being written for wartime radio broadcast after the Nazis destroyed the Czechoslovakian town of Lidice and slaughtered its male inhabitants. *The Murder of Lidice* cannot be considered as more than hastily written propaganda at best, and *Conversation at Midnight* suffers if one looks for the conflict and engagement of drama in it. Millay conceded after its completion that it was not really a play but a series of poems with a fixed setting.

In addition to working with dramatic forms, Millay, in the beginning years of her career, wrote topical commentaries for the New York weekly *Vanity Fair* under the pseudonym Nancy Boyd; they were collected in a 1924 volume as *Distressing Dialogues*, the title used by the magazine as the pieces appeared. Although these early essays helped to support the young poet, Millay was never willing to have them published under her name. She was, however, proud of her collaboration with George Dillon on *The Flowers of Evil* (1936), a translation of Charles Baudelaire's *Les Fleurs du mal* (1857, 1861, 1868; *Flowers of Evil*, 1909), although scholars find more of Millay in the translations than the original may warrant. Millay's letters have been collected and published.

Achievements

Edna St. Vincent Millay's meteoric rise as a popular poet seems to have been, in part, a product of her times and the independent style of life that she represented. This fact may account for the later critical dismissal of her work. Millay's poetry is, in many ways, conventional in its formal aspects, often showing strict attention to rhyme and traditional metrical patterns. Her nineteenth century literary forebears were Alfred, Lord Tennyson and A. E. Housman. She showed no interest in the experimental work being done by T. S. Eliot, Ezra Pound, and others of her generation. In her strong allegiance to the lyric, to traditional verse forms, and to conventional diction, she guaranteed that she would not take her place in the mainstream of influential twentieth century poets, although she was very much aware of contemporary currents. Once her initial popularity waned, Millay's work was judged to be something of a sport in a century in which the breaking of forms was thought to be the best representation of the breaking of traditional views of the world.

Ironically, much of Millay's early popularity came from her image as a rebel and nonconformist—a representative of emancipated Greenwich Village culture, a perfect example of the liberated woman of the 1920's. This reputation was primarily promoted by the publication of *A Few Figs from Thistles*, a collection of flippant and audacious poems that seemed a manifesto for the new woman and her independent, nontraditional attitude toward modern life. The image of the short-lived candle burning at both ends and giving its lovely light forged an identity for Millay that her serious poems could never alter, and the proverbial candle seems in retrospect almost an ironic paradigm for Millay's own poetic career.

In spite of Millay's waning popularity in the last decades of her life and the harsh judgment of critics who were suspicious of her early widespread popularity, Millay's poetic accomplishment is considerable. She was awarded the Pulitzer Prize in 1923 for *The Ballad of the Harp-Weaver*, the Levinson Prize from *Poetry* magazine in 1931, and the Frost Medal in 1943.

Millay is very much an American poet in her eclecticism. As a champion of the individual and of freedom from tyranny of any kind, she deserves a place in the American tradition beside poets as widely divergent as Walt Whitman and Archibald MacLeish. As a poet willing to insist on the validity and strength of real emotion and thought in women and on their individuality in relationships, Millay replaced hitherto largely convention-bound material with fresh insights. In her frank introspection and exploration of psychological states, she opened the way for the modern confessional poets who followed her.

Biography

Although Edna St. Vincent Millay is not usually thought of as a New England poet, she was born in Maine and spent the first twenty years of her life there, most of them in Camden, where her mother moved with her three young girls after a divorce in 1900. Millay and her sisters were encouraged to develop their musical and poetic talents and to read widely in the classics and in English and American literature. Millay's mother supported the family by working as a nurse, and from her example, Millay learned early the independence and self-reliance that were to influence her poetry. She learned to value and trust her personal voice, leading many of her readers to search her poems for the details of her personal life that they were thought to reveal.

With the aid of a patron, Millay was able to attend Vassar College the year after the publication of "Renascence," the beginning of her public career as a poet. After graduation from Vassar, Millay moved to New York and, living in poverty, began her association with Greenwich Village and the Provincetown Players. This period of five or six years before her marriage provides the backdrop against which Millay is remembered and with which she is identified, although it represents a very small portion of her life. It was during this period that her famous friendships and love affairs with Floyd Dell, Arthur Fricke, and Edmund Wilson, among others, began, and during which the Provincetown Players produced *Aria da Capo*. She won fame and national popularity with the publication of *A Few Figs from Thistles* in 1920. After several years in Europe, marked by the beginning of the bad health that was to plague her for the rest of her life, Millay returned to the United States and in 1923 became the first woman to win a Pulitzer Prize in poetry. In the same year, she married a Dutch importer who gave up his business to provide a stable environment for her—on a farm at Austerlitz, New York, and in an island home off the coast of Maine.

Taking an active part in the general outcry of American intellectuals and artists against the death sentencing of Nicola Sacco and Bartolomeo Vanzetti, Millay called on the governor of Massachusetts and wrote public statements and several poems, including "Justice Denied in Massachusetts." She was arrested along with others keeping vigil at the time of the execution. In this, as in everything she did, Millay acted with total conviction and unflinching courage—qualities that give strength to her poems, although these same unabashed qualities set her apart in an age that increasingly demanded ironic distance as a prerequisite for serious verse.

Millay received several honorary doctorates and was elected to both the National Institute of Arts and Letters and the American Academy of Arts and Letters. By the end of the 1930's, however, after publication of *Conversation at Midnight*, her reputation had suffered a serious decline, a decline accelerated by the work that she published too hurriedly in the service of wartime propaganda: *Make Bright the Arrows* and *The Murder of Lidice* represent the lowest ebb in her reputation as a serious poet. In the summer of 1944, she suffered a severe nervous breakdown accompanied by serious "writer's block" that lasted for more than two years. Just as she was beginning to take up her work again in 1949, her husband died suddenly. The shock resulted in hospitalization again. She returned later that year alone to her farm in Steepletop, New York, where she died of heart failure a little more than a year after her husband's death. A volume of new poems, *Mine the Harvest*, was published in 1954 and her *Collected Poems* in 1956.

ANALYSIS

The theme of individual liberty and the frank acknowledgment of emotion are ever-present in Edna St. Vincent Millay's poems. She speaks as clearly for a democracy of persons, in whatever relationship, as Whitman does and with no hint of snobbery or elitism. She values the simple and common in nature; the reader never finds her straining after exotic effects. Millay is a realist in her expectations, and she refuses conventional romantic attitudes—a refusal that often results in the ironic tone of some of her love poems. It is not surprising that she acknowledged her fondness for Andrew Marvell, the poet of "The Passionate Shepherd to His Love" and "The Nymph's Reply."

Millay's volumes of poetry contain no "major" poems that have entered the canon of literature in the way in which those of Robert Frost, T. S. Eliot, or William Butler Yeats have. Her early volume, *Renascence, and Other Poems*, with its title poem written before she entered Vassar, may hold little interest for contemporary readers, although it was highly praised by Harriet Monroe, the editor of *Poetry* magazine. Much of the strength of the other volumes lies in the sustained effect of sonnet sequences and collections of lyrics. There is evidence of growth, however uneven, in Millay's development as a poet, as her work moves from the devil-may-care irony and unabashed emotion of the early poems to a more considered and mature production.

The one form in which Millay excelled is the sonnet, both Shakespearean and Petrarchan. She has been described as a transitional poet, and this is nowhere better borne out than in her control of a conventional and circumscribed form in which she was equally comfortable with traditional or modern subject matter and attitudes.

"EUCLID ALONE HAS LOOKED ON BEAUTY BARE"

"Euclid Alone Has Looked on Beauty Bare," published in *The Harp-Weaver, and Other Poems*, is an accomplished classical Petrarchan sonnet written early in Millay's career. It takes as its subject the holy, dazzling beauty of pure form or idea available only to the Greek mathematician, Euclid, who perceived a pure beauty that has not been matched by the prattling of subsequent generations seeking imitations of beauty clothed in human form. The octave ends with a command to let the geese gabble and hiss (an allusion both to the use of geese as watchdogs in ancient times and to those who mistakenly cry out that they have sighted Beauty). The sestet presents a vivid description of the blinding and terrible light that Euclid bore when he "looked on Beauty bare," suggesting that lesser men are fortunate that they have not seen Beauty whole, as it would be too much for them to bear. (In the sestet, the word "bare" has become an adjective of personification as well as one carrying its original meaning of "pure," "unadorned.") Lesser men are lucky if they have even once heard Beauty's sandal on a distant rock; those seekers after Beauty who are not Euclids are doubly fortunate to have heard only a distant echo of Beauty's step, for they could not have borne the blinding intensity of Euclid's vision.

This sonnet is seemingly simple and straightforward. It is more complex than it first appears, however, for by the poet's own personification of Beauty (now clothed, in sandals at least), she acknowledges herself to be one of those lesser mortals who followed Euclid. She ironically accepts her own conventional restrictions. Euclid's vision is of "light anatomized," not of Beauty in the traditional, personified female form.

FATAL INTERVIEW

Fatal Interview, the chronicling of a love affair from inception through intense passion to sad conclusion, represents Millay's longest sustained sonnet sequence. The book's title comes from John Donne's sixteenth elegy in a series about a tragic affair, beginning, "By one first strange and fatal interview." Although the sonnets do not evince the full range of intense emotion that one might expect, Millay manages to treat her subject with the objectivity, control, and irony that mark her love poems as the products of the modern woman, freed from the stereotype of woman as the passive, overwhelmed love object. The passions of love and sexual ecstasy find their way into these poems, but always present too is an awareness of the fleeting nature of even the most passionate relationships and a refusal to accept a bondage that involves the loss of individual integrity. She knows that love can be "stung to death by gnats."

"Well, I have lost you; and I lost you fairly" is the initial line of sonnet 47, and there is a pride expressed in losing well on the speaker's own terms. Nights of weeping she will not deny, but day finds her dry-eyed and fully operative in the world that goes on after love is lost. A more slyly played relationship or one of lesser intensity might have preserved the relationship through another summer, but at too high a cost for lovers who have experienced so much intensity and honesty. The price in "words I value highly" is one that Millay as poet and woman will not, cannot, pay. "Well, I have lost you" is simple and straightforward; a sign of control over pain and grief. Sonnet 30 and others preceding it have made it clear that Millay's realism, her defense against the grief of loss, is a reaction inherent in her philosophical stance in the world; this fact, however, does not lessen the real poignancy of the sonnet. These are the statements of a highly intelligent and sensitive woman who suffers because of the awareness that never leaves her. In "Love is not all: it is not meat nor drink" (sonnet 30) the speaker is conscious that men have died for lack of love even though it is not technically one of the physical necessities of life such as food, drink, and shelter. The sonnet accepts love as a dear necessity for life, but there is in the concluding lines the nagging realization that if it were necessary, she might sell this love for peace, or these passionate memories for food. Although at this moment she is inclined to think she would not, the acknowledgment of the possibility clearly marks the distance between Millay's poem and Elizabeth Barrett Browning's "How do I love thee?" In a more flippant early lyric titled "Thursday," the gulf between Millay and the more conventional Browning is absolute and unbridgeable.

"The Ballad of the Harp-Weaver"

Among Millay's poems for her mother, "The Ballad of the Harp-Weaver" and "In the Grave No Flower" are two that display careful simplicity and controlled depth of feeling. "The Ballad of the Harp-Weaver" was criticized by Wilson for being slight, superficial, and sentimental. He characterized it as a poem for a woman's magazine. The poem is more effective than Wilson suggested and wholly appropriate to its subject: the rich gifts of the spirit given to a child by a mother who, in her poverty, cannot provide the material food and clothing that her child needs. The ballad form controls the simple narrative of the parable, and if the reader accepts the perfect union of form and subject that Millay achieves, the poem is more than a modest success.

"In the Grave No Flower"

"In the Grave No Flower" names with loving specificity common weeds that, by their rank fecundity and stubborn resistance to the plow, inherit the earth, in contrast to the barren grave where there is and can be no flower. This lyric demonstrates Millay's control of intense grief, heightened by her ability to express it with devastating simplicity. The reader has only to compare "In the Grave No Flower" to the early "Elegy Before Death," written on the death of a close friend, to see the distance that Millay has come in her growth as a poet.

"Menses"

Millay's best poems may be love sonnets or lyrics of passion or elegy (even "The Buck in the Snow" is an elegy of sorts), but as a poet she is willing to risk the most ordinary of subjects. A poem called simply "Menses," although not one of her best, is an interesting example of the risk-taking that marked Millay both in her personal and in her poetic life. This poem celebrates the settled relationship, the accommodations made between two people out of the love and understanding that comes with adjustments to an unglamorous cycle of life.

The occasion of the poem is a surface duel between a man and a woman who is undergoing the emotional upheaval associated with her monthly menstrual cycle. The poem is, for the most part, an interior dramatic monologue spoken by the man ("to himself, being aware how it is with her"), who turns aside an incipient quarrel, having "learned/ More things than one in our few years together." Millay's risk-taking in this poem is found with her decision to give to the man the voice in this special situation, and with the woman, driven by physical forces, half-awaiting the relief his understanding will bring her. A simple rendering of the symbiotic daily relationship of two people, this poem is deeply meaningful and, in its own way, as spectacular and surprising as a moment of passion might be in one of Millay's love sonnets.

Millay's poetic subjects thus range more widely than her reputation suggests, for the complexity of her poetry has been obscured by the personal image created during the early years of her career. She is not only the poet whose candle consumes itself and the night and "gives a lovely light!"; she is also an accomplished poet of a wide range of complex emotions, themes, and forms.

OTHER MAJOR WORKS

PLAYS: *The Princess Marries the Page*, pr. 1917; *Two Slatterns and a King*, pr. 1917; *Aria da Capo*, pr. 1919; *The Lamp and the Bell*, pr., pb. 1921; *The Wall of Dominoes*, pb. 1921; *Three Plays*, 1926; *The King's Henchman*, pr., pb. 1927 (libretto; music by Deems Taylor).

NONFICTION: *Distressing Dialogues*, 1924 (as Nancy Boyd); *Letters*, 1952.

TRANSLATION: *The Flowers of Evil*, 1936 (of Charles Baudelaire; with George Dillon).

BIBLIOGRAPHY

Brittin, Norman A. *Edna St. Vincent Millay*. Rev. ed. Boston: Twayne, 1982. Brittin has rewritten his 1967 biography of Millay (he uses the name Vincent, as her friends and family called her, in the earlier edition), providing more discussion of her prose works and less space to the biography. He brings out her feminist ideas and her relation to the poetic movement of high modernism. An essential reference. Includes chronology and useful annotated bibliography.

Constantakis, Sara, ed. *Poetry for Students*. Vol. 31. Detroit: Thomson/Gale Group, 2010. Contains an analysis of "An Ancient Gesture" by Edna St. Vincent Millay plus a brief biography.

Cucinella, Catherine. "Textual and Corporeal Convergence: Edna St. Vincent Millay." In *Poetics of the Body: Edna St. Vincent Millay, Elizabeth Bishop, Marilyn Chin, and Marilyn Hacker*. New York: Palgrave Macmillan, 2010. Examines the poetical treatment of the human body in Millay's work, as well as in that of Elizabeth Bishop, Marilyn Chin, and Marilyn Hacker.

Epstein, Daniel Mark. *What Lips My Lips Have Kissed: The Loves and Love Poems of Edna St. Vincent Millay*. New York: Henry Holt, 2001. Although the author's emphasis is on Millay's love affairs and their connection to specific love poems, he discusses *Aria da Capo* and Millay's career as an actor in part two.

Freedman, Diane P., ed. *Millay at One Hundred: A Critical Reappraisal*. Carbondale: Southern Illinois University Press, 1995. A collection of essays by critics of poetry and women's writing that reinterpret the themes of Millay's poetry. Includes bibliographical references and an index.

Galens, David, ed. *Poetry for Students*. Vol. 17. Detroit: Thomson/Gale, 2003. Contains an analysis of Millay's "Wild Swans" as well as a brief biography.

Meade, Marion. *Bobbed Hair and Bathtub Gin: Writers Running Wild in the Twenties*. New York: Nan A. Talese/Doubleday, 2004. Examines the literary and social triumphs of Millay, Edna Ferber, Dorothy Parker, and Zelda Fitzgerald, their liberated lifestyles, the men in their lives, and their substance abuse and mental problems.

Milford, Nancy. *Savage Beauty: The Life of Edna St. Vincent Millay*. New York: Random House, 2001. The author was the first biographer to have access to Millay's private papers, and she also discussed them extensively with Norma Millay.

Miller, Brett C. *Flawed Light: American Women Poets and Alcohol*. Urbana: University of Illinois Press, 2009. Miller studies how drinking and alcoholism affected prominent American women poets, and how their struggles were reflected in their poetry. Contains an informative chapter on Millay.

Thesing, William B., ed. *Critical Essays on Edna St. Vincent Millay*. New York: Maxwell Macmillan International, 1993. A comprehensive collection of both early reviews and modern scholarly essays.

Donna Gerstenberger

MARIANNE MOORE

Born: Kirkwood, Missouri; November 15, 1887
Died: New York, New York; February 5, 1972

PRINCIPAL POETRY
Poems, 1921
Observations, 1924
Selected Poems, 1935
The Pangolin, and Other Verse, 1936
What Are Years, 1941
Nevertheless, 1944
Collected Poems, 1951
Like a Bulwark, 1956
O to Be a Dragon, 1959
Tell Me, Tell Me, 1966
The Complete Poems of Marianne Moore, 1967, 1981
Becoming Marianne Moore: The Early Years, 1907-1924, 2002 (Robin G. Schulze, editor)
The Poems of Marianne Moore, 2003 (Grace Schulman, editor)

OTHER LITERARY FORMS

Marianne Moore left a voluminous correspondence with literary figures in the United States and England. She also wrote occasional reviews and lectured on campuses and at poetry centers. This work, too, shows her imaginative daring, the "idiosyncrasy and technique" that she valued. A sampling of her prose as well as of her verse was published as *A Marianne Moore Reader* (1961). A selection of essays, *Predilections*, appeared in 1955.

The words "collected" and "complete" in a title may promise more than the book delivers; in Moore's case, the contents are only those examples of her work that she wished to keep in circulation. Because she frequently revised extensively, a genuinely complete edition must be variorum. Her poems have been collected in *The Complete Poems of Marianne Moore* and *The Poems of Marianne Moore*. Most of Moore's manuscripts and correspondence, as well as a collection of her furnishings and personal items, are housed in the museum of the Philip H. and A. S. W. Rosenbach Foundation, Philadelphia. *The Complete Prose of Marianne Moore* (1986) includes all of Moore's published prose work, from her early stories to her mature essays and reviews; as editor of *The Dial* from 1921 to 1929, and later, as her poetic reputation grew, she had the opportunity to write on a broad range of twentieth century poets and fiction writers.

Achievements

If Marianne Moore had lived longer, she would have sympathized with the aims, if not with the more fervid rhetoric, of the revived feminist movement, but in her day Moore sought recognition without regard to gender. Her daring paid off because her work impresses most critics, male or female, as that of a major figure among poets of modernism; she is considered to be an artist on a par with Wallace Stevens, William Carlos Williams, and Ezra Pound.

Praised by Eliot as "one of those few who have done the language some service," Moore quickly made a reputation among other poets. She won the *Dial* Award in 1924, and in 1925 was the object of discussion in five consecutive issues of *The Dial*. Her work, however, long remained little known to the public. The "beauty" that she sought was the product of an individualistic decorum, a discipline of self and art that yielded the quality she admired in the poem "The Monkey Puzzle" (*Selected Poems*, 1935) as "porcupinequilled, complicated starkness." The quilled and stark imagery was slow to attract admirers other than the *cognoscenti*, but she won the Levinson Prize from *Poetry* magazine in 1933 and the Shelley Memorial Award in 1941. She became a member of the American Academy of Arts and Letters in 1947.

By the 1950's, her work was receiving wide recognition. She had, indeed, a year of wonder in 1952, winning the National Book Award, the Bollingen Prize, and the Pulitzer Prize. She served as chancellor for the Academy of American Poets from 1952 to 1964. She received the Academy of American Poets Fellowship in 1965 and the Frost Medal from the Poetry Society of America in 1967. Some of her poems have appeared in every reasonably comprehensive anthology of modern verse. Either the 1935 or the 1967 version of "Poetry" is almost always included. Other choices vary: "The Pangolin," "What Are Years?," "Virginia Britannia," and "A Grave" are among those poems most frequently anthologized.

Biography

The relaxation in Marianne Craig Moore's later verse and the rise of public acclaim demonstrate that late in her life the poetic self that had begun in a reticence that approached diffidence, that had armored itself as much against temptation from within as against threat from without, had burst through its early encasements to take on the role of moralist and even of sociopolitical adviser. A degree of tolerance for the self and the world perhaps made her choices easier, although it did not always benefit her art.

Moore seems to have had an inborn disdain for the self-indulgent. After a girlhood in Missouri and Pennsylvania and an education at Bryn Mawr College, she taught commercial subjects at the United States Indian School in Carlisle, Pennsylvania, for three and a half years while perfecting her art as a poet. Her verse began to appear in *The Egoist* (London), *Poetry*, and other journals of the new poetry. By 1918, she had settled in Manhattan and become a member of the literary circle that included William Carlos

Marianne Moore
(Library of Congress)

Williams, Wallace Stevens, and Alfred Kreymborg. Her first volume, *Poems*, was brought out in London in 1921. The period of the Dial Award was followed by her appointment in 1925 as an editor—soon to be editor-in-chief—of *The Dial*. She guided the journal through its heyday as the premier American periodical of literature and the arts. The work excited her, demonstrated her firm taste, and made her acquainted with most of the prominent writers of the time. After *The Dial* was discontinued in 1928, Moore never again worked at a salaried job. Although she earned occasional small checks for verse and reviews, her career as a writer, according to Driver, was subsidized by the former backers of *The Dial*. In the same year that the publication ended, Moore and her mother—a close adviser until her death in 1947—moved to Brooklyn, where the poet's brother John, a Navy chaplain, was stationed.

Useful though it was, the period with *The Dial* was an interruption. Moore had published *Observations* before going to work on the journal; her next book, *Selected Poems*, did not appear until 1935. This volume reprinted several pieces from earlier books and also some more recent work from magazines. The slim *The Pangolin, and Other Verse* appeared in 1936. Moore lived quietly for the next two decades, publishing additional thin volumes. In the 1950's, the growing acceptance of modernism and the approval indicated by her numerous awards helped bring public attention; she became, indeed, something of a celebrity. Doubtless interest was furthered by her darting and witty conversation with interviewers, as well as her shrewd adoption of a three-cornered hat as a badge of eccentricity. It became routine to see a photo story in *Life* magazine on Moore's trip to the zoo, to read of her as unofficial hostess for the mayor of New York, and to find *The New Yorker* printing the hilarious exchange of letters that resulted from the request in 1955 that she think up names for a new model from Ford. (The final choice—not one of her suggestions—was "Edsel.") When in 1965 she left her Brooklyn apartment for one in Manhattan, the move was recorded on the front page of *The New York Times*.

However, Moore could never be accused of self-importance. She enjoyed attention, but was wary—"I am often taken advantage of," she said—and continued to work at essays, reviews, and poetry. In some of her late verse, she is sententious or playful. In other pieces, she continues to focus on an object, a "thing" that provides her with observable fact that she can carpenter into an aesthetic stairway, a means of rising to discovery. Readers will frequently find in the work of her early and middle decades, and sometimes even in her late poems, the delight, the quilled beauty that is her legacy.

Analysis

In Marianne Moore's best work the imagined and the perceived are interdependent; she merges the two to create her usefully idiosyncratic reality. Often she finds in her universe suggestions of ethical principle. When she integrates statement of principle with sufficient circumstance, she makes the presentation seem not merely a lesson but also a fundamental component of the aesthetic structure of her world.

That "we"—speakers of English, one supposes—have not successfully integrated the world of imagination with that of the senses is part of the closing observation in her best-known poem, the 1935 version of "Poetry." This piece unfortunately has been the victim of ill-advised revision. Its argument was clear in the 1921 printing; after publishing a much-altered version in her 1924 book, Moore in 1935 returned to the 1921 version. The 1935 printing, however, introduced an ambiguity that illustrates how much may depend on so supposedly trivial a device as a punctuation mark.

The 1935 version, the one that became well known, opens with a first line that seems to dismiss poetry as "all this fiddle." This is best taken as a bit of rueful humor about Moore's own dedication, since she clearly was in no way contemptuous of her art. The poetry she likes is that which contains the "genuine," a quality that she shows by example and then by assertion to be equivalent to "useful." In what is perhaps a caution against the dangers of her own frequent practice of working from pictures or written descriptions rather than from firsthand experience, she remarks that the too "derivative" may become "unintelligible," and adds that people do not admire "what they cannot understand." In the 1921 version, a period followed "understand," making it clear that the next several examples that the poem gives are included in the "phenomena" mentioned in line 18. After "understand" in the 1935 version, Moore puts a colon, seeming to indicate that the content of the following lines is to be taken as examples of objects that, because they are unintelligible, are not admired. This material, however, consists of several notations of the sort of exact reality that Moore likes to use—a "tireless" wolf, a "twitching critic"—and lines 16 to 18 accept the usefulness of such detail by declaring that, together with other matter, all such "phenomena" are important.

The reader not deterred by the apparent contradiction will next find a warning that mere specification of "phenomena" does not make art, followed by the observation that real poetry is not yet with "us," that it will arise only when poets become "literalists of the imagination" who produce "imaginary gardens with real toads in them." This much-discussed phrase is a careful statement of her own intention: to disclose the universe ("imaginary gardens") suggested by the objects perceived by the senses (such as "real toads"). The ending remark is that "in the meantime" the reader will have to be satisfied with one or the other of the two components of true art: raw material in "all its rawness" and "the genuine." The real poet, it appears, will be the one who merges these elements.

"Poetry" is uncharacteristically broad in its interests. Moore's usual stance in her early work is that of one on guard against threat, controlling and armoring the self. She sees humankind as living in danger, as though over an abyss, an emptiness largely composed of people's ignorance of purpose or significances, together with a suggestion that the universe, insofar as it may heed humankind at all, is indifferent or hostile. One must be rock-hard, alert, wary. In "The Fish" (*Poems*) she portrays the dark colorations, the lack of hiding places, the "iron edge" of the forces that impel life-forms into seemingly chaotic motion. Yet these life-forms represent the intelligence, the consciousness of an enduring cliff of reality and of spirit that withstands all "abuse" and "accident." The view is ultimately optimistic; but the optimism is sparse, the opponent determined, grim, almost victorious. The sense of threat, of a necessary caution in attempts to profit from or even to understand the oceanic indifference that surrounds humankind, is emphasized in "A Grave" (*Observations*). Here the "sea," the abyss of, perhaps, the universe, society, or self-indulgence, offers the incautious nothing but a grave; it subdues the rapacious with its own superior rapacity; it lies under all activity of humans and bird and shell, and, though people may at times create a harmony that seems to deny its power, in the end it extinguishes all that is "dropped," that thoughtlessly stumbles into it.

One protection is decorum, a discipline that keeps focus on the essential, that avoids all gluttony and greed. Moore frequently celebrates objects, creatures, and places that exemplify this spare rectitude. Thus, she presents as an appropriate home for humankind the town that has an abundance of delights but no excess, the town of "The Steeple-Jack" (*Selected Poems*). The excess that Moore criticizes is that of the artifice that is too clever, too luxuriant in ornament and ingenuity. In "The Jerboa" (*Selected Poems*), stanzas headed "Too Much" condemn the wealth of Egyptian courtiers who accumulated luxuries while poverty and drought afflicted the common people; stanzas headed "Abundance" celebrate the true wealth of the jerboa, the self-sufficient rodent that, unlike the pharaoh's overindulged mongoose, knows a natural "rest" in its desert home. In such early poems, Moore finds in the relatively uncomplicated lives of animals, usually exotic ones that have no traditional symbolism in the English-speaking world, and occasionally in examples from the worlds of flora and of human craftsmanship, the delight that arises from the primary values she recommends. These are the values that make for survival in a world of hard requirements: honesty in function and behavior, modest simplicity in bearing, and courage.

STYLE

The combination of discipline and excitement, of decorum and ardor, is supported by Moore's style. Instead of using the accentual-syllabic measure that determines the length of lines in most poetry in English—a repetitive arrangement of stressed syllables that gives verse a sound quite different from prose—Moore counts syllables. This gives her the freedom to use the syntax normal to prose. Her syntax is at times exotic, but this results from her fondness for ellipses and abrupt juxtapositions that require of the reader some of the dexterity of her own perception. The syllabic measure enables her to use feminine rhyme, which puts the stress on syllables other than those that rhyme. She commonly parallels line lengths from stanza to stanza. In "The Jerboa," for example, the first and second lines of each stanza have five syllables, the third lines each have six, the fourth lines have eleven, and similar parallelism is maintained throughout. She also indents to put together those lines that rhyme. Internal correspondences of sound are frequent. Despite this workmanship, however, the effects are almost entirely visual: Read aloud, a Moore poem sounds like thoughtful prose. Yet the suggestion of verse is there; and it is strengthened by Moore's obvious delight in accumulating specific, colorful detail. Fastidious, seemingly reticent, avoiding the glaring and the grotesque, gaining impact by conveying the sense of tightly controlled, unsentimental emotion, the style suggests possibilities for a verse that English has not yet fully exploited.

THEMES

The theme of most of Moore's early work is summed up in "An Octopus" (*Selected Poems*) as "relentless accuracy." Although in the poetry that she published in mid-career she continues to emphasize need for discipline and heroic behavior, she begins to relent a bit, to add to her exposition an emphasis on love and spiritual grace. She always gives particulars, grounding cautionary generalization firmly in sensory reality. She no longer limits her typical poem to one "thing," one animal or object, however, and she more often considers directly the human behavior that is the underlying subject.

THE PANGOLIN, AND OTHER VERSE

The broadening of range shows in the great poem "The Pangolin" (*The Pangolin, and Other Verse*), an admiration of the interrelationships of grace as that quality is seen in the observed features of the animal, the architecture and stone ornamentation of a cathedral, and the behavior of humans when "kindly" toward one another. In such "splendour," Moore finds a suggestion of the spiritual. The poem is a marvelous interweaving of delighted observations of the animal, appreciative examination of the cathedral, recognition of humanity's "vileness" but also of its "excellence," and intimation, by question and by assertion of renewal, of the existence of a grace beyond the mundane.

Other poems from *The Pangolin, and Other Verse* show similar acceptance of a world beyond the self. Intricate and skillful interweaving of detail and unobtrusive comment makes "Virginia Britannia" a celebration of the possibilities of the American continent, leading to the question: "How could man ignore and destroy?" In "Smooth Gnarled Crape Myrtle"—the title hints at paradox—the poet ends with a rueful "Alas!" for humankind, the creatures who in artifice honor the peace, plenty, and wisdom, the friendship and love, that they do not in fact allow to direct their behavior. In "Spenser's Ireland" (*What Are Years*), a gentler humor accepts certain peculiarities as native to the Irish (among whom the poet lists herself), even while the poem renews Moore's frequent assertion that one is never really free until or unless one is "captive" to a "supreme belief."

"WHAT ARE YEARS?"

The poem "What Are Years?" is Moore's most direct presentation of her values. Perhaps too direct for some tastes, it appeals to others by its accessibility. After noting that people cannot understand the nature of their guilt or innocence, but that all are "naked" to the dangers of existence, the speaker moves on to define courage as "resolute doubt," the strength of spirit to remain strong even when defeated. The chief exponent of such strength is the one who "accedes to mortality," who accepts the fact of death and yet struggles to live, keeps returning to the struggle even though imprisoned in a world of mortality. An ambiguous "So" begins the last stanza: One who feels strongly, who is intensely aware of mortality, "behaves," keeps the ego disciplined. The pattern is that of the caged bird who, though captive, continues to sing. Despite his lack of "satisfaction," presumably of desire for flight and freedom, he knows "joy," the spiritual strength to go on living and to triumph over circumstance. This joyous discipline, it appears, "is" mortality, is knowledge of death, yet also "is" eternity, awareness of something beyond the mortal.

"NEVERTHELESS"

Survival calls, above all, for fortitude, the quality honored in "Nevertheless" (*Nevertheless*). Here the speaker's admiring delight in the way plant life manages to survive, not by withdrawing but by reaching out, by extending its growth, leads to the observation that to achieve "victory" one cannot be merely passive; one must "go/ to it." Two of Moore's most delightful poems are "A Carriage from Sweden," applauding the "unannoying/ romance" of the decorative yet functional cart that the speaker has seen in a museum; and "The Mind Is an Enchanting Thing," celebrating the play of the human mind that is both "trued" by belief and complex enough to experience "conscientious inconsistency."

"In Distrust of Merits"

"In Distrust of Merits" praises the sacrifices of Allied soldiers in World War II; the speaker contrasts hate and love, declares that the worst of enemies is the self, and, vowing never to hate people of other skin colors or religions, decries the error of hate and egocentrism. The speaker then backs up: Presumably those who love are "not competent" to make such vows until they have replaced with "life" the scene of death that has resulted from their neglect of others. The guilt is shared by everyone, for wars are "inward." The speaker must learn to live for the beauty that arises from patient (that is, thoughtful and loving) action, not as the "dust," the human being who lives in arrogance.

The 1950's

Moore wrote no long poems. Although in her work of the 1950's she appears to have moved away from reticence, she still often prefers to attribute declarative or striking statements to someone else: Few poets have been as given to the indirect, sometimes oblique, view of experience afforded by use of quotations, photographs, and other products of someone else's observation. Moore likes to approach at second hand, so to speak, to comment on and to expand the significance that she finds suggested or confirmed by others. Most such material she takes from her reading, but in some cases one may suspect that she puts quotation marks around a phrase of her own that she wants to hold up for inspection without seeming to impose herself on the reader. This fondness for operating at one remove from the subject is one reason that she would find work as a translator congenial.

Selected Fables of La Fontaine

It is not surprising to note that in 1945, after W. H. Auden proposed to a publisher that Moore translate the *Fables choisies, mises en vers* (1668-1694) of the French poet Jean de La Fontaine, Moore began what became an eight-year labor of translation, amounting to two and a half times as much verse as she printed in the *Collected Poems* (1951).

Moore's approach is not the literal translation often demanded by the language teacher, but it remains closer to the original than do most of the translations of, for example, Ezra Pound or Robert Lowell. She was attracted to the task because of La Fontaine's craftsmanship and, one may assume, because his skeptical, world-weary examples of competitive behavior in a sophisticated world of affairs provided vicarious experience of a world with which Moore had little direct contact. Hugh Kenner praised her for discovering "a badly needed idiom, urbane without slickness and brisk without imprecision"; and Donald Hall found that her versions have a "fire of visual imagery" that is lacking in the originals. Laurence Stapleton observed that, good as they are, *Selected Fables of La Fontaine* (1955) took her on "a detour from her own best work."

Whatever her hopes that *Selected Fables of La Fontaine* might expand her scope, Moore's last three volumes continue to explore her familiar themes: resistance to threat and intrusion, admiration for the disciplined and delightful. She adds, however, much of what used to be called occasional verse, prompted by some event of the moment.

LIKE A BULWARK

The poems of *Like a Bulwark* show these late tendencies. The title poem admires one "firmed" by the assault of fate, leaned and strengthened by his sturdy resistance. Delight in a certain complexity in existence appears in "Then the Ermine": In a quotation that Moore may have devised, she describes the ermine's color as "ebony violet." In "The Sycamore," this pleasure in the parti-colored expands to glorification of "anything in motley." Too often overlooked is "Apparition of Splendor," wherein works of art, the forests of the earth, and traditional fairy tales all contribute to celebrate the courage of the porcupine, which defends itself without aggression. Observation of particulars in skating, tennis, dancing, music, canoeing, pomology, and painting lead in "Style" to an exclamation of joy as the speaker rapturously contemplates artistry wherever it occurs.

CHRISTIAN IMAGES

Several poems make direct use of Christian tradition, although their intention is not to argue specific doctrine but to use this tradition as a vehicle for values. In "Rosemary," Moore represents beauty and love as enwreathed to form "a kind of Christmas-tree," a celebration of Christ's birth. "Blessed Is the Man" may be viewed as a version of the beatitudes, Moore's metrical objections to the intemperate and her praise of the "unaccommodating" man who has faith in the unseen.

TELL ME, TELL ME

In some poems of *Tell Me, Tell Me*, Moore's last book made up primarily of new poems, ardor is as warm as ever. "Arthur Mitchell," a brief admiration of a dancer, shapes its stanzas to imitate the twirl of the performer. The closing imagery of "Sun" (a poem first published in 1916) implies comparison of the power of the sun—standing, one deduces, for courage of spirit—to a work of spiritual art, a gorgeously wrought hour-glass. The poem is almost a prayer: The speaker appeals to "Sun" to eradicate the "hostility"

163

found in "this meeting-place of surging enmity," this world, or, even, one's own soul.

The reprinting of "Sun" implies a continuity of thought and feeling. Moore seems, however, to have been conscious of a lessening of her powers. "The Mind, Intractable Thing" is, despite its seemingly playful title, a saddening poem when compared with the sprightly dance of feeling in the earlier "The Mind Is an Enchanting Thing." In the late poem, the speaker still exclaims over her subject, but the details are autumnal, the delight colored by near despair as she complains that the "mind" does not help her, that she does not know how to "deal with" terror and wordcraft. One need not take the poem too literally for, as the several good poems in the volume show, Moore retained great abilities to the end of her life.

CRITICAL RECEPTION

Following the discovery in the 1960's that Moore's work was not, after all, impenetrable, book-length studies are accumulating, and the school anthologies that give most Americans the only experience they have with good poetry regularly print some of her poems. The proselike surface of her art is now understood to be supported by a skill with diction and metrics that, as she put it, is "galvanized against inertia." Most poet-critics have continued to be admiring. Randall Jarrell declared that Moore discovered "a new sort of subject" and "a new sort of connection and structure for it," and John Ashbery speculated that she would eventually be ranked as the best American modernist poet.

Moore has had detractors, of course. In her early years, such traditionalists as Louis Untermeyer and Margaret Anderson denigrated her work because it does not have the marked rhythm and heightened language that their Romantic taste demanded. Somewhat later, such middle-of-the-road critics as Oscar Cargill and Babette Deutsch gave her writing only carefully qualified praise. Feminists have struggled to accommodate Moore in their systems. Emily Stipes Watts declared that her reputation was "evaporating" because she followed what are in Watts's view masculine standards. Helen Vendler and Bonnie Costello admire her greatly and are rather possessive about her as a fellow member of what they see as their beleaguered gender, but they are bothered by male critics' applause, suspicious that such praise is only another tactic for putting a woman on a pedestal. Moore's work will survive the obtuse and the silly. Quilled beauty may put off the timid, but it will nevertheless prevail, because by its rigor, grace, and artistry, it achieves aesthetic triumph.

OTHER MAJOR WORKS

PLAY: *The Absentee*, pb. 1962.
NONFICTION: *Predilections*, 1955.
TRANSLATION: *Selected Fables of La Fontaine*, 1955.
MISCELLANEOUS: *A Marianne Moore Reader*, 1961; *The Complete Prose of Marianne Moore*, 1986.

Bibliography

Bloome, Harold, ed. *Marianne Moore: Comprehensive Research and Study Guide.* Philadelphia: Chelsea House, 2004. A collection of essays on Moore's poetry and life. Contains critical analysis of "Poetry" and "Marriage."

Goodrich, Celeste. *Marianne Moore and Her Contemporaries.* Iowa City: University of Iowa Press, 1989. In some respects a study for specialists, this work does document the interactions between Moore and her more conspicuous male colleagues T. S. Eliot, Wallace Stevens, Ezra Pound, and William Carlos Williams. Fully documented and indexed, and includes a selected bibliography.

Gregory, Elizabeth, ed. *The Critical Response to Marianne Moore.* Westport, Conn.: Praeger, 2003. This volume brings together the critics' comments on Moore's work, from her earlier to later work, and also on her work as a whole.

Holley, Margaret. *The Poetry of Marianne Moore: A Study in Voice and Value.* New York: Cambridge University Press, 1987. This mainstay standard scholarly commentary on Moore's poetry is more readable and useful than most. It provides insights and persuasive interpretations. The biographical sketch is separate and concise, and the text also includes a chronology of publication, notes, an accurate bibliography, and an index.

Joyce, Elisabeth W. *Cultural Critique and Abstraction: Marianne Moore and the Avant-Garde.* Lewisburg, Pa.: Bucknell University Press, 1998. A critical assessment of Moore's work and her association with the avant-garde. Includes bibliographical references and index.

Leavell, Linda, Cristanne Miller, and Robin G. Schulze, eds. *Critics and Poets on Marianne Moore: "A Right Good Salvo of Barks."* Lewisburg, Pa.: Bucknell University Press, 2005. A collection of essays and other works on Moore and her works.

Miller, Cristanne. *Marianne Moore: Questions of Authority.* Cambridge, Mass.: Harvard University Press, 1995. Takes a feminist approach to reading Moore's poetry, analyzing how her female voice counters masculine views of poetic "authority."

Molesworth, Charles. *Marianne Moore: A Literary Life.* New York: Atheneum, 1990. Access to Moore's letters to her mother and brother provided Molesworth with valuable biographical material. The story of Moore's life revealed here shows how carefully she made decisions about each step she took. Sixteen pages of photographs, notes, and an index complete the work.

Stamy, Cynthia. *Marianne Moore and China: Orientalism and a Writing of America.* New York: Oxford University Press, 1999. Criticism and interpretation of Moore's poetry. Bibliography, index.

Stapleton, Laurence. *Marianne Moore: The Poet's Advance.* 1978. Reprint. Princeton, N.J.: Princeton University Press, 1999. Stapleton chronicles the continuity of Moore's "courageous act of self-exploration" in a detailed examination of her poems, essays, and translations. Includes notes and an index.

Willis, Patricia C., ed. *Marianne Moore: Woman and Poet*. Orono: National Poetry Foundation, University of Maine, 1990. This major work is invaluable for making possible an uncluttered view of the poet. It collects essays about Moore's life and writings from a kaleidoscopic array of perspectives and by a formidable battery of scholars. It also contains a complete and useful annotated bibliography.

Bernard F. Engel

THYLIAS MOSS

Born: Cleveland, Ohio; February 27, 1954

PRINCIPAL POETRY
Hosiery Seams on Bowlegged Women, 1983
Pyramid of Bone, 1989
At Redbones, 1990
Rainbow Remnants in Rock Bottom Ghetto Sky, 1991
Small Congregations: New and Selected Poems, 1993
Last Chance for the Tarzan Holler, 1998
Slave Moth: A Narrative in Verse, 2004
Tokyo Butter: A Search for Forms of Deirdre, 2006

OTHER LITERARY FORMS

Known primarily as a poet, Thylias Moss has also written a memoir, *Tale of a Sky-Blue Dress* (1998), and a children's picture book titled *I Want to Be*, published by Dial Books for Young Readers in 1993. Her *Slave Moth* is a novel written in verse.

ACHIEVEMENTS

Thylias Moss first won a poetry prize for "Coming of Age in Sandusky," which she entered in the Cleveland Public Library Poetry Contest in 1978. In 1983, her poems were collected into *Hosiery Seams on Bowlegged Women*, a volume commissioned by the Cleveland State University Poetry Center. She received a fellowship from the Artists Foundation of Massachusetts in 1987 and won a grant from the National Endowment for the Arts two years later. In 1989, *Pyramid of Bone* was a finalist for a National Book Critics Circle Award. Moss's "Interpretation of a Poem by Frost" appeared in *The Pushcart Prize XIV: Best of the Small Presses, 1989-1990*. In 1991, she won the Witter Bynner Prize for Poetry from the American Academy of Arts and Letters, the Whiting Writers' Award, and the Dewar's Profiles Performance Artist Award. Her *Rainbow Remnants in Rock Bottom Ghetto Sky* was selected for the National Poetry Series in 1990 and earned the Ohioana Book Award for Poetry in 1992. In 1995, she received a Guggenheim Fellowship and a MacArthur Fellowship. In 1998, *Last Chance for the Tarzan Holler* was named Best Book by the Village Voice and was a finalist for a National Book Critics Circle Award. In 2006, she received the Frederick Bock Prize from *Poetry* magazine.

BIOGRAPHY

Thylias Rebecca Brasier Moss was the only child of Calvin Brasier, a tire recapper, and Florida Brasier, a maid, both of whom adored her. In her memoir, *Tale of a Sky-Blue*

Dress, she describes how she learned about the dark side of human nature from a babysitter who abused the young girl emotionally, physically, and sexually. She was happy in school until the age of nine, when her family moved and her new surroundings caused her to become withdrawn. She married at the age of nineteen and spent two unhappy years at Syracuse University before leaving to work at a Cleveland business. She received a B.A. from Oberlin College in 1981 and an M.A. from the University of New Hampshire in 1983.

She was an instructor at Phillips Academy in Andover, Massachusetts, from 1984 to 1992, then joined the faculty of the University of Michigan at Ann Arbor in 1993. She settled in Ann Arbor with her husband and two sons. Moss has also served as a visiting professor at the University of New Hampshire at Durham and as a visiting poet at Brandeis University in Waltham, Massachusetts.

Analysis

Thylias Moss's poems have changed over the years, exhibiting an astonishing growth in control and complexity as well as new forms. Moss's early work is marked by strong portraits of racial bitterness and despair. *Hosiery Seams on Bowlegged Women*, her first book, attracted relatively little attention but was representative of the themes that Moss would pursue in later work: deep concern over the roles of women and minorities in society, a religious sensibility that is critical of the social and intellectual repression of conventional religion, and an examination of her own emotional states as she comes into contact with the various facets of life.

At Redbones

From the rage and honesty of her first two books, Moss moved to the slightly less negative tone of *At Redbones*, a collection that reflects the events and influences of her early years. These include the church she attended as a child and the family kitchen on Saturday nights, where her father would hold court, sipping whiskey and asking forbidden questions regarding the soul. "Redbones" is the mythical place that holds the poems, full of racial images and protest, together. It portrays a world dominated by old-fashioned racist images such as the character of Mammy in the film *Gone with the Wind* (1939) and the Aunt Jemima logo on maple syrup bottles. Moss's style began to receive critical praise with this book, due to her facility with puns and other kinds of wordplay. Her later work reflects a more tranquil mind and a strong interest in experimentation, as well as an acute grasp of psychology as shown in *Slave Moth*.

Small Congregations

The themes of *Small Congregations* are the ways religious symbolism informs everyday life, the mythology of African American life, and racism. Although the book is divided into three parts, there is a great overlap of subject matter between the sections.

Religious imagery informs many of them, including the opening poem of the collection, "Washing Bread," in which the children eat their crosses; "One Year Sonny Stabs Himself," an ironic poem of a child who stabs himself on the Christmas tree star; "The Manna Addicts," about the mysterious biblical substance; and "Spilled Sugar," a poem about her father in which Moss redefines the concept of God. The idea of "God" also appears in the closing poem of the anthology, "One for All Newborns," in which Moss states:

> The miracle was not birth but that I lived
>   despite my crimes.
> I treated God badly also; he is another parent
> watching his kids through a window, eager
>   to be proud
> of his creation, looking for signs of spring.

Some of her use of mythology turns the myth upside down. In "The Adversary," she says that Satan is the original Uncle Tom; in "The Wreckage on the Wall of Eggs," Moss interprets the nursery rhyme of Humpty Dumpty as a tale of segregation in which it is she who sits on the segregated wall, where life is not easy. In "November and Aunt Jemima," Aunt Jemima shows up at the Thanksgiving table as a guest, the target of pancakes thrown at her by whites whose sins are as invisible as her pain is.

Early signs of Moss's formal experimentation occur in this early collection, in such prose poems as "The Warmth of Hot Chocolate," "Renegade Angels," and "Denial." Included are an epistolary poem, "Dear Charles," which condenses all the experiences of African Americans into the answer to a letter; poems that are interspersed by choruses; and "The Best of the Body," in which sections named for "Spleen" and "Liver" are followed by a glorious linguistic riff on "Heart to Heart Talk."

SLAVE MOTH

Slave Moth is that rare literary item: a novel told in verse that has all the range and density of a novel combined with the sublime language of poetry. From the very first words of this remarkable novel, "My master is a collector/ Rare things delight him," readers know they are in an extraordinary environment. Varl, the fourteen-year-old daughter of Mamalee, turns out to be that rare thing herself, a slave who can read and write because her mother taught her. Mamalee is an educated slave who chooses to stay in captivity so that she can educate other slaves and help them escape. Varl was named after her master's horse of the same name, which died at the precise moment that the infant girl uttered her first birth cry, yet she shows nothing of the race horse's tamed spirit. In love with words, she stitches her thoughts into squares of cloth that she sews together and wears under her dress, a cocoon that she believes will someday turn into luna wings.

The other characters in *Slave Moth* are also unusual. Varl's master, Peter Perry, recognizes that Varl is a rare thing and delights in her, but because he made a vow to her mother to keep his hands off the girl, he has not touched her physically. Still, the dramatic tension between him and Varl is one of the axes around which the book revolves. Varl speaks her mind to Master Peter, going beyond the permitted level of expression allowed to slaves in antebellum Tennessee, yet he not only permits it but also is inflamed by it. In a remarkable scene in which Master Peter and his nephew, Bishop Adler, discover Varl embroidering her words on cloth in the woods, Peter comes so close to Varl that she becomes afraid yet is still defiant. The bolder she becomes, the greater his delight in her, until she finally calls Mamalee. The quarrel continues between Varl and her master, until Bishop Adler grows enraged at the liberties the slave is taking. As the scene rises in a crescendo, it combusts of its own energy and sears everyone involved. Varl realizes now just how much her master loves her and understands the depth of his threat.

Tokyo Butter

Tokyo Butter is more generous, detailed, and experimental than Moss's previous poetry collections. Bits of information from science, technology, the arts, and many other areas of life are juxtaposed in this rich stew of twenty-five poems, which is Moss's attempt to make sense of the sudden death of her cousin and friend, Deirdre. "Deirdre: A Search Engine," a ten-page poem that seems to be the center of the collection, is aptly named because the poem might indeed be the result of a search engine, which searches the Internet for any word or phrase the user might want to find that relates to a certain subject.

In long lines that seem to be tied together by free association, as items found in a search engine would be, Moss moves from Deirdre's wedding to her husband to the ghost of butter, which includes a basic recipe for herb butter that the writer tells us she brings to family gatherings, mostly funerals. The long poem about Deirdre includes some smaller poems rendered in italics that sometimes suggest another viewpoint, erratic spacing on the page, distracting asides, and a strong emphasis on the "butter" theme. The poem does not recognize boundaries and lacks any kind of prolonged connection. It is instead an exercise in radical inclusion of topics, tied together at the beginning and the end by the late Deirdre.

Moss's interest in experimental poetry has led her to create limited fork poetics, a theory of interacting language systems (mixing vision, sound, touch, and smell). In accordance with this theory, Moss has begun writing what she calls poams, products of acts of making. This theory is described in an afterword to *Tokyo Butter*, although it is not fully employed.

Other major works

NONFICTION: *Tale of a Sky-Blue Dress*, 1998 (memoir).
PLAYS: *The Dolls in the Basement*, pr. 1984; *Talking to Myself*, pr. 1984.
CHILDREN'S LITERATURE: *I Want to Be*, 1993.

Bibliography

Friedman, Paula. Review of *Tale of a Sky-Blue Dress*. *The New York Times Book Review*, September 13, 1998, p. 26. Praises the impressionistic writing in this memoir and discusses how the language enhances the experiences depicted.

Kitchen, Judith. "Poetry Reviews." Review of *Last Chance for the Tarzan Holler*. *Georgia Review* (Winter, 1998): 763-765. This extended review provides an in-depth discussion of Moss's style and technique.

Morris, Daniel Charles, and Felicia Friendly-Thomas. "The Poetry of Thylias Moss." In *Masterplots II: African American Literature*, edited by Tyrone Williams. Rev. ed. Pasadena, Calif.: Salem Press, 2009. Provides analysis of Moss's poetry, with attention to themes and meanings and the critical context.

Tracy, D. H. Review of *Tokyo Butter*. *Poetry* 189, no. 6 (March, 2007): 495-498. This reviewer's first impression is of an "avalanche of stuff," because of Moss's diverse topics and context shifts, and Tracy suggests that the poems might be better in a multimedia presentation. Moss's theory of limited fork poetics is discussed briefly.

Winston, Jay. "The Trickster Metaphysics of Thylias Moss." In *Trickster Lives: Culture and Myth in American Fiction*, edited by Jeanne Campbell Reesman. Athens: University of Georgia Press, 2001. This essay offers an analysis of Moss's work within the context of trickster literature. The trickster figure originated in Native American and African American traditions, and is used also in Asian American and Latino writing.

Sheila Golburgh Johnson

ALICIA SUSKIN OSTRIKER

Born: Brooklyn, New York; November 11, 1937

PRINCIPAL POETRY
Songs, 1969
A Dream of Springtime, 1979
The Mother/Child Papers, 1980
A Woman Under the Surface: Poems and Prose Poems, 1982
The Imaginary Lover, 1986
Green Age, 1989
The Crack in Everything, 1996
The Little Space: Poems Selected and New, 1968-1998, 1998
The Volcano Sequence, 2002
No Heaven, 2005

OTHER LITERARY FORMS

Alicia Suskin Ostriker (AHS-trih-kur) is as well known for her critical writings as she is for her poetry. Her doctoral dissertation became her first book, *Vision and Verse in William Blake* (1965). Ostriker's nonfiction books explore many of the same themes that influence her poetry. Her study of the poems of Sylvia Plath, Anne Sexton, H. D., May Swenson, and Adrienne Rich appeared in *Writing Like a Woman* (1983).

In her major study, *Stealing the Language: The Emergence of Women's Poetry in America* (1986), Ostriker probes the meanings of contemporary women's poetry since the 1960's. She traces the struggle of woman poets of the period to achieve self-definition in the context of a tradition designed to repress the female voice. *Stealing the Language* examines this new poetry in relation to its female roots and as an alternative to academic modernism, examining the poetics of body, anger, and violence as revisionist mythmaking in women's poetry.

In *The Nakedness of the Fathers: Biblical Visions and Revisions* (1994), Ostriker creates her own feminist midrash, and in *For the Love of God: The Bible as an Open Book* (2007), she reinterprets the Song of Songs, the Book of Ruth, Psalms, Ecclesiastes, Jonah, and Job. *Dancing at the Devil's Party: Essays on Poetry, Politics, and the Erotic* (2000) defines the difference between poetry and propaganda and surveys the aesthetic accomplishments of women's poetry. Other essays in this collection discuss politics, love, and the spiritual lives in the work of several prominent American poets.

ACHIEVEMENTS

Alicia Suskin Ostriker won the William Carlos Williams Award of the Poetry Society of America for *The Imaginary Lover*. *The Crack in Everything* was a National Book

Award finalist in 1996 and earned her the Paterson Poetry Award (1997) and the San Francisco State Poetry Center Award (1996). *The Little Space* was a 1998 National Book Award finalist.

Biography

Alicia Suskin Ostriker was born Alicia Suskin in Brooklyn, New York, to David Suskin and Beatrice Linnick Suskin. Both parents held degrees in English from Brooklyn College. Her father worked as a playground director for the New York City Department of Parks, and her mother tutored students in English and math, and later taught folk dancing. Her mother wrote poetry and read William Shakespeare and Robert Browning to her two daughters, Alicia, and a younger sister, Amy David, born in 1948.

Ostriker received a B.A. from Brandeis University in 1955, and in 1958, she married the astronomer Jeremiah P. Ostriker, with whom she had three children: Rebecca (1963), Eve (1965), and Gabriel (1970). She earned her M.A. (1961) and her Ph.D. (1964) from the University of Wisconsin. In 1965, she began to teach in the Rutgers University English Department, where she became a full professor.

Analysis

Alicia Suskin Ostriker has become an idol of the feminist movement, and she has also been called a Jewish poet, a visionary, a revolutionist, and an iconoclast. Her poetry fits into all these categories and yet transcends them. She is in love with both the natural and human-constructed world and somehow includes more of both in her work than most other poets do; however, there is an intimate thread that runs through each collection. By themselves, Ostriker's poems are alternately perceptive, startling, and beautiful, but in each collection, her poetry achieves a certain momentum, each poem building on the last to create a more complex reading experience than is found in any single poem.

The Mother/Child Papers

The Mother/Child Papers, written in the 1970's after the birth of her son during the Vietnam War and after four young people were killed at Kent State University by U.S. National Guards, has become a feminist classic. In this work, Ostriker confronts her personal tumult as she considers the world into which she has brought her son. Having a son during wartime was difficult for Ostriker, but she recounts that during his actual delivery, she experienced her own personal invasion: Medical staff overruled her wish for a natural childbirth, partially numbing her and exhibiting their need for control and domination. Worse yet, those in charge claimed that the procedure was for her own good. The thin volume was originally published by the small press Momentum Books but was reprinted in 2009 as part of the prestigious Pitt Poetry series by the University of Pittsburgh Press, with a new preface by the author.

The Volcano Sequence

The Volcano Sequence, a much later collection of poetry, reveals Ostriker's considerable knowledge of the Hebrew Bible, Jewish customs, and feminist theory. She explores the relationship between the human and divine, and considers profound spiritual questions. Although she deplores the Bible's historic marginalization of women, rather than abandoning the Bible, she challenges the tradition, argues with it, and somehow transforms it. This volume has identified Ostriker as one of the most important contemporary poets working in the visionary tradition of Blake and Allen Ginsberg, two poets who have had an influence on her work.

The Crack in Everything

The title of *The Crack in Everything* is taken from "Anthem," a song by the Canadian poet/songwriter Leonard Cohen, which contains the lines: "There is a crack, a crack in everything/ That's how the light gets in." The volume is divided into four uneven parts: Section 1 draws readers in with the first poem, "The Dogs at Live Oak Beach, Santa Cruz," a deceptively simple poem about dogs as they leap and plunge into the foaming sea, "for absolutely nothing but joy." However, the tone of the collection grows darker quickly. In such poems as "Surfer Days," "Migrant," "The Boys, the Broom Handle, the Retarded Girl," and especially the often anthologized "The Eighth and Thirteenth," Ostriker deals with death, depravity, and the scourge of war. Pain also is frequently present here, as in "Somalia" and "Disco."

Section 2 is one long poem, "The Book of Life," dedicated to Ostriker's friend, Sheila Solomon, that was written on Yom Kippur and uses the second-person singular, "you." Although the poem mentions many facets of Solomon's life, it also includes meditations on the Days of Awe, the role of women artists, and another deceased friend, Cynthia. Both personal and universal, the poem is interspersed with biblical quotations that Ostriker uses to comment on the place of women and the mysteries of religion.

The last section of the book, "The Mastectomy Poems," is a remarkable collection of poems that take readers through the most intimate details of the author's surgery. Through poems such as "The Bridge," "The Gurney," "Riddle: Post-Op," and "What Was Lost," readers follow Ostriker's inmost thoughts through the stages of the operation so closely that they are almost able to experience it with her. However, in "Normal," a poem near the end of the book, Ostriker presents an excruciating description of her wound and ends the poem with an ironic reference to the lost breast: "Never invite my colleagues/ To view it pickled in a mason jar."

The Little Space

The Little Space provides an excellent introduction to Ostriker's work as it contains the best poems from different stages of her career. The work collects poems from *A Dream of Springtime*, *The Mother/Child Papers*, *A Woman Under the Surface*, *The*

Imaginary Lover, *Green Age*, and *The Crack in Everything*, as well as nine poems under the heading "Uncollected and New Poems (1980-1998)."

In "April One," the first of the uncollected and new poems, the poet, who is in her mid-forties, is bicycling through Princeton on a sunny day following four days of rain and snow. Ostriker savors the beautiful spring day, telling us she feels "capacious and insatiable as the sea." She even mentions her students, "the ones who are not idiotic, who write poetry like whipped cream," as part of the joy she is experiencing. She is giddy with spring, and she is not nursing her grievances, which she lists; she even describes the errand she is doing, visiting her mother on Witherspoon Street to give back her mother's poems. A flower motif runs through "April One": Ostriker notices the crocuses she passes on her bicycle, chats with her mother about her flowers, and by the end of the poem, admits, "I am this blue-veined crocus/ straightening up on her spine/ today without effort I hold up my half of the sky." Written on April 1, 1980, the poem is ecstatic and visionary; yet in true Ostriker style, she cannot resist the dark note. The poem ends with the lines, "And under the ground/ Even the lost people are combing their hair."

NO HEAVEN

In *No Heaven*, which begins by repeating the lyrics from John Lennon's song "Imagine" on its dedication page—"Imagine there's no heaven/ it's easy if you try,/ No hell below us/ Above Us Only Sky"—Ostriker is as iconoclastic, ironic, and honest as an older woman can be, having survived the ups and downs of a long life. *No Heaven* is organized into four parts, each of which forms a thematic whole. The first section, "Here and Now," includes nostalgic poems of marriage and the city. The next, brief section, "Archival," is made up of previously uncollected poems, several of which extend the motif of conjugal relations. This section ends with two lovely nature poems, "Mid-February" and "Coastal Dawn," which suggest transience while intimately drawing in the reader.

The third section, "Material Density," contains poems inspired by various art forms and their creators, seen through a poet's astute eyes. Ostriker depicts the creations of various artists—paintings by Pierre Bonnard, Jean-Baptiste-Camille Corot, and Caravaggio as well as musical compositions by Robert Schumann and Maurice Ravel—in words that almost challenge the power of these works in their original media. In every one of these poems, Ostriker not only makes the reader wish to experience the artwork in the original but also creates a linguistic analogue.

The final section, "Tearing the Poem Up," engages the dark side of American life. In "Walker in the City," Ostriker catalogs New York crimes so appalling that the reader may remember them from old newspaper headlines. Fury at the killing of Vietnam War protesters, the horrors of World War II, and the ironies of deaths in Israel all find a place in this section. The theme of this final section is what it means to be an "innocent" American in a world racked by violence. The last poem, "Daffodils," brings readers to the war in Iraq. As she often does, Ostriker creates a synthesis, fusing the sublime and the base. On the day the war started, the poet tells the reader, she was photographing flowers, and she suggests that it is people's business to defend the sublime, even on the day a war starts. For this accomplished writer, poetry itself is the defense of life in the midst of debilitating horrors.

Other major works

NONFICTION: *Vision and Verse in William Blake*, 1965; *Writing Like a Woman*, 1983; *Stealing the Language: The Emergence of Women's Poetry in America*, 1986; *Feminist Revision and the Bible*, 1992; *The Nakedness of the Fathers: Biblical Visions and Revisions*, 1994; *Dancing at the Devil's Party: Essays on Poetry, Politics, and the Erotic*, 2000; *For the Love of God: The Bible as an Open Book*, 2007.

EDITED TEXT: *William Blake: The Complete Poems*, 1977.

Bibliography

Barron, Jonathan N., and E. Murphy Selinger, eds. *Jewish American Poetry: Poems, Commentary, and Reflections.* Hanover, N.H.: University Press of New England, 2000. This work, part of the Brandeis series in American Jewish History, includes Ostriker's "The Eighth and Thirteenth," along with a remarkable commentary by the poet, dealing with the question of what makes Jewish poetry "Jewish."

Frost, Elisabeth A., and Cynthia Hogue, eds. *Innovative Women Poets: An Anthology of Contemporary Poets and Interviews.* Iowa City: University of Iowa Press, 2006. Contains an interview by Hogue of Ostriker and a brief biography of Ostriker and a selection of her poems. Provides a look at Ostriker's views of poetry.

Kelly, David, ed. *Poetry for Students.* Vol. 26. Detroit: Thomson/Gale, 2007. Contains an analysis of Ostriker's poem "Mastectomy."

Ostriker, Alicia. Interview by Gary Pacernick. In *Meaning and Memory: Interviews with Fourteen Jewish Poets*, edited by Pacernick. Columbus: Ohio State University Press, 2001. Ostriker discusses the loneliness of the writer, the many facets of language, and other provocative topics.

_____. Introduction to *Poetry After 9/11: An Anthology of New York Poets*, edited by Dennis Loy Johnson and Valerie Merians. Hoboken, N.J.: Melville House, 2002. Discusses the importance of poetry as a medium that stretches and contracts to mirror the age.

Sheila Golburgh Johnson

SYLVIA PLATH

Born: Boston, Massachusetts; October 27, 1932
Died: London, England; February 11, 1963
Also known as: Victoria Lucas

PRINCIPAL POETRY
The Colossus, and Other Poems, 1960
Three Women, 1962
Ariel, 1965 (revised as *Ariel: The Restored Edition*, 2004)
Uncollected Poems, 1965
Crossing the Water, 1971
Crystal Gazer, 1971
Fiesta Melons, 1971
Lyonesse, 1971
Winter Trees, 1971
Pursuit, 1973
The Collected Poems, 1981 (Ted Hughes, editor)
Selected Poems, 1985
Sylvia Plath: Poems, 2000 (Hughes, editor)

OTHER LITERARY FORMS

Sylvia Plath was a prolific writer of poetry and prose. Her first publication was a short story, "Sunday at the Mintons'," which appeared in *Mademoiselle* in 1952. Throughout the remainder of her life, her stories and prose sketches appeared almost yearly in various journals and magazines. Ted Hughes edited a selection of these prose works, *Johnny Panic and the Bible of Dreams* (1977-1979). Plath's extensive diaries and journals were also edited by Hughes; they were published as *The Journals of Sylvia Plath* in 1982. Her mother has edited a collection of letters written by Plath to her between 1950 and 1963, *Letters Home* (1975). Plath's work in other forms included a poetic drama, *Three Women*, that was aired on the BBC on August 19, 1962; an autobiographical novel, *The Bell Jar*, published under the pseudonym Victoria Lucas (1963); and a popular children's book, *The Bed Book* (1976).

ACHIEVEMENTS

Sylvia Plath's poetry, like that of Hart Crane, will be read, studied, and known for two reasons: for its intrinsic merit, and for its bearing on her suicide. In spite of efforts to disentangle her poetry from her life and death, Plath's reputation and impact have fluctuated with public interest in her suicide. Almost immediately after her death, she was adopted by many members of the feminist movement as an emblem of the female in a male-dominated world; her death was lamented, condemned, criticized, and analyzed as a symbolic gesture as well as an inevitable consequence of her socialization. Explanations for her acute mental anguish were often subsumed in larger arguments about her archetypal sacrifice.

With the publication of *The Bell Jar* and the posthumous collections of poetry, however, her audience grew in diversity and appreciation. She received the Bess Hokin Prize from *Poetry* magazine in 1957, and *The Collected Poems* was awarded the Pulitzer Prize in poetry in 1982. Although she never lost her value to the feminist movement, she gained other sympathetic readers who attempted to place her in a social and cultural context that would help to explain—although certainly not definitively—her artistic success and her decision to end her life.

It is not difficult to understand why Plath has won the respect of a wider audience. Her poems transcend ideology. Vivid, immediate re-creations of mental collapse, they are remnants of a psyche torn by severely conflicting forces. However, Plath's poems are not merely re-creations of nightmares; were they only that, they would hardly be distinguishable from reams of psychological case histories. Plath's great achievement was her ability to transform the experience into art without losing its nightmarish immediacy.

To retain that immediacy, Plath sometimes exceeded what many readers consider "good taste" or "aesthetic appropriateness"; she has even been convicted of trivializing universal suffering to the level of individual "bitchiness." The texture of her poetry demands closer scrutiny than such judgments permit, for Plath was one of the few poets to adhere to Theodor Adorno's dictum: "To write lyric poetry after Auschwitz is barbaric." In one sense, Plath redefined lyric by using that mode in a unique way. Plath's Auschwitz was personal but no less terrifying to her than was the horror of the German death camps to the millions who died there and the millions who learned of them later. For Plath, as for the inmates of Auschwitz, survival became paramount, but her Nazis were deep in her own psyche and her poetry became a kind of prayer, a ritual to remind her of her identity in a world gone mad. As a record of such experiences, Plath's poetry is unexcelled in any tradition.

Biography

Few poets demand that we know as much about their lives as Sylvia Plath does. Her intensely personal poetry was often rooted in everyday experiences, the knowledge of which can often open obscure references or cryptic images to fuller meaning for the reader.

Plath's father, Otto, was reared in the German town of Grabow and emigrated to the United States at the age of fifteen. He spoke German, Polish, and French, and later majored in classical languages at Northwestern University. In 1928, he received his doctor of science degree in applied biology from Harvard University. He taught at Boston University, where he met Aurelia Schober, whom he married in January, 1932. In 1934, his doctoral thesis was published by Macmillan as *Bumblebees and Their Ways*, and he became recognized as an authority on this subject. Beginning about 1935, Otto's health declined; he stubbornly refused any kind of medical treatment, assuming his illness to be lung cancer. When, in August, 1940, he stubbed his toe and suffered immediate complications, he submitted to medical examination. He was diagnosed as suffering from diabetes mellitus, a disease he could possibly have conquered had he sought treatment earlier. The condition of his toe worsened, however, and on October 12, his leg was amputated. He died on November 5 from a pulmonary embolus.

Plath's mother had also been a teacher—of English and German. At Otto's request, she gave up her career and devoted her time to housekeeping. Of Austrian ancestry, she too spoke German as a child and took great interest in Otto's scientific research and writing as well as in her own reading and in the teaching of her children.

Plath's early years were spent near the sea in her native Massachusetts, where she passed much of her time with her younger brother, Warren, exploring the beaches near their home. A very bright student, she consistently received high grades in virtually all her subjects and won many awards.

In September, 1950, Plath began her freshman year at Smith College in Massachusetts, the recipient of a scholarship. She continued her brilliant academic record, and at the end of her third year, she was named guest managing editor of *Mademoiselle* and given a month's "working vacation" in New York. In August, 1953, after returning from New York, she suffered a nervous breakdown and attempted suicide. She was hospitalized and given shock treatments and psychotherapy. She returned to Smith for her senior year in February, 1954.

Plath won a full scholarship to study German at Harvard in the summer of 1954. She returned to Smith in September; in January, 1955, she submitted her English honors thesis, "The Magic Mirror: A Study of the Double in Two of Dostoevsky's Novels," and graduated summa cum laude in June. She won a Fulbright Fellowship to study at Newnham College, Cambridge University, and sailed for England in September.

After one semester of study, she briefly toured London and then went to Paris to spend the Christmas break. Back in Cambridge, she met Ted Hughes at a party on February 25, 1956. They were married on June 16 in London. That summer, she and Hughes toured France and Spain. She was awarded a second year on her Fulbright; Hughes began teaching at a secondary school. She completed her year of study, and in 1957, she submitted her manuscript of poetry, "Two Lovers and a Beachcomber," for the English tripos and M.A. degree at Newnham College. In June, 1957, she and Hughes sailed for the United States, where she would be an instructor in freshman English at Smith College. She enjoyed her teaching and was regarded as an excellent instructor, but the strain of grading essays led her to abandon the academic world after one year. She and Hughes remained in Boston for the following year, both trying to earn a living by writing and part-time work. In the spring of 1959, Hughes was given a Guggenheim Fellowship; meanwhile, Plath was attending Robert Lowell's seminars on poetry at Boston University.

In December of 1959, the couple returned to England, settling in London after a brief visit to Hughes's Yorkshire home. Plath was pregnant with her first child, and it was during these months in early spring that she learned of the acceptance by William Heinemann of her first book of poems, *The Colossus, and Other Poems*, for publication in the fall. On April 1, Plath gave birth to her daughter, Frieda. Her book was published in October, to generally favorable reviews.

In February, 1961, Plath suffered a miscarriage, and in March, she underwent an appendectomy. That summer, Plath and Hughes purchased a house in Croton, Devon, and went to France for a brief vacation. In August, they moved into their house in Devon, and in November, Plath was given a grant to enable her to work on *The Bell Jar*.

On January 17, 1962, Plath gave birth to her second child, Nicholas. Within a period of ten days in April, she composed six poems, a sign of her growing desire to fit into the village life of Croton and of her returning poetic voice.

In June, Plath's mother arrived from the United States and remained until August. In July, Plath learned of Hughes's affair with Assia Gutman. On September 11, Plath and Hughes journeyed to Ireland; almost immediately Hughes left Plath and went to London to live with Gutman. Plath returned alone to Devon, where, with her children, she attempted to rebuild her life. She wrote extensively: twenty-three poems in October, ten in November. She decided, however, that she could not face another winter in Devon, so she found a flat in London and moved there with her children in the middle of December.

That winter proved to be one of the worst on record, and life in the flat became intolerable. The children were ill, the weather was cold, there was little heat, the pipes had frozen, and Plath was suffering extremes of depression over her separation from Hughes. On January 14, 1963, *The Bell Jar* was published to only lukewarm reviews. Plath's mood worsened. On February 11, 1963, she committed suicide in the kitchen of her flat.

Analysis

In many ways, Sylvia Plath as a poet defies categorization. She has been variously described as a lyricist, a confessionalist, a symbolist, an imagist, and a mere diarist, but none of these terms can adequately convey the richness of approach and content of her work. Perhaps the proper way to identify Plath is not through a process of exclusive labeling but through inclusion and synthesis. All these terms aptly describe the various modes of discourse that work effectively in her poetry and her prose.

She was definitely a lyricist, capable of creating great verbal beauty to match feelings of peace and tranquillity. Her lyricism can range from a simple but effective evocation of a Spanish sunrise ("Southern Sunrise") in which adjectives and metaphors balance finely against the simple intent of the word-picture, to a very Hopkinsian ode for her beloved ("Ode for Ted"), in which a blending of delicacy of emotion with startling diction is achieved. Even toward the end of her tortured life, she was able to return to this mode in a few of her last poems, the finest of which is "Nick and the Candlestick," in which transcending not only the usual maudlin and mawkish treatment of maternal love but her own emotional plight as well, she is able to re-create a moment of genuine tenderness that emerges from her wholly realistic viewing of herself and her young son. This lyrical trait was not restricted to whole poems; quite often, in the midst of utter frustration and despair, Plath creates images or sounds of great beauty.

Plath's poetry is largely confessional, even when it is lyrical. Most of her confessional poetry, however, is not at all lyrical. Especially in her last years, she used this mode frequently, personally, and often viciously. She seldom bothered to create a persona through whom she could project feelings; rather, she simply expressed her feelings in open, exposed, even raw ways, leaving her self equally exposed. One such poem is "The Jailer," written after her separation from Hughes. The focus is the authorial "I," which occurs twelve times (together with the pronouns "my" and "me," which occur thirteen times) within the poem's forty-five lines. This thinly disguised persona imagines herself captive of her lover/husband (the jailer of the title), who has not only drugged her but also raped her; she has become, in her degradation, a "Lever of his wet dreams." She then imagines herself to be Prometheus; she has been dropped from great heights to be smashed and consumed by the "beaks of birds." She then projects herself in the role of a black woman being burned by her captor with his cigarettes. Then she sees herself as a starved prisoner, her ribs showing after her meals of only "Lies and smiles." Then she sees herself as persecuted by him because of her rather frail religious belief (her "church of burnt matchsticks"). She is killed in several ways: "Hung, starved, burned, hooked." In her impotence to wish him the harm she feels he deserves, she retreats to slanders against his sexuality, making him impotent as well. She is paralyzed: unable to attain freedom through his death (by her wishes) and unable to escape her own imagination and her own psyche's fears. She ends the poem by unconsciously revealing her worst fear: "What would the light/ Do without eyes to knife, what would he/ Do, do, do without me?" She seems reconciled to the pain and suffering that awareness brings, but, by repeating "d" three times, she shows that she cannot face her awareness that her lover has already assumed another active role, that he is performing on his new victim the same deeds he performed on her. Written only four months before her death, this poem shows Plath at both her strongest and her weakest. She is in command of the poetic form and language, but the emotions running through the words are in control of her. This same phenomenon occurs in many of Plath's other confessional poems, but especially in "Daddy," perhaps her most infamous poem. There she also seems able to control the artistic expression within the demands of the poem, but she ultimately resorts to "screaming" at her father, who is transformed into a "Panzer-man," a "Fascist," and a "bastard."

Plath used many symbols throughout her poetry, some assuming the value of motifs. Although her mode was not, in the strictest literary sense of the word, symbolic, she frequently resorted to symbols as primary conveyors of meaning, especially in some of her most personal and most obscure poems. The moon held a special fascination for her, and it recurs throughout her entire poetic output. Colors—especially white—take on greater significance with each appearance. In the same manner, trees become larger and more significant in her later poems. Fetuses and corpses, although less often used, are two prominent symbols in her poetry. Animals move in and out of symbolic meaning in both her poetry and prose. The sea is second only to the moon as one of her favorite symbols. Other recurring symbols include bees, spheres (skulls, balloons, wombs, heads), mirrors, flowers, and physical wounds. This is only a partial list, and the meaning of each of these symbols in any particular context is governed by many factors; but the mere repetition shows that Plath allowed them to assume special value in her own mind and imbued them with special meaning in her poems.

Plath was also capable of creating Imagistic poems, word-pictures intended to evoke a specific emotional response. Using an economy of words and an artist's eye (Plath did sketch and draw for a brief period), she could present a picture from her travels in Spain ("Fiesta Melons"), ships tied up at a wharf in winter ("A Winter Ship"), or a beach scene in which her eye is attracted by an incongruous figure ("Man in Black").

Perhaps Plath's greatest talent lay in her ability to transform everyday experiences—the kind that would be appropriate entries in a diary—into poems. Her poetry is a journal, recording not only full-fledged experiences but also acute perceptions and a wide range of moods. One such poem based on an everyday happening is "Medallion," in which the persona tells of discovering a dead snake. In fact, if the lines of the poem were simply punctuated as prose, the piece would have very much the appearance of a diary entry. This style in no way lessens the value of the piece as poetry. It is, indeed, one of Plath's most successful works because it is elegantly easy and colloquial, exemplifying one more mode of expression in which the poet excelled.

As Plath developed as a poet, she attempted to fuse these various modes, so that, by the end of her life, she was writing poems that combined any number of symbols and images into a quasi-lyrical confessional poem. What remains constant throughout her life and the various modes in which she wrote, however, is the rooting of the poem in her own experience. If Plath is to be faulted, this quality is perhaps her greatest weakness: She was not able to project her personae a great distance from herself. Plath was aware of this limitation (she once wrote: "I shall perish if I can write about no one but myself"), and she attempted to turn it into an advantage. She tried to turn her personal experiences and feelings into a vision. Her vision was in no way comprehensive, nor did it ever receive any systematic expression in prose, but it did govern many of her finest creations, especially in her later poetry, and it does account for the "lapses of taste" that many readers find annoying in her.

"Mary's Song"

One of Plath's last poems will serve as an example of how this vision both limited and freed her expression. "Mary's Song" is a complex of religious imagery and the language of war, combined to express feelings of persecution, betrayal, impending destruction, and, at the same time, defiant hope. The poem is very personal, even though its language works to drown the personal voice. An everyday, ordinary scene—a Sunday dinner in preparation, a lamb cooking in its own fat—suddenly provokes violent associations. It is the Sunday lamb whose fat sacrifices its opacity. The fire catches the poet's attention—fire that crystallizes window panes, that cooks the lamb, that burned the heretics, that burned the Jews in Poland. The poet re-creates the associations as they occurred to her, as it was prompted by this everyday event of cooking. Her vision of the world—bleak, realistic, pessimistic—demands that the associations follow each other and that the poem then turn on the poet herself, which it does. The victims of the fire do not die, she says, implying that the process has somehow transformed them, purified them. She, however, is left to live, to have the ashes of these victims settle on her eye and in her mouth, forcing her to do a psychic penance, during which she sees the smokestacks of the ovens in Poland as a kind of Calvary. The final stanza returns the poet to her immediate plight: Her own heart is a holocaust through which she must travel; it too has been victimized by fathers, mothers, husbands, men, gods. She ends by turning to her own child—her golden child—and lamenting that he too will be "killed and eat[en]" by this same world.

This poem shows how Plath's vision worked to take a moment in her day and, rather than merely entering it mechanically in her journal, transform it into a statement on suffering. The horror of death by fire for heretics and Jews in Poland is no less intense, she says, because her horror—a heart that is a holocaust—is as real as theirs was; nor is her horror any the less horrible because other victims' horror was so great or so real. Plath's vision works to encapsulate this statement with its corollary in virtually all her later confessional pieces.

Although Plath's vision remained, unfortunately for her, fairly consistent, the personae through whom she expressed that vision often varied widely. In some poems there is no reason to assume the presence of any persona; powerful, sometimes psychotic emotions brush aside any obstacle between Plath and her reader. This shortened distance can be seen in such poems as "The Disquieting Muses," "On the Decline of Oracles," "Full Fathom Five," "Lesbos," and "Lady Lazarus," all poems written with a specific person in mind as both the subject of the poem and the object of the feeling, usually anger, expressed therein. In these works, Plath does little to create a mask behind which she could create feelings analogous to her own. Rather, she simply charges frontally and attacks whoever she feels has somehow wronged her. As a result of too much frontal assault and too little consideration for the poetic mode, some of these poems are not as successful as those in which she is at least in control of the poetic medium.

"Maudlin"

On the other hand, Plath could at times be a bit too detached from her persona, trying to force personal sentiment into a statement intended to have universal significance. One example of this kind of distancing is "Maudlin," a poem rooted in Plath's experience but one that attempts to moralize without sufficiently providing the moral, or literal, groundwork. Its cryptic images—a sleep-talking virgin, "Faggot-bearing Jack," and "Fish-tailed girls"—drive the reader to hunt for clues outside the poem, weakening the basis for the moralizing that takes place in the last two lines. The poem seems to be based on a birth that Plath witnessed during one of her visits to a hospital with a medical student. The "sleep-talking virgin" is the expectant mother (thus Plath indulged her love of dark and comic irony), rambling on in her drug-induced stupor. "Jack" is the child, reluctant to emerge from the mother (hence, "in his crackless egg"), a male bearing a "faggot" (a penis). He finally emerges with his "claret hogshead" (the placenta) to take his place with the dominant sex in the world ("he kings it"). This scene is behind the poem, but it cannot be reconstructed from the poem itself: The reader must turn to *The Bell Jar* and other prose. Without an understanding of this scene—knowledge of what is literally occurring—the reader is not only unprepared for the moral at the end of the poem, but is also unwilling to accept such a pat bit of overt sermonizing, especially after pondering the cryptic clues. The poet simply warns her readers, especially women, that such pain as the mother suffers in childbirth results from the loss of the maidenhead. "Maudlin" is one of the few poems by Plath that actually needs less distance between the poet and her persona; it stands as an example of the other extreme to which Plath occasionally went, confusing her readers in an attempt to "depersonalize" her poems. A similar poem is "Among the Narcissi," about her ailing neighbor in Devon: It lacks the presence of the persona, it lacks a perspective, and it lacks a reason for its stark diction.

"By Candlelight"

Such failures, however, were not typical: Few of her poems suffer from excessive detachment. Rather, her recurring struggle was against uncontrolled subjectivity and self-dramatization. Two poems written in October, 1962, demonstrate the difficulties Plath faced when her poetic persona was simply herself, and her poetry less an act of communication than a private rite of exorcism. The first poem, "By Candlelight," presents a winter night's scene of a mother and her young son. The first stanza represents the exterior environment as threatening to break through the windows and overwhelm the two characters in cold and darkness. The next stanza focuses on the reality given the child by the light that fights the darkness (the candlelight of the title). The next stanza presents the awakening of the child and the poet's gazing on a brass figure supporting the candle. That figure is the focus of the final stanza, in which the little Atlas figure becomes the child's sole heirloom, his sole protection "when the sky falls." The poem is Plath's lamentation on her inadequacy as a mother, as a human being, and as a poet to ward off the world that threatens to break through the window. Her perception is made graphic and horrifying, as the surroundings take on an autonomy beyond human control. The tone of this poem is submissive, not even rebellious; the poet writes as therapy for her wounded self, as justification for resorting to words when all else fails.

"NICK AND THE CANDLESTICK"

"Nick and the Candlestick," written five days later, reveals changes in the poet's psyche that make the poem more assertive and alter its tone. Even the very beginning of the poem reflects this change of tone: "I am a miner." At least now the poet has assumed some sort of active role, she is doing something other than resorting to mere words to ward off mortality. She does, in fact, assume the role of a target, a lightning rod to attract the overwhelming forces toward her and away from the child. Even her small gestures—decorating their "cave" with rugs and roses and other Victoriana—have taken on great significance as acts to ward off the reality outside the window. The poet is able to end on a note of strengthened resignation, almost challenging the world to hurl its worst at her, for her child has been transformed by her into her own messiah, "the baby in the barn." The process by which this quasi-religious transformation and salvation has occurred accounts for the major differences in tone in these two poems; but, again, without reference to Plath's life, the reader cannot be expected to grasp this process.

The tonal fluctuation and the inconsistent and varied personae in Plath's poems are rooted in her personality, which is capable of adopting numerous, almost infinite, masks. Plath played at many roles in her life: wronged daughter, brilliant student, coy lover, settled housewife, poet of promise, and mentally disturbed woman. Her life reflects her constant attempt to integrate these masks into what she could consider her identity—an irreproachable and independent psyche that needed no justification for its existence. Her life was spent in pursuit of this identity. She attempted to reassemble her shattered selves after her first suicide attempt, to exorcize selves that seemed to her too horrible, and to invent selves that she felt she should possess. Her poetry overwhelms its readers with its thematic consistency, drafted into this battle by Plath to help her survive another day, to continue the war against a world that seemed always on the verge of undoing the little progress she had made. Her personae were created from her and by her, but they were also created for her, with a very specific intent: survival of the self as an integrated whole.

In her quest for survival, Plath uncannily resembled Hedda Gabler, the title character of the 1890 Henrik Ibsen play. Like Hedda, Plath viewed the feminine self as a product created and manipulated by traditions and bindings far beyond the control of the individual woman. Also like Hedda, Plath felt that by rejecting the traditional demands placed on women, she could take one step toward assertion of an independent self. Plath's reactions to these traditional demands can be seen in "All the Death Dears," "The Ghost's Leavetaking," and "Magi," but the bulk of her poetry deals not so much with rejection of demands as with the whole process of establishing and maintaining identity. Masks, roles, charades, lies, and veils all enter Plath's quest and all recur throughout her poems.

"Channel Crossing"

In "Channel Crossing," an early poem, Plath uses the excitement of a storm at sea to suspend temporarily the identity of the persona, who reassumes her identity when the poem ends and she picks up her luggage. Identity is depicted as a fragile, dispensable entity. The nature of identity is also a theme in "The Lady and the Earthenware Head," in which the head is a tangible mask, a physically separate self that the persona seeks unsuccessfully to destroy. Here, instead of fragility, Plath emphasizes the oppressive durability of a prefabricated self. Identity's endurance, if it violates one's personal sense of self, is a terrible burden. That quality is displayed in "The Bee Meeting." Here the persona is a naked, vulnerable self that assumes identity only when the villagers surrounding her recognize her need for clothing, give her the clothing, and respond to the new self. The poem ends with the implication that her perceived identity will prove to be permanent, despite any efforts she might make to alter these perceptions. Identity becomes a matter of perception, as is clearly stated in "Black Rook in Rainy Weather." In this poem, the persona concedes to the artist's perception the very power to establish the artist's identity. The dynamic of power between perceived and perceiver is finely balanced in this poem. In "A Birthday Present," the balance is tipped by the duplicity of veils and what they hide in identities that are established within personal relationships.

"Lady Lazarus" and "Daddy"

Toward the end of her life, Plath's concern with identity became rebellious. In "Daddy," she openly declares her rebellion, severing the demands and ties of tradition that so strangled her earlier in her life and in her poetry. She adopts several methods to achieve her end of freedom: name calling, new identities, scorn, humiliation, and transfer of aggression. Her freedom rings false, however; the ties are still there. "Lady Lazarus" reveals Plath's awareness of the lingering ties and stands as an encapsulation of her whole life's quest for identity—from passivity, to passive resistance, to active resistance, and finally to the violently imagined destruction of those people who first gave and then shattered her self: men. This poem contains meaning within meaning and exposes much about Plath's feelings on where her identity arose. She saw herself as a product of a male society, molded by men to suit their particular whims or needs. Her contact with women in this context led inevitably to conflict and competition. This duality in her self was never overcome, never expelled, or, worse, never understood. Having failed to manipulate her manipulators, she tried to find identity by destroying her creators. Set free from the basis she had always known even if she despised it, she had nowhere else to go but to the destruction of the self as well.

"Words"

Plath realized this quandary. In "Words," a poem written ten days before her death, she looked back:

> Years later I
> Encounter them on the road—
> Words dry and riderless,
> The indefatigable hoof-taps.
> While
> From the bottom of the pool, fixed stars
> Govern a life.

The words with which she had striven to create a self—a meaningful self that would integrate her various sides in a harmonious whole and not merely reflect "daddy's girl," "mommy's girl," "big sister," "sorority Sue," or "Mrs. Hughes"—these words had turned "dry and riderless." They too had failed her, just as her family, friends, husband, and her own self had failed her. She had sought identity in traditional places—parents, school, marriage, and work—but had not found enough strands to weave her various selves together. She had sought identity in unorthodox places—the mind, writing, Devon, and hope—but even these failed her.

Plath finally conceded her failure to create a self that would satisfy her and the world about her. She reviewed a life that she had tried to end earlier. Even then she had been forced to regroup, forced to continue inhaling and exhaling. The truth of the real world that had threatened to overwhelm her collection of masks throughout her life had finally yielded to her on one point. She asked ten days before her death: "Once one has seen God, what is the remedy?" The perfection of death that had haunted her throughout her life seemed the only answer. Her final act was her ultimate affirmation of self in a world that would not let her or her words assume their holistic role.

Other major works

LONG FICTION: *The Bell Jar*, 1963 (originally published under the name Victoria Lucas).

SHORT FICTION: *Johnny Panic and the Bible of Dreams*, 1977-1979 (prose sketches).

NONFICTION: *Letters Home*, 1975; *The Journals of Sylvia Plath*, 1982 (Ted Hughes and Frances McCullough, editors); *The Unabridged Journals of Sylvia Plath, 1950-1962*, 2000 (Karen V. Kukil, editor).

CHILDREN'S LITERATURE: *The Bed Book*, 1976.

Bibliography

Bassnett, Susan. *Sylvia Plath: An Introduction to the Poetry.* 2d ed. New York: Palgrave Macmillan, 2005. This second edition of an important work in Plath scholarship makes use of later scholarship. Provides intriguing and controversial analysis of Plath's work, breaking from traditional interpretations.

Gill, Jo. *The Cambridge Introduction to Sylvia Plath.* New York: Cambridge University Press, 2008. A comprehensive guide to Plath's poetry, prose, and autobiographical writings. Provides a critical overview to key readings and debates.

_____, ed. *Cambridge Companion to Sylvia Plath.* New York: Cambridge University Press, 2006. A two-prong approach to Plath and her works. One section deals with "Context and Issues" and the other "Works." The student of Plath will find both sections invaluable.

Helle, Anita, ed. *The Unraveling Archive: Essays on Sylvia Plath.* Ann Arbor: University of Michigan Press, 2007. Eleven original essays that draw on correspondence and manuscript drafts to discuss the life and writing of Plath. Includes family photographs and full-page reproductions of her paintings.

Kirk, Connie Ann. *Sylvia Plath: A Biography.* Amherst, N.Y.: Prometheus Books, 2009. A concise biography created using archives at Smith College and University of Indiana, Bloomington, and the unabridged journals published in 2000. Tries to present a balanced view of Hughes, her husband.

Kroll, Judith. *Chapters in a Mythology: The Poetry of Sylvia Plath.* Stroud, Gloucestershire, England: Sutton, 2007. This work looks at Plath's use of the theme of the divided self and argues that its basis can be found in mythology rather than in her mental state.

Middlebrook, Diane. *Her Husband: Hughes and Plath—A Marriage.* New York: Viking, 2003. Middlebrook brings insight and empathy to a probing examination of the literary marriage of the century.

Miller, Ellen. *Releasing Philosophy, Thinking Art: A Phenomenological Study of Sylvia Plath's Poetry.* Aurora, Colo.: Davies Group, 2008. A phenomenological analysis of Plath's poetry. Includes sections on "Mystic," "Ariel," "The Moon and the Yew Tree," and "The Arrival of the Bee Box."

Steinberg, Peter K. *Sylvia Plath.* Philadelphia: Chelsea House, 2004. Part of the Great Writers series, this work provides a biographical introduction and close analyses of the poems "The Colossus," "The Arrival of the Bee Box," "Ariel," "Daddy," and "Lady Lazarus." Also contains bibliographies.

Wagner-Martin, Linda. *Sylvia Plath: A Literary Life.* 2d ed. New York: Palgrave, 2003. Plath's work in the 1960's is examined closely through her reading and apprenticeship writing. The revised edition examines the aftermath of her death, the publication of the *Collected Poems*, Hughes's *Birthday Letters*, and various biographies.

Richard F. Giles

ADRIENNE RICH

Born: Baltimore, Maryland; May 16, 1929

PRINCIPAL POETRY
A Change of World, 1951
The Diamond Cutters, and Other Poems, 1955
Snapshots of a Daughter-in-Law, 1963
Necessities of Life, 1966
Selected Poems, 1967
Leaflets, 1969
The Will to Change, 1971
Diving into the Wreck, 1973
Poems: Selected and New, 1950-1974, 1975
Twenty-one Love Poems, 1976
The Dream of a Common Language, 1978
A Wild Patience Has Taken Me This Far: Poems 1978-1981, 1981
Sources, 1983
The Fact of a Doorframe: Poems Selected and New, 1950-1984, 1984
Your Native Land, Your Life, 1986
Time's Power: Poems, 1985-1988, 1989
An Atlas of the Difficult World: Poems, 1988-1991, 1991
Collected Early Poems, 1950-1970, 1993
Dark Fields of the Republic: Poems, 1991-1995, 1995
Selected Poems, 1950-1995, 1996
Midnight Salvage: Poems, 1995-1998, 1999
Fox: Poems, 1998-2000, 2001
The School Among the Ruins: Poems, 2000-2004, 2004
Telephone Ringing in the Labyrinth: Poems, 2004-2006, 2007

OTHER LITERARY FORMS

Adrienne Rich is known primarily for her poetry, but she has produced essays on writing and politics as well: *Of Woman Born: Motherhood as Experience and Institution* (1976) is an analysis of the changing meanings of childbirth and motherhood in Anglo-American culture, in which Rich draws on personal experience as well as sources in mythology, sociology, economics, the history of medicine, and literature to develop her analysis. *On Lies, Secrets, and Silence: Selected Prose, 1966-1978* (1979) is a collection of essays on women writers (including Anne Bradstreet, Anne Sexton, Charlotte Brontë, and Emily Dickinson) and feminism. *Blood, Bread, and Poetry: Selected*

Prose, 1979-1985 (1986) followed with further essays on women writers and feminist criticism. *What Is Found There: Notebooks on Poetry and Politics* (1993) delivers just what the title promises. For several years Rich also coedited, with Michelle Cliff, the lesbian feminist journal *Sinister Wisdom*.

Achievements

Adrienne Rich's work has been at the vanguard of the women's movement in the United States. Her poems and essays explore her own experience and seek to develop a "common language" for women to communicate their values and perceptions. She has received numerous awards, including two Guggenheim Fellowships, the National Institute of Arts and Letters Award for Poetry (1960), the Shelley Memorial Award of the Poetry Society of America (1971), and the National Book Award (1974) for *Diving into the Wreck*. Other recognitions include the Ruth Lilly Poetry Prize (1986), the Northern California Book Award in poetry (1989), the Bill Whitehead Award (1990), Lambda Literary Awards (1991, 1995, 2001), the Lenore Marshall Poetry Prize (1992), the Academy of American Poets Fellowship (1992), the *Los Angeles Times* Book Prize (1992), the Frost Medal (1992), a MacArthur Fellowship, the Poets' Prize (1993), the Fred Cody Award for lifetime achievement (1994), the Wallace Stevens Award (1996), the Lifetime Achievement Award from the Lannan Foundation (1999), the Bollingen Prize (2003), and the Medal for Distinguished Contribution to American Letters from the National Book Foundation (2006). In 2004, *The School Among the Ruins* earned Rich the National Book Critics Circle Award, the Gold Medal from the Commonwealth Club of California, and the Poetry Center Book Award. She served as chancellor for the Academy of American Poets from 1999 to 2001.

Biography

Adrienne Cecile Rich was born in 1929, into a white, middle-class southern family. Her Jewish father, Arnold Rice Rich, taught medicine at The Johns Hopkins University. Her southern Protestant mother, Helen Jones Rich, was trained as a composer and concert pianist but gave up her career to devote herself to her husband and two daughters. She carried out their early education at home, until the girls began to attend school in fourth grade. Her father encouraged his daughter to read and to write poetry. In his library, she found the work of such writers as Matthew Arnold, William Blake, Thomas Carlyle, John Keats, Dante Gabriel Rossetti, and Alfred, Lord Tennyson. Rich graduated from Radcliffe College in 1951, the year her first volume of poetry was published. She traveled in Europe and England on a Guggenheim Fellowship in 1952-1953.

Rich married Alfred H. Conrad in 1953 and in the next few years gave birth to three sons, David (1955), Paul (1957), and Jacob (1959). She lived with her family in Cambridge, Massachusetts, from 1953 to 1966, but spent 1961-1962 in the Netherlands on

Adrienne Rich
(Library of Congress)

another Guggenheim Fellowship. In 1964, Rich began her involvement in the New Left, initiating a period of personal and political growth and crisis. In 1966, the family moved to New York, where Conrad taught at City College of New York. Rich also began to teach at City College, where she worked for the first time with disadvantaged students. In 1970, Rich ended her marriage, and later the same year, Conrad ended his life. Rich continued teaching at City College and then Rutgers University until 1979, when she moved to western Massachusetts. Poems of these years explore her lesbian relationships.

Rich eventually moved to northern California to continue her active career as poet, essayist, and sought-after speaker. Rich spent time in the 1980's and early 1990's at numerous California colleges and universities, acting as visiting professor and lecturer. Her stops included Scripps College, San Jose State University, and Stanford University. In 1992, she accepted the National Director of the National Writer's Voice Project. In the 1990's, she joined several advisory boards, including the Boston Woman's Fund, National Writers Union, Sisterhood in Support of Sisters in South Africa, and New Jewish Agenda.

Analysis

Adrienne Rich's successive volumes of poetry chronicle a contemporary female artist's odyssey. Her earliest work is a notable contribution to modern poetry. Her later work has broken new ground as she redefines and reimagines women's lives to create a female myth of self-discovery. In her life and work, she has been struggling to break out of patriarchal social and literary conventions, to redefine herself and to create new traditions. W. H. Auden praised her first volume for its stylistic control, its skillful use of traditional themes such as isolation, and its assimilation of influences such as the work of Robert Frost and William Butler Yeats. He wrote: "The poems . . . in this book are neatly and modestly dressed, speak quietly but do not mumble, respect their elders but are not cowed by them, and do not tell fibs."

Since then, however, Rich has been reshaping poetic conventions to develop her own themes and to create her own voice, often a radical (and sometimes a jarring) one. Reviewer Helen Vendler termed *Diving into the Wreck* "dispatches from the battlefield." Central concerns of Rich's poetry include the uses of history and language, the relationship of the individual to society, and the individual's quest for identity and meaning. The home is often a site for the working out of these themes.

A Change of World

Auden chose Rich's first volume of poetry, *A Change of World*, for the Yale Younger Poets Award. Despite the title, the poems have to do with resisting change. Rich's early training at her father's hands reinforced her allegiance to a literary tradition of meticulous craft, of "beauty" and "perfection." Accordingly, these poems are objective, carefully crafted, and rhymed, with echoes of W. H. Auden, T. S. Eliot, and Robert Frost. A recurring image is that of the home as a refuge that is threatened by social instability ("The Uncle Speaks in the Drawing Room") or natural forces ("Storm Warnings"). The women in these poems remain at home, occupied with women's tasks such as embroidering ("Aunt Jennifer's Tigers"), weaving ("Mathilde in Normandy"), and caring for their families ("Eastport to Block Island"). A central theme of these poems is the use of art as a technique for ordering experience ("Aunt Jennifer's Tigers" and "At a Bach Concert"). "At a Bach Concert" is written in a musically complex form, a variant of the intricate terza rima stanza used by Dante. Rich's poem weaves together many strands of poetic technique (assonance, consonance, internal rhyme, off-rhyme, alliteration) and rhetorical devices (oxymoron and parallelism) into a rich textural harmony to develop the theme that formal structure is the poet's gift of love: "Form is the ultimate gift that love can offer—/ The vital union of necessity/ With all that we desire, all that we suffer."

The Diamond Cutters

The theme of artistic control and craft is repeated in Rich's second book, *The Diamond Cutters*. Written when Rich was traveling in Europe as the recipient of a

Guggenheim Traveling Fellowship, this volume is a tourist's poetic diary. Landscape and scenery are prominent. The book blends two moods, nostalgia for a more beautiful past and ironic disillusionment with a present that falls short of perfection (as in "The Ideal Landscape," "Lucifer in the Train," or "The Strayed Village." In a profound way, all the characters in this book are exiles, aliens, uneasy in the places they inhabit. The heroines of poems such as "Autumn Equinox," "The Prospect," and "The Perennial Answer" are dissatisfied with their lives but unable to change. They hold on to history and to the social structures it has produced, refusing to question present conditions. Suppressed anger and unacknowledged tensions lie just beneath the surface of all the poems; the book's tone is passive, flat. Eight years passed before Rich's next book appeared. Its stylistic and thematic changes reflect changes in her outlook.

SNAPSHOTS OF A DAUGHTER-IN-LAW

In her next two books, *Snapshots of a Daughter-in-Law* and *Necessities of Life*, Rich begins to move from conventional poetic forms, to develop her own style, and to deal more directly with personal experience. Her attitudes toward literary tradition, history, and the home have changed markedly. She questions traditional attitudes toward home and family. As she found the patriarchal definitions of human relationships inadequate, her work became more personal and more urgent.

Snapshots of a Daughter-in-Law is written in a looser form than Rich's previous work. Language is simpler, texture less dense. The title poem is a series of vignettes of women's experiences. It fairly bristles with quotations drawn from Rich's wide-ranging reading. According to the poem, male authorities have always defined women in myths and literature. Thus, women lacked a literature of their own in which to define themselves. Rich wrote that she composed the poem "in fragments during children's naps, brief hours in a library, or at 3 A.M. after rising with a wakeful child." Because of these interruptions, she wrote the poem over a two-year period. In this poem, she wrote, "for the first time, directly about experiencing myself as a woman" rather than striving to be "universal." As the title indicates, these are static, fixed vignettes: The women are trapped, denied scope for action and choice.

Another poem in this volume, "The Roofwalker," speaks again of entrapment. The poem's speaker is a builder or architect who is no longer satisfied with the enclosure he has built. The role of the artist is here redefined. Whereas "At a Bach Concert" celebrated the need for objectivity, distance, and form, the speaker of "The Roofwalker" feels constrained by forms: "Was it worth while to lay—/ with infinite exertion—/ a roof I can't live under?" The poet begins to wonder whether her tools—rhyme, alliteration, meter, poetic conventions—are stifling her imagination.

The well-planned house that Rich rejects in "The Roofwalker" is the house of formalist poetry as well. She finds the measured stanzas, rhymed couplets, and blank verse rhythms of her earlier books too rigid for her present purposes. Writing a poem no longer means finding a form for a preconceived idea. Instead, each experience informs its own expression; the poem is not product, but process. The poet, like "The Roofwalker," must break out of the stultifying traditional structure. Like most of her contemporaries, she has come to write in freer forms. Yet Rich never abandons rational structure or rootedness in social context as do some experimental writers.

NECESSITIES OF LIFE

Rich's next book, *Necessities of Life*, continues her movement toward a freer poetic line and toward subjectivity. Where she formerly spoke of history in terms of objects and products of tradition, she now identifies with historical persons (Antinous, Emily Dickinson, and others). A struggle between death and life, between winter and spring, is in process. Indoor-outdoor imagery carries the weight of these tensions. Poems of death and disappearance take place indoors; the expansive, life-enhancing experiences occur outdoors.

These poems are a retreat from the angry stance of "Snapshots of a Daughter-in-Law" and the daring escape of "The Roofwalker." In *Necessities of Life*, Rich feels oppressed by the human world, so she turns to nature for sustenance. *Necessities of Life* establishes a deep relationship with the world of nature; it is one of the "bare essentials" that preserve the heroine in her difficulties. Through a bond with the vegetable and animal world, the world of warmth and light, the book is able to bring life to bear against death and darkness. Nature's cyclical pattern provides clues for survival. Plants move from winter's icy grip into spring's renewal by learning to exist on little. To achieve similar rebirth, humans must consciously will change and force themselves into action. This is the pattern of death and rebirth that structures the book.

LEAFLETS

Rich's first four books are built on linear oppositions. Balanced groups of stanzas articulate dichotomies between art and emotion, control and chaos, passivity and action, indoors and outdoors. Often characters must choose between alternatives. Tension between polarities becomes a controlling force, focusing the poems' energies. In her next books of poetry, Rich would modify the dualistic structure of the earlier books. At the end of *Leaflets*, she introduces the *ghazal*, a series of two-line units that conflate many ideas. These poems are collagelike, offering multiple perspectives.

Prompted by her increasing social concern and the leftist political critique evolving in the middle and later 1960's, Rich turned from personal malaise to political struggle, from private meditation to public discourse. Her jarring tone reflects her anger and impatience with language. Rhythms are broken, speech is fragmented. The poems suggest hurried diary entries. Images of violence, guerrilla warfare, and global human suffering suggest an embattled society. Yet anger is close kin to hope: It asserts the wish to effect change. Therefore, alongside the destruction, symbols of fertility and rebirth appear.

Rich writes of an old tradition dying and a new one struggling to be born. Fear of change dominated her earlier books, but the "will to change" is paramount here. The poems of this period describe Rich's heroines casting off traditional roles and preparing for journeys. The titles of the next three books represent steps in this process. *Leaflets* is a manifesto for public involvement, *The Will to Change* is the determination to move forward, and *Diving into the Wreck*, the first title to contain a verb, is the act itself.

The evolution of *Leaflets* epitomizes Rich's movement from the personal to the political. The first poem, "Orion," is written in regular six-line stanzas and built on a typical pattern of balanced contrast. Indoors and outdoors, feminine and masculine, stagnation and adventure are the poles. The poem is a monologue in which the speaker blames herself for her failures as a woman. In contrast, the last poem in the book, "Ghazals," is a series of unrhymed couplets arranged in a seemingly random conflation of ideas and images. "Ghazals" is a multivoiced political critique of contemporary America. The heroes and heroines of the book are revolutionaries, protesters, and challengers of an old order: Frantz Fanon, Walt Whitman, Galileo, LeRoi Jones (Amiri Baraka), Eldridge Cleaver, and Dian Fossey. Turning her back on a political tradition that she now equates with death and destruction, Rich is saddened and estranged. However, she not only wants to last until the new tradition begins but also will attempt to create that new tradition. To do so, she must substitute new ideas and modes of expression for the old, wishing "to choose words that even you/ would have to be changed by" ("Implosions"). Because the values and attitudes she wants to modify are so deeply entrenched in people's most fundamental assumptions, language itself must be reshaped to provide a vocabulary equal to her task of reconstruction. Consequently, language becomes a crucial issue.

Rich believes that "only where there is language is there world" ("The Demon Lover"). She fears, however, that the English language is "spoiled." If the poet is using the "oppressor's language," how may her words avoid contamination?

THE WILL TO CHANGE

Rich's powerful meditation on language and power "The Burning of Paper Instead of Children" (in *The Will to Change*) draws on her classroom experience with disadvantaged students. Unlike the poet, whose privileged childhood opened the possibilities of language to her, the children of the ghetto find the worlds of literacy and power closed to them. Rich quotes a student whose grammatical awkwardness lends his description of poverty a pointed eloquence: "a child steal because he did not have money to buy it: to hear a mother say she do not have money to buy food for her children . . . it will make tears in your eyes." Because she mistrusts rhetoric, the poet closes her meditation with a prose passage of bald statement.

> I am in danger. You are in danger. The burning of a book arouses no sensation in me. I know it hurts to burn. There are flames of napalm in Catonsville, Maryland. I know it hurts to burn.

The typewriter is overheated, my mouth is burning, I cannot touch you and this is the oppressor's language.

Her simple syntax affirms her identification with the disadvantaged student, the oppressed. In her refusal to use complex diction or traditional metrics she argues by implication for a rhetoric of honesty and simplicity.

DIVING INTO THE WRECK

Rich's poetry revises the heroic myth to reflect women's experiences. *Diving into the Wreck* presents questing female heroes for the first time in her work. On their quests, they reconnect with lost parts of themselves, discover their own power, and build commonality with other women. Women's lives are the central focus as Rich's project becomes that of giving voice to women's experience, developing a "common language" that will bring the "dark country" of women's lives into the common light of day. Yet Rich also claims another task for women: They must struggle to redeem an endangered society. She argues that patriarchy's exaggerated aggressiveness, competition, and repression of feeling have led Western civilization to the brink of extinction. The task of reconstruction must be taken up by women. Working for change, the women in this book seek to turn civilization from its destructive paths by persuasion, creation of new myths, or redirection of anger.

To understand and overcome patriarchy's suicidal impulses, Rich attempts to open a dialogue. Almost all the poems in *Diving into the Wreck* are cast as dialogue. Conversation is the book's central metaphor for poetry. The book begins with "Trying to Talk with a Man," a poem that deals with the dangers of an accelerating arms race but also has a deeper subject: the creation of a dialogue between men and women. Considering gender a political issue, Rich calls on men to join her in rethinking gender questions.

The book, however, comes to question the possibility of real communication. "Translations" examines the gulf between the languages spoken by women and men. In "Meditations for a Savage Child," the concluding poem, scientists cannot teach the child to speak.

POEMS: SELECTED AND NEW, 1950-1974

Poems: Selected and New, 1950-1974 includes early unpublished poems and several new ones. In the final poem of this book, "From an Old House in America," Rich uses the home image as a starting point for a reconsideration of American history from a woman's point of view. She reimagines the lives of women, from immigrants to pioneers to the new generation of feminist activists. All are journeying. Simple and direct in language, written in stanzas of open couplets, the poem is a stream-of-consciousness meditation that builds in force as it imagines the unwritten history of North American women and reaches a profound celebration of sisterhood.

Thus, by the end of the book, the woman at home is transformed from the cautious door-closer of "Storm Warnings" (*A Change of World*) into the active participant in history and the questing adventurer eager to define herself by exploration and new experience.

THE DREAM OF A COMMON LANGUAGE

Transformation is the cornerstone of *The Dream of a Common Language* and *A Wild Patience Has Taken Me This Far*. The poet wishes to effect fundamental changes in social arrangements, in concepts of selfhood, in governmental politics, in the meanings of sexuality, and in language. To that end, transformation supplants her earlier idea of revolution.

The title *The Dream of a Common Language* suggests vision, community, and above all a language in which visions and shared experience may be conceived and expressed. Dream is the voice of the nocturnal, unconscious self breaking into daytime existence. The terrain Rich explores here is the unknown country of the self, discovered in dream, myth, vision, and ritual. Like dreams, the poems telescope time and space to make new connections among past, present, and future, between home and world. "Common" signifies that which is communal, habitual, shared, widely used, and ordinary. Rich sets great value on the common, choosing it over the extraordinary.

In *The Dream of a Common Language*, the poet affirms that poetry stems from "the drive/ to connect. The dream of a common language." The book's central section, "Twenty-One Love Poems," orchestrates the controlling themes of women's love, power, language, world. Images of light and dark, dream and reality, speech and silence, home and wanderer structure the sequence. There are in fact twenty-two poems, for Rich has included an unnumbered "Floating Poem." Drawing from the sonnet tradition, Rich breaks formal conventions by varying the poems' lengths and departing from strict rhyme and meter. The sequence records a particular lesbian relationship, its joyous beginnings, the difficulties encountered, and the termination of the relationship. The poems ask questions about the meanings of self, language, and love between women, and about the possibilities of sustaining love in a hostile world. Rich insists on grounding her explorations in the quotidian as well as the oneiric world. To be "at home" in the world requires coming to terms with the ugliness and brutality of the city, the pain and wounds, as well as the beauty of love and poetry. Deliberately, Rich situates the first sonnet of her sequence "in this city," with its "rainsoaked garbage."

Because she wishes to escape false romanticism, Rich seeks to connect the poems firmly to the world of daily life, to avoid sentimentality, and to speak honestly of her feelings. Because she wishes to transform the self-effacing behavior that has typically characterized women in love, she stresses self-awareness and deliberate choice. Caves and circles—images of roundness, completeness, and wholeness—are dominant. Like the homes of Rich's earlier work, they are enclosures; however, the meaning of encirclement has been transformed, for in her new vision, the poet no longer escapes from the world in her narrow room but reaches out to include the world, to bring it within her protected circle.

Poem 21, the final poem of the sequence, is a complex network of dreamlike associations, of ritual and archetypal memory. In the sonnet, Rich moves from dark into light, from the prehistoric into the present, from inanimate nature ("the color of stone") into purposeful consciousness ("more than stone"). She becomes by choice "a figure in the light." The clarity of intelligence–"a cleft of light"—shapes her purpose. In drawing the circle, she deliberately chooses her place.

Particularly in the last three poems of the book, there is a sacramental quality, as Rich affirms her fusion with a world of women working together throughout time. Weaving, cooking, and caring for children, they are crafting beautiful and utilitarian objects such as ceramic vessels, quilts, and clothing. Through these tasks, they create mementos of their lives and carry out the work of making a world.

"Transcendental Etude" is a long meditative poem of great richness and power. It traces the course of birth, death, and rebirth through a creativity that heals splits in the natural world and within the self. The poem begins in the pastoral imagery of an August evening and ranges over the realms of nature and of human life. Rich's vision here transforms the poet's craft. As a poet, she need not be, as she had once feared, an egocentric artist seeking undying fame at the expense of those she loves. Instead, through participation in the life of the physical universe, she articulates the patterns of her own being, of life itself. Thus, Rich's new metaphor of the poet is at once the most daring and the most simple: The poet is a common woman.

Achieving a selfhood that encompasses both creative work and human relationships, egotism and altruism, Rich and her women heal their psychic split in the symbolic return to home, to the full self represented by the circle. The voyage into history, the unconsciousness, the mind is completed in the return.

EXPLORING WOMEN'S SHARED PASTS

The next group of books—*A Wild Patience Has Taken Me This Far, Sources, The Fact of a Doorframe, Your Native Land, Your Life,* and *Time's Power*—continue to develop the themes broached in *The Dream of a Common Language*: exploration of women's shared past, the struggle to be "at home" in a strife-torn world, the vision of transforming the self and the world. Here again the imagery is that of simple, ordinary objects important to women's lives: books, kettles, and beets. Yet these books speak in a more muted voice, the voice of resolution, acceptance, accomplishment, with less anger.

A Wild Patience Has Taken Me This Far is to a large extent a dialogue with nineteenth century women writers and thinkers: the Brontës, Susan B. Anthony, Elizabeth Barrett Browning. "Culture and Anarchy" takes its title from Matthew Arnold's essay on nineteenth century culture. Arnold longed for a literate, elite, verbal culture; Rich, on the other hand, celebrates a world of women's work, both verbal and nonverbal. Here, growing and cooking vegetables, responding to nature's seasonal rhythms, the simple tasks of women's lives, form a valuable cultural matrix out of which arise the heroic actions of individual women.

Rich's poem is a quilting together of the words of historical women (derived from the diaries and letters of Emily Dickinson, Susan B. Anthony, Elizabeth Barrett Browning, and Jane Addams) and meditation on her own life and work. The women's voices here replace the quotations of male words in "Snapshots of a Daughter-in-Law." Again, Rich telescopes time, bringing the earlier women into the circle of her life, joining them in their acts and visions.

In *Sources*, Rich returns to her past and engages in a dialogue with her dead father and husband. She is trying to come to terms with her own life and to put the lives of the others into perspective. *Your Native Land, Your Life* and *Time's Power* continue to develop the persona of the poet as representative woman facing the issues of her country and time. Language and poetry and their relation to history remain foci of concern: in "North American Time" she writes

> Poetry never stood a chance
> of standing outside history.
> . . . .
> We move   but our words stand
> become responsible
> for more than we intended

In the ruefully ironic "Blue Rock" she writes

> Once when I wrote poems they did not change
> left overnight on the page
> . . . .
> But now I know what happens while I sleep
> and when I wake the poem has changed:
> the facts have dilated it, or cancelled it.

Time's Power is a book of dialogue, with the poet's mother, her lover, and a cast of historical figures. "Letters in the Family" is a series of imagined letters written by fictionalized historical persons, such as a friend of the Hungarian partisan Chana Senesh or a South African mother writing to her child. The book ends with "Turning," a poem of quest for knowledge. It articulates a question the poet-speaker asks as she tries to understand her ongoing quest: "So why am I out here, trying/ to read your name in the illegible air?"

MIDNIGHT SALVAGE

Rich subtly moves toward a quieter wisdom in *Midnight Salvage,* passing the torch and trying to impart to future readers and writers what she has learned and how she learned it. In doing so, she reminisces of her girlhood and her past selves' varied goals and causes, perhaps best captured in the title poem, an ambitious, eight-section piece that sorts through her history. Her experience with aging and illness brings forth the subject matter of physical torture. "Shattered Head" ranges from one body's devastation ("a life hauls itself uphill") to the betrayal of the many, and by the end of the poem, to the victims of torture or warfare ("who did this to us?"). Her work continues to be combative, yet in this volume, it is in a quiet, more indirect way.

FOX

Fox continues to meld Rich's art with conviction, her familiar attentions to social injustice and intense personal introspection still present. She praises, commemorates, and questions friends and public figures, while also probing what political action means. Her usual strident tone makes a small retreat here, however, and her voice is less edgy, a little more malleable, than in previous collections. As she declares in "Regardless," a poem about loving a man, "we'd love/ regardless of manifestoes I wrote or signed." Yet familiar themes are present, whether she is writing about war in the long, provocative poem "Veterans Day," female identity in the searing title poem, or the violence witnessed by a woman in "Second Sight," and Rich continues to give voice to the most fundamental of feelings.

POETIC EVOLUTION

Rich's successive volumes of poetry reveal her development as poet and as woman. As she breaks out from restrictive traditions, her voice is achieving power and authenticity. From a poet of isolation and withdrawal, of constraint and despair, she has become a seer of wide-ranging communal sympathy and great imaginative possibility. She is redefining in her life and poetry the meanings of language, poetry, love, power, and home. In her earlier life and work, she accepted patriarchal definitions. Consequently, she felt trapped in personal and poetic conventions: a marriage that curbed her creativity, an aesthetic that split form and feeling, a language that ignored her experience, a position of powerlessness.

At first, she spoke in a derivative voice, the language of the "universal." Reluctant to speak as a woman, she echoed the tone of her male poetic ancestors. Because she hesitated to voice her own experience, her early poems are highly polished but avoid emotional depth. She grew to mistrust a language that seemed alien. The fragmented, provisional, stark poems of *Leaflets, The Will to Change,* and *Diving into the Wreck* record her groping toward a new language in which to voice her deepest concerns. In subsequent books, she wrote in a freer form, viewing poems as "speaking to their moment."

This stance is particularly noticeable in such works of the 1990's as *An Atlas of the Difficult World*, with its powerhouse title poem, *Dark Fields of the Republic*, and *Midnight Salvage*. These volumes, produced almost on schedule every three or four years, also suggest less urgency and a more relaxed authority as a voice at once personal and representative. In *Fox*, there seems to be a gradual falling off of intensity, a quieter wisdom, as Rich moves into her seventies.

Through the major phases of her career, the transformations of Rich's home imagery parallel her growth of poetic force and political awareness. In early poems, the home was entrapping, because patriarchal voices defined women's roles. As Rich's women became more self-defining, the old relationships were abandoned or modified to fit the real needs of the persons involved. Achieving selfhood, Rich's female heroes came to seize control of their homes, their lives. Through metaphorical journeys exploring the world, women's history, and their own psychic heights and depths, they struggle for knowledge and self-mastery. Healing their tormenting self-division, they grow more "at home" in the world. They recognize and cherish their links to a women's tradition of great power and beauty and to the natural world. In this process, the idea of home has acquired new significance: from frail shelter or painful trap it has grown to a gateway, the starting point for journeys of self-exploration, and the magic circle to which women return so that they may participate in the work of "making and remaking" the world.

OTHER MAJOR WORKS

NONFICTION: *Of Woman Born: Motherhood as Experience and Institution*, 1976; *On Lies, Secrets, and Silence: Selected Prose, 1966-1978*, 1979; *Blood, Bread, and Poetry: Selected Prose, 1979-1985*, 1986; *What Is Found There: Notebooks on Poetry and Politics*, 1993, 2003; *Arts of the Possible: Essays and Conversations*, 2001; *Poetry and Commitment: An Essay*, 2007; *A Human Eye: Essays on Art in Society, 1997-2008*, 2009.

EDITED TEXTS: *The Best American Poetry, 1996*, 1996; *Selected Poems / Muriel Rukeyser*, 2004.

MISCELLANEOUS: *Adrienne Rich's Poetry and Prose: Poems, Prose, Reviews, and Criticism*, 1993 (Barbara Chartesworth Gelpi and Albert Gelpi, editors).

BIBLIOGRAPHY

Cooper, Jane Roberta, ed. *Reading Adrienne Rich: Review and Re-visions, 1951-1981*. Ann Arbor: University of Michigan Press, 1984. A useful collection of reviews and critical studies of Rich's poetry and prose. It includes Auden's foreword to *A Change of World* and other significant essays. The aim is for breadth and balance.

Dickie, Margaret. *Stein, Bishop, and Rich: Lyrics of Love, War, and Place*. Chapel Hill: University of North Carolina Press, 1997. Examination of the poets Rich, Gertrude Stein, and Elizabeth Bishop. Three of the book's nine chapters are devoted to Rich. Bibliography, index.

Estrin, Barbara L. *The American Love Lyric After Auschwitz and Hiroshima*. New York: Palgrave, 2001. Estrin finds a connection between the language of the love lyric and hate speech. Using the specific examples of Rich, Wallace Stevens, and Robert Lowell, she expresses a revisionist critique of twentieth American poetry, supporting the theory that the love lyric is political.

Gelpi, Barbara Charlesworth, and Albert Gelpi, eds. *Adrienne Rich's Poetry and Prose*. New York: W. W. Norton, 1993. This volume in the Norton Critical Edition series presents a significant sampling of Rich's work, biographical materials, and a carefully representative selection of essays (sometimes excerpted) and reviews. It provides a chronology and a list of selected criticism for further study.

Keyes, Claire. *The Aesthetics of Power: The Poetry of Adrienne Rich*. Athens: University of Georgia Press, 1986. Keyes discusses Rich as a feminist poet. Introduction provides a biographical and historical overview. Each of the ten chapters discusses one of Rich's books, from *A Change of World* through *A Wild Patience Has Taken Me This Far*.

Langdell, Cheryl Colby. *Adrienne Rich: The Moment of Change*. Westport, Conn.: Praeger, 2004. This biography of Rich traces her several transformations through analyses of her poems.

Ratcliffe, Krista. *Anglo-American Feminist Challenges to the Rhetorical Traditions: Virginia Woolf, Mary Daly, Adrienne Rich*. Carbondale: Southern Illinois University Press, 1996. A feminist perspective on the rhetoric and literary devices of writers-critics Rich, Virginia Woolf, and Mary Daly. Bibliography, index.

Templeton, Alice. *The Dream and the Dialogue: Adrienne Rich's Feminist Poetics*. Knoxville: University of Tennessee Press, 1994. Templeton finds each of Rich's volumes both responsive to and party to the dominant critical issues at the time of publication. Templeton's exploration of Rich's "feminist poetics" posits feminism as a way of reading literature, so that reading in itself becomes a political act.

Waddell, William S., ed. *"Catch If You Can Your Country's Moment": Recovery and Regeneration in the Poetry of Adrienne Rich*. Newcastle, England: Cambridge Scholars, 2007. A collection of eight essays on Rich's poetry that focuses on the themes of recovery and regeneration. Looks at her development from a poet dealing with feminist personal topics to one dealing with public, political issues.

Yorke, Liz. *Adrienne Rich: Passion, Politics, and the Body*. Newbury Park, Calif.: Sage, 1998. This accessible introduction to Rich's work reviews the process and development of her ideas, tracing her place in the major debates within second-wave feminism. Yorke assesses Rich's contribution to feminism and outlines her ideas on motherhood, heterosexuality, lesbian identity, Jewish identity, and issues of racial and sexual otherness.

Karen F. Stein; Philip K. Jason
Updated by Sarah Hilbert

MURIEL RUKEYSER

Born: New York, New York; December 15, 1913
Died: New York, New York; February 12, 1980

PRINCIPAL POETRY
Theory of Flight, 1935
Mediterranean, 1938
U.S. 1, 1938
A Turning Wind, 1939
The Soul and Body of John Brown, 1940
Wake Island, 1942
Beast in View, 1944
The Green Wave, 1948
Elegies, 1949
Orpheus, 1949
Selected Poems, 1951
Body of Waking, 1958
Waterlily Fire: Poems, 1935-1962, 1962
The Outer Banks, 1967
The Speed of Darkness, 1968
Twenty-nine Poems, 1972
Breaking Open: New Poems, 1973
The Gates, 1976
The Collected Poems, 1978
Out of Silence: Selected Poems, 1992
Selected Poems, 2004 (Adrienne Rich, editor)
The Collected Poems of Muriel Rukeyser, 2005 (Janet E. Kaufman and Anne F. Herzog, editors)

OTHER LITERARY FORMS

In addition to her own poetry, Muriel Rukeyser (ROOK-iz-ur) published several volumes of translations (including work by the poets Octavio Paz and Gunnar Ekelöf), three biographies, two volumes of literary criticism, a number of book reviews, a novel, five juvenile books, and a play. She also worked on several documentary film scripts. The translations were exercises in writing during dry spells; the biographies, like her poetic sequence "Lives," combine her interests in the arts and sciences. The two volumes of literary criticism (along with her uncollected book reviews) are central to understanding her views concerning poetry and life.

Achievements

With the publication of *Theory of Flight* in the Yale Series of Younger Poets in 1935, Muriel Rukeyser began a long and productive career as a poet and author. Her work earned for her the first Harriet Monroe Poetry Award (1941), a National Institute of the Arts and Letters Award (1942), a Guggenheim Fellowship (1943), the Levinson Prize from *Poetry* magazine (1947), the Shelley Memorial Award (1977), the Copernicus Award (1977), a grant from the Eric Mathieu King Fund (1996), an honorary D.Litt. from Rutgers, and membership in the National Institute of Arts and Letters. She won the Swedish Academy Translation Award (1967) and the Anglo-Swedish Literary Foundation Award (1978) for her translations.

Biography

Muriel Rukeyser was born on December 15, 1913, in New York City, the daughter of Lawrence B. Rukeyser, a cofounder of Colonial Sand and Stone, and Myra Lyons, a former bookkeeper. Her childhood was a quiet one, her protected, affluent life a source of her insistence on experience and communication in her poetry. In *The Life of Poetry* (1949), she tells of recognizing the sheltered nature of her life: "A teacher asks: 'How many of you know any other road in the city except the road between home and school?' I do not put up my hand. These are moments at which one begins to see."

Rukeyser's adult life was as eventful as her childhood was sheltered. In 1933, at age nineteen, she was arrested and caught typhoid fever while attending the Scottsboro trials in Alabama; three years later, she investigated at firsthand the mining tragedy at Gauley Bridge, West Virginia; and in 1936, she was sent by *Life and Letters Today* to cover the Anti-Fascist Olympics in Barcelona as the Spanish Civil War broke out around her. These crusades dramatize her intense conviction on the sanctity of human life and her desire to experience life actively, and they all served as inspiration for her poetry, fulfilling her declaration in "Poem out of Childhood" to "Breathe-in experience, breathe-out poetry."

Throughout the remainder of a life filled with traveling and speaking for causes in which she intensely believed, Rukeyser never stopped learning, teaching, and writing; she declared that she would never protest without making something in the process. The wide range of knowledge in her poetry and criticism and the large volume of poetry and prose she published testify to this fact. She attended the Ethical Culture School and Fieldston School, Vassar College, Columbia University, and the Roosevelt School of Aviation in New York City, and she learned film editing with Helen Van Dongen. Besides conducting poetry workshops at a number of different institutions, she taught at the California Labor School and Sarah Lawrence College and later served as a member of the board of directors of the Teachers-Writers Collaborative in New York.

Rukeyser made her home in New York City, except for the nine years she spent in California and the time she was traveling. She moved to California in 1945 and shortly

Muriel Rukeyser
(Library of Congress)

afterward married painter Glynn Collins (although the marriage was soon annulled). Three years later, she had an illegitimate son and was disowned by her family, experiences that figure prominently in her poetry after this date. She moved back to New York in 1954 to teach at Sarah Lawrence College.

Rukeyser left Sarah Lawrence College in 1967. Although in failing health, she continued to write and protest. For the Committee for Solidarity, she flew to Hanoi in 1972 to demonstrate for peace, and later that year, she was jailed in Washington, D.C., for protesting the Vietnam War on the steps of the Capitol. In 1974, as president of the American center for PEN, a society that supports the rights of writers throughout the world, she flew to Korea to plead for the life of imprisoned poet Kim Chi-Ha. Rukeyser died in New York City on February 12, 1980.

Analysis

While Muriel Rukeyser has been linked to W. H. Auden, Stephen Spender, and other political poets, her work more clearly evolves from that of Ralph Waldo Emerson, Herman Melville, and Walt Whitman. From Emerson and the Transcendental tradition, she developed her organic theory of poetry, from Melville, her poetry of outrage. From Whitman, however, she obtained perhaps her most distinguishing characteristics: her belief in possibility; her long, rhythmic lines; her need to embrace humanity; and her expression of the power and beauty of sexuality. Her feminist views link her with Denise Levertov and Adrienne Rich, while her experimentation with the poetic line and the visual appearance of the poem on the page remind one at times of May Swenson. Both the quality and quantity of her work and the integrity of her feminist and mythic vision suggest that she will come to be seen as a significant figure in modern American poetry.

THEORY OF FLIGHT

"Look! Be: leap," Rukeyser writes in the preamble to the title poem of her first collection, *Theory of Flight*. These imperatives identify her emphasis on vision, her insistence on primary experience, and her belief in human potential. Focusing on this dictum, Rukeyser presents to her readers "the truths of outrage and the truths of possibility" in the world. To Rukeyser, poetry is a way to learn more about oneself and one's relations with others and to live more fully in an imperfect world.

The publication of *Theory of Flight* immediately marked Rukeyser as, in Stephen Vincent Benét's words, "a Left Winger and a revolutionary," an epithet she could never quite shake, although the Marxists never fully accepted her for not becoming a Communist and for writing poems that tried to do more than simply support their cause. Indeed, Rukeyser did much more than write Marxist poems. She was a poet of liberty, recording "the truths of outrage" she saw around her, and a poet of love, writing "the truths of possibility" in intimate human relationships. With the conviction of Akiba (a Jewish teacher and martyr who fought to include the Song of Songs in the Bible and from whom, according to family tradition, Rukeyser's mother was descended), Rukeyser wrote with equal fervor about social and humane issues such as miners dying of silicosis, the rights of minorities, the lives of women and imprisoned poets, and about universals such as the need for love and communication among people and the sheer physical and emotional joy of loving.

U.S. 1

Unlike many political poets, Rukeyser tried to do more than simply espouse: to protect, but also to build and to create. For Rukeyser, poetry's purpose is to sustain and heal, and the poet's responsibility is to recognize life as it is and encourage all people to their greatest potential through poetry.

Refusing to accept the negation of T. S. Eliot's *The Waste Land* (1922), Rukeyser uses images of technology and energy extensively in her early volumes to find, in a positive way, a place for the self in modern technological society, thus identifying herself with Hart Crane and with the poets of the Dynamo school. "Theory of Flight" centers on the airplane and the gyroscope. The dam and the power plant become the predominant symbols in "The Book of the Dead" in *U.S. 1*, her next collection.

U.S. 1 also contains a series of shorter, more lyrical poems titled "Night-Music."

While these poems are still strongly social in content, they are more personal and are based on what Rukeyser refers to as "unverifiable fact" (as opposed to the documentary evidence in "Theory of Flight" and "The Book of the Dead"). This change foreshadows the shifting emphasis throughout her career on the sources of power about which she writes—from machinery to poetry to the self. It is this change in conception that allowed Rukeyser to grow poetically, to use fewer of the abstractions for which many critics have faulted her, and to use instead more personal and concrete images on which to anchor her message.

A Turning Wind

This movement is evident in *A Turning Wind*. She begins to see the power and the accompanying fear of poetry, and her poetic voice becomes increasingly personal, increasingly founded in personal experience. Poetry becomes the means, the language, and the result of looking for connections or, in Jungian terms, a kind of collective unconscious. Rukeyser notices, however, that poetry is feared precisely because of its power: "They fear it. They turn away, hand up palm out/ fending off moment of proof, the straight look, poem." The fear of poetry is a fear of disclosure to oneself of what is inside, and this fear is "an indication that we are cut off from our own reality." Therefore, Rukeyser continually urges her readers to use poetry to look within themselves for a common ground on which they can stand as human beings.

"Lives"

The poetic sequence "Lives" (which extends through subsequent volumes as well as *A Turning Wind*) identifies another of Rukeyser's growing interests—"ways of getting past impossibilities by changing phase." Poetry thus becomes a meeting place of different ideas and disciplines. It is a place where the self meets the self, diving to confront unchallenged emotions in the search for truth, and a place where the self can face the world with newly discovered self-knowledge. Using the resources they discover both inside and outside themselves, people can grow to understand themselves and the world better. The subjects of the "Lives" exemplify values and traditions Rukeyser believes are important to the search.

Rukeyser's growth as a person and as a poet, then, has been a growth of the self, realizing her capabilities and her potential and, in turn, the capabilities and potential of those around her. She becomes increasingly open in her later poems, discussing her failed marriage, her illegitimate son and subsequent disinheritance, her son's exile in Canada during the Vietnam War, and her feelings about age and death. Although these poems may seem confessional, she is not a confessional poet such as Robert Lowell or W. D. Snodgrass. The details of her life, she tells the reader, are events she must consider from various angles as she dives within herself, looking for the essence of being. "The universe of poetry is the universe of emotional truth." Rukeyser writes in her critical work

The Life of Poetry, and it is the "breaking open" of her preconceived emotions to discover emotional truth that allows her to become closer to the humanity around her. "One writes in order to feel," she continues. "That is the fundamental mover."

"AJANTA"

In "Ajanta," Rukeyser makes perhaps her first statement of inner emotional truth, according to poet-critic Virginia R. Terris. In this mythic journey within the self, Rukeyser realizes that self-knowledge is the prerequisite for all other kinds of knowledge. Yet behind her search for self-knowledge and expansion of the self into the world is her belief in the necessity of communication. The silence she experienced at home as a child had a profound effect on her, and in many early poems, such as "Effort at Speech Between Two People," communication is ultimately impossible. This same silence appears to be at the root of many of the world's problems, and Rukeyser's open outrage and inner searching are attempts to right the problem, to achieve communication. By the time she wrote "Ajanta," silence had become a positive force, allowing her the opportunity to concentrate on her journey within.

ARTIST AND AUDIENCE

Rukeyser has at times been criticized for combining disparate images within the same poem, as in "Waterlily Fire," from her collection by the same name, but this seems unjust. Far from being unrelated elements, her images grow, change, and develop throughout a poem and throughout her poetic canon. She puts the responsibility for making connections on the reader; she gives clues but does not take all the work out of the poem: "Both artist and audience create, and both do work on themselves in creating." Rukeyser is not an easy poet, and one cannot read her poetry passively. Yet she is a rewarding poet for those who take the time to look at and listen to what she is doing.

POETIC SEQUENCES

Another distinguishing mark of Rukeyser's poetry is the numerous poetic sequences (such as "Lives") which are connected by a common situation, theme, or character. "Waterlily Fire," for example, is a group of five poems about the burning of Claude Monet's *Waterlilies* at the Museum of Modern Art in New York City. "Elegies" is a collection of ten poems extending over three volumes. "Poem out of Childhood" is a cluster of fifteen poems, of which one is also a cluster of three, centered on Rukeyser's childhood—what she learns from it and how she uses it poetically.

Rukeyser's interest in poetic sequences grew from her training as a film editor:

> The work with film is a terribly good exercise for poetry... the concept of sequences, the cutting of sequences of varying length, the frame by frame composition, the use of a traveling

image, traveling by the way the film is cut, shot, projected at a set speed, a sound track or a silent track, in conjunction with the visual track but can be brought into bad descriptive verbal things and brought into marvelous juxtapositions.

The sequence makes more apparent to readers the necessity of looking for connections among poems—recurring images, phrases, and sounds—than could separate poems.

THE SPEED OF DARKNESS

In *The Speed of Darkness*, Rukeyser returns to her preoccupation with silence, expressing it structurally both in and as a subject. From her earliest poems, she used space within lines (often combined with a proliferation of colons) to act as a new type of punctuation—a metric rest—but in *The Speed of Darkness*, she places greater emphasis on the placement of the poem on the page to achieve this metric rest, for space on the page "can provide roughly for a relationship in emphasis through the eye's discernment of pattern."

MOVING TOWARD SHORTER LINES

Rukeyser's verse has often been characterized as half poetry, half prose because of the long, sweeping, encompassing, Whitmanesque free-verse lines especially noticeable in her early poems. In *The Speed of Darkness* and later poems, however, she moves toward shorter lines and works with smaller units of meaning to compensate for breathing. At times, her arrangement of these poems ("The War Comes into My Room," "Mountain: One from Bryant," and "Rune," for example) approaches Swenson's iconographs in their experimentation with the visual and physical movement of the line.

Perhaps another reason for the new, shorter lines is that they are more suited for the introspective journeys of Rukeyser's later work than are the long, flowing, altruistic lines she used earlier. They also help her to control more effectively her penchant for verbosity and maintain the development of her images. Yet the length and conclusion of the later lines are not without precedent. Many of the most powerful passages in the early poems were journalistic or cinematic passages, not yet matured but still effective in their performance. "The Book of the Dead" is especially noteworthy in this respect, for it contains the seeds of the concrete image and colloquial diction fully realized later.

DICTION

Rukeyser's diction also gives ample reason for labeling her poetry half prose. Yet as startling as it may be to encounter words such as "eugenically," "silicosis," and "cantillations" in her poems, these words make the reader pay attention. She also employs words and even sounds as physical, musical, and thematic ties within and among poems in the same way other poets use rhyme and in the same way she uses image sequences.

With the variety of line length and placement evident in Rukeyser's work, it is not surprising that her canon is characterized by a rich variety of styles. Her experiments with language, line length, and rhythm easily lend themselves to experiments with different verse styles, including but extending beyond elegies, sonnets, odes, rounds, and rondels.

"Letter, Unposted"

While Rukeyser uses traditional as well as nontraditional verse patterns, she often treats even her most traditional subjects untraditionally. Because of her belief in the community of humankind, she has written many love poems, yet she approaches even the most personal subjects in an unexpected way. A notable example is "Letter, Unposted" from *Theory of Flight*, which is centered on the traditional theme of waiting for a lover. Yet it is distinguished from other such poems by the speaker's refusal to languish in love and to see nature languishing along with her. The letter remains unposted because the speaker cannot write all the traditional sentimental foolishness expected of her. Instead, as in even the bleakest situations about which Rukeyser writes, she sees the positive side: "But summer lives,/ and minds grow, and nerves are sensitized to power . . . and I receive them joyfully and live: but wait for you." The speaker rejoices in life rather than feeling sorry for herself.

Feminist outlook

Although a feminine consciousness is evident in every volume of Rukeyser's poetry, *The Speed of Darkness* also begins a new and more imperative feminist outlook. In the same way that she refused to be simply a Marxist poet, neither is she simply a feminist poet. Rukeyser sees with a feminist point of view, but rather than rejecting the masculine, she retains valuable past information and revisualizes history and myth with female vitality. For example, in "Myth," one learns that Oedipus was not as smart as he thought he was; he did not answer the Sphinx's riddle correctly after all: "'You didn't say anything about woman.'/ 'When you say Man,' said Oedipus, 'you include women/ too. Everyone knows that.' She said, 'That's what/ you think.'" "Ms. Lot" adds another perspective to the biblical story of Lot and his wife, and in "Painters" (*The Gates*) she envisions a woman among the primitive cave painters.

Other poems written throughout her career on more contemporary issues reveal the strength of women while upholding their nurturing role. The mother in "Absalom" ("The Book of the Dead") will "give a mouth to my son" who died of silicosis, and Kim Chi-Ha's mother in "The Gates" is portrayed as a pitchfork, one of Rukeyser's few uses of simile or metaphor. She also refuses to let women take the easy way out as some have been trained to do: "More of a Corpse than a Woman" and "Gradus Ad Parnassum," for example, display the vapidity of the stereotypical passive rich woman.

While women are strong in Rukeyser's verse, they are still human. Sex is one of the driving forces in Rukeyser's work, and she frequently expresses the joys of love and sex, especially in *Breaking Open*. Significant examples are the powerful eroticism of "Looking at Each Other," the honesty of "In Her Burning" and "Rondel," and the power of sexual renewal in "Welcome from War." Giving birth is also a powerful image in many of the poems.

"THE GATES"

"The Gates," a fifteen-poem sequence organized around Rukeyser's trip to Korea to plead for the release of imprisoned poet Kim Chi-Ha, synthesizes her recurring images and messages in a final, powerful poetic statement. Like "Night-Music," this sequence is at once social commentary and personal discovery, but it takes a much stronger stance in demanding freedom of speech and assessing Rukeyser's own development as a poet in the light of Kim Chi-Ha's life.

LEGACY

"Breathe-in experience, breathe-out poetry" begins "Poem out of Childhood," the first poem in Rukeyser's first collection. Muriel Rukeyser wrote a poetry developing organically from personal experience and self-discovery, a poetry bringing the anguish, miseries, and misfortunes of human beings around the world to her readers' attention, a poetry demonstrating her exhilaration with life and love. Readers cannot hide from reality in her poetry, nor can they hide from themselves. There is always the journey, but possibility always lies at its end: "the green tree perishes and green trees grow." Rukeyser's challenge to the world she left behind is found near the end of "Then" (in "The Gates"): "When I am dead, even then,/ I will still love you, I will wait in these poems . . . I will still be making poems for you/ out of silence." The silence and passivity against which she fought throughout her life will not triumph if her readers are alive to her words and to the world around them.

OTHER MAJOR WORKS

LONG FICTION: *The Orgy*, 1965.

PLAYS: *The Colors of the Day: A Celebration for the Vassar Centennial, June 10, 1961*, pr. 1961; *Houdini*, pr. 1973.

NONFICTION: *Willard Gibbs*, 1942; *The Life of Poetry*, 1949; *One Life*, 1957; *Poetry and the Unverifiable Fact: The Clark Lectures*, 1968; *The Traces of Thomas Hariot*, 1971.

CHILDREN'S LITERATURE: *Come Back, Paul*, 1955; *I Go Out*, 1961; *Bubbles*, 1967; *Mazes*, 1970; *More Night*, 1981.

TRANSLATIONS: *Selected Poems*, 1963 (of Octavio Paz's poems); *Sun Stone*, 1963 (of Paz's poems); *Selected Poems*, 1967 (with Leif Sjöberg; of Gunnar Ekelöf's poems); *Three Poems*, 1967 (of Ekelöf's poems); *Early Poems, 1935-1955*, 1973 (of

Paz's poems); *Uncle Eddie's Moustache*, 1974 (of Bertolt Brecht's poems); *A Mölna Elegy*, 1984 (of Ekelöf's poem).

MISCELLANEOUS: *A Muriel Rukeyser Reader*, 1994.

BIBLIOGRAPHY

Dayton, Tim. *Muriel Rukeyser's "The Book of the Dead."* Columbia: University of Missouri Press, 2003. Provides a close look at "The Book of the Dead" and describes its critical reception. A radio interview of Rukeyser by Samuel Sillen is included.

Gardinier, Suzanne. "A World That Will Hold All People: On Muriel Rukeyser." *Kenyon Review* 14 (Summer, 1992): 88-105. An in-depth discussion of Rukeyser's poetry as reflecting her life experiences and her political beliefs. Gardinier states that Rukeyser wrote "the poetry of a believer—in an age of unbelief." Many quotations from Rukeyser's early and later poems.

Goodman, Jenny. "'Presumption' and 'Unlearning': Reading Muriel Rukeyser's 'The Book of the Dead' as a Woman's American Epic." *Tulsa Studies in Women's Literature* 25, no. 2 (Fall, 2006): 267. Goodman argues that Rukeyser uses the epic convention to create a narrative of national redemption centered on women.

Herzog, Anne F., and Janet E. Kaufman, eds. *How Shall We Tell Each Other of the Poet? The Life and Writing of Muriel Rukeyser.* New York: St. Martin's Press, 1999. A collection of tributes and essays regarding Rukeyser by poets and literary scholars. Includes bibliographical references and an index.

Kertesz, Louise. *The Poetic Vision of Muriel Rukeyser.* Baton Rouge: Louisiana State University Press, 1980. Kertesz provides the first book-length critical evaluation of Rukeyser's work. This book is flawed in that much of Kertesz's analysis is abandoned in favor of an angry defense of Rukeyser's work against critics who misunderstood it. However, Kertesz puts Rukeyser in the context of her time and place and so provides a valuable study for all Rukeyser students.

Rich, Adrienne. "Beginners." *Kenyon Review* 15 (Summer, 1993): 12-19. In this beautifully written essay, Rich, a prominent poet herself, discusses Rukeyser, Walt Whitman, and Emily Dickinson, calling them all "beginners . . . openers of new paths . . . who take the first steps . . . and therefore seem strange and 'dreadful.'"

Rukeyser, Muriel. *The Life of Poetry.* Rev. ed. Foreword by Jane Cooper. Williamsburg, Mass.: Paris Press, 1996. Rukeyser's explanation of her conception of the role of the poet in society, drawing on such diverse authorities as English mathematician/philosopher Alfred North Whitehead, Austrian psychoanalyst Sigmund Freud, German philosopher Georg Hegel, and American physicist Willard Gibbs. As the title suggests, Rukeyser believed that poetry should be a way of life.

Thurston, Michael. *Making Something Happen: American Political Poetry Between the World Wars.* Chapel Hill: University of North Carolina Press, 2001. Thurston examines the political poetry of Rukeyser, Edwin Rolfe, Langston Hughes, and Ezra

Pound, arguing that the poetry is worth reading for its aesthetic qualities as well as its message.

Ware, Michele S. "Opening *The Gates*: Muriel Rukeyser and the Poetry of Witness." *Women's Studies* 22 (June, 1993): 297-308. An extensive analysis of *The Gates*, the last volume of Rukeyser's new poetry to be published before her death. Praises her oracular characteristics and lyricism while maintaining the integrity of her political and social messages.

Kenneth E. Gadomski

ANNE SEXTON

Born: Newton, Massachusetts; November 9, 1928
Died: Weston, Massachusetts; October 4, 1974

PRINCIPAL POETRY
To Bedlam and Part Way Back, 1960
All My Pretty Ones, 1962
Selected Poems, 1964
Live or Die, 1966
Poems, 1968 (with Thomas Kinsella and Douglas Livingston)
Love Poems, 1969
Transformations, 1971
The Book of Folly, 1972
The Death Notebooks, 1974
The Awful Rowing Toward God, 1975
Words for Dr. Y.: Uncollected Poems with Three Stories, 1978 (Linda Gray Sexton, editor)
The Complete Poems, 1981
Selected Poems of Anne Sexton, 1988

OTHER LITERARY FORMS

In addition to several articles on the craft and teaching of poetry, Anne Sexton wrote a play that ran successfully at the American Place Theatre of New York and several children's books produced in collaboration with Maxine Kumin. The play, *45 Mercy Street* (pr. 1969), presents the struggle of a woman named Daisy to find meaning in a past and present dominated by religious and sexual conflicts objectified as demons and disembodied voices. Its success suggests that the poet also had talent as a playwright, and critics find the thematic material important biographically and artistically in an analysis of Sexton's career. An important collection of her prose is *Anne Sexton: A Self-Portrait in Letters* (1977); also, a recording of twenty-four poems read by the poet is available as *Anne Sexton Reads Her Poetry*, recorded June 1, 1974.

ACHIEVEMENTS

With little formal training in literature, Anne Sexton emerged as a major modern voice, transforming verse begun as therapy into poetic art of the first order. Important for refining the confessional mode, experimenting with new lyrical forms, and presenting themes from the female consciousness, Sexton had the controversial impact of any pioneering artist. Despite periodic hospitalization for depression, ultimately culminat-

Anne Sexton
(Library of Congress)

ing in her suicide at age forty-six, Sexton contributed richly to her craft, receiving much critical recognition and traveling widely.

Awarded fellowships to most of the major writing conferences, Sexton worked closely with John Holmes, W. D. Snodgrass, Robert Lowell, Kumin, and others. She taught creative writing at Harvard, Radcliffe, and Boston University, and she served as editorial consultant to the *New York Poetry Quarterly* and as a member of the board of directors of *Audience* magazine. She won the Levinson Prize from *Poetry* magazine in 1962, and her second collection of poetry, *All My Pretty Ones*, was nominated for a National Book Award in 1963. In 1967, she received the Shelley Memorial Award and a Pulitzer Prize for her fourth collection, *Live or Die*. Sexton also received a Guggenheim Fellowship in 1969 and many honorary degrees from major universities.

Although most critics believe the quality of her work deteriorated toward the end of her life, by that time, she had achieved success with a new, highly personal voice in poetry and expanded the range of acceptable subjects to include the intimate concerns of women. In presenting the theme of female identity, Sexton began with a careful lyric formalism and then progressed throughout her career to experiment with open, dramatic forms, moving from the confessional to the surreal. She explored the limits of sanity and the nature of womanhood more fully than any poet of her generation.

Biography

Anne Sexton was born Anne Gray Harvey, the daughter of upper-middle-class parents. She attended the public schools of Wellesley, Massachusetts and spent two years at Rogers Preparatory School and one year at Garland Junior College before marrying Alfred Muller Sexton, whose nickname, Kayo, provides the dedication for her first volume of poems. Although a strictly biographical approach to Anne Sexton's work is dangerously limiting, the significant events of her life serve as major subjects and impetus for her art.

After her marriage, she worked briefly as a model at the Hart Agency of Boston. Then, when she was twenty-five, her first daughter, Linda Gray Sexton, was born. The next year, Anne Sexton was hospitalized for emotional disturbance, and several months later, she suffered the loss of her beloved great-aunt, Anna Ladd Dingley, nicknamed Nana, in various poems and remembrances. The next year, Joyce Ladd Sexton was born, but within months, her mother was again hospitalized for depression culminating in a suicide attempt on her twenty-eighth birthday.

Following her first suicide attempt, Sexton began writing poetry on the advice of her psychiatrist, Martin Orne, whose name appears in her first collection of poems. On the strength of her first work, she received a scholarship to the Antioch Writer's Conference where she worked with W. D. Snodgrass. Then she was accepted into Robert Lowell's graduate writing seminar at Boston University, soon developing friendships with Sylvia Plath, Maxine Kumin, and George Starbuck. The next year, Sexton's parents died in rapid succession. She continued her work, attending the Bread Loaf Writer's Conference and delivering the Morris Gray Poetry Lecture at Harvard, although she was hospitalized at intervals for pneumonia, an appendectomy, and an ovariectomy. In 1960, Sexton studied with Philip Rahv and Irving Howe at Brandeis University and developed a friendship with James Wright. She was appointed, with Maxine Kumin, to be the first scholars in poetry at the Radcliffe Institute for Independent Study. In 1962, she was again hospitalized for depression, but by the end of the year, she had recovered and toured Europe on the first traveling fellowship of the American Academy of Arts and Letters. She also received a Ford Foundation grant for residence with the Charles Playhouse in Boston.

In 1966, Sexton began a novel that was never completed. She again attempted suicide in July, 1966. In August, she took an African safari with her husband, but in November, she was hospitalized again when she broke her hip on her thirty-eighth birthday. In May of 1967, she received the Pulitzer Prize for *Live or Die* and the Shelley Memorial Award from the Poetry Society of America. She taught poetry as a visiting professor in many schools and received many honorary degrees before again attempting suicide in 1970. In 1973, she divorced her husband during another period of hospitalization for depression. She continued to write and teach despite frequent intervals of hospitalization. In 1974, she committed suicide by carbon monoxide poisoning in the garage of her home.

Analysis

Anne Sexton's poetry presents a search for self and meaning beyond the limits of conventional expression and form. Although viewing her work autobiographically limits critical understanding of it, readers discover in her work a chronicle of experience that is intensely personal and genuine. Her poems are confessional in that they present statements about impulses formerly unknown or forbidden. Begun for self-revelation in therapy and initially sustained for the possible benefit of other troubled patients, Sexton's poems speak with penetrating honesty about the experience of mental illness, the temptation of suicide, and the dynamics of womanhood. Although less strident in tone than the work of Sylvia Plath, Sexton's work occasionally alienates readers who, like James Dickey, find her work too personal for literary evaluation. At its best, however, Sexton's poetry develops the confessional lyric into an effective modern form.

To Bedlam and Part Way Back

In her first collection, *To Bedlam and Part Way Back*, scenes from an asylum are set against those of life before and after the speaker's hospitalization. The perspective of these early poems is a daring interior one, underscored by the book's epigraph taken from a letter of Arthur Schopenhauer to Johann Wolfgang von Goethe, including the phrase "But most of us carry in our heart the Jocasta who begs Oedipus for God's sake not to inquire further." Sexton's poems pursue the inquiry into the mental hospital and the mind of the patient as well. In the chantlike poem "Ringing the Bells," for example, Sexton projects the senseless rhythm of institutional life through the consciousness of a patient in the bell choir of a mental ward. The troubled women who "mind by instinct" assemble, smile, ring their bells when pointed to, and disperse, no better for their weekly music lesson. Another well-known portrayal of institutional life, "Lullaby," shows the figure of the night nurse arriving with the sleeping pills that, like splendid pearls, provide a momentary escape for the patients who receive them. Observing the moths which cling to window screen, the patient of "Lullaby" imagines that he will become like them after taking the sedative. "You, Doctor Martin" presents other figures in the mental hospital, including the large children who wait in lines to be counted at dinner before returning to the labor of making moccasins all day long. Although the portrayal of the mental hospital from an insider's perspective provides a fresh subject for experimental lyrics, Sexton's poems of the journey and return (suggested by the volumes title) are among her most complex and effective.

"The Double Image," for example, is a composite of experiences parallel to Sexton's own biography. In the poem, the speaker's hospitalization brings about a separation from her young daughter; the speaker's return to live in the home of her childhood coincides with the final illness of her own mother. Weaving together the present moment of her return home for a reunion with her daughter and events of the past, the speaker reflects on the guilt bounded by past and present sorrow. The three autumns explain her trouble better than any medical theories, and she finds that despair and guilt transform attempts at ordinary life into artifice. Portrait painting becomes a metaphor for control of time and emotions through the rest of the poem. Unable to adjust to the awkward period spent as a grown child in her parents' home, the speaker states repeatedly, "I had my portrait done instead." The same response belongs to her mother, who cannot forgive the speaker's attempt at suicide and so chooses to have the daughter painted as a measure of control. A double image forms when the mother learns of her own incurable illness and has her portrait done "instead." The portraits, facing each other in the parental home, serve as a mirror reflection with the figure of the speaker's child moving between them. As the speaker had been "an awkward guest" returning to her mother's home, so the young daughter arrives "an awkward guest" for the reunion with her recovering mother. The child provides both a measure of final identity and guilt.

In "The Division of Parts," the bitterness of inheritance replaces grief as a response to the death of the speaker's mother. As in "The Double Image," the coincidence of the speaker's recovery with her mother's suffering suggests an apparent exchange of death for life. Equipped with the lost one's "garments" but not with grief, the speaker recalls the suffering of her mother, overshadowed now by the ceremonies of the Lenten season. Division of property replaces the concerns of the Christ who waits on the crucifix for the speaker. Her dreams recall only the division of ways: the separation of death and inevitable division of property.

Other poems in the first volume experiment with the voices of those whose experiences differ from those of the poet. "The Farmer's Wife," for example, reveals the isolation and loneliness of a young wife on an Illinois farm. The poem presents the ambivalence of the woman toward her husband, whose work and bed are her lifelong habit. "Unknown Girl in the Maternity Ward" attempts to voice the feelings of an unmarried girl who has just given birth. The emotions and imagery are generalized and undefined in presenting the setting of an urban hospital and the typical unmarried girl in trouble. According to Sexton, the poem marks a pivotal moment in her career, for after reading it, Robert Lowell advised her to develop the more personal voice that gives her finest poetry its power. A poem reflecting conflicting advice is "For John, Who Begs Me Not to Enquire Further." John Holmes, Sexton's teacher for a Boston University poetry workshop, recommended that she avoid the self-revelation becoming characteristic of her work. The directly personal voice won out, not only in this poem of apology to Holmes but also throughout her career. Another early poem, "Kind Sir: These Woods," indicates an awareness that readers in general may disapprove her probing of the psyche, "this inward look that society scorns." The speaker finds in her inward search, however, nothing worse than herself, "caught between the grapes and the thorns," and the search for herself continued to the end of her life.

ALL MY PRETTY ONES

An epigraph for Sexton's second collection, *All My Pretty Ones*, suggests a reason for the poet's insistence on inner exploration. According to a letter of Franz Kafka, "a book should serve as the ax for the frozen sea within us." Sexton similarly asserted in a later interview that "poems of the inner life can reach the inner lives of readers in a way that anti-war poems can never stop a war." The inner life revealed in *All My Pretty Ones* is primarily the experience of grief, the response to loss of the most precious others expressed in the lines from *Macbeth* (pr. 1606) that form the title. "The Truth the Dead Know" and the title poem deal with the death of Sexton's parents during the same year. The first poem eliminates personal references except for a dedication to the parents and simply contrasts the intensity of life and grief with the emptiness and stoniness of the dead. "All My Pretty Ones" addresses the lost father with memories of his belongings, his habits, and his hopes. Disposition of scrapbook photographs provides a way to accept and forgive the disappointments of the past, including the secret alcoholism his daughter can never forget.

The strongest poems of the second volume arise from Sexton's own experience. In "The Operation," the speaker's confrontation with death parallels the illness of her mother, and the speaker considers the uncertainty of life as much as the reality of death. Knowing that cancer, the disease of her mother, the "historic thief" that plundered her mother's home is now invading her own domain, the speaker proceeds helplessly through the preparations for surgery, the experience of losing consciousness, and the recovery phase in doubt of her survival. Then, pronounced better, perhaps cured, by the doctors, she is sent home like a child, the stitches in her abdomen reminding her of the lacing on a football ready for the game. A similar sense of vulnerability appears in "The Fortress," wherein the speaker admits to her sleeping child that a mother has no ability to control life and that eventually it will overtake the child through the suffering of "bombs or glands" ending in death. Beyond the sense of relationships, especially those connected with motherhood, controlling many of Sexton's poems, there looms a sense of dark knowledge gained through poetry as a secret or forbidden art. In "The Black Art," for example, the speaker asserts that a woman who writes will not fit into society, for she "feels too much, these trances and portents." Home, family, social life are inadequate expressions for the one who wishes to know and control the mysterious forces of existence. The poem recalls an earlier statement of identity, "Her Kind," in which the speaker presents herself as a witch who is lonely, misunderstood, insane, and unashamed to die in the course of her journey. The comparison of Sexton's poetry with the black arts places her work on the level of myth, particularly in her pursuit of death itself.

LIVE OR DIE

Live or Die, Sexton's third collection, marks a high point in her career for handling intimate or despairing material with sure control and an element of self-irony. The epigraph for this book, taken from Saul Bellow's *Herzog* (1964), records the admonition to "Live or die, but don't poison everything." Certainly, the poems of this group reflect the impulse toward love and life as well as the impulse toward despair and death. The institutional setting appears in the volume but so does the home and family relationships of Sexton. "Flee on Your Donkey," one of her best-known poems, develops the tension between the worlds of private and institutional life. In the poem, a flood of scenes from the hospital culminates in a desire to escape back to the normal world that patients enter the hospital to avoid. Similarly, in "For the Year of the Insane," structured as a prayer to Mary, the speaker struggles to escape her mental as well as physical confinement. No longer at peace in the refuge of therapy, a mind that believes itself "locked in the wrong house" struggles in vain for expression and release. Poems of similar desperation, "The Addict" and "Wanting to Die," develop other means of escape. The speaker of the former poem yearns for the hallucinatory realm where drugs parcel out moments of deathlike experience. "Wanting to Die," another of Sexton's best-known poems, strives to explain for the uninitiated the hunger for death haunting the potential suicide. The obsession with methods of dying replaces the desire for experience of life. Love itself becomes "an infection" to those seeking the secret pleasure that final escape from the body will bring.

Poems of the third collection that deal with survival include those concerned with children and birth. In "Little Girl, My String Bean, My Lovely Woman," the speaker identifies with the approaching womanhood of her daughter Linda, beautiful even in the uncertain changes adolescence creates. The poem celebrates the body in its growth and capacity for becoming; the figure of mother and daughter share the mystery of reproduction that is spiritual, "a white stone," as well as physical, "laughter," and joy. In "Pain for a Daughter," the mother discovers in her injured child's suffering a universal misery that transcends their relationship. The child's foot torn by the hoof of a horse, she cries out to God, not her mother, and the isolation of the cry suggests not childhood misery but the future pangs of childbirth and death itself. The decision to survive, for the moment at least, appears in "Live," the final statement of the volume. The speaker recounts a shift from life as a dark pretense or game to a moment when the sun rose within her, illuminating the figures of her husband and daughters. The speaker determines herself no longer to be the murderer she thought, allowing the newborn Dalmatian puppies to live and deciding to survive herself.

LOVE POEMS

Love Poems, Sexton's fourth collection, examines the cycle of roles women play in life and love. Poems of separation and return, for example, include "Touch" and "Eighteen Days Without You," lyrics in which love between a woman and her lover controls survival and existence beyond their union. Throughout the volume, individual body parts achieve significance beyond their function in the physical realm. "Touch" begins, "For months my hand had been sealed off/ in a tin box." Following the arrival of her lover, life rushes into the fingers, spreading across the continent in its intensity. Other celebrations of physical contact include "The Kiss," "The Breast," and "In Celebration of My Uterus." In this last poem, Sexton develops a great song that a whole catalog of women sing as they go about their daily work carrying the "sweet weight" of the womb. The negative side of experience returns in poems such as "The Break," which recounts the depression preceding a fall down the stairs that broke Sexton's hip and forced another lengthy hospitalization. Although the bones are sure to heal, the speaker's heart begins another building process to create a "death crèche," ready for the zeal of destruction when it returns.

TRANSFORMATIONS

The theme of self-destruction is hidden in *Transformations*, Sexton's collection of rewritten fairy tales narrated by a "middle-aged witch," the poet's name for her persona in the tales. For some critics, this collection provides a more objective scheme for Sexton's mythic quest; for others, the subject matter is quaint and unoriginal. Certainly the retold tales are entertaining and effective in the dark, modern twists Sexton creates. "Snow White," for example, tortures the wicked queen without mercy before returning to gaze triumphantly in her mirror "as women do." "Rumpelstiltskin" develops the figure of the dark one within, the doppelgänger trying to escape every man. Failing to gain the queen's child, he splits in two, "one part papa/ one part Doppelganger," completing the division of the psyche. "Briar Rose (Sleeping Beauty)" becomes a tortured insomniac after being awakened by her prince and never knows the sleep of death.

LAST YEARS

Sexton's last collections, *The Book of Folly*, *The Death Notebooks*, and *The Awful Rowing Toward God* contain many of her previous themes developed in experimental forms, including dramatic changes in style. Critics note a looser structure in the poems written late in Sexton's career; some believe it reflects a deterioration of her creative powers, while others find the experimentalism valuable for its innovation.

One of the well-known late poems, "Hurry Up Please It's Time," reflects the variety of thematic material, the variable stanza lengths, and the intrusion of dialogue, such as those between "Anne" and "The Interrogator." The poem reworks the approach of death and the obsessive derision of life on the part of the dying one. "Ms. Dog," one of Sexton's nicknames for herself, as well as "God" spelled backward, figures in the poem as the troubled one facing guilt and rejection as well as the mystery and futility of death. In "Frenzy," another of the last poems, the speaker describes herself "typing out the God/ my typewriter believes in."

Through the last years of Sexton's life, her writing sustained her even as her quest darkened. At the end of her life, she sought God when doctors, friends, and family were unable to help her; and her work reflected an outwardly religious search that had formerly been hidden. Although she never revealed that she found God within or without the lines of her poetry, she left behind a brilliant record of her heroic search.

OTHER MAJOR WORKS

PLAY: *45 Mercy Street*, pr. 1969.

NONFICTION: *Anne Sexton: A Self-Portrait in Letters*, 1977 (Linda Gray Sexton and Lois Ames, editors); *No Evil Star: Selected Essays, Interviews, and Prose*, 1985.

CHILDREN'S LITERATURE (WITH MAXINE KUMIN): *Eggs of Things*, 1963; *More Eggs of Things*, 1964; *Joey and the Birthday Present*, 1971; *The Wizard's Tears*, 1975.

BIBLIOGRAPHY

Furst, Arthur. *Anne Sexton: The Last Summer*. New York: St. Martin's Press, 2000. A collection of Furst's photos of Sexton with letters and unpublished drafts of Sexton's poems written during the last months of her life, as well as previously unpublished letters to her daughters.

Gill, Jo. *Anne Sexton's Confessional Poetics*. Gainesville: University Press of Florida, 2007. Gill applies postconstructionalist literary theory to provide new readings of Sexton's poetry. She examines the place of Sexton's works in the larger body of confessional poetry.

Hall, Caroline King Barnard. *Anne Sexton*. Boston: Twayne, 1989. This useful introduction to Sexton examines her poetry and its chronological development. Worth noting is the chapter *"Transformations*: Fairy Tales Revisited."

McGowan, Philip. *Anne Sexton and Middle Generation Poetry: The Geography of Grief*. Westport, Conn.: Praeger, 2004. An upper-level, advanced analysis of Sexton's poetry with little biographical focus. Includes a bibliography and index.

Middlebrook, Diane Wood. *Anne Sexton: A Biography*. Boston: Houghton Mifflin, 1991. Middlebrook's biography of Sexton is based on audiotapes from Sexton's therapy sessions and the intimate revelations of Sexton's family. Middlebrook explores Sexton's creativity and the relationship between art and mental disorder.

Salvio, Paula A. *Anne Sexton: Teacher of Weird Abundance*. Albany: State University of New York Press, 2007. Examines how Sexton taught poetry, using the personal in teaching and learning.

Sexton, Linda Gray, and Lois Ames, eds. *Anne Sexton: A Self-Portrait in Letters*. Boston: Houghton Mifflin, 1977. A compilation of the best and most representative letters written by Sexton, who was an exceptional correspondent. Contains a wonderful collection of letters, arranged chronologically and interspersed with biographical details, and providing much insight about this poet's imagination.

Wagner-Martin, Linda, ed. *Critical Essays on Anne Sexton*. Boston: G. K. Hall, 1989. A volume of selected critical essays, gathering early reviews and modern scholarship, including essays on Sexton's poems and her life. All the essays offer significant secondary material on Sexton; the introduction by Wagner-Martin is helpful, giving an overview of Sexton's poems.

Chapel Louise Petty

GERTRUDE STEIN

Born: Allegheny (now in Pittsburgh), Pennsylvania; February 3, 1874
Died: Neuilly-sur-Seine, France; July 27, 1946

PRINCIPAL POETRY
Tender Buttons: Objects, Food, Rooms, 1914
Before the Flowers of Friendship Faded Friendship Faded, 1931
Two (Hitherto Unpublished) Poems, 1948
Bee Time Vine, and Other Pieces, 1913-1927, 1953
Stanzas in Meditation, and Other Poems, 1929-1933, 1956

OTHER LITERARY FORMS

Most of Gertrude Stein's works did not appear until much later than the dates of their completion. Much of her writing, including novelettes, shorter poems, plays, prayers, novels, and several portraits, appeared posthumously in the Yale Edition of the Unpublished Writings of Gertrude Stein, in eight volumes edited by Carl Van Vechten. A few of her plays have been set to music, the operas have been performed, and the later children's books have been illustrated by various artists.

ACHIEVEMENTS

Gertrude Stein did not win tangible recognition for her literary achievements, though she did earn the Medal of French Recognition from the French government for services during World War II. Nevertheless, her contribution to art, and specifically to writing, is as great as that of Ezra Pound or James Joyce. It is, however, diametrically opposed to that of these figures in style, content, and underlying philosophy of literature. She advanced mimetic representation to its ultimate, doing away progressively with memory, narration, plot, the strictures of formalized language, and the distinction among styles and genres. Her view of life was founded on a sense of the living present that shunned all theorizing about meaning and purpose, making writing a supreme experience unto itself. For the first fifteen years of her artistic life, she worked at her craft with stubborn persistence while carrying on an active social life among the Parisian avant-garde. She became influential as a person of definite taste and idiosyncratic manners rather than as an artist in her own right. Her parlor became legend, and writers as diverse as Ernest Hemingway and Sherwood Anderson profited from her ideas. In the 1920's, she was the matron of the American expatriates, and her work, by then known to most writers, was either ferociously derided or enthusiastically applauded.

It was the poetry of *Tender Buttons* that first brought Gertrude Stein to the attention of the public. After 1926, however, her novels, critical essays, and prose portraits in-

Gertrude Stein
(Library of Congress)

creasingly circulated. She secured a place in American letters with the publication of *The Autobiography of Alice B. Toklas* (1933), which was also a commercial success. She did not receive any official recognition during her lifetime, except as a curiosity in the world of letters.

Literary criticism has traditionally simply skirted the "problem" of Gertrude Stein, limiting itself to broad generalizations. There exists a group of Stein devotees responsible for preserving the texts; this group includes Robert Bartlett Haas, Carl Van Vechten, Donald Gallup, and Leon Katz. Stein's work has been illuminated by two indispensable scholar-critics, Richard Bridgman and Donald Sutherland; and there are useful interpretive suggestions in studies by Rosalind Miller, Allegra Stewart, Norman Weinstein, and Michael J. Hoffman. Stein's major impact has been on writers of later generations, especially in the late 1950's, through the 1960's, and up to the present time; the poetry of Aram Saroyan, Robert Kelly, Clark Coolidge, Jerome Rothenberg, and Lewis Welch is especially indebted to Stein. New insights into this revolutionary writer in the wake of global revisions of the notion of writing and critical thinking have been offered in short pieces by S. C. Neuman, William H. Gass, and Neil Schmitz. Today, a place of eminence is accorded to Stein's fairy tales and children's stories, the theoretical writings, the major works *The Autobiography of Alice B. Toklas* and *The Making of Ameri-*

cans: *Being a History of a Family's Progress* (1925, 1934), the shorter works *Three Lives* (1909) and *Ida, a Novel* (1941), and finally *Tender Buttons*, considered by many to be a masterpiece of twentieth century literature.

Biography

Gertrude Stein was born in Allegheny, Pennsylvania, on February 3, 1874. Her grandfather, Michael Stein, came from Austria in 1841, married Hanna Seliger, and settled in Baltimore. One of his sons, Daniel, Gertrude's father, was in the wholesale wool and clothing industry. Daniel was mildly successful and very temperamental. He married Amelia Keyser in 1864 and had five children, Michael (born in 1865), Simon (1867), Bertha (1870), Leo (1872), and Gertrude (1874). In 1875, the family moved to Vienna, and three years later, Daniel returned to the United States, leaving his family for a one-year stay in Paris. In 1879, the family moved back to the United States and spent a year in Baltimore with Amelia Keyser's family. In 1880, Daniel found work in California, and the family relocated again, to Oakland. Memories of these early moves would dot Gertrude's mature works. Leo and Gertrude found that they had much in common, took drawing and music lessons together, frequented the Oakland and San Francisco public libraries, and had time to devote to their intellectual and aesthetic interests. When their mother died of cancer in 1888, Leo and Gertrude found themselves more and more detached from the rest of the family. In 1892, Daniel Stein died, and the eldest son, Michael, took the family back to Baltimore, but the Steins began to scatter. In 1892, Leo entered Harvard, while Gertrude and Bertha stayed with their aunt, Fannie Bachrach. Michael, always patriarchal and the image of stability, married Sarah Samuels and later moved to Paris, where he became a respected member of the intellectual elite, maintaining a Saturday night open house at their apartment in rue Madame. Matisse's portrait of Michael is now in San Francisco.

Gertrude was a coddled and protected child. At sixteen, she weighed 135 pounds, and later in college she hired a boy to box with her every day to help her lose weight. Her niece, Gertrude Stein Raffel, recalls that her heaviness "was not unbecoming. She was round, roly-poly, and angelic looking." During her adolescent years, she became very introspective and critical, and was often depressed and concerned with death. Already emotionally independent, owing to her mother's protracted invalidism and her father's neglect and false representation of authority, Gertrude saw in her brother Leo her only friend. Their bond would not be broken for another twenty years, and she would follow him everywhere, the two delving into matters of mutual interest.

In 1893, Gertrude Stein entered the Harvard Annex, renamed Radcliffe College the following year. She gravitated toward philosophy and psychology, and took courses with such luminaries as George Santayana, Josiah Royce, Herbert Palmer, and William James. In 1894, she worked in the Harvard Psychological Laboratory with Hugo Münsterberg. Her interest in psychology expanded, and in 1896, she published, together with Leon Solomons, a paper on "Normal Motor Automatism," which appeared in the *Psychological Review*. A second article, "Cultivated Motor Automatism," appeared two years later. In 1897, Stein followed her brother to The Johns Hopkins University and began the study of medicine. She specialized in brain research and was encouraged to continue, even though by 1901 her dedication had waned. She attempted four examinations, failed them, and withdrew without a degree.

In 1902, Stein began her travels, first to Italy and then to London, where she met philosopher Bertrand Russell. She spent much time in the British Museum Library studying the Elizabethans, especially William Shakespeare. In the meantime, Leo also abandoned his studies, reverting to an earlier passion for history. A specialist in Renaissance costume, he was drawn to contemporary art, and when, in 1904, he and his sister saw a Paul Cézanne exhibit in Florence, they started buying paintings; Leo would became a major collector of Henri Matisse. The two settled in the now-famous apartment at 27 rue de Fleurus, where Gertrude's literary career began, though her first sustained effort, *Q.E.D.*, written in 1903, remained unpublished until 1950 (as *Things as They Are*). In 1905, while working on a translation of Gustave Flaubert's *Trois contes*, she wrote *Three Lives*. During that period, she met Pablo Picasso, who would be very influential in her thinking about art and with whom she would remain friends for decades. The following year, he painted the famous portrait now at the Metropolitan Museum. These days of intense work and thinking saw Stein fast at work on her first major long novel, *The Making of Americans*, which she completed in 1910.

Gertrude's trips abroad and throughout France from her home base in Paris became an essential part of her existence. In 1907, her brother Michael introduced her to Alice B. Toklas, who soon became her secretary, going to work on the proofs of *Three Lives*. Toklas learned to use a typewriter, and the following year, in Fiesole, Italy, she began to copy parts of the manuscript of *The Making of Americans*. Leo, intellectually independent, was moving toward his own aesthetic, though he was still busy promoting new American and French talents. As a painter, Leo was not successful, and he came eventually to dislike all contemporary painters except the cubists. In 1913, he moved from the rue de Fleurus apartment, and with him went all the Renoirs and most of the Matisses and Cézannes, while Gertrude kept the Picassos. Leo's place had been taken by Toklas, who stayed with Gertrude until her death in 1946.

The writer first began to be noticed as a result of Alfred Stieglitz's publication of her "portraits" of Matisse and Picasso in *Camera Work* in 1912. She spent the summer of that year in Spain, capturing the sense of her idea of the relationship between object and space, with which she had been struggling. Here she began the prose poem *Tender Buttons*, which brought her to the attention of most of her contemporaries, eliciting varying reactions. She continued to write "portraits" while visiting Mabel Dodge in Florence, at the Villa Curonia. At the Armory Show in New York in 1913, Stein was responsible for the presentation of the Pablo Picasso exhibit. When the war broke out, she was in London, where she met the philosopher Alfred North Whitehead. She continued to work intensely, mostly on poetry and plays, and visited Barcelona and Palma de Majorca. In 1916, Stein and Toklas returned to France and the next year did voluntary war relief work in the south. In 1922, Stein was awarded a Medaille de la Reconnaissance Française.

With the appearance of her first collected volume, *Geography and Plays*, in 1922, Stein's fame among the cognoscenti was assured, together with a lively controversy over her truly original style. She was invariably visited by the younger expatriate artists from the United States, and her parlor became a focal point for the exchange of ideas. Sherwood Anderson introduced her to Hemingway in 1922, and the younger writer learned much from her about the craft of writing. Hemingway was influential in securing publication of parts of *The Making of Americans* in Ford Madox Ford's magazine, *Transatlantic Review*. (The nine-hundred-page work was later abridged to half its size by her translator into French, and the shorter version was published in 1925 by Contact Editions, Paris.) Her relationship with Hemingway, however, because of conflicting temperaments, was short-lived; their friendship soon degenerated into bickering.

Stein entered another phase of her life when she was asked to lecture in Oxford and Cambridge in 1926. The text of the conference, "Composition as Explanation," constituted her first critical statement on the art of writing; she subsequently returned to a personal exposition of her ideas in *How to Write* (1931), breaking new ground at the stylistic level. This period of major intellectual and thematic upheaval witnessed several transformations in her art. She began to devote more time to the theater and eventually tackled the difficult task of writing about ideas in the little known *Stanzas in Meditation, and Other Poems, 1929-1933* (not published until 1956). In 1929, she left Paris and moved to Bilignin. Her *Lucy Church Amiably* (1930) had not pleased her, but *Four Saints in Three Acts* (pr., pb. 1934), with music by Virgil Thomson, was successfully produced in New York. After publication of the well-received *The Autobiography of Alice B. Toklas* in 1933, she traveled to the United States for a lecture tour. Her *Lectures in America* (1935) dealt with her philosophy of composition.

Compelled to close her apartment at rue de Fleurus shortly after her return to France, Stein moved with Toklas to rue Christine; with the onset of the war in 1939, however, they returned to Bilignin. During the war, the two women lived for a time in Culoz, where they first witnessed the German occupation and then the arrival of the Americans, which would be recounted in *Wars I Have Seen* (1945). In December, 1944, she returned to Paris, only to leave soon afterward to entertain U.S. troops stationed in occupied Germany. Her views on the U.S. soldier and the society that produced him changed considerably during these two years. In October, 1945, she traveled to Brussels to lecture. Weary and tired, she decided to visit her friend Bernard Fay in the country. Her trip was abruptly interrupted by her illness, and she entered the American Hospital in Neuilly-sur-Seine, where, after an unsuccessful cancer operation, she died on July 27, 1946.

Analysis

It is customary to refer to Gertrude Stein's poetry—and her work in general—with the qualifiers "abstract," "repetitive," and "nonsensical," terms that do little if any justice to a most remarkable literary achievement. The proper evaluation of Stein's work requires a willingness to rethink certain basic notions concerning art, discourse, and life, a task that is perhaps as difficult as the reading of Stein's voluminous production itself. Her work, however, is really not excessively abstract, especially when one considers that her poetic rests on the fundamental axiom of "immediate existing." Nothing could be more concrete than that. Whatever she may be describing, each unit is sure to be a complete, separate assertion, a reality immediately given—in the present, the only time there is.

Repetition is insistence: A rose is a rose is a rose is a rose. Each time it is new, different, unique, because the experience of the word is unique each time it is uttered. Stylistically, this entails the predominance of parataxis and asyndeton, words being "so nextily" in their unfolding. Repetition of the same is often supplanted by repetition of the different, where the juxtaposition is in kind and quality. An example of the latter is the following passage from *A Long Gay Book* (1932):

> All the pudding has the same flow and the sauce is painful, the tunes are played, the crinkling paper is burning, the pot has cover and the standard is excellence.

Whether operating at the syntagmatic or at the paradigmatic level, as above, the repetition serves the purpose of emphasizing and isolating a thing, not simply anything. The break with all previous associations forces one to consider this pudding and this sauce, allowing a concretization of the experience in this particular frame of the present. If the content appears to have no "logical" coherence, it is because it is not meant to, since the experience of the immediate does not warrant ratiocination or understanding of any sort. Art in Stein is perception of the immediate, a capturing of the instantaneity of the word as event, sense, or object. The notion is clearly nonreferential in that art does not need a world to know that it exists. Although it occasionally refers to it, it does not have to—in fact, the less it does, the better. What is of paramount importance is that this self-contained entity comes alive in the continuous present of one's experience of it, and only then. The influence of Stein's painter friends was unequivocal. Not all discourse that links the work of art to history and other realms of life is, properly speaking, a preoccupation of the artist: It does not constitute an aesthetic experience, remaining just that—criticism, sociology, and philosophy. Meaning is something that comes after the experience, thanks to reflection, the mediation of reason, and the standardization of logic and grammar; it is never given in the immediacy of the poetic expression. Stein's writings attempt to produce the feeling of something happening or being lived—in short, to give things (objects, emotions, ideas, words) a sense that is new and unique and momentary, independent and defiant of what an afterthought may claim to be the "true" meaning or sense of an experience or artistic event. From this perspective, can it still be honestly said that Stein's work is "nonsense," with all the negative implications usually associated with the epithet?

THINGS AS THEY ARE

Stein had from very early in her career a keen sense of the distance that naturally exists between objects and feelings as perceived, and their transposition into conventional formalized speech. Her first novel, *Q.E.D.* (for the Latin *quod erat demonstrandum*, meaning "which was to be proved"), written in 1903 and known after 1950 as *Things as They Are*, dealt with the then taboo topic of lesbianism in a ménage à trois of three women. However, the work is already shorn of such typical narrative features as symbolism, character development, climax, and descriptions of setting, though it is cast in an intelligible variation of standard prose. At the limits of the (Henry) Jamesian novel, what happens among the characters and the space of emotional relatedness is more important than the characters as characters. The focal point is the introspection of these human natures, and all elaborations and complications of feelings remain internal, intimate, within the consciousness of the individual being described or, most often, within the dialectic of the relationship. Doing away with all contingent background material meant zooming in on the poetic process itself; but for all practical purposes the author is still struggling within the precincts of the most sophisticated naturalism: She is still representing, in the tradition of Henry James and Gustave Flaubert, two authors whom she admired greatly. The characters are at odds with the author: They are white American college women constantly preoccupied with the propriety of their relationship and therefore demand of the author a polite, cultivated, and literary realization.

THREE LIVES

The problem of the language to employ in writing is dealt with in the next work, *Three Lives*, where the progressive abandonment of inherited expressive forms is much stronger and can be said to constitute a first milestone in Gertrude Stein's stylistic development, especially in "Melanchta," the last of the three stories. Here Stein describes a love story set among lower-class blacks, where she can explore the intensity of "uneducated" speech and where, as Donald Sutherland quite aptly points out, there exists "a direct relationship between feeling and word." Typical of her entire literary career, at the time of publication the printer inquired whether the author really knew English. In *Three Lives*, Stein was "groping for a continuous present and for using everything again and again." This continuous present is immediate and partakes of the human mind as it exists at any given moment when confronted with the object of writing. It is different from the prolonged present of duration, as in Henri Bergson, where aspects of human nature may enter. At the stylistic level, punctuation is rare and the present participle is employed as a substantive for its value in retaining the sense of process, of continuity in a present mode that knows no before and no after. This "subjective time" of writing is paralleled by similar developments in the visual and plastic arts, from which Stein drew copiously. Her admiration and appreciation of what Cézanne had done for painting was matched by the unrelenting support that she bestowed on the upcoming younger generation of artists, such as Picasso, Matisse, Juan Gris, and Francis Picabia. Cézanne had taught her that there are no less important areas on a canvas vis-à-vis the theme or figure that traditionally dominated representational painting, and he returned to "basics," such as color, tone, distribution, and the underlying abstractions, reaching out for those essentials in the welter of external detail to capture a sense without which there would be no painting. Picasso went even further, forsaking three-dimensional composition for the surface purity of plane geometry, ushering in cubism. For Stein, perception takes place against the tabula rasa of immediate consciousness, and cubism offered the flatness of an interior time that could be brought to absolute elementalism, simplicity, and finality.

TENDER BUTTONS

Things as They Are and *Three Lives*, for all their stylistic experimentation, are clearly works of prose. In *Tender Buttons*, however, Stein blurs the distinction between prose and poetry. She works with "meaningless" babble, puns, games, rhymes, and repetitions. Much as in Lewis Carroll and Tristam Tzara, the word itself is seen as magic. In a world of pure existence, dialogue disappears, replaced by word lists and one-word utterances. Interactions of characters are no longer tenable, and people give way to objects. The portrait is supplanted by the still life, and the technique of composition is reminiscent of Picasso's collages, not of automatic writing. The intention seems to be to give the work its autonomy independent of both writer and reader: One sees and reads what one sees and reads, the rest being reconstruction from memory or projections of the viewer's intellect. The effort is ambitious: to see language being born. Disparate critical ideas have been invoked to "interpret" *Tender Buttons*, and it is likely that Norman Weinstein (*Gertrude Stein and the Literature of Modern Consciousness*, 1970) comes closest when he summons the studies of Jean Piaget, the Sapir-Whorf language hypothesis, R. D. Laing, and the dimension of schizophrenia. On the opposite bank, Allegra Stewart (*Gertrude Stein and the Present*, 1967) reads the work as a Jungian mandala and relates the alchemical correspondences to all the literary movements of the epoch, such as Dada, Futurism, and so on.

"A jack in kill her, a jack in, makes a meadowed king, makes a to let." The plastic use of language permits the bypassing of the rule where, for example, a substantive is the object of a preposition. The infinitive "to let" appears as the object of a verb and is modified by the indefinite article "a." If analysis emphasizes the dislocation, the derangement, of standard usage, suggesting that alternative modes of expression are possible and even revealing, no matter how unwieldy, it should also note the foregrounding of "events" in an atemporal framework, where even nouns are objects that do not need the passing of ages to be what they are. Sense, if not altogether certain meanings, can be obtained only in the suspended perception of the reading, especially aloud.

This effort to see and write in the "continuous present" requires, Stein said, a passionate identification with the thing to be described: A steady, trance-like concentration on the object will first of all divest it of all its customary appellations and then permit the issuing forth of words and structures that alone can speak as *that* thing in front of the observer.

"Poetry and Grammar"

In "Poetry and Grammar" (1935), Stein says, "Poetry is concerned with using with abusing, with losing with wanting, with denying with avoiding with adoring with replacing the noun.... Poetry is doing nothing but using losing refusing and pleasing and betraying and caressing nouns." In this spirit of reevaluation of the nature and process of naming things she will then go all out in making sure that the things she looks at will by themselves elicit the way they are to be called, never being for a moment worried that such a process may be at odds with the limited range of possibilities offered by conventional reality; she wanted not only to rename things but also to "find out how to know that they were there by their names or by replacing their names." As Shakespeare had done in Arden, the goal was to create "a forest without mentioning the things that make a forest."

With this new discovery, for the ensuing twenty years Stein kept busy revisiting timeworn forms and models of poetic expression, charging them with fresh blood and impetus. The underlying magic would be constant: "looking at anything until something that was not the name of that thing but was in a way that actual thing would come to be written." This process was possible because Stein had arrived at a particular conception of the essence of language: It is not "imitation either of sounds or colors or emotions," but fundamentally an "intellectual recreation." The problem of mimesis and representation was forever behind her, and the idea of play became fundamental in her work.

1920's and 1930's

The third stage of Stein's poetry came in the late 1920's and early 1930's, when she was both very happy at receiving some recognition and much depressed about some new problems of her craft. Of the three materials that she felt art had to deal with—sight, sound, and sense, corresponding to the spatial, the temporal, and the conceptual dimensions of the mind—she had up to then worked intensely on the first two, relegating the third to the background by ignoring it or by simply rejecting it as a response to conventional grammatical and logical sense. At times, she handled the problem of sense by mediating it through her theoretical writings, especially after 1925.

With the ending of the Roaring Twenties, however, much of the spatiality in literature also disappeared. Painting became intellectual, poets became religious or political, and the newer waves did not seem to hold much promise. Stein had also reached a conclusion concerning works of art: that there are no masterpieces containing ideas; in philosophy, there are no masterpieces. Ideas and philosophy require almost by definition a mediated, sequential array of items over time and in history, ideas being about something or other. For a poetic of the unique, concrete thing—again, against all claims that Stein's is a poetic of the abstract—the task of dealing with ideas, which are by nature abstract, posed no small problem. Still, owing also to her attention to religious thought and the artistic implications of meditation, communion, trance, and revelation, she felt the need to come to terms with this hitherto untrodden ground.

STANZAS IN MEDITATION

Stein set about writing a poem of ideas without all the historical and philosophical underpinnings and referents that accompany works such as Ezra Pound's *The Cantos* (1925-1972) and T. S. Eliot's *The Waste Land* (1922). True to the credo that art is immanent and immediate, she wrote *Stanzas in Meditation*, a long poem made up of five parts and running to 163 stanzas, some a line long, others extending over several pages.

Remarkably little has been written about this forgotten but truly major composition, for the difficulty once again is the unpreparedness of criticism to deal with another of Stein's innovations: Instead of writing about ideas, she writes the ideas themselves: Thinking, in other words, does not occur in the mind after reading the words on the page, but the words themselves are the ideas, making ideas partake of the human mind instead of human nature. The old reliable technique of stopping the momentous thoughts on the page as consciousness becomes aware of them creates once again the typical situation with Stein's art: One experiences ideas as one reads; one cannot lean back and expect to put together a "coherent" whole. There are in fact no philosophical terms in the traditional sense and no organization as such. Norman Weinstein writes that "The poem is not *about* philosophy, but *is* philosophy set into motion by verbal action." The disembodied, fragmentary, and discontinuous vision of the cubists is here interwoven with the process-philosophy of William James and Whitehead.

Stylistically, each line tends to be objective and stable and corresponds to what in prose is the sentence. As the lines build up into a stanza, they swell with tension, and, like the paragraph, constitute a specific unit of attention. The poem will occasionally evidence images and allow symbols, but these are accidental, perhaps because the idea itself can best or only be expressed in that particular fashion. According to Sutherland, the poem can be entered in a tradition that lists Plato, Pindar, the English Metaphysicals, and Gerard Manley Hopkins. The poem can be read by simply beginning at random, which is perhaps the best way for the uninitiated to get a "sense" of it and familiarize themselves with the tone, lyricism, and surprisingly deceiving content. The technique of repetition is still present, revealing new contexts for given words, and Stein coins new expressions for ancient truisms. The text is a gold mine of brilliant aphorisms: "There is no hope or use in all," or "That which they like they knew."

THE AUTOBIOGRAPHY OF ALICE B. TOKLAS

Between the time of the appearance of *The Autobiography of Alice B. Toklas* and the publication, shortly before her death, of *The Gertrude Stein First Reader and Three Plays* (1946), thirteen other books came out, among which were the highly successful and important *The Geographical History of America* (1936) and *Everybody's Autobiography* (1937). During these years, Stein's major efforts were directed to the problem of self-presentation and the formal structure of autobiography. She put the writer on the same ground as the reader, ending the privileged position of both biographer and autobiographer. She continued to elaborate the poetic of impersonal, timeless, and spaceless writing, ensuring that experience, flow, and place remain within the confines of the continuous present of perception. Her poetry during this period was chiefly written for children, rhymed and chanted and playful, with no pretense at being anything more than a momentary flash in the continuum of life, a diversion, a game. Many of these works were published either as limited editions or posthumously in the Yale edition of her uncollected writings, where they can now be read in chronological sequence.

OTHER MAJOR WORKS

LONG FICTION: *Three Lives*, 1909; *The Making of Americans: Being a History of a Family's Progress*, 1925 (abridged, 1934); *Lucy Church Amiably*, 1930; *A Long Gay Book*, 1932; *Ida, a Novel*, 1941; *Brewsie and Willie*, 1946; *Blood on the Dining-Room Floor*, 1948; *Things as They Are*, 1950 (originally known as *Q.E.D.*); *Mrs. Reynolds and Five Earlier Novelettes, 1931-1942*, 1952; *A Novel of Thank You*, 1958.

SHORT FICTION: *As Fine as Melanctha*, 1954; *Painted Lace, and Other Pieces, 1914-1937*, 1955; *Alphabets and Birthdays*, 1957.

PLAYS: *Geography and Plays*, pb. 1922; *Operas and Plays*, pb. 1932; *Four Saints in Three Acts*, pr., pb. 1934; *In Savoy: Or, Yes Is for a Very Young Man (A Play of the Resistance in France)*, pr., pb. 1946; *The Mother of Us All*, pr. 1947; *Last Operas and Plays*, pb. 1949; *In a Garden: An Opera in One Act*, pb. 1951; *Lucretia Borgia*, pb. 1968; *Selected Operas and Plays*, 1970.

NONFICTION: *Composition as Explanation*, 1926; *How to Write*, 1931; *Matisse, Picasso, and Gertrude Stein, with Two Shorter Stories*, 1933; *The Autobiography of Alice B. Toklas*, 1933; *Portraits and Prayers*, 1934; *Lectures in America*, 1935; *Narration: Four Lectures*, 1935; *The Geographical History of America*, 1936; *Everybody's Autobiography*, 1937; *Picasso*, 1938; *Paris, France*, 1940; *What Are Masterpieces?*, 1940; *Wars I Have Seen*, 1945; *Four in America*, 1947; *Reflections on the Atomic Bomb*, 1973;

How Writing Is Written, 1974; *The Letters of Gertrude Stein and Thornton Wilder*, 1996 (Edward Burns and Ulla E. Dydo, editors); *Baby Precious Always Shines: Selected Love Notes Between Gertrude Stein and Alice B. Toklas*, 1999 (Kay Turner, editor).

CHILDREN'S LITERATURE: *The World Is Round*, 1939.

MISCELLANEOUS: *The Gertrude Stein First Reader and Three Plays*, 1946; *The Yale Edition of the Unpublished Writings of Gertrude Stein*, 1951-1958 (8 volumes; Carl Van Vechten, editor); *Selected Writings of Gertrude Stein*, 1962; *The Yale Gertrude Stein*, 1980.

BIBLIOGRAPHY

Curnutt, Kirk, ed. *The Critical Response to Gertrude Stein*. Westport, Conn.: Greenwood Press, 2000. This guide includes quintessential pieces on Stein by Carl Van Vechten, William Carlos Williams, and Katherine Anne Porter, as well as previously obscure estimations from contemporaries such as H. L. Mencken, Mina Loy, and Conrad Aiken.

Dydo, Ulla E., with William Rice. *Gertrude Stein: The Language That Rises, 1923-1934*. Evanston, Ill.: Northwestern University Press, 2003. Dydo, a renowned Stein scholar, provides a comprehensive analysis of the letters, manuscripts, and notebooks Stein generated in a twenty-year period.

Kellner, Bruce, ed. *A Gertrude Stein Companion*. New York: Greenwood Press, 1988. Kellner supplies a helpful introduction on how to read Stein. The volume includes a study of Stein and literary tradition, her manuscripts, and her various styles; and biographical sketches of her friends and "enemies." Includes an annotated bibliography of criticism.

Knapp, Bettina. *Gertrude Stein*. New York: Continuum, 1990. A general introduction to Stein's life and art. Discusses her stylistic breakthrough in the stories in *Three Lives*, focusing on repetition and the use of the continuous present. Devotes a long chapter to *Tender Buttons* as one of Stein's most innovative and esoteric works; discusses the nonreferential nature of language in the fragments.

Malcolm, Janet. *Two Lives: Gertrude and Alice*. New Haven, Conn.: Yale University Press, 2007. Malcolm examines the good and the bad in the life shared by Stein and Alice B. Toklas.

Mitrano, G. F. *Gertrude Stein: Woman Without Qualities*. Burlington, Vt.: Ashgate, 2005. A study of Stein's writing and a look at why it remains relevant to twenty-first century readers.

Murphy, Marguerite S. *A Tradition of Subversion: The Prose Poem in English from Wilde to Ashbery*. Amherst: University of Massachusetts Press, 1992. Devotes a chapter to *Tender Buttons*. Argues that Stein borrowed her genre from painting. Discusses the experimental nature of Stein's prose poems in the collections.

Pierpont, Claudia Roth. *Passionate Minds: Women Rewriting the World*. New York:

Alfred A. Knopf, 2000. Evocative, interpretive essays on the life paths and works of twelve women, including Stein, connecting the circumstances of their lives with the shapes, styles, subjects, and situations of their art.

Simon, Linda. *Gertrude Stein Remembered.* Lincoln: University of Nebraska Press, 1994. Consists of short memoirs of the modernist writer by her colleagues and contemporaries. Selections include pieces by Daniel-Henri Kahnweiler, Sylvia Beach, Sherwood Anderson, Cecil Beaton, and Eric Sevareid, each of whom offer intimate and often informal views of Stein.

Wineapple, Brenda. *Sister Brother: Gertrude and Leo Stein.* Lincoln: University of Nebraska Press, 2008. Wineapple looks at the long and close relationship between Stein and her brother, Leo, and the emergence of her writing voice, which may been in part responsible for the rift between the two siblings.

Peter Carravetta

ALICE WALKER

Born: Eatonton, Georgia; February 9, 1944

PRINCIPAL POETRY
Once, 1968
Five Poems, 1972
Revolutionary Petunias, and Other Poems, 1973
Good Night, Willie Lee, I'll See You in the Morning, 1979
Horses Make a Landscape Look More Beautiful, 1984
Her Blue Body Everything We Know: Earthling Poems, 1965-1990 Complete, 1991
Absolute Trust in the Goodness of the Earth: New Poems, 2003
A Poem Traveled Down My Arm: Poems and Drawings, 2003

OTHER LITERARY FORMS

Although Alice Walker's poetry is cherished by her admirers, she is primarily known as a fiction writer. The novel *The Color Purple* (1982), generally regarded as her masterpiece, achieved both popular and critical success, winning the Pulitzer Prize and the National Book Award. The Steven Spielberg film of the same name, for which Walker acted as consultant, reached an immense international audience.

Other Walker fiction has received less attention. Her first novel, *The Third Life of Grange Copeland* (1970), depicts violence and family dysfunction among people psychologically maimed by racism. *Meridian* (1976) mirrors the Civil Rights movement, of which the youthful Walker was actively a part. Later novels, *The Temple of My Familiar* (1989), *Possessing the Secret of Joy* (1992), and *By the Light of My Father's Smile* (1998) have employed narrative as little more than a vehicle for ideas on racial and sexual exploitation, abuse of animals and the earth, and New Age spirituality. *In Love and Trouble: Stories of Black Women* (1973) and *You Can't Keep a Good Woman Down* (1981) revealed Walker to be one of the finest of late twentieth century American short-story writers. She also has written an occasional children's book (*To Hell with Dying*, 1988, is particularly notable) and several collections of essays (*In Search of Our Mothers' Gardens: Womanist Prose*, 1983, is the most lyrical) that present impassioned pleas for the causes Walker espouses.

ACHIEVEMENTS

At numerous colleges, as a teacher and writer-in-residence, Alice Walker established herself as a mentor, particularly to young African American women. Her crusades became international. To alert the world to the problem of female circumcision in Africa, she collaborated with an Anglo-Indian filmmaker on a book and film. She has been a voice for artistic freedom, defending her own controversial writings and those of others, such as Salman Rushdie. In her writings and later open lifestyle, she affirmed lesbian and bisexual experience. However, the accomplishment in which she took the most pride was her resurrection of the reputation of Zora Neale Hurston, a germinal African American anthropologist and novelist, whose books had gone out of print.

Walker won the Rosenthal Award of the National Institute of Arts and Letters for *In Love and Trouble* and received a Charles Merrill writing fellowship, a National Endowment for the Arts award, and a Guggenheim Fellowship. Her second book of poetry, *Revolutionary Petunias, and Other Poems*, received the Lillian Smith Award and was nominated for a National Book Award. Her highest acclaim came with the novel *The Color Purple*, for which she won the National Book Award and the 1983 Pulitzer Prize. She received the Fred Cody Award for lifetime achievement in 1990. Walker was inducted into the California Hall of Fame in 2006.

Biography

Alice Malsenior Walker was the youngest of eight children born to a Georgia sharecropper and his wife. Her father earned about three hundred dollars per year, while her mother, the stronger figure, supplemented the family income by working as a maid. Walker herself was a bright, confident child until an accident at age eight blinded her in one eye and temporarily marred her beauty. At this time, she established what was to become a lifelong pattern of savoring solitude and making the most of adversity. She started reading and writing poetry.

Because of her partial blindness and her outstanding high school record, Walker qualified for a special scholarship offered to disabled students by Spelman College, the prestigious black women's college in Atlanta. When she matriculated there in 1961, her neighbors raised the bus fare of seventy-five dollars to get her to Atlanta.

As a Spelman student, Walker was "moved to wakefulness" by the emerging Civil Rights movement. She took part in demonstrations downtown, which brought her into conflict with the conservative administration of the school. Finding the rules generally too restrictive and refreshed with her new consciousness, she secured a scholarship at Sarah Lawrence College in Bronxville, New York. She then felt closer to the real action that was changing the country. At Sarah Lawrence College, she came under the influence of the poet Muriel Rukeyser, who recognized her talent and arranged for her first publications. She also took a summer off for a trip to her "spiritual home," Africa. She returned depressed and pregnant, contemplated suicide for a time, but instead underwent an abortion and poured her emotions into poetry.

After graduation, Walker worked for a time in the New York City Welfare Department before returning to the South to write, teach, and promote voter registration. She married Melvyn Leventhal, a white Jew, and worked with him on desegregation legal cases and Head Start programs. Their child, Rebecca, was born during this highly productive period. By the time the marriage ended in 1976, Walker was already becoming recognized as a writer, though she did not become internationally famous until after the publication of *The Color Purple*.

Walker continued to write during the 1980's and 1990's, though never again achieving the acclaim or the notoriety that *The Color Purple* brought her. Critics complained of her stridency, the factual inaccuracies in her writings, and her tendency to turn her works of fiction into polemics. Many African Americans felt that her writings cast black society in a grim light. Walker moved to California and lived for several years with Robert Allen, the editor of *Black Scholar*. Times had changed; the motto was no longer "black and white together": marriages between Jews and African Americans were out, and black-black relationships were in.

Walker also became more alert to the problems women of color faced throughout the world. Taking a female partner, she decided to devote her time and talents to celebrating women and rectifying wrongs committed against them. In March of 2003, Walker was arrested for protesting the Iraq War. In 2009, Walker visited Gaza to promote peace and friendlier relations between Egypt and Israel. Walker has always encouraged awareness of important issues in her writing, but she has attracted attention to issues such as problems in the black culture, violence against women, and the ravages of war by personally participating in or protesting events about which she feels passionately.

Analysis

Alice Walker writes free verse, employing concrete images. She resorts to few of the conceits, the extended metaphors, the Latinate language, and other common conventions of poetry. Readers frequently say that her verses hardly seem like poetry at all; they resemble the conversation of a highly articulate, observant woman. Although her poetry often seems like prose, her fiction is highly poetic. The thoughts of Miss Celie, the first-person narrator of *The Color Purple*, would not have been out of place in a book of poetry. Boundaries between prose and poetry are minimal in the work of Walker. Her verse, like her prose, is always rhythmic; if she rhymes or alliterates, it seems to be by accident. The poetry appears so effortless that its precision, its choice of exact image or word to convey the nuance the poet wishes, is not immediately evident. Only close scrutiny reveals the skill with which this highly lettered poet has assimilated her influences, chiefly E. E. Cummings, Emily Dickinson, Robert Graves, Japanese haiku, Li Bo, Ovid, Zen epigrams, and William Carlos Williams.

Walker's poetry is personal and generally didactic, generated by events in her life, causes she has advocated, and injustices over which she has agonized. The reader feels that it is the message that counts, before realizing that the medium is part of the message. Several of her poems echo traumatic events in her own life, such as her abortion. She remembers the words her mother uttered over the casket of her father, and she makes a poem of them. Other poems recall ambivalent emotions of childhood: Sunday school lessons which, even then, were filled with discrepancies. Some poems deal with the creative process itself: She calls herself a medium through whom the Old Ones, formerly mute, find their voice at last.

Some readers are surprised to discover that Walker's poems are both mystical and socially revolutionary, one moment exuberant and the next reeking with despair. Her mysticism is tied to reverence for the earth, a sense of unity with all living creatures, a bond of sisterhood with women throughout the world, and a joyous celebration of the female principle in the divine. On the other hand, she may lament that injustice reigns in society: Poor black people toil so that white men may savor the jewels that adorn heads of state.

ONCE

Walker's first collection of poetry, *Once*, communicates her youthful impressions of Africa and her state of mind during her early travels there and the melancholy and thoughts of death and suicide she felt on her return to United States, where racism persisted. Perhaps the epigram from French philosopher Albert Camus, which prefaces the book, expresses its mood best: "Misery kept me from believing that all was well under the sun, and the sun taught me that history wasn't everything."

The title poem of the collection contains several loosely connected scenes of injustice in the American South, small black children run down by vans because "they were in the way," Jewish Civil Rights workers who cannot be cremated because their remains cannot be found, and finally a black child waving an American flag, but from "the very/ *tips*/ of her/ fingers," an image perhaps of irony or perhaps of hope. There are meditations on white lovers—blond, Teutonic, golden—who dare kiss this poet who is "brown-er/ Than a jew." There are memories of black churches, where her mother shouts, her father snores, and she feels uncomfortable.

The most striking poem is certainly "African Images," an assortment of vignettes from the ancestral homeland: shy gazelles, the bluish peaks of Mount Kenya, the sound of elephants trumpeting, and rain forests with red orchids. However, even when viewed in the idealism of youth, Africa is not total paradise. The leg of a slain elephant is fashioned into an umbrella holder in a shop; a rhinoceros is killed so that its horn may be made into an aphrodisiac.

REVOLUTIONARY PETUNIAS, AND OTHER POEMS

Revolutionary Petunias, and Other Poems is divided into two parts. The first is titled "In These Dissenting Times . . . Surrounding Ground and Autobiography." She proposes to write "of the old men I knew/ And the young men/ I loved/ And of the gold toothed women/ Mighty of arm/ Who dragged us all/ To church." She writes also "To acknowledge our ancestors" with the awareness that "we did not make/ ourselves, that the line stretches/ all the way back, perhaps, to God; or/ to Gods." She recalls her baptism "dunked . . . in the creek," with "gooey . . . rotting leaves,/ a greenish mold floating." She was a slight figure, "All in white./ With God's mud ruining my snowy/ socks and his bullfrog spoors/ gluing up my face."

The last half of the collection, "Revolutionary Petunias . . . the Living Through," begins with yet another epigram from Camus, reminding the reader that there will come a time when revolutions, though not made by beauty, will discover the need for beauty. The poems, especially those referred to as "Crucifixions," become more anguished, more angered. Walker becomes skeptical of the doctrine of nonviolence, hinting that the time for more direct action may have come. The tone of the last poems in the collection may be expressed best by the opening lines to the verse Walker called "Rage." "In me," she wrote, "there is a rage to defy/ the order of the stars/ despite their pretty patterns."

GOOD NIGHT, WILLIE LEE, I'LL SEE YOU IN THE MORNING

Good Night, Willie Lee, I'll See You in the Morning expands on earlier themes and further exploits personal and family experiences for lessons in living. The title poem is perhaps the most moving and characteristic of the collection. Walker shared it again on May 22, 1995, in a commencement day speech delivered at Spelman College. As a lesson in forgiveness, she recalled the words her mother, who had much to endure and much to forgive, uttered above her father's casket. Her last words to the man with whom she had lived for so many years, beside whom she had labored in the fields, and with whom she had raised so many children were, "Good night, Willie Lee, I'll see you in the morning." This gentle instinctive act of her mother taught Walker the enduring lesson that "the healing of all our wounds is forgiveness/ that permits a promise/ of our return/ at the end."

HORSES MAKE A LANDSCAPE LOOK MORE BEAUTIFUL

Horses Make a Landscape Look More Beautiful took its title from words of Lame Deer, an Indian seer who contemplated the gifts of the white man—chiefly whiskey and horses—and found the beauty of horses almost made her forget the whiskey. This thought establishes the tone of the collection. These are movement poems, but as always, they remain intensely personal and frequently elegiac. The poet seems herself to speak:

> I am the woman
> with the blessed
> dark skin
> I am the woman
> with teeth repaired
> I am the woman
> with the healing eye
> the ear that hears.

There is also lamentation for lost love:

> When I no longer have your heart
> I will not request your body
> your presence
> or even your polite conversation.
> I will go away to a far country
> separated from you by the sea
> —on which I cannot walk—
> and refrain even from sending
> letters
> describing my pain.

Her Blue Body Everything We Know

Her Blue Body Everything We Know contains a selection of poems written between 1965 and 1990, along with a few new verses and revealing commentary. This collection includes poems from *Once*; *Revolutionary Petunias, and Other Poems*; *Good Night, Willie Lee, I'll See You in the Morning*; and *Horses Make a Landscape Look More Beautiful*. Walker provides readers with insights on the art of poetry (in poems such as "How Poems Are Made: A Discredited View" and "I Said to Poetry"). In her introduction to the final section of the collection, Walker relates how she once felt jealous of how musicians connect with their work and seem to be one with it, but that during career as a writer, she has learned that poets share a similar relationship with their poetry. Walker, a woman of passion, shows how her personal beliefs about Africa (in the first section of this collection, "African Images: Glimpses from a Tiger's Back"), multiracial relationships (in the poem "Johann"), and the pangs of love (in poems such as "Did This Happen to Your Mother? Did Your Sister Throw Up a Lot?") are intricately intertwined and evident in her poetic creations.

Walker calls the final section "We Have a Beautiful Mother: Previously Uncollected Poems." The poems in this section, including "Some Things I Like About My Triple Bloods," "If There Was Any Justice," "We Have a Map of the World," and "Telling," are deeply personal and challenge readers to think about boundaries between cultures, countries, and hearts.

Absolute Trust in the Goodness of the Earth

In the preface to *Absolute Trust in the Goodness of the Earth*, Walker confides that she thought that she had reached the end of her career as a poet and was at peace with this, but after the terrorist attacks of September, 11, 2001, on the United States, Walker found herself writing poems regularly. After the attacks, Walker feared imminent war, and her poems in this book reflect that anxiety, including pieces such as "Thousands of Feet Below You," "Not Children," and "Why War Is Never a Good Idea." The narrator of "Thousands of Feet Below You" mentions a boy, running away from the bombs of war, who eventually is shredded to pieces in a violent explosion. Walker shares similar feelings about the concept of war in "Not Children," in which she refers to war as a cowardly act and an event that the world can do without. The title of "Why War Is Never a Good Idea" is self-explanatory, the subtitle of which ("A Picture Poem for Children Blinded by War") emphasizes Walker's stance on the issue.

Walker also continuously challenges readers to think about race relations in the United States, and how they might be improved. For example, "Patriot" encourages readers to respect all Americans, no matter what their country of origin is (she mentions Middle Eastern men, American Indian men, and African women, in particular), because these people all combine to make and define the United States. "Projection" encourages readers to look beyond the stereotypes associated with certain ethnicities (such as Indians, Germans, and Arabs) and remember that, inside each person, exists an innocent child.

In the preface to *Absolute Trust in the Goodness of the Earth*, Walker also shares her interest in and admiration for the environment and plants in particular. These feelings about the natural world are represented clearly in the title of this collection, which praises the earth for its beauty and righteousness. Walker, like many writers, associates nature with an inherent sense of peace. Natural imagery abounds in this collection, appearing in poems such as "Even When I Walked Away," "Red Petals Sticking Out," "Inside My Rooms," and "The Tree." Walker's plant and flower images remind readers of her belief that humankind is deeply rooted in and connected to the earth.

A Poem Traveled Down My Arm

In the introduction to *A Poem Traveled Down My Arm*, Walker explains that her publisher sent her blank pages to autograph; these pages would later be bound into copies of *Absolute Trust in the Goodness of the Earth* to save Walker time at forthcoming book signings. Tired of signing her own name so many times, Walker says that she suddenly started drawing little sketches on the pieces of paper. Soon, she was scrambling to keep up with writing down poems that sprang to mind, inspired by the images she had drawn. Walker feels this collection is strange when compared with her others, especially because she thought she was done writing poetry a few years earlier. Instead, she published two collections of poetry in a single year.

The poems in *A Poem Traveled Down My Arm* typically hover around ten words each. These succinct poetic creations address topics prevalent in the rest of Walker's canon, including love, peace, nature, and war. The untitled poems function almost like a series of proverbs, offering her readers advice about living a healthy spiritual life while respecting Earth and all of humanity.

OTHER MAJOR WORKS

LONG FICTION: *The Third Life of Grange Copeland*, 1970; *Meridian*, 1976; *The Color Purple*, 1982; *The Temple of My Familiar*, 1989; *Possessing the Secret of Joy*, 1992; *By the Light of My Father's Smile*, 1998; *Now Is the Time to Open Your Heart*, 2004.

SHORT FICTION: *In Love and Trouble: Stories of Black Women*, 1973; *You Can't Keep a Good Woman Down*, 1981; *The Complete Stories*, 1994; *Alice Walker Banned*, 1996 (stories and commentary).

NONFICTION: *In Search of Our Mothers' Gardens: Womanist Prose*, 1983; *Living by the Word: Selected Writings, 1973-1987*, 1988; *Warrior Marks: Female Genital Mutilation and the Sexual Blinding of Women*, 1993 (with Pratibha Parmar); *The Same River Twice: Honoring the Difficult*, 1996; *Anything We Love Can Be Saved: A Writer's Activism*, 1997; *The Way Forward Is with a Broken Heart*, 2000; *Sent by Earth: A Message from the Grandmother Spirit After the Attacks on the World Trade Center and Pentagon*, 2001; *We Are the Ones We Have Been Waiting For: Light in a Time of Darkness*, 2006; *The World Has Changed: Conversations with Alice Walker*, 2010 (Rudolph P. Byrd, editor).

CHILDREN'S LITERATURE: *Langston Hughes: American Poet*, 1974; *To Hell with Dying*, 1988; *Finding the Green Stone*, 1991; *There Is a Flower at the Tip of My Nose Smelling Me*, 2006; *Why War Is Never a Good Idea*, 2007.

EDITED TEXT: *I Love Myself When I Am Laughing . . . and Then Again When I Am Looking Mean and Impressive: A Zora Neale Hurston Reader*, 1979.

BIBLIOGRAPHY

Bates, Gerri. *Alice Walker: A Critical Companion*. Westport, Conn.: Greenwood Press, 2005. A well-crafted biography that discusses Walker's major works, tracing the themes of her novels to her life.

Bloom, Harold, ed. *Alice Walker*. New York: Chelsea House, 1989. An important collection of critical essays examining the fiction, poetry, and essays of Walker from a variety of perspectives. The fourteen essays, including Bloom's brief introduction, are arranged chronologically. Contains useful discussions of her first three novels, brief analyses of individual short stories, poems, and essays, and assessments of Walker's social and political views in connection with her works and other African American female authors. Chronology and bibliography.

Bloxham, Laura J. "Alice (Malsenior) Walker." In *Contemporary Fiction Writers of the South*, edited by Joseph M. Flora and Robert Bain. Westport, Conn.: Greenwood Press, 1993. A general introduction to Walker's "womanist" themes of oppression of black women and change through affirmation of self. Provides a brief summary and critique of previous criticism of Walker's work.

Gates, Henry Louis, Jr., and K. A. Appiah, eds. *Alice Walker: Critical Perspectives Past and Present.* New York: Amistad, 1993. Contains reviews of Walker's first five novels and critical analyses of several of her works of short and long fiction. Also includes two interviews with Walker, a chronology of her works, and an extensive bibliography of essays and texts.

Gentry, Tony. *Alice Walker.* New York: Chelsea House, 1993. Examines the life and work of Walker. Includes bibliographical references and index.

Lauret, Maria. *Alice Walker.* New York: St. Martin's Press, 2000. Provocative discussions of Walker's ideas on politics, race, feminism, and literary theory. Of special interest is the exploration of Walker's literary debt to Zora Neale Hurston, Virginia Woolf, and even Bessie Smith.

Simcikova, Karla. *To Live Fully, Here and Now: The Healing Vision in the Works of Alice Walker.* Lanham, Md.: Lexington Books, 2007. Simcikova focuses on Walker's spirituality, her relationship with nature, and how these beliefs and connections present themselves in her oeuvre of work.

Smith, Lindsey Claire. "Alice Walker's Eco-'Warriors.'" In *Indians, Environment, and Identity on the Borders of American Literature: From Faulkner and Morrison to Walker and Silko.* New York: Palgrave Macmillan, 2008. Smith analyzes boundaries delineating cultural, geographical, and racial differences in Walker's canon.

Walker, Rebecca. *Black, White, and Jewish: Autobiography of a Shifting Self.* New York: Riverhead, 2001. A self-indulgent but nevertheless insightful memoir by Alice Walker's daughter, Rebecca Walker. She describes herself as "a movement child," growing up torn between two families, two races, and two traditions, always in the shadow of an increasingly famous and absorbed mother.

White, Evelyn C. *Alice Walker: A Life.* New York: Norton, 2004. The life and accomplishments of Walker are chronicled in this biography through interviews with Walker, her family, and friends.

Allene Phy-Olsen
Updated by Karley K. Adney

MITSUYE YAMADA

Born: Fukuoka, Kyushu, Japan; July 5, 1923

PRINCIPAL POETRY
Camp Notes, and Other Poems, 1976

OTHER LITERARY FORMS

Mitsuye Yamada (yah-mah-dah) published two short stories in *Desert Run: Poems and Stories* and, in addition to producing her own work, has collaborated with others in editing poetry collections. Her essays on literature, personal history, and human rights have appeared in anthologies and periodicals, and she compiled a teachers' guide for Amnesty International. In 1981, the Public Broadcasting Service aired a documentary, *Mitsuye and Nellie: Two Asian-American Poets*, featuring Yamada and Chinese American writer Nellie Wong.

ACHIEVEMENTS

Mitsuye Yamada is one of the first writers to publish a personal account of the United States' internment of citizens of Japanese descent. Publication of the "Camp Notes" poems also marked an important event in the resurgence of feminist literature in the 1970's. Yamada has served on the national board of Amnesty International on the organization's Committee on International Development. She has received numerous awards for her writing, teaching, and human rights work.

BIOGRAPHY

Mitsuye May Yamada was born in Fukuoka, Kyushu, Japan, the third child and only daughter of Jack Yasutake and Hide Yasutake. She was brought to the United States at age three. At the age of nine, she went to Japan to live with her father's family for eighteen months. She lived with her parents and three brothers in Seattle until she was nineteen. Her high school education was curtailed in 1941 when her father, a translator for the United States Immigration Service, was imprisoned as an enemy alien. Mitsuye, her mother, and her brothers were later removed to internment camps in Puyallup, Washington, and Minidoka, Idaho. She spent eighteen months in the camps, finally leaving to work and study at the University of Cincinnati. She completed her bachelor's degree at New York University and a master of arts degree in English literature at the University of Chicago.

She was able to become a naturalized American citizen following passage of the McCarran-Walter Immigration Act and received citizenship in 1955. In 1950, she married chemist Yoshikazu Yamada (becoming Mitsuye Yasutake Yamada). They lived in

New York, where their four children were born, until the early 1960's, when the family moved to Southern California. In 1966, she began teaching in community colleges and was professor of English at Cypress Community College from 1968 until her retirement in 1989. Following publication of *Camp Notes, and Other Poems*, she held many university appointments as visiting professor, artist-in-residence, and consultant.

A lifelong commitment to human rights emerged as Yamada's response to her incarceration, and she has related her sense of urgency on the subject to years of living with a diagnosis of incurable emphysema when her children were very young. She was an early member of Amnesty International and has served on the executive board and national committees in that organization. Her poetry was published by feminist presses; she organized a multicultural women writers group and has participated in numerous projects addressed to the concerns of women, ethnic groups, and environmental awareness.

Analysis

Originally published by Shameless Hussy, a struggling feminist press, Mitsuye Yamada's *Camp Notes, and Other Poems* is a personal volume involving family participation. The cover illustration, by the author's older daughter, Jeni Yamada, is a line drawing of a female figure in three stages: a shy little girl, an older girl walking forward, and a striding woman carrying either a briefcase or suitcase. The ambiguity of the last figure can refer to the camp experience, where internees were able to bring only what they could carry, or to the author's professional life as writer, teacher, and activist. The author's husband contributed the book's calligraphy, and the volume is dedicated to Yamada's parents, husband, two daughters, and two sons. The actual "Camp Notes" poems center the volume and are bracketed by an opening section on the author's parents and a closing series of poems looking to the present and future.

The seven poems in the section "My Issei Parents, Twice Pioneers, Now I Hear Them" were written after the central "camp notes" set, and they look back to parents, grandparents, and great-grandparents. The section opens with a folk saying: "What your Mother tells you now/ in time/ you will come to know." The text appears first in brush-stroke ideograms, then in transliterated Japanese, and finally in the author's translation. Thetheme permeates the author's work, which engages with the ways that origins—"the mother"—shape a person, through both acceptance and resistance.

The next poem offers a portrait of "Great Grandma" figured in her orderly collection of ordinary objects: "colored stones," "parched persimmons," "powdery green tea." Great Grandma's static world and calm acceptance of fate stand in contrast to the turmoil, pain, and conflict documented in much of Yamada's work.

"Marriage Was a Foreign Country" and "Homecoming" are narrated in the voice of the persona's mother; they tell stories of pain and difficulty of life as a Japanese immigrant woman in a country both alien and hostile. Following these poems are two poems relating to the speaker's father. Contrasting the mother's monologues, these dialogues comment on traditional Japanese wisdom that the father is attempting to impart.

The section titled "Camp Notes" highlights poems composed while Yamada was imprisoned with her mother and brothers in the Minidoka camp. Thirty years later, the poems were culled from their early inscription in a large writing tablet, one of the few possessions the author could take with her to the camp. The section opens with another line drawing by Jeni Yamada, picturing a small child clutching a stuffed animal and seated amid piles of luggage. The first poems tally the upheaval of the removal experience with titles such as "Evacuation," "Curfew," and "On the Bus." The title of "Harmony at the Fair Grounds" reflects the irony in many of these brief, acrid poems: The "grounds" on which the Japanese Americans were imprisoned were anything but "fair." The last lines offer a stark picture of concentration camp life: "Lines formed for food/ lines for showers/ lines for the john/ lines for shots."

A secondary subheading, "Relocation," designates poems about life in the Minidoka camp. The author continues to document the grim, degrading aspects of prison life, where monotony and uncertainty intensified the physical stresses of primitive, cramped quarters and the denial of amenities such as radios and cameras. Even more demoralizing are the irrationality, stupidity, and lies of the bureaucratic internment system. As the family huddles under bedclothes to survive a "Desert Storm," the speaker observes

> This was not
> im
> prison
> ment.
> This was
> re
> location.

Likewise, the opening of "Block 4 Barrack 4 'Apt' C" demolishes the excuse that relocation benefited the imprisoned, noting that barbed wire protected the inmates from "wildly twisted/ sagebrush." In two poems, the persona notes the paradox of guards locked inside their watchtowers. Hedi Yamada, the author's younger daughter, illustrated "The Watchtower" with a silhouette drawing of an adult holding a child's hand and gazing at such a tower; it is impossible to tell whether they are looking out of or into the prison area. The double bind of Nisei (second-generation Japanese American) citizens emerges in the protest to the "Recruiting Team":

> Why should I volunteer!
> I'm an American
> I have a right to be
> drafted.

As the persona notes in "The Trick Was," notwithstanding propaganda or disinformation, "the mind was not fooled."

Several poems return with poignancy to the theme of family. The author translates two *senryu* poems (three-line unrhymed Japanese poems) written by her father, at that time incarcerated at a camp in New Mexico. "The Night Before Good-Bye" pictures the mother performing the intimately caring task of mending her daughter's clothes. "Cincinnati," written after the actual camp experience, comes to terms with a racist assault, in which the speaker loses a lace handkerchief given her by her mother.

The remaining poems in this volume reflect the author's life from the end of the war through the 1950's and 1960's and introduce themes of personal challenge, illness, raising children, education, and activism. The section opens with another drawing by Jeni Yamada, suggesting a serene Japanese village scene of a cove surrounded by woods and mountains with small boats at anchor and a line of houses on the beach. The past is still important: The author recollects, in the twinned poems "Here" and "There," being taunted as an "outsider" by classmates in both Japan and the United States. "Freedom in Manhattan" opens particularly feminist concerns, depicting police officers' indifference to attempted rape.

DESERT RUN

The professional production of Yamada's second collection, published by Kitchen Table: Women of Color Press, testifies to recognition of the author and establishment of ethnic and women's cultural institutions in the twelve years after the appearance of *Camp Notes, and Other Poems*. The later volume is professionally typeset, pages are numbered, and a single thematic illustration—a calligraphy of the author's name—appears on the cover, section divisions, and end of each poem. The author's husband again contributed the calligraphy, and the book is dedicated to her three brothers.

The poems in *Desert Run* extend themes introduced in *Camp Notes, and Other Poems*, now developed in more discursive, meditative modes. The initial set, headed "Where I Stay," is a sequence completed after a camping trip in the Southern California desert. The experience was unique: Part of an experimental college course co-taught with a biologist to connect creative writing and natural science, it marked for the author a reexamination of the "desert" experience of internment. The title poem, "Desert Run," meditates on the fragility, power, and beauty of the desert ecology, the author's contrast of her present interest in the desert with the earlier rancor and hatred of the apparently barren landscape and her continuing sense of the irreparable injustice of arbitrary imprisonment. The address of this poem—the author's longest—embodies the speaker's difficult ruminations as she speaks sometimes as a meditative "I" and at other times addresses a "you" that appears in other poems and that implies the "other," the "dominant" or "mainstream" or "official" American perspective. In this section, "Lichens" and "Desert Under Glass" are also notable close observations of nature.

Titles of the three remaining sections—"Returning," "Resisting," and "Connecting"—express the author's continuing project of synthesizing the disparate elements of her life. The poems and short story in "Returning" revisit experience and heritage in Japan. The grandmother's ambivalent pride and resentment over the emigration of the author's father emerges in "American Son," which with "Obon: Festival of the Dead" recollects the months Yamada spent as a child being tutored in Japanese language and culture.

A thread of women's stories and women's plight runs through the "Resisting" section. Two poems are framed in the personas of other women. "Jeni's Complaint," presented as in the voice of the author's daughter, captures the chaos of a multigeneration, multicultural family celebration. "I Learned to Sew" tells, in the Japanese Hawaiian cadence of the author's mother-in-law, a story of immigration, hardship, endurance, and survival; this poem contains a brief retelling of the Japanese folktale of Urashima Taro. The short story "Mrs. Higashi Is Dead" elaborates the anecdote briefly referred to in the poem "Homecoming" in *Camp Notes, and Other Poems*.

The "Connecting" section of *Desert Run* contains half the poems in the volume and recapitulates the major themes: nature, human dignity, family, and roots. Several poems in this section are voiced by "fictional" personas, notably "The Club," a woman's narration of her husband's abuse. "Connecting" also refers to the links between the author's personal experience of injustice with those of others: a Holocaust survivor, a battered wife, even animals sacrificed for fur.

Camp Notes, and Other Writings

Camp Notes, and Other Writings (1998) continues a canonization process. The volume reprints both *Camp Notes, and Other Poems* and *Desert Run*. Although it contains no previously unpublished work, the poems and dedication of *Camp Notes, and Other Writings* have been professionally typeset; also, the order of the poems has been substantially altered and the illustrations eliminated. One important addition is the cover illustration. A photograph taken around 1908 of Yamada's mother as a child, it commemorates a grade-school dramatization of the legend of Urashima Taro with Yamada's mother in the title role. (In the legend, Urashima Taro is rewarded for saving a turtle by a visit to the underseas palace of the Dragon King, where he spends a few days in the company of a beautiful princess. The young man returns home to see his parents, but the few days underseas were hundreds of years in his village, and everyone he knew is gone and everything has changed.) A historical and documentary return to the author's origins, complementing anecdotal and personal connections, the photograph also serves as a return and gloss to the translation of the mother's folk saying that opens *Camp Notes, and Other Writings*.

OTHER MAJOR WORKS
EDITED TEXTS: *The Webs We Weave: Orange County Poetry Anthology*, 1986 (with others); *Sowing Ti Leaves: Writings by Multi-Cultural Women*, 1990 (with Sarie Sachie Hylkema).

MISCELLANEOUS: *Desert Run: Poems and Stories*, 1988; *Camp Notes, and Other Writings*, 1998 (includes *Camp Notes, and Other Poems* and *Desert Run*).

BIBLIOGRAPHY
Cheng, Scarlet. "Foreign All Your Life." Review of *Desert Run*, by Mitsuye Yamada, and *Seventeen Syllables*, by Hisaye Yamamoto DeSoto. *Belles Lettres* 4, no. 2 (Winter, 1989). The reviewer finds Yamada's poetry nostalgic and filled with lyricism but notes the way in which poems consistently confront pain and alienation.

Harth, Erika. *Last Witnesses: Reflections on the Wartime Internment of Japanese Americans*. New York: Palgrave/St. Martin's Press, 2001. Contains "Legacy of Silence I," by Yamada, which gives *gaman*, the virtue of endurance, as a cultural reason for why the Japanese Americans are not more vocal about their experiences, and "Legacy of Silence II," by Jeni Yamada, in which she explains how her marriage to a Jew exposed her to a group that is not as reluctant to speak about past injustices.

Patterson, Anita Haya. "Resistance to Images of the Internment: Mitsuye Yamada's *Camp Notes*." *MELUS* 23, no. 3 (Fall, 1998): 103-128. Examines poems in *Camp Notes, and Other Writings* in light of the concept of "obligation" and the problematic issue of the seeming nonresistance by Americans of Japanese ancestry to unconstitutional imprisonment in concentration camps. The essay contains photographs from newspapers and other sources to illustrate images of Japanese Americans as visualized in American popular culture during and after World War II.

Schweik, Susan. "A Needle with Mama's Voice: Mitsuye Yamada's *Camp Notes* and the American Canon of War Poetry." In *Arms and the Woman: War, Gender, and Literary Representation*, edited by Helen M. Cooper, Adrienne Auslande Munich, and Susan Merrill Squier. Chapel Hill: University of North Carolina Press, 1989. Examination of Yamada's poems in the context of war poetry by women. The author considers the silencing of Yamada's voice between the writing of the "camp notes" poems and their publication thirty years later and maintains that such silence was brought about by the unique situation of Japanese American women—especially Issei women—who were considered "enemy aliens." The discussion compares mother-daughter and father-daughter expressions in the difference between retelling of transmitted oral tales versus translation of the father's poems.

Srikanth, Rajini, and Esther Y. Inwanaga, eds. *Bold Words: A Century of Asian American Writing*. New Brunswick, N.J.: Rutgers University Press, 2001. This anthology contains several poems by Yamada. The introduction to the poetry section provides context for understanding Yamada.

Woolley, Lisa. "Racial and Ethnic Semiosis in Mitsuye Yamada's 'Mrs. Higashi Is Dead.'" *MELUS* 24, no. 4 (Winter, 1999): 77-92. Using poems from *Camp Notes, and Other Poems*, the author analyzes Yamada's short story "Mrs. Higashi Is Dead" according to a theory called ethnic semiosis. The theory postulates that Americans realize "ethnicity" through performance in instances of contact between individuals from different ethnic backgrounds; these relational moments both define and contest characteristics considered as belonging to particular ethnicities. The analysis of Yamada's story examines how it reflects "ethnic semiosis" in the different ways that a mother and daughter interpret a request from a woman of a different ethnicity.

Yamada, Mitsuye. "A *MELUS* Interview: Mitsuye Yamada." Interview by Helen Jaskoski. *MELUS* 15, no. 1 (Spring, 1988): 97-108. The poet reflects on family influences in her writing (her father founded a society devoted to the Japanese *senryu* poem) and the impact of the concentration camp experience on her life and work. Also mentioned are women's writing, human rights activism, political persecution of poets, and formal aspects of poetry.

Helen Jaskoski

YOSANO AKIKO

Born: Sakai, Japan; December 7, 1878
Died: Tokyo, Japan; May 29, 1942

PRINCIPAL POETRY
Dokusō, 1901
Midaregami, 1901 (*Tangled Hair*, 1935, 1971)
Koōgi, 1904
Koi goromo, 1905
Mai hime, 1906
Yume-no-hana, 1906
Hakkō, 1908
Tokonatsu, 1908
Sabo hime, 1911
Shundeishū, 1911
Seikainami, 1912
Pari yori, 1913
Sakura Sō, 1915
Maigoromo, 1916
Shubashū, 1916
Myōjōshū, 1918
Wakakiotome, 1918
Hinotori, 1919
Tabi-no-uta, 1921
Taiyō-to-bara, 1921
Kusa-no-yume, 1922
Nagareboshi-no-michi, 1924
Ningen ōrai, 1925
Ruriko, 1925
Kokoro no enkei, 1928
Shiro zakura, 1942
The Poetry of Yosano Akiko, 1957
Tangled Hair: Selected Tanka from "Midaregami," 1971
Akiko shukasen, 1996
River of Stars: Selected Poems of Yosano Akiko, 1996

OTHER LITERARY FORMS

Although the married name of Yosano Akiko (yoh-sah-noh ah-kee-koh) was Yosano (placed before her personal name, in the normal Japanese order), she is commonly called Akiko, which is her "elegant name." Among her many translations and modernizations, the most enduringly popular is her modern Japanese version of the greatest Japanese novel, *Genji monogatari* (early eleventh century; *The Tale of Genji*, 1881), written by Murasaki Shikibu. Akiko's version was published in 1912 and 1939. This monumental work revived general interest in Murasaki and other classical authors; it is included with Akiko's autobiography, novels, fairy tales, children's stories, essays, and original and translated poetry in the standard Japanese edition of her works, *Yosano Akiko zenshū* (1972).

Achievements

Yosano Akiko is generally admired as the greatest female poet and *tanka* poet of modern Japan, as an influential critic and educator, and as the grand embodiment of Romanticism, feminism, pacifism, and social reform in the first three decades of the twentieth century. She has been called a princess, queen, and goddess of poetry. In fact, Japanese Romanticism in the early twentieth century has been called the age of Akiko. She also influenced feminist writers internationally. She infused erotic and imaginative passion into the traditional *tanka* form (a poem of five lines containing five, seven, five, seven, and seven syllables respectively) at a time when it had grown lifelessly conventional, having lost the personal vitality of ancient times; in the same way, she revived certain classical qualities of the *Manyōshū* (mid-eighth century; *The Collections of Ten Thousand Leaves*; also as *The Ten Thousand Leaves*, 1981, and as *The Manyoshu*, 1940) and other ancient collections, while introducing stunning innovations of style. Projecting her own life and spirit into the form, she insisted that every word be charged with emotion. Such intensity is rarely transmitted through English translations, but Kenneth Rexroth's translations are fine poems in their own right as well as the most expressive renditions of Akiko's strong but subtle art.

Akiko's first book, *Tangled Hair*, was an immediate success and remains her most popular collection. It contains 399 *tanka* about her tempestuous love for the man who became her husband, Yosano Hiroshi (known as Tekkan). Her sequence of poems dramatically reveals the agonizing and sometimes ecstatic interactions among Akiko; Tekkan, his second wife (whom he was divorcing), and Yamakawa Tomiko. Tomiko, a beautiful poet beloved by both Tekkan and Akiko, was the leader of Shinshisha (the new poetry society) and edited its journal, *Myōjō* (the morning star), the chief organ of Japanese Romanticism.

Altogether, Akiko published seventy-five books, of which more than twenty are collections of original poetry. She wrote approximately seventeen thousand *tanka* as well as five hundred poems in free verse, which she devoted primarily to social issues such as pacifism and feminism. One of her outstanding poems of this kind, "Kimi shinitamō koto nakare" ("Never Let Them Kill You, Brother!"), was addressed to her own brother, who participated in the attack on Port Arthur in 1904 during the Russo-Japanese War.

Akiko disliked war, observing that it brought nothing but suffering and death. Her rhetorical question—How can the emperor, who does not fight, allow his subjects to die like beasts?—was so outrageously subversive at the time that people stoned her house. It was, in fact, the first criticism of the emperor, aside from political prose, that had been published. She was defended by Mori Ōgai and other writers, and this most famous of all Japanese antiwar poems has been revived periodically by antimilitarists. Akiko also courageously defended radicals who were executed in 1912.

Another often-quoted poem in free verse, "Yama no ugoku hi kitaru" ("The Day When Mountains Move"), was one of twelve of her poems to appear in *Seitō* (bluestocking) when that feminist journal was founded in 1916, establishing Akiko as the leading poet of women's consciousness in Japan. In 1921, with Tekkan, Akiko founded the Bunka Gakuin (culture school) for girls, where she worked as a teacher and dean, while also advancing the cause of women's education and social emancipation in essays in *Taiyō* and other journals. Between 1925 and 1931, with Tekkan and a third editor, she edited and published an authoritative fifty-volume set of Japanese classics, a work that helped to democratize the study of literature and gave her and her husband financial security. Her literary and financial success never interfered with her struggle for justice, which in her view was inseparable from literature. In "Kogan no shi" ("Death of Rosy-Cheeked Youth"), for example, she mourned the slaughter of Chinese boy-soldiers by the Japanese in Shanghai.

Some conservative critics ruthlessly denounced both Akiko and Tekkan for their scandalous lives and writings, which violated so many conventions, both literary and social. Undeterred by such attacks, Akiko struggled ceaselessly against prejudice and abuse to attain a high place among major Japanese poets of all eras.

BIOGRAPHY

Yosano Akiko was born in Sakai, Japan, December 7, 1878. Her father, Hō Sōshichi, owned a confectionery shop in Sakai, a suburb of Osaka. Both Akiko's father and her mother imposed traditional constraints on her, but she soon developed precocious literary enthusiasms and talents, thanks to the libraries of her great-grandparents; her great-grandfather was called the "master's master" of the town because of his knowledge of Chinese literature and his skilled composition of haiku. Akiko read all the literature that she could find from France and England, as well as from ancient and modern Japan—especially such classics as *The Manyoshu*, Sei Shōnagon's *Makura-no-sōshi* (early eleventh century; *Pillow Book*, 1928), and *The Tale of Genji* (which Akiko eventually translated from the archaic style into modern Japanese).

At age nineteen, Akiko published her first poem in a local journal, and within three years, she became prominent in Kansai-area literary activities. In 1900, Tekkan, the poet-leader of the new Romanticism, discovered Akiko's genius, began teaching her literature, brought her into his Shinshisha in Tokyo, and had her work published in the journal *Myōjō*; Akiko helped to edit the journal from 1901 until its demise in 1908, and again during its revival from 1921 to 1927. In 1901, Tekkan also edited and arranged publication for Akiko's first book, *Tangled Hair*. Her immediate success ensured her impact as a feminist and a pacifist, as well as the popularity of her many other books of poetry and prose, the royalties from which helped to finance Tekkan's three-year trip to France. Akiko was able to join him for six months in 1912, also visiting Germany, Holland, England, and Manchuria. She was inspired by European writers and artists, especially Auguste Rodin. She was also intrigued by the relative freedom of European women, and her tour strengthened her determination to change Japanese life through the power of the creative word. Her husband died in 1935, and two years later, she began working on a collection of others' poetry, *Shin Manyōshū* (1937-1939). In addition to her vigorous cultural activities, she gave birth to thirteen children, rearing eleven of them to adulthood. She died in 1942, of a stroke.

Analysis

Not even the finest translations can fully convey the subtle nuances of tone, the delicacy of imagery, and the great suggestiveness and complex allusiveness of Yosano Akiko's poetry—or indeed of most Japanese literature; English simply does not have the "feel" of Japanese, in sound, diction, grammar, or prosody. For example, there are no English equivalents for poignant sighs at the ends of many poems, or exclamations such as *ya!* and *kana!*

Fortunately, Rexroth's masterful renditions reveal Akiko's sensibility, passion, and imagination in English poems that are themselves enduring works of art. In the selections from her work included in his *One Hundred More Poems from the Japanese* (1974)—in which each English version is followed by the poem in romanized Japanese—Rexroth captures the erotic intensity that shocked Akiko's first readers. Other poems in this selection poignantly foreshadow separation—as a man fondles his lover in the autumn, as lovers gaze at each other without speaking or thinking of the future, or as a woman smells her lover's clothes in the darkness as he says good-bye. In others, the poet remembers writing a poem with her lover before separating from him, looks back on her passion like a blind man unafraid of the dark, contemplates sorrow as if it were hail or feathers falling, and watches cherry blossoms fall as stars go out in a false dawn. Such poems suggest the intricate, heartbreaking love story that comes alive, as in a novel, in hundreds of Akiko's original poems, many of them arranged to be read in a kind of narrative sequence. Most of them, however, are still unavailable in English.

Akiko also wrote many poems that calmly contemplate nature—poems in which, for example, snow and stars shine on her disheveled hair; an old boat reflects the autumn sky; ginkgo leaves scatter in the sunset; the nightingale sleeps with doubled-up jeweled claws; a white bird flying over the breakers becomes an obsessive dream; and cranes fly crying across Waka Bay to the other shore (an image traditionally suggesting Nirvana).

In his 1977 anthology, *The Burning Heart: Women Poets of Japan*, Rexroth included additional translations of Akiko's poetry. This collection illustrates how Akiko's influence has enabled women poets to speak out in a country whose literary tradition has been dominated by men. Some of Akiko's *tanka* included in the volume concern the love triangle in which Tomiko—Akiko's friend and her husband's lover—appears as a lily or queen in summer fields; Akiko's heart is envisioned as the sun drowned in darkness and rain. One of Akiko's poems in free verse, "Labor Pains," is also included; in it, the birth of her baby is likened to truth pushing outward from inwardness.

Rexroth usually renders Akiko's *tanka* in five lines, and he often approximates the normal syllable count without distorting sound or sense; his cadences, as well as his melodies and imagery, evoke the tone of the Japanese much more reliably than does H. H. Honda's rhymed quatrains, which seem more akin to A. E. Housman's verse than to Akiko's. Honda's *The Poetry of Yosano Akiko* is useful, however, for readers with even an elementary knowledge of Japanese, for the original poem is given in Japanese script as well as in romanized Japanese under each translation; Honda's selections from nineteen of Akiko's books are arranged so the reader can follow the overall development of the poet's work and her growing consciousness of aging, of her children, and of her place in society and in the universe. Although he bypasses the explicitly erotic passages that attracted Rexroth, Honda does convey something of Akiko's sensuousness in poems that show her cherishing her five-foot-long hair after a bath or rain, gazing at herself in a mirror for an hour, caressing herself, and floating like a serene lily in a pond. Some of Honda's best renditions are "The Cherries and the Moon," a snow scene in Kyoto; "Upon the Bridge of Shijo," where twilight hail falls on the brow of a dancer; "Down in the Ocean of My Mind," where fish wave jewel-colored fins; "Like Open-Eyed Fish," in which the fish are compared to the poet, who is unable to sleep; "There Side by Side," about being a slave to love; and the satirical poems "O That I Could," a defiance of Japanese conventionality, and "Naught Knowing the Blissful Touch," in which Akiko teases a youthful Buddhist monk.

Akiko's poetry is characterized by lyric, rhetorical, dramatic, and narrative strength. Each poem expresses an intense feeling of a particular moment in the poet's life, a feeling that is often too subtle, complex, or ambiguous to be fully comprehended by Westerners unfamiliar with the nuances of Japanese sensibility. The rhetorical thrust of many of Akiko's poems can readily be understood, however, especially in those poems concerned with dramatic conflicts between lovers, with the plight of women generally, and with protests against social conventions. The drama of Akiko's stormy life, concentrated in the *tanka*, reveals the intricate story of her romance, marriage, and literary career; thus, a study of her collections as unified works is usually more fruitful than formal analysis of individual poems. The narrative dimension of her work does not unfold chronologically, as a rule, but evolves cyclically from poem to poem, as she returns periodically to the dominant images and themes of her life. Indeed, the details of her life are inseparable from her poems, which require far more biographical knowledge on the part of the reader than is usually required for Western poetry. Such themes as love, jealousy, fear, loneliness, rebellion against oppression, and death are, however, universal, and may be directly and deeply appreciated by any reader.

Tangled Hair

The best English translations of Akiko's work, besides Rexroth's, are those by Sanford Goldstein and Shinoda Seishi. Their 1971 translation of *Tangled Hair* (which includes 165 of the 399 *tanka* in the collection, along with the Japanese originals) is supplemented by an excellent biographical introduction and useful notes based in part on the pioneering commentaries by Satake Kazuhiko. Goldstein and Shinoda's free-verse translations (usually in five lines, but without the conventional syllable count) are sensitive, vivid, and faithful to the meaning and feeling of the original, though not as intense. In "Yawahada no" ("You Have Yet to Touch"), the translators convey Akiko's seductive, sarcastic, teasing tone, as she asks an "Expounder of the Way" if he is not lonely for her blood and flesh. Satake's commentary on this poem identifies the "Expounder" as Tekkan; in Satake's reading, the poem reflects Akiko's impatience with Tekkan before he divorced his second wife and married her. Satake disagreed with Akiko's own interpretation of the poem as a generalized polemic against society, but its attack on hypocritical moralizing is surely as universal as it is personal. Akiko's rival Tomiko also figures in many poems in *Tangled Hair*. In "Sono namida" ("Tears in Your Eyes"), Akiko turns away from Tomiko's tears and gazes at the waning moon (always an image of sadness) reflected in a lake. The poignancy is heightened by knowledge that Akiko has just discovered that Tekkan still loves Tomiko, although he intends to marry Akiko.

Other poems evolve from customs such as the Dolls' Day celebration in "Hitotsu hako ni" ("Laying"), in which Akiko, in adolescence, sighs with some strange sexual awareness after putting the emperor and empress dolls together in a box; in an amazing image, she is afraid of her sigh being heard by peach blossoms. Sometimes Akiko identifies herself with women in ancient times, such as courtesans. In "Nakade isoge" ("Complain Not"), she tells a man to hurry on his way to other women who will undress him. Buddhism enters many of her poems in original ways. In "Wakaki ko no" ("Only the Sculptor's Fame"), she writes that she was attracted to the artist (probably Tekkan) because of his reputation when he was young, but now she is drawn to the face of the Buddha that he has carved (perhaps Tekkan's Buddha nature).

Sakanishi Shio's *Tangled Hair* (1935) includes translations not only from Akiko's first book but from eleven others as well, along with an informative introduction and a sketch of Akiko that might be compared to the photograph in Honda's volume. Sakanishi's versions are much more aesthetically subtle than Honda's and deserve close attention for their suggestively vivid imagery, natural speech rhythms, and artfully controlled syntax, all of which help to convey Akiko's tone. The sensuous and psychological implications of her hair are spun out in a variety of startling images. Her hair, for example, sweeps the strings of her koto, and its breaking strands recall the sound of the koto's strings; elsewhere, nightingales sing in a nest made from her fallen hair. Her discontent with traditional religions is manifest in her turning from the gods toward natural beauties, from the sutras to her own song, to the attractive flesh of a young monk, or to her loving husband. At other times, she prays to bodhisattvas while cherry blossoms fall on them and returns to sutras in bewilderment and despair, or sees the Buddha in the rising sun—a traditional image of Shingon Buddhism. Many of Akiko's poems included in Sakanishi's selection explicitly detail her life with Tekkan—her ambivalence about their original romance, resentful memories, ecstasies, the sadness of separation during his years in France, reunions, the agony of childbirth as three hearts beat in her body and one twin dies there, despair, children burning in volcanic eruptions, and renewed joy in rearing her children, to whom she gives her great-grandmother's prayer beads.

Thus, while the nuances of Akiko's verse remain resistant to translation, much of her artistry is accessible to English-speaking readers, who are now able to appreciate her significant contribution to the development of modern poetry in Japan.

OTHER MAJOR WORKS
LONG FICTION: *Genji monogatari*, 1912, 1939 (modern version); *Akarumi e*, 1913.
NONFICTION: *Nyonin sōzō*, 1920 (essays); *Yushosha to nare*, 1934; *Uta no tsukuriyō*, 1948; *Gekido no naka o yuku*, 1991; *Ai resei oyobi yuki*, 1993; *Travels in Manchuria and Mongolia: A Feminist Poet from Japan Encounters Prewar China*, 2001.
CHILDREN'S LITERATURE: *Watakushi no oitachi*, 1915.
MISCELLANEOUS: *Yosano Akiko zenshū*, 1972.

BIBLIOGRAPHY
Beichman, Janine. *Embracing the Firebird: Yosano Akiko and the Birth of the Female Voice in Modern Japanese Poetry*. Honolulu: University of Hawaii Press, 2002. This book-length biography of Akiko looks at her life, from birth to death, and analyzes her poetry at length, especially *Tangled Hair*. Contains an appendix with the poems in the original Japanese.
Morton, Leith. *The Alien Within: Representations of the Exotic in Twentieth-Century Japanese Literature*. Honolulu: University of Hawaii Press, 2009. Contains two chapters on Akiko: One argues that Akiko adapted ideas drawn from translations of Western poetry in revitalizing the *tanka* form, the other discusses Akiko's descriptions of childbirth in her poems, a subject not previously used in poetry.
_____. "The Birth of the Modern: Yosano Akiko and Tekkan's Verse Revolution." In *Modernism in Practice: An Introduction to Postwar Japanese Poetry*. Honolulu: University of Hawaii Press, 2004. Describes how Akiko and Tekkan helped modernize Japanese poetry.

Okada, Sumie. "The Visit by Hiroshi (1873-1935) and Akiko Yosano (1878-1942) to France and England in 1912." In *Japanese Writers and the West*. New York: Palgrave Macmillan, 2003. Discusses Akiko's impressions of French women and her resulting belief that Japanese women could have a more independent existence.

Rowley, Gillian Gaye. *Yosano Akiko and "The Tale of Genji."* Ann Arbor: University of Michigan Press, 2000. A critical analysis of Akiko's modern Japanese version of *The Tale of Genji*. Includes bibliographical references and index.

Takeda, Noriko. "The Japanese Reformation of Poetic Language: Yosano Akiko's *Tangled Hair* as Avant-Garde Centrality." In *A Flowering Word: The Modernist Expression in Stéphane Mallarmé, T. S. Eliot, and Yosano Akiko*. New York: Peter Lang, 2000. This comparative study of modernism examines Akiko's most famous work for its poetic language.

Morgan Gibson and Keiko Matsui Gibson

CHECKLIST FOR EXPLICATING A POEM

I. The Initial Readings

A. Before reading the poem, the reader should:
   1. Notice its form and length.
   2. Consider the title, determining, if possible, whether it might function as an allusion, symbol, or poetic image.
   3. Notice the date of composition or publication, and identify the general era of the poet.

B. The poem should be read intuitively and emotionally and be allowed to "happen" as much as possible.

C. In order to establish the rhythmic flow, the poem should be reread. A note should be made as to where the irregular spots (if any) are located.

II. Explicating the Poem

A. *Dramatic situation.* Studying the poem line by line helps the reader discover the dramatic situation. All elements of the dramatic situation are interrelated and should be viewed as reflecting and affecting one another. The dramatic situation serves a particular function in the poem, adding realism, surrealism, or absurdity; drawing attention to certain parts of the poem; and changing to reinforce other aspects of the poem. All points should be considered. The following questions are particularly helpful to ask in determining dramatic situation:
   1. What, if any, is the narrative action in the poem?
   2. How many personae appear in the poem? What part do they take in the action?
   3. What is the relationship between characters?
   4. What is the setting (time and location) of the poem?

B. *Point of view.* An understanding of the poem's point of view is a major step toward comprehending the poet's intended meaning. The reader should ask:
   1. Who is the speaker? Is he or she addressing someone else or the reader?
   2. Is the narrator able to understand or see everything happening to him or her, or does the reader know things that the narrator does not?
   3. Is the narrator reliable?
   4. Do point of view and dramatic situation seem consistent? If not, the inconsistencies may provide clues to the poem's meaning.

C. *Images and metaphors.* Images and metaphors are often the most intricately crafted vehicles of the poem for relaying the poet's message. Realizing that the images and metaphors work in harmony with the dramatic situation and point of view will help the reader to see the poem as a whole, rather than as disassociated elements.
1. The reader should identify the concrete images (that is, those that are formed from objects that can be touched, smelled, seen, felt, or tasted). Is the image projected by the poet consistent with the physical object?
2. If the image is abstract, or so different from natural imagery that it cannot be associated with a real object, then what are the properties of the image?
3. To what extent is the reader asked to form his or her own images?
4. Is any image repeated in the poem? If so, how has it been changed? Is there a controlling image?
5. Are any images compared to each other? Do they reinforce one another?
6. Is there any difference between the way the reader perceives the image and the way the narrator sees it?
7. What seems to be the narrator's or persona's attitude toward the image?

D. *Words.* Every substantial word in a poem may have more than one intended meaning, as used by the author. Because of this, the reader should look up many of these words in the dictionary and:
1. Note all definitions that have the slightest connection with the poem.
2. Note any changes in syntactical patterns in the poem.
3. In particular, note those words that could possibly function as symbols or allusions, and refer to any appropriate sources for further information.

E. *Meter, rhyme, structure, and tone.* In scanning the poem, all elements of prosody should be noted by the reader. These elements are often used by a poet to manipulate the reader's emotions, and therefore they should be examined closely to arrive at the poet's specific intention.
1. Does the basic meter follow a traditional pattern such as those found in nursery rhymes or folk songs?
2. Are there any variations in the base meter? Such changes or substitutions are important thematically and should be identified.
3. Are the rhyme schemes traditional or innovative, and what might their form mean to the poem?
4. What devices has the poet used to create sound patterns (such as assonance and alliteration)?
5. Is the stanza form a traditional or innovative one?
6. If the poem is composed of verse paragraphs rather than stanzas, how do they affect the progression of the poem?

7. After examining the above elements, is the resultant tone of the poem casual or formal, pleasant, harsh, emotional, authoritative?

F. *Historical context.* The reader should attempt to place the poem into historical context, checking on events at the time of composition. Archaic language, expressions, images, or symbols should also be looked up.

G. *Themes and motifs.* By seeing the poem as a composite of emotion, intellect, craftsmanship, and tradition, the reader should be able to determine the themes and motifs (smaller recurring ideas) presented in the work. He or she should ask the following questions to help pinpoint these main ideas:
1. Is the poet trying to advocate social, moral, or religious change?
2. Does the poet seem sure of his or her position?
3. Does the poem appeal primarily to the emotions, to the intellect, or to both?
4. Is the poem relying on any particular devices for effect (such as imagery, allusion, paradox, hyperbole, or irony)?

BIBLIOGRAPHY

GENERAL REFERENCE SOURCES

BIOGRAPHICAL SOURCES
Colby, Vineta, ed. *World Authors, 1975-1980*. Wilson Authors Series. New York: H. W. Wilson, 1985.
_____. *World Authors, 1980-1985*. Wilson Authors Series. New York: H. W. Wilson, 1991.
_____. *World Authors, 1985-1990*. Wilson Authors Series. New York: H. W. Wilson, 1995.
Cyclopedia of World Authors. 4th rev. ed. 5 vols. Pasadena, Calif.: Salem Press, 2003.
International Who's Who in Poetry and Poets' Encyclopaedia. Cambridge, England: International Biographical Centre, 1993.
Seymour-Smith, Martin, and Andrew C. Kimmens, eds. *World Authors, 1900-1950*. Wilson Authors Series. 4 vols. New York: H. W. Wilson, 1996.
Thompson, Clifford, ed. *World Authors, 1990-1995*. Wilson Authors Series. New York: H. W. Wilson, 1999.
Wakeman, John, ed. *World Authors, 1950-1970*. New York: H. W. Wilson, 1975.
_____. *World Authors, 1970-1975*. Wilson Authors Series. New York: H. W. Wilson, 1991.
Willhardt, Mark, and Alan Michael Parker, eds. *Who's Who in Twentieth Century World Poetry*. New York: Routledge, 2000.

CRITICISM
Brooks, Cleanth, and Robert Penn Warren. *Understanding Poetry*. 4th ed. Reprint. Fort Worth, Tex.: Heinle & Heinle, 2003.
Day, Gary. *Literary Criticism: A New History*. Edinburgh, Scotland: Edinburgh University Press, 2008.
Habib, M. A. R. *A History of Literary Criticism: From Plato to the Present*. Malden, Mass.: Wiley-Blackwell, 2005.
Jason, Philip K., ed. *Masterplots II: Poetry Series, Revised Edition*. 8 vols. Pasadena, Calif.: Salem Press, 2002.
Lodge, David, and Nigel Wood. *Modern Criticism and Theory*. 3d ed. New York: Longman, 2008.
Magill, Frank N., ed. *Magill's Bibliography of Literary Criticism*. 4 vols. Englewood Cliffs, N.J.: Salem Press, 1979.
MLA International Bibliography. New York: Modern Language Association of America, 1922- .

Poetry Dictionaries and Handbooks

Carey, Gary, and Mary Ellen Snodgrass. *A Multicultural Dictionary of Literary Terms.* Jefferson, N.C.: McFarland, 1999.

Deutsch, Babette. *Poetry Handbook: A Dictionary of Terms.* 4th ed. New York: Funk & Wagnalls, 1974.

Drury, John. *The Poetry Dictionary.* Cincinnati, Ohio: Story Press, 1995.

Kinzie, Mary. *A Poet's Guide to Poetry.* Chicago: University of Chicago Press, 1999.

Lennard, John. *The Poetry Handbook: A Guide to Reading Poetry for Pleasure and Practical Criticism.* New York: Oxford University Press, 1996.

Matterson, Stephen, and Darryl Jones. *Studying Poetry.* New York: Oxford University Press, 2000.

Packard, William. *The Poet's Dictionary: A Handbook of Prosody and Poetic Devices.* New York: Harper & Row, 1989.

Preminger, Alex, et al., eds. *The New Princeton Encyclopedia of Poetry and Poetics.* 3d rev. ed. Princeton, N.J.: Princeton University Press, 1993.

Shipley, Joseph Twadell, ed. *Dictionary of World Literary Terms, Forms, Technique, Criticism.* Rev. ed. Boston: George Allen and Unwin, 1979.

Indexes of Primary Works

Frankovich, Nicholas, ed. *The Columbia Granger's Index to Poetry in Anthologies.* 11th ed. New York: Columbia University Press, 1997.

_____. *The Columbia Granger's Index to Poetry in Collected and Selected Works.* New York: Columbia University Press, 1997.

Guy, Patricia. *A Women's Poetry Index.* Phoenix, Ariz.: Oryx Press, 1985.

Hazen, Edith P., ed. *Columbia Granger's Index to Poetry.* 10th ed. New York: Columbia University Press, 1994.

Hoffman, Herbert H., and Rita Ludwig Hoffman, comps. *International Index to Recorded Poetry.* New York: H. W. Wilson, 1983.

Marcan, Peter. *Poetry Themes: A Bibliographical Index to Subject Anthologies and Related Criticisms in the English Language, 1875-1975.* Hamden, Conn.: Linnet Books, 1977.

Poetics, Poetic Forms, and Genres

Attridge, Derek. *Poetic Rhythm: An Introduction.* New York: Cambridge University Press, 1995.

Brogan, T. V. F. *Verseform: A Comparative Bibliography.* Baltimore: Johns Hopkins University Press, 1989.

Fussell, Paul. *Poetic Meter and Poetic Form.* Rev. ed. New York: McGraw-Hill, 1979.

Hollander, John. *Rhyme's Reason.* 3d ed. New Haven, Conn.: Yale University Press, 2001.

Jackson, Guida M. *Traditional Epics: A Literary Companion*. New York: Oxford University Press, 1995.

Padgett, Ron, ed. *The Teachers and Writers Handbook of Poetic Forms*. 2d ed. New York: Teachers & Writers Collaborative, 2000.

Pinsky, Robert. *The Sounds of Poetry: A Brief Guide*. New York: Farrar, Straus and Giroux, 1998.

Preminger, Alex, and T. V. F. Brogan, eds. *New Princeton Encyclopedia of Poetry and Poetics*. 3d ed. Princeton, N.J.: Princeton University Press, 1993.

Spiller, Michael R. G. *The Sonnet Sequence: A Study of Its Strategies*. Studies in Literary Themes and Genres 13. New York: Twayne, 1997.

Turco, Lewis. *The New Book of Forms: A Handbook of Poetics*. Hanover, N.H.: University Press of New England, 1986.

Williams, Miller. *Patterns of Poetry: An Encyclopedia of Forms*. Baton Rouge: Louisiana State University Press, 1986.

WOMEN WRITERS

Adelaide, Debra. *Bibliography of Australian Women's Literature, 1795-1990: A Listing of Fiction, Poetry, Drama, and Non-fiction Published in Monograph Form Arranged Alphabetically by Author*. Port Melbourne: Thorpe with National Centre for Australian Studies, 1991.

Blum, Cinzia Sartini, and Lara Trubowitz, eds. and trans. *Contemporary Italian Women Poets: A Bilingual Anthology*. New York: Italica Press, 2001.

Boland, Eavan, ed. and trans. *After Every War: Twentieth-Century Women Poets*. Princeton, N.J.: Princeton University Press, 2004.

Chapman, Alison, ed. *Victorian Women Poets*. Cambridge, England: D. S. Brewer, 2003.

Chapman, Dorothy Hilton, comp. *Index to Poetry by Black American Women*. Bibliographies and Indexes in Afro-American and African Studies 15. New York: Greenwood Press, 1986.

Classen, Albrecht, ed. and trans. *Late-Medieval German Women's Poetry: Secular and Religious Songs*. Rochester, N.Y.: D. S. Brewer, 2004.

Colman, Anne Ulry. *Dictionary of Nineteenth-Century Irish Women Poets*. Galway: Kenny's Bookshop, 1996.

Davidson, Phebe, ed. *Conversations with the World: American Women Poets and Their Work*. Pasadena, Calif.: Trilogy Books, 1998.

Davis, Gwenn, and Beverly A. Joyce, comps. *Poetry by Women to 1900: A Bibliography of American and British Writers*. Toronto: University of Toronto Press, 1991.

Dowson, Jane, and Alice Entwistle. *A History of Twentieth-Century British Women's Poetry*. New York: Cambridge University Press, 2005.

Drake, William. *The First Wave: Women Poets in America, 1915-1945*. New York: Macmillan, 1987.

Frabotta, Biancamaria, ed. *Italian Women Poets*. Translated by Corrado Federici. Toronto: Guernica Editions, 2002.

Gray, F. Elizabeth. *Christian and Lyric Tradition in Victorian Women's Poetry*. New York: Routledge, 2009.

Gray, Janet, ed. *She Wields a Pen: American Women Poets of the Nineteenth Century*. Iowa City: University of Iowa Press, 1997.

Hampton, Susan, and Kate Llewellyn, eds. *The Penguin Book of Australian Women Poets*. New York: Penguin Ringwood, 1986.

Harper, Anthony, and Margaret C. Ives. *Sappho in the Shadows: Essays on the Work of German Women Poets of the Age of Goethe, 1749-1832*. New York: Peter Lang, 2000.

Jackson, J. R. de J. *Romantic Poetry by Women: A Bibliography, 1770-1835*. Oxford: Clarendon-Oxford University Press, 1993.

Lee, Valerie, ed. *The Prentice Hall Anthology of African American Women's Literature*. Upper Saddle River, N.J.: Pearson Prentice Hall, 2006.

McBreen, Joan, ed. *The White Page = An Bhileog Bhán: Twentieth-Century Irish Women Poets*. Cliffs of Moher, Ireland: Salmon, 1999.

Mark, Alison, and Deryn Rees-Jones. *Contemporary Women's Poetry: Reading, Writing, Practice*. New York: St. Martin's Press, 2000.

Reardon, Joan, and Kristine A. Thorsen. *Poetry by American Women, 1900-1975: A Bibliography*. Metuchen, N.J.: Scarecrow Press, 1979.

―――. *Poetry by American Women, 1975-1989: A Bibliography*. Metuchen, N.J.: Scarecrow Press, 1990.

Sartori, Eva Martin, and Dorothy Wynne Zimmerman. *French Women Writers: A Biobibliographical Source Book*. New York: Greenwood Press, 1991.

Shapiro, Norman R., ed. and trans. *French Women Poets of Nine Centuries: The Distaff and the Pen*. Baltimore: Johns Hopkins University Press, 2008.

Stortoni, Laura A., and Mary P. Lillie, eds. *Women Poets of the Italian Renaissance: Courtly Ladies and Courtesans*. New York: Italica, 1997.

Weekes, Ann Owens. *Unveiling Treasures: The Attic Guide to the Published Works of Irish Women Literary Writers: Drama, Fiction, Poetry*. Dublin: Attic Press, 1993.

GUIDE TO ONLINE RESOURCES

WEB SITES

The following sites were visited by the editors of Salem Press in 2010. Because URLs frequently change, the accuracy of these addresses cannot be guaranteed; however, long-standing sites, such as those of colleges and universities, national organizations, and government agencies, generally maintain links when their sites are moved.

Academy of American Poets
http://www.poets.org

The mission of the Academy of American Poets is to "support American poets at all stages of their careers and to foster the appreciation of contemporary poetry." The academy's comprehensive Web site features information on poetic schools and movements; a Poetic Forms Database; an Online Poetry Classroom, with educator and teaching resources; an index of poets and poems; essays and interviews; general Web resources; links for further study; and more.

A Celebration of Women Writers
http://digital.library.upenn.edu/women

This site is an extensive compendium on the contributions of women writers throughout history. The "Local Editions by Authors" and "Local Editions by Category" pages include access to electronic texts of the works of numerous writers. Users can also access biographical and bibliographical information by browsing lists arranged by writers' names, countries of origin, ethnicities, and the centuries in which they lived.

Contemporary British Writers
http://www.contemporarywriters.com/authors

Created by the British Council, this site offers profiles of living writers of the United Kingdom, the Republic of Ireland, and the Commonwealth. Information includes biographies, bibliographies, critical reviews, and news about literary prizes. Photographs are also featured. Users can search the site by author, genre, nationality, gender, publisher, book title, date of publication, and prize name and date.

LiteraryHistory.com
http://www.literaryhistory.com

This site is an excellent source of academic, scholarly, and critical literature about eighteenth, nineteenth, and twentieth century American and English writers. It provides individual pages for twentieth century literature and alphabetical lists of authors that link to articles, reviews, overviews, excerpts of works, teaching guides, podcasts, and other materials.

Literary Resources on the Net
http://andromeda.rutgers.edu/~jlynch/Lit

Jack Lynch of Rutgers University maintains this extensive collection of links to Web sites that are useful to researchers, including numerous sites about American and English literature. This collection is a good place to begin online research about poetry, as it links to other sites with broad ranges of literary topics. The site is organized chronologically, with separate pages about twentieth century British and Irish literature. It also has separate pages providing links to Web sites about American literature and to women's literature and feminism.

LitWeb
http://litweb.net

LitWeb provides biographies of hundreds of world authors throughout history that can be accessed through an alphabetical listing. The pages about each writer contain a list of his or her works, suggestions for further reading, and illustrations. The site also offers information about past and present winners of major literary prizes.

The Modern Word: Authors of the Libyrinth
http://www.themodernword.com/authors.html

The Modern Word site, although somewhat haphazard in its organization, provides a great deal of critical information about writers. The "Authors of the Libyrinth" page is very useful, linking author names to essays about them and other resources. The section of the page headed "The Scriptorium" presents "an index of pages featuring writers who have pushed the edges of their medium, combining literary talent with a sense of experimentation to produce some remarkable works of modern literature."

Outline of American Literature
http://www.america.gov/publications/books/outline
-of-american-literature.html

This page of the America.gov site provides access to an electronic version of the ten-chapter volume *Outline of American Literature*, a historical overview of poetry and prose from colonial times to the present published by the Bureau of International Information Programs of the U.S. Department of State.

Poetry Foundation
http://www.poetryfoundation.org

The Poetry Foundation, publisher of *Poetry* magazine, is an independent literary organization. Its Web site offers links to essays; news; events; online poetry resources, such as blogs, organizations, publications, and references and research; a glossary of literary terms; and a Learning Lab that includes poem guides and essays on poetics.

Poet's Corner
http://theotherpages.org/poems

The Poet's Corner, one of the oldest text resources on the Web, provides access to about seven thousand works of poetry by several hundred different poets from around the world. Indexes are arranged and searchable by title, name of poet, or subject. The site also offers its own resources, including "Faces of the Poets"—a gallery of portraits—and "Lives of the Poets"—a growing collection of biographies.

Representative Poetry Online
http://rpo.library.utoronto.ca

This award-winning resource site, maintained by Ian Lancashire of the Department of English at the University of Toronto in Canada, has several thousand English-language poems by hundreds of poets. The collection is searchable by poet's name, title of work, first line of a poem, and keyword. The site also includes a time line, a glossary, essays, an extensive bibliography, and countless links organized by country and by subject.

Voice of the Shuttle
http://vos.ucsb.edu

One of the most complete and authoritative places for online information about literature, Voice of the Shuttle is maintained by professors and students in the English Department at the University of California, Santa Barbara. The site provides countless links to electronic books, academic journals, literary association Web sites, sites created by university professors, and many other resources.

Voices from the Gaps
http://voices.cla.umn.edu/

Voices from the Gaps is a site of the English Department at the University of Minnesota, dedicated to providing resources on the study of women artists of color, including writers. The site features a comprehensive index searchable by name, and it provides biographical information on each writer or artist and other resources for further study.

ELECTRONIC DATABASES

Electronic databases usually do not have their own URLs. Instead, public, college, and university libraries subscribe to these databases, provide links to them on their Web sites, and make them available to library card holders or other specified patrons. Readers can visit library Web sites or ask reference librarians to check on availability.

Canadian Literary Centre

Produced by EBSCO, the Canadian Literary Centre database contains full-text content from ECW Press, a Toronto-based publisher, including the titles in the publisher's Canadian fiction studies, Canadian biography, and Canadian writers and their works series; *ECW's Biographical Guide to Canadian Novelists*; and *George Woodcock's Introduction to Canadian Fiction*. Author biographies, essays and literary criticism, and book reviews are among the database's offerings.

Literary Reference Center

EBSCO's Literary Reference Center (LRC) is a comprehensive full-text database designed primarily to help high school and undergraduate students in English and the humanities with homework and research assignments about literature. The database contains massive amounts of information from reference works, books, literary journals, and other materials, including more than 31,000 plot summaries, synopses, and overviews of literary works; almost 100,000 essays and articles of literary criticism; about 140,000 author biographies; more than 605,000 book reviews; and more than 5,200 author interviews. It contains the entire contents of Salem Press's MagillOnLiterature Plus. Users can retrieve information by browsing a list of authors' names or titles of literary works; they can also use an advanced search engine to access information by numerous categories, including author name, gender, cultural identity, national identity, and the years in which he or she lived, or by literary title, character, locale, genre, and publication date. The Literary Reference Center also features a literary-historical time line, an encyclopedia of literature, and a glossary of literary terms.

MagillOnLiterature Plus

MagillOnLiterature Plus is a comprehensive, integrated literature database produced by Salem Press and available on the EBSCOhost platform. The database contains the full text of essays in Salem's many literature-related reference works, including *Masterplots, Cyclopedia of World Authors, Cyclopedia of Literary Characters, Cyclopedia of Literary Places, Critical Survey of Poetry, Critical Survey of Long Fiction, Critical Survey of Short Fiction, World Philosophers and Their Works, Magill's Literary Annual*, and *Magill's Book Reviews*. Among its contents are articles on more than 35,000 literary works and more than 8,500 poets, writers, dramatists, essayists, and philosophers; more than 1,000 images; and a glossary of more than 1,300 literary terms. The biographical essays include lists of authors' works and secondary bibliographies, and hundreds of overview essays examine and discuss literary genres, time periods, and national literatures.

Rebecca Kuzins; updated by Desiree Dreeuws

GEOGRAPHICAL INDEX

CANADA
    Atwood, Margaret, 17

ENGLAND
    Behn, Aphra, 31
    Levertov, Denise, 127
    Mew, Charlotte, 141

FRANCE
    Stein, Gertrude, 224

GREAT BRITAIN
    Behn, Aphra, 31
    Levertov, Denise, 127
    Mew, Charlotte, 141

IRELAND
    Boland, Eavan, 54

JAPAN
    Yamada, Mitsuye, 246
    Yosano Akiko, 253

UNITED STATES
    Allen, Paula Gunn, 11
    Bishop, Elizabeth, 42
    Cervantes, Lorna Dee, 71
    Forché, Carolyn, 79
    Fulton, Alice, 89
    H. D., 97
    Hirshfield, Jane, 107
    Howe, Susan, 115
    Levertov, Denise, 127
    Millay, Edna St. Vincent, 146
    Moore, Marianne, 155
    Moss, Thylias, 167
    Ostriker, Alicia Suskin, 172
    Plath, Sylvia, 177
    Rich, Adrienne, 189
    Rukeyser, Muriel, 203
    Sexton, Anne, 214
    Stein, Gertrude, 224
    Walker, Alice, 237
    Yamada, Mitsuye, 246

CATEGORY INDEX

AFRICAN AMERICAN CULTURE
    Moss, Thylias, 167
    Walker, Alice, 237
ASIAN AMERICAN CULTURE
    Yamada, Mitsuye, 246
AVANT-GARDE POETS
    Stein, Gertrude, 224

BLACK ARTS MOVEMENT
    Walker, Alice, 237
BLACK MOUNTAIN POETS
    Levertov, Denise, 127

CHILDREN'S/YOUNG ADULT POETRY
    Stein, Gertrude, 224
CONFESSIONAL POETS
    Plath, Sylvia, 177
    Sexton, Anne, 214
CUBISM
    Stein, Gertrude, 224

DRAMATIC MONOLOGUES
    Mew, Charlotte, 141
    Millay, Edna St. Vincent, 146

EKPHRASTIC POETRY
    Bishop, Elizabeth, 42
    Boland, Eavan, 54
    Ostriker, Alicia Suskin, 172
ELEGIES
    Behn, Aphra, 31
EXPERIMENTAL POETS
    Howe, Susan, 115
    Moss, Thylias, 167
    Sexton, Anne, 214
    Stein, Gertrude, 224

GAY AND LESBIAN CULTURE
    Allen, Paula Gunn, 11
    Bishop, Elizabeth, 42
    Feminist Criticism, 1
    Mew, Charlotte, 141
    Rich, Adrienne, 189
    Stein, Gertrude, 224
    Walker, Alice, 237
GHAZALS
    Rich, Adrienne, 189

IMAGISM
    H. D., 97
    Moore, Marianne, 155
    Plath, Sylvia, 177

JEWISH CULTURE
    Levertov, Denise, 127
    Ostriker, Alicia Suskin, 172
    Rich, Adrienne, 189
    Rukeyser, Muriel, 203
    Stein, Gertrude, 224

LANGUAGE POETRY
    Howe, Susan, 115
LATINO CULTURE
    Cervantes, Lorna Dee, 71
LOST GENERATION
    Stein, Gertrude, 224
LOVE POETRY
    Millay, Edna St. Vincent, 146
    Sexton, Anne, 214
    Yosano Akiko, 253
LYRIC POETRY
    Behn, Aphra, 31
    Hirshfield, Jane, 107

Levertov, Denise, 127
Millay, Edna St. Vincent, 146
Plath, Sylvia, 177

MODERNISM
H. D., 97
Mew, Charlotte, 141
Millay, Edna St. Vincent, 146
Moore, Marianne, 155

NARRATIVE POETRY
Forché, Carolyn, 79
Levertov, Denise, 127

NATIVE AMERICAN CULTURE
Allen, Paula Gunn, 11
Cervantes, Lorna Dee, 71

NATURE POETRY
Walker, Alice, 237

OCCASIONAL VERSE
Behn, Aphra, 31
Moore, Marianne, 155

ODES
Rukeyser, Muriel, 203

PETRARCHAN SONNETS
Millay, Edna St. Vincent, 146

POLITICAL POETS
Behn, Aphra, 31
Cervantes, Lorna Dee, 71
Forché, Carolyn, 79
Levertov, Denise, 127
Millay, Edna St. Vincent, 146
Moss, Thylias, 167
Rich, Adrienne, 189

Rukeyser, Muriel, 203
Walker, Alice, 237
Yamada, Mitsuye, 246
Yosano Akiko, 253

POSTCONFESSIONAL POETS
Bishop, Elizabeth, 42
Rich, Adrienne, 189

POSTMODERNISM
Boland, Eavan, 54
Cervantes, Lorna Dee, 71
Fulton, Alice, 89
Levertov, Denise, 127
Rukeyser, Muriel, 203

PROSE POETRY
Forché, Carolyn, 79
Moss, Thylias, 167
Ostriker, Alicia Suskin, 172

RELIGIOUS POETRY
Hirshfield, Jane, 107
Ostriker, Alicia Suskin, 172

RESTORATION
Behn, Aphra, 31

ROMANTICISM
Yosano Akiko, 253

SONGS
Behn, Aphra, 31

SONNETS
Millay, Edna St. Vincent, 146

VERSE DRAMATISTS
Millay, Edna St. Vincent, 146

VICTORIAN ERA
Mew, Charlotte, 141

SUBJECT INDEX

Abdelazar (Behn), 37
"About Marriage" (Levertov), 135
Absolute Trust in the Goodness of the Earth (Walker), 242
After (Hirshfield), 112
Against Love Poetry (Boland), 66
"Ajanta" (Rukeyser), 208
Alaya (Hirshfield), 109
All My Pretty Ones (Sexton), 219
Allen, Paula Gunn, 11-16
    A Cannon Between My Knees, 13
    Shadow Country, 14
Amis, Aphara. *See* Behn, Aphra
Angel of History, The (Forché), 86
Animals in That Country, The (Atwood), 22
Astrea. *See* Behn, Aphra
At Redbones (Moss), 168
Atwood, Margaret, 17-30
    The Animals in That Country, 22
    The Circle Game, 20
    The Door, 28
    Interlunar, 27
    The Journals of Susanna Moodie, 23
    Morning in the Burned House, 27
    Power Politics, 25
    Procedures for Underground, 24
    True Stories, 26
    Two-Headed Poems, 26
    You Are Happy, 25
Autobiography of Alice B. Toklas, The (Stein), 234

"Ballad of the Harp-Weaver, The" (Millay), 152
"Bananas" (Cervantes), 77
Bayn, Aphra. *See* Behn, Aphra

Behn, Aphra, 31-41
    Abdelazar, 37
    "The Disappointment," 37
    "Love in fantastic triumph sate," 37
    "On the Death of Edmund Waller," 38
    "On the Death of the Late Earl of Rochester," 38
"Beneath the Shadow of the Freeway" (Cervantes), 74
Bishop, Elizabeth, 42-53
    "The Fish," 45
    "In the Waiting Room," 50
    "The Man-Moth," 46
    "The Map," 49
    "The Monument," 48
    "Objects and Apparitions," 45
    "Over 2000 Illustrations and a Complete Concordance," 46
    Questions of Travel, 46
    "The Riverman," 47
    "Sandpiper," 44
Blue Hour (Forché), 86
Boland, Eavan, 54-70
    Against Love Poetry, 66
    Domestic Violence, 67
    In Her Own Image, 58
    In a Time of Violence, 65
    The Journey, and Other Poems, 63
    The Lost Land, 65
    Night Feed, 56
Boyd, Nancy. *See* Millay, Edna St, Vincent
"By Candlelight" (Plath), 184

Camp Notes, and Other Writings (Yamada), 250
Cannon Between My Knees, A (Allen), 13

Cascade Experiment (Fulton), 93
Cervantes, Lorna Dee, 71-78
   "Bananas," 77
   "Beneath the Shadow of the Freeway," 74
   "Coffee," 77
   Drive, 76
   Emplumada, 72
   "Freeway 280," 74
   From the Cables of Genocide, 75
   "Oaxaca, 1974," 73
   "Poem for the Young White Man . . . ," 75
   "Refugee Ship," 72
Change of World, A (Rich), 192
"Channel Crossing" (Plath), 186
Circle Game, The (Atwood), 20
"Coffee" (Cervantes), 77
Country Between Us, The (Forché), 84
Crack in Everything, The (Ostriker), 174

"Daddy" (Plath), 186
Desert Run (Yamada), 249
Diamond Cutters, The (Rich), 193
"Disappointment, The" (Behn), 37
Diving into the Wreck (Rich), 196
Domestic Violence (Boland), 67
Door, The (Atwood), 28
Dream of a Common Language, The (Rich), 197
Drive (Cervantes), 76

Emplumada (Cervantes), 72
"Euclid Alone Has Looked on Beauty Bare" (Millay), 150

Farmer's Bride, The (Mew), 143
Fatal Interview (Millay), 151
Feminist criticism, 1-10
"Fish, The" (Bishop), 45
"Fix" (Fulton), 91
Forché, Carolyn, 79-88

The Angel of History, 86
Blue Hour, 86
The Country Between Us, 84
Gathering the Tribes, 82
Fox (Rich), 200
"Freeway 280" (Cervantes), 74
"From an Old House in America" (Rich), 196
From the Cables of Genocide (Cervantes), 75
Fulton, Alice, 89-96
   Cascade Experiment, 93
   "Fix," 91
   "Fuzzy Feelings," 92
   "The Orthodox Waltz," 92
"Fuzzy Feelings" (Fulton), 92

"Gates, The" (Rukeyser), 211
Gathering the Tribes (Forché), 82
Gendered discourse, 5
Given Sugar, Given Salt (Hirshfield), 111
Good Night, Willie Lee, I'll See You in the Morning (Walker), 241
Gynocriticism, 2

H. D., 97-106
   "Oread," 99
Her Blue Body Everything We Know (Walker), 242
Hirshfield, Jane, 107-114
   After, 112
   Alaya, 109
   Given Sugar, Given Salt, 111
   The Lives of the Heart, 111
   The October Palace, 110
   Of Gravity and Angels, 109
Horses Make a Landscape Look More Beautiful (Walker), 241
Howe, Susan, 115-126
   The Liberties, 119
   The Midnight, 123
   The Nonconformist's Memorial, 122

Subject Index

Pierce-Arrow, 122
Pythagorean Silence, 120
Souls of the Labadie Tract, 124

"In Distrust of Merits" (Moore), 162
In Her Own Image (Boland), 58
In a Time of Violence (Boland), 65
"In the Grave No Flower" (Millay), 152
"In the Waiting Room" (Bishop), 50
Interlunar (Atwood), 27

Johnson, Aphra. *See* Behn, Aphra
Journals of Susanna Moodie, The (Atwood), 23
Journey, and Other Poems, The (Boland), 63

"Lady Lazarus" (Plath), 186
Lakoff, Robin, 6
Language, 2
Language and Woman's Place (Lakoff), 6
Leaflets (Rich), 194
"Letter, Unposted" (Rukeyser), 210
Levertov, Denise, 127-140
　"About Marriage," 135
　"Listening to Distant Guns," 134
　"On the Edge of Darkness," 134
　"Those Who Want Out," 132
　"To the Muse," 132
Liberties, The (Howe), 119
Like a Bulwark (Moore), 163
"Listening to Distant Guns" (Levertov), 134
Little Space, The (Ostriker), 174
Live or Die (Sexton), 220
"Lives" (Rukeyser), 207
Lives of the Heart, The (Hirshfield), 111
Lost Land, The (Boland), 65
Love Poems (Sexton), 220
"Love in fantastic triumph sate" (Behn), 37
Lucas, Victoria. *See* Plath, Sylvia

"Man-Moth, The" (Bishop), 46
"Map, The" (Bishop), 49
"Mary's Song" (Plath), 183
"Maudlin" (Plath), 184
"Menses" (Millay), 152
Mew, Charlotte, 141-145
　The Farmer's Bride, 143
　The Rambling Sailor, 144
Midaregami. *See Tangled Hair*
Midnight, The (Howe), 123
Midnight Salvage (Rich), 200
Millay, Edna St. Vincent, 146-154
　"The Ballad of the Harp-Weaver," 152
　"Euclid Alone Has Looked on Beauty Bare," 150
　Fatal Interview, 151
　"In the Grave No Flower," 152
　"Menses," 152
"Monument, The" (Bishop), 48
Moore, Marianne, 155-166
　"In Distrust of Merits," 162
　Like a Bulwark, 163
　"Nevertheless," 161
　The Pangolin, and Other Verse, 161
　Selected Fables of La Fontaine, 162
　Tell Me, Tell Me, 163
　"What Are Years?," 161
Morning in the Burned House (Atwood), 27
Moss, Thylias, 167-171
　At Redbones, 168
　Slave Moth, 169
　Small Congregations, 168
　Tokyo Butter, 170
Mother/Child Papers, The (Ostriker), 173

Necessities of Life (Rich), 194
"Nevertheless" (Moore), 161
"Nick and the Candlestick" (Plath), 185
Night Feed (Boland), 56

No Heaven (Ostriker), 175
Nonconformist's Memorial, The (Howe), 122

"Oaxaca, 1974" (Cervantes), 73
"Objects and Apparitions" (Bishop), 45
October Palace, The (Hirshfield), 110
Of Gravity and Angels (Hirshfield), 109
"On the Death of Edmund Waller" (Behn), 38
"On the Death of the Late Earl of Rochester" (Behn), 38
"On the Edge of Darkness" (Levertov), 134
Once (Walker), 240
"Oread" (H. D.), 99
"Orthodox Waltz, The" (Fulton), 92
Ostriker, Alicia Suskin, 172-176
   The Crack in Everything, 174
   The Little Space, 174
   The Mother/Child Papers, 173
   No Heaven, 175
   The Volcano Sequence, 174
"Over 2000 Illustrations and a Complete Concordance" (Bishop), 46

Pangolin, and Other Verse, The (Moore), 161
Phallocentricism, 2
Pierce-Arrow (Howe), 122
Plath, Sylvia, 177-188
   "By Candlelight," 184
   "Channel Crossing," 186
   "Daddy," 186
   "Lady Lazarus," 186
   "Mary's Song," 183
   "Maudlin," 184
   "Nick and the Candlestick," 185
   "Words," 187
"Poem for the Young White Man . . ." (Cervantes), 75
Poem Traveled Down My Arm, A (Walker), 243
Poems (Rich), 196
"Poetry and Grammar" (Stein), 232

Pound, Ezra, 98
Power Politics (Atwood), 25
Procedures for Underground (Atwood), 24
Pythagorean Silence (Howe), 120

Questions of Travel (Bishop), 46

Rambling Sailor, The (Mew), 144
"Refugee Ship" (Cervantes), 72
Revolutionary Petunias, and Other Poems (Walker), 240
Rich, Adrienne, 189-202
   A Change of World, 192
   The Diamond Cutters, 193
   Diving into the Wreck, 196
   The Dream of a Common Language, 197
   Fox, 200
   "From an Old House in America," 196
   Leaflets, 194
   Midnight Salvage, 200
   Necessities of Life, 194
   Poems, 196
   Snapshots of a Daughter-in-Law, 193
   Time's Power, 199
   "Transcendental Etude," 198
   A Wild Patience Has Taken Me This Far, 198
   The Will to Change, 195
   Your Native Land, Your Life, 199
"Riverman, The" (Bishop), 47
Room of One's Own, A (Woolf), 4
Rukeyser, Muriel, 203-213
   "Ajanta," 208
   "The Gates," 211
   "Letter, Unposted," 210
   "Lives," 207
   The Speed of Darkness, 209
   Theory of Flight, 206
   A Turning Wind, 207
   U.S. 1, 206

"Sandpiper" (Bishop), 44
Saturday Market. See *Farmer's Bride, The*
Second Sex, The (Beauvoir), 3
Selected Fables of La Fontaine (Moore), 162
Sexton, Anne, 214-223
   All My Pretty Ones, 219
   Live or Die, 220
   Love Poems, 220
   To Bedlam and Part Way Back, 217
   Transformations, 221
Shadow Country (Allen), 14
Showalter, Elaine C., 2
Slave Moth (Moss), 169
Small Congregations (Moss), 168
Snapshots of a Daughter-in-Law (Rich), 193
Souls of the Labadie Tract (Howe), 124
Speed of Darkness, The (Rukeyser), 209
Spivak, Gayatri Chakravorty, 6
Stanzas in Meditation (Stein), 233
Stein, Gertrude, 224-236
   The Autobiography of Alice B. Toklas, 234
   "Poetry and Grammar," 232
   Stanzas in Meditation, 233
   Tender Buttons, 231
   Things as They Are, 230
   Three Lives, 230

Tangled Hair (Yosano Akiko), 258
Tell Me, Tell Me (Moore), 163
Tender Buttons (Stein), 231
Theory of Flight (Rukeyser), 206
Things as They Are (Stein), 230
"Those Who Want Out" (Levertov), 132
Three Lives (Stein), 230
Time's Power (Rich), 199
To Bedlam and Part Way Back (Sexton), 217
"To the Muse" (Levertov), 132
Tokyo Butter (Moss), 170

"Transcendental Etude" (Rich), 198
Transformations (Sexton), 221
True Stories (Atwood), 26
Turning Wind, A (Rukeyser), 207
Two-Headed Poems (Atwood), 26

U.S. 1 (Rukeyser), 206

Vietnam War, 134
Volcano Sequence, The (Ostriker), 174

Walker, Alice, 237-245
   Absolute Trust in the Goodness of the Earth, 242
   Good Night, Willie Lee, I'll See You in the Morning, 241
   Her Blue Body Everything We Know, 242
   Horses Make a Landscape Look More Beautiful, 241
   Once, 240
   A Poem Traveled Down My Arm, 243
   Revolutionary Petunias, and Other Poems, 240
"What Are Years?" (Moore), 161
Wild Patience Has Taken Me This Far, A (Rich), 198
Will to Change, The (Rich), 195
Woolf, Virginia, 4
"Words" (Plath), 187
World War II, 134, 250

Yamada, Mitsuye, 246-252
   Camp Notes, and Other Writings, 250
   Desert Run, 249
Yosano Akiko, 253-260
   Tangled Hair, 258
You Are Happy (Atwood), 25
Your Native Land, Your Life (Rich), 199